George W. Cox, Eustance Hinton Jones

Popular romances of the middle ages

George W. Cox, Eustance Hinton Jones

Popular romances of the middle ages

ISBN/EAN: 9783742836601

Manufactured in Europe, USA, Canada, Australia, Japa

Cover: Foto ©Andreas Hilbeck / pixelio.de

Manufactured and distributed by brebook publishing software (www.brebook.com)

George W. Cox, Eustance Hinton Jones

Popular romances of the middle ages

POPULAR ROMANCES OF THE

MIDDLE AGES.

BY

GEORGE W. COX, M.A.

AUTHOR OF 'THE MYTHOLOGY OF THE ARYAN NATIONS' ETC.

and

EUSTACE HINTON JONES.

LONDON:
LONGMANS, GREEN, AND CO.
1871.

PREFACE.

THE GENIUS of a great poet has in our own time shed a new lustre on the story of Arthur; but with this exception the romances which delighted Englishmen of the Middle Ages are known to their descendants, generally, little more than in name. Yet these stories must possess an interest for all who welcome any evidence which throws light on the growth of the human mind, if only from the mere fact that for generations these tales carried with them an irresistible charm; but even to this day the heroes whose names they bear still exercise over us in some faint measure the power of old associations. The wisdom of Merlin, the bravery of Bevis and Guy, have almost passed into proverbs: and to not a few, probably, the name of Olger will bring up the image of the mighty Dane, wrapped in the charmed slumber in which he lifts his mace once only in seven years. But a more potent spell is linked with the thought of Roland the brave and true, the peerless Paladin who fell on Roncesvalles.

If the rudest traditions of savage tribes have acquired a new value and a new interest as supplying materials for the history of human culture, the inference is justified that from the traditions in which our forefathers took delight we also may reap no scanty harvest of pleasure and instruction. But these traditions are partly contained in books not easily accessible, or have assumed forms which tend to make them monotonous and wearisome. To this monotonous character of mediæval romances generally we cannot shut our eyes: but all probably will feel that in the Arthur story, as related especially by Sir Thomas Malory, the evil becomes well-nigh intolerable. Still, as we toil wearily through endless details of justs and tournaments which present no distinguishing features, and through adventures of knight-errantry which simply repeat each other, we cannot be blind to the beauty of the scenes in which from time to time we find ourselves, or deaf to the tones which, at intervals, strike a chord in our hearts.

Hence the thought that these old romances may be presented to Englishmen of the present day in a form which shall retain their real vigour without the repulsive characteristics impressed on them by a comparatively rude and ignorant age, may not, perhaps, be regarded as inexcusably presumptuous. With greater confidence it may be affirmed that, if we turn to these old legends or romances at all, it should be for the purpose of learning what they really were, and not with any wish of seeing them through a glass which shall reflect chiefly our own thoughts about them and throw over them a colouring borrowed from the sentiment of the nineteenth century.

These two conditions have, it is hoped, been strictly observed in the versions here given of some of the great romances of mediæval Europe. While special care has been taken to guard against the introduction even of phrases not in harmony with the original narratives, not less pains have been bestowed on the task of preserving all that is essential in the narrative; and thus it may perhaps be safely said that the readers of this volume will obtain from it an adequate knowledge of these time-honoured stories, without having their attention and their patience overtaxed by a multiplicity of superfluous and therefore utterly irksome details.

The result is that nine romances are given in a space scarcely more than half that which the Arthur story alone occupies in the pages of Sir Thomas Malory. Of the present version of the Arthur myth it may be enough to say that it relates many important episodes which have been omitted in some of the versions recently published, while no attempt has been made to impart a more historical complexion to the romance than that which it received at the hands of Caxton's friend. From first to last this alleged historical character of the myth is precisely the feature which, as we analyse the story, becomes more and more dim and vague. But as the connexion of the myth with the affairs of men becomes more shadowy, the real meaning and beauty and pathos of the legend will, it can scarcely be doubted, be brought out into a clearer and more enduring light.

If the reception given to this volume should warrant the undertaking, it is proposed to include in another volume the more important Teutonic romances which, appearing in earlier days as the story of the Helgis and Volsungs, grew up into the Lay of the Nibelungs and the stories of Gudrun, of Walthar of Aquitaine, and other heroes whose features we recognise in other portions of the wide field of Aryan mythology.

I must add that for the Introduction and for the story of Arthur and his Knights I am alone responsible. The versions here given of the stories of Merlin, Tristrem, Bevis, Guy of Warwick, Roland, Olger, Havelok and Beowulf, have been contributed by Mr. EUSTACE HINTON JONES.

G. W. C.

CONTENTS.

INTRODUCTION:—

	PAGE
The story of Arthur	1
Alleged historical character of King Arthur	1
Supposed historical residuum in the myth of Arthur	4
Victories of Arthur and Herakles	6
Origin of the Arthur romance	7
Limits of the inquiry	8
Growth of popular tradition	8
The source of human fancy	8
Myths of savage tribes	9
Etymological explanations of myths	10
Parallelisms in the incidents of mythical tales	11
Illustrations from myths in which the names do not translate each other	12
Classifications of popular stories	14
Tests for the detection of mythical elements in popular tradition	15
Birth and early years of Arthur	16
The loves of King Arthur	18
Arthur and his destroyer	19
Arthur's sword	19
The scabbard of Arthur's sword	20
Repetition of myths in the Arthur story	21
Arthur and the fatal children	21
The story of Balin the poor knight	22
The two brothers	23

* A 5

x *Contents.*

INTRODUCTION—*continued.*

	PAGE
The invisible knight	23
The sacrifice of Sir Percivale's sister	23
The marriage of Arthur and Guenevere	24
The dower of Guenevere	25
Symbols of wealth	27
The toils and wanderings of Arthur	27
Imagery of solar myths	29
The weird sisters	30
Mythical cycles in the Arthur romance: (I) ARTHUR, (II) BALIN, (III) LANCELOT	31
The fourth cycle—GARETH	31
Repetition of the myth of Gareth in the episode of the Knight of the Ill-shapen Coat	33
The knights who fail, and the knight who wins	34
The snake-leaves	35
The magic ring	36
The fifth cycle—TRISTRAM	36
The child born to be great	36
Tristram the hunter and musician	38
The poisoned weapons	39
Parallelisms in the myths of Arthur, Tristram, and Lancelot	40
Physical powers of mythical heroes	43
The madness of Tristram and Lancelot	44
Subordination of Arthur in the myths of Balin, Lancelot, and Tristram	44
Talismanic tests	46
The ship of the dead	46
The Sangreal	48
Introduction of Christian sentiment	51
The two Elaines and Guenevere	52
Arthur and Mordred	56
The departure of Arthur to the vale of Avilion	58
Composition of the Arthur romance	60
The story of Bevis of Hampton	61
The story of Guy of Warwick	63
The tale of Roland	65
The legend of Olger the Dane	68
The story of Havelok	70
The loves of Argentile and Curan	72
Havelok and Hamlet	73
Hamlet and his uncle	74
The genealogy of Hamlet	76
The saga of Beowulf	78
General results of the inquiry	79

Contents.

THE STORY OF KING ARTHUR AND HIS KNIGHTS:—

		PAGE
Chapter I.—The crowning of Arthur	. . .	81
" II.—The story of Balin and Balan	. . .	88
" III.—The wedding of Arthur and Guenevere	.	96
" IV.—The treason of Morgan le Fay	. .	99
" V.—The crowning of Arthur at Rome	. .	110
" VI.—The exploits of Sir Lancelot du Lake	.	112
" VII.—The story of Sir Gareth of Orkney	.	117
" VIII.—The history of Sir Tristram	. .	135
" IX.—The madness of Sir Tristram	. .	145
" X.—The treasons of King Mark and Palamides	.	152
" XI.—The birth of the good knight Galahad	.	161
" XII.—The finding of Lancelot	. . .	169
" XIII.—The shriving of Sir Lancelot	. .	173
" XIV.—The temptation of Sir Percivale	.	182
" XV.—The vision of Sir Lancelot	. .	185
" XVI.—The trial of Sir Bors	. . .	188
" XVII.—The achieving of the Sangreal	. .	193
" XVIII.—The story of the Maid of Astolat	.	202
" XIX.—The judgment of Queen Guenevere	.	209
" XX.—The siege of Joyous Gard	. .	215
" XXI.—The last days of Arthur, Guenevere, and Lancelot	225

MERLIN	. . . . .	234
SIR TRISTREM	. . .	245
BEVIS OF HAMTOUN	. .	268
GUY OF WARWICK	. . .	297
ROLAND	. . . .	340
OLGER THE DANE	. . . .	348
HAVELOK	. . .	369
BEOWULF	. . .	382
INDEX	. . . .	399

Errata.

Page 2, line 22, *for* Kyklópes *read* Kyklôpes.
Page 76, lines 6 and 7 of note, *for* declaration *read* declamation.

POPULAR ROMANCES

OF THE

MIDDLE AGES.

INTRODUCTION.

THE proposition that King Arthur either is or is not an historical personage will be disputed by none. Happily the answer to this question, whether it be given in the affirmative or the negative, has really nothing to do with the origin of the world-renowned story as told by Jeffrey of Monmouth, or by Sir Thomas Malory. Whatever may have been the deeds of the real Arthur, if Arthur ever really lived, they exhibit scarcely a single feature in common with the fortunes and exploits of the lord of the Round Table, and the illustrious knights who went in search of the Holy Grail. *The story of Arthur.*

The historical character of the legend of King Arthur must, even by those who accept it, be taken with a qualification. If Lappenberg, in his chivalrous defence of the story, myth, or fiction (whichever it be), can argue that the rapid spread of Jeffrey's work over great part of Europe proves that the belief in the hero of it was deeply rooted,[1] it may be *Alleged historical character of King Arthur.*

---

[1] *England under the Anglo-Saxon Kings* (translated by Benjamin Thorpe), i. 102.

answered that the same profound faith alone explains the wide circulation of the stories of Valentine and Orson or Jack the Giant-killer. If the same historian can even infer the historical existence of Arthur from the many local memorials which, throughout the whole of the Christian part of Europe, are made to bear his name, it may be urged that the same method will prove the existence of Aineias, or Odysseus, or Achilleus, whose relics or sepulchres are thickly strewn along the shores of the Mediterranean; and that the story of Aineias, in particular, was attested beyond all possibility of dispute, even in the days of Cato, by the relics of the marvellous sow kept in pickle at Lavinium.[1] If, again, Lappenberg lays stress on the more measured veneration of the Welsh poets, who esteem his general Geraint more highly than the king himself, and even relate that the latter, far from being always victorious, surrendered Hampshire and Somersetshire to the Saxons, this plea for the existence of the great Celtic hero has as much and as little value as the argument which would infer the historical character of the Odyssey from the defeats or injuries sustained by Odysseus at the hands of Kyklôples or Laistrygonians, of Skylla or Charybdis, and from the more straightforward and honest bearing of Telemachos or Eumaios, who certainly do not fight with poisoned arrows, or boast of stabbing men behind their back. If Lappenberg seeks to impart a faint historical hue to the expedition of Arthur against the Roman emperor, on the ground that a real expedition was undertaken in the year 468 on the demand of Anthemius by the British general, Riothamus, the device is neither better nor worse than that of the historian who should claim as fact the expedition of Herakles against the Eastern tyranny of Ilion, on the ground that there was at a later time a real victory of the Greeks over the Eastern tyranny of Persia.

[1] Lewis, *Credibility of Early Roman History*, i. 334.

If Lappenberg can insist that the discovery of Arthur's long-concealed grave is mentioned by credible contemporaries, and excited at the time no suspicion of any religious or political deception, it may be answered not only that the discoveries of relics rarely rouse such suspicions, but that the discovery of forgotten or unknown sepulchres is too common an incident to carry much weight either in favour of a story or against it. The final argument that Henry II., if he wished merely through an artifice to convince the Welsh of the death of their national hero, 'would hardly himself have acted so conspicuous a part on the occasion,' may be dismissed partly with the reply that we are perhaps scarcely competent to pronounce on his motives, and in part with the retort that some portions of the story even of Henry II. pass into the cloud-land of mythology, and that the maze of Woodstock bears too suspicious a likeness to the labyrinth of Daidalos to allow any but the most credulous to receive without misgiving the tale of Queen Eleanor's vengeance against Fair Rosamond. In all this ingenious or desperate pleading Lappenberg is in truth defending a breach which was long ago surrendered as untenable by William of Malmesbury. If we choose to say with him that 'poem and tradition bear witness to the spirit, and his ashes and the gravestone to the life and name of Arthur,' how much more may it be said that the discovery of the books written by the sacred hands of Numa bear witness to the existence of the great Roman representative of Drakon, or Zaleukos, or Lykourgos? There is, indeed, but one way of escape out of this vicious circle, and this rather apparent than real. When we have a story in which gods and goddesses mingle visibly among men, in which the great heroes are invulnerable except in one part of their bodies, in which the leaders are sons of the Heaven, or the Dawn, or the Morning, it may seem possible to get at the historical evidence by cutting away all the mar-

vellous features, and accepting the remaining incidents
as fact. It is the old cheat which Euêmeros practised on
himself, and which his followers have diligently applied
in all ages; and, like Milton, Lappenberg quietly sur-
renders himself to the delusion. 'Faith in the existence
of this Christian, Celtic Hector,' he asserts, 'cannot be
shaken by short-sighted doubt; though much must be
yet done for British story, to render the sense latent in the
poems of inspired bards, which have in many cases
reached us only in spiritless paraphrases, into the sober
language of historical criticism.' In other words, it will
be no easy task to achieve for the great Celtic legend
that which Thucydides, much to his own satisfaction,
accomplished for the story of the Trojan war. But the
meagre skeleton to which Thucydides reduces the myth
of Ilion is not the story as told by the poets of the Iliad
or the Odyssey, or by the lyric and tragic poets of Hellas,
most of whom lived nearer to the times in which the
incidents are supposed to have taken place than the great
historian. From his narrative, which is unquestionably
conveyed in the 'sober language of historical criticism,'
all the old familiar features of the legend have vanished
utterly away. We see neither Helen with her griefs and
woes, nor Memnon, nor Sarpédôn; neither Eôs, nor Zeus,
nor Athênê, nor Aphroditê. We have but a ghastly *caput
mortuum* of bare incidents, of which, in Mr. Grote's words,
we can but say that as the possibility of such events cannot be denied, so neither can the reality be affirmed.

No other judgment can be given of any historical
residuum extracted from any of the versions into which
the story of Arthur has passed. No other judgment was given practically seven hundred years
ago by William of Malmesbury, when he speaks
of the many fables told about him by the Britons, even
in his own day. William, it is true, mentions Arthur
as a man who deserved to be celebrated, not by idle fiction,

but by genuine history; but he has no other mode of constructing or reconstructing this history than that which had been applied by Euémeros before him or Dr. Lappenberg after him. If he hesitates to believe other parts of the narrative, he can readily believe that 'at the siege of Mount Badon, Arthur, trusting in an image of the Virgin, engaged nine hundred of the enemy, single handed, and turned them to flight with fearful slaughter.' The Virgin's image, it may be safely said, rendered this incident credible to William, who would have rejected with contempt the notion that Grettir, in the Icelandic Saga which bears his name, should, without aid from any other, slay eighty men who attack him while he is asleep. In striking contrast with the special pleading of Lappenberg is the testimony of Lingard, who has no hesitation in asserting that, 'if we divest his memory of the fictitious glory which has been thrown round it by the imagination of the bards and minstrels, he will sink into equal obscurity with his fellows. We know neither the period when he lived, nor the district over which he reigned. He is said to have fought and to have gained twelve battles. In most of these, from the names of the places, he seems to have been opposed to the Angles in Lincolnshire,—from the last, at Mount Badon, to the Saxons under Cerdic or Cynric. This, whether it was fought under Arthur or not, was a splendid and useful victory, which for forty years checked the advances of the strangers. Perhaps, when the reader has been told that Arthur was a British chieftain, that he fought many battles, that he was murdered by his nephew, and was buried at Glastonbury, where his remains were discovered in the reign of Henry II., he will have learned all that can be ascertained at the present day of that celebrated warrior.'[1]

[1] *History of England*, i. 72. Ed. 4. Mr. Freeman, having insisted on the totally different character of the story of the English conquest as told by

He can scarcely be said to know so much. In the case of a chieftain, with whose life mythology, by universal consent, has been busy, the twelve victories which he wins provoke comparison with the twelve labours which Herakles brought to a successful end, while the chronology which marks the result of the battle of Mount Badon is as little to be trusted as any other part of the legend. The annals of the Æscingas of Kent are constructed on an eight times recurring cycle of eight years; and Lappenberg, who upholds the historical character of King Arthur, traces this number through every stage in the career of the English conquerors.[1] The remaining incidents, which Dr. Lingard is content that the reader should believe, if he likes to do so, are, of course, perfectly possible; but if our knowledge of them be derived solely from the legendary narratives of his exploits, it is worth neither more nor less than the chronology of the events which took place in the House that Jack built. We may learn the truth of these facts, if they be facts, from other sources, as we learn from Eginhard that Hruodland (Roland), the prefect of the British march, fell at Roncesvalles. From the legend we learn nothing.

The ground is at once in a great measure cleared before

marginal note: Victories of Arthur and Herakles.

the English Chronicles and by Jeffrey of Monmouth, has not thought it worth while to take any notice of the Arthur legend.

[1] The battle of Crayford is fought eight years after the landing of the Teutonic invaders; eight years later Hengest won the battle of Wippedesfleot. The next eighth year is marked by another victory. Twice eight years after this battle, or in the fortieth year after his arrival, Hengest dies. His successor, Eric, reigns three times eight years; and so onwards to Æthelberht, who reigns six times eight years, and his successors Eadbald and Earconberht, who each reign three times eight years.—Lappenberg, *England under the Anglo-Saxon Kings*, i. 75.

The artificial chronology of the early Roman kings is far more elaborated. That of the Assyrians ranges over a wider field, and is more cumbrous and less ingenious. See the *Edinburgh Review*, January 1867, No. 255, fol. 128-130.

us. The question of the historical residuum contained in the stories at the head of which may be placed the myth of Arthur loses all importance and all interest. The question even of the times in which they have taken shape becomes comparatively insignificant. But the stories themselves still remain; and we are driven to ask—What are they, and whence come the materials which have been wrought into these shapes? and the question must be asked till it receives an answer. If, then, in these stories we find incidents which seem to be the same—if they occur in the same or nearly the same sequence—if they are astonishing or improbable in character. or even impossible—if again, we find incidents or sequences precisely similar in the popular stories or the epical literature of other ages and countries—is it possible to avoid entering on the task of comparison, in the hope of reaching a definite source for narratives which, amidst so many variations, still exhibit so much likeness? This course is justified, apart from all considerations of comparative philology. In identity or resemblance of names we have unquestionably the strongest evidence for the identity or affinity of legends which profess to relate different events, or to belong to different countries; but it is obvious that, if we have half-a-dozen tales which repeat the same set of extraordinary incidents in the same order, we must regard them all as versions of a single story, even though two or three may possess no names in common, or though the difference extend to all. The original story thus reached may, of course, have an historical foundation; but probably long before we have reached this stage of the inquiry, we shall see on all sides evidence which will drive us more and more to the conclusion that the history is that of Cloudland.

My present task, therefore, is confined wholly to the matter of the stories contained in this volume. That some of the men who are named in them may have lived, or that

marginal note: Origin of the Arthur romance.

some of the events which are related in them may have happened, I do not in any way deny. The Persian Cyrus is unquestionably historical; the whole story of his birth and childhood is unquestionably unhistorical. But when we find that this story is repeated in the history of Romulus and Remus, of Oidipous, Perseus, and Telephos, of Chandragupta and many more, the conclusion follows that, so far as these stories are concerned, they are all the same; and while I leave altogether on one side the possible historical reality of any or all of these personages, I am bound to ask again, how this story came into being.

<small>Limits of the inquiry.</small>

To a certain extent I have answered this question already; and an examination of the mediæval romances of Europe will, I think, tend greatly to strengthen the position which I have felt no hesitation in laying down, that together with the whole genuine epical literature of the Aryan race, that is, with all the poems which are strictly of popular growth, they relate a story which has its origin in the phenomena of the natural world and the course of the day and the year.[1] I welcome with pleasure the vast amount of evidence, extending beyond the bounds of the Aryan race, over the whole area of human life, which has been gathered by Mr. Tylor in his learned and valuable work on Primitive Culture, and which, I venture to think, renders it impossible to maintain any other conclusion than that which I had reached already.

<small>Growth of popular tradition.</small>

In speaking of the Hellenic mythology, Mr. Gladstone asserted that man may embellish, but that he can not create, the inference being that as the Hellenic tribes had not created their mythology, it must have its roots in an original revelation from which it was a degradation and a depravation. The reasons which

<small>The source of human fancy.</small>

[1] *Mythology of the Aryan Nations.* i. vi.

Introduction.   9

render such a theory untenable have been already given.[1] Mr. Tylor, fully sharing Mr. Gladstone's scepticism with regard to the inventive power of the mind of man, and holding that 'among those opinions which are produced by a little knowledge, to be dispelled by a little more, is the belief in an almost boundless creative power of the human imagination,' asserts that ' the superficial student, mazed in a crowd of seemingly wild and lawless fancies, which he thinks to have no reason in nature nor pattern in this material world, at first concludes them to be new births from the imagination of the poet, the tale-teller and the seer. But little by little, in what seemed the most spontaneous fiction, a more comprehensive study of the sources of poetry and romance begins to disclose a cause for each fancy, an education that has led up to each train of thought, a store of inherited materials from out of which each province of the poet's land has been shaped and built over and peopled. Backward from our own times, the course of mental history may be traced through the changes wrought by modern schools of thought and fancy, upon an intellectual inheritance handed down to them from earlier generations. And through remote periods, as we recede more nearly toward primitive conditions of our race, the threads which connect new thought with old do not always vanish from our sight. It is in large measure possible to follow them as clues leading back to that actual experience of nature and life, which is the ultimate source of human fancy.'[2]

Mr. Tylor has, accordingly, brought together a vast number of myths from existing savage tribes, whose 'clear and fresh mythic conceptions may serve as a basis in studying the nature-myths of the world at large;'[3] and his classification of these myths is based distinctly on a judgment of 'the characteristics of the

<small>Myths of savage tribes.</small>

---
[1] *Aryan Mythology*, Book I. ch. i. [2] *Primitive Culture*, i. 248.
[3] *Ib.* i. 331.

10 *Popular Romances of the Middle Ages.*

episodes themselves as to the ideas which suggested them.'[1] His conclusion is that the evidence so gathered countenances ' a strong opinion as to the historical development of legends which describe in personal shape the life of nature.'[2]

In the road to which we are thus brought, we have to a certain extent the sure guidance of etymology. All is clear so long as we deal with legends such as that of Endymion, whose name denotes simply the plunging sun, and which represents him as the child of Protogeneia, the early dawn, and of Aethlios, the sun who struggles through the clouds or against the darkness, and as the husband of Selênê, the moon, or of Asterodia, who wanders among the stars with her fifty children whose forms are seen in the star-lit heavens. There is no room for doubt, while we have before us such a myth as that of Prokris, whose name carries us to the Sanscrit root which furnished a name for the dew—whose mother Hersê is dew even to the Greek, and who is unwittingly smitten by the spear of Kephalos, the head of the sun, as the solar rays kill or drink up the dew drops. We can have no misgivings lest we be on the wrong path, as we read how Sarpêdôn, the light which creeps along the sky, came from Lykia, the land of light, with his friend Glaukos the shining one; how he was slain far away in the West, and how Thanatos and Hypnos, Sleep and Death, bore him homewards through the silent hours of night, and laid him on his threshold by the banks of Xanthos, the golden river, as the first streak of dawn shot along the blue fields of heaven. We can move with confidence, as we hear how Persephone, the daughter of the Earth-Mother or the Dawn-mother, was stolen away by Hades Polydegmon, the King of the unseen land which swallows all living things; how Helios, the Sun, saw her borne away, and Hekatê, the Moon, heard her cry; how while she lay in

[Sidenote: Etymological explanations of myths.]

[1] *Primitive Culture,* i. 309. [2] *Ib.* i. 331.

the dark land beneath the earth, the flowers refused to bloom, the grass would not grow, and the trees would not put forth leaves or fruits; and how the heavens were glad and the earth laughed when the fair maiden was brought back by Hermes, the lord of the moving air, to the Mourning Mother at Eleusis, the trysting-place.

Why should we move with less confidence, or be less sure of our ground when we come to the myth of the Teutonic Iduna, of whom the same story is told, how Wuotan and all the Æsir mourn when she is stolen away; how the trees shed frozen tears, and the sun withdraws his face, until Loki brings her back in the form of a quail?[1] Why should we feel any misgiving when we have to handle stories in which all things are held in a dreamless sleep, while a beautiful maiden slumbers either within a fortress of ice, or walls of flame, or an impenetrable hedge of briars? When Iduna and Persephonê are brought back, the whole world rejoices. When Dornroschen awakes from her slumber at the kiss of the brave knight who has found his way to her chamber, the scullion boy receives the blow which the cook had raised his hand to inflict a hundred years ago, and the maid goes on with the process of basting the meat, in which she had been interrupted when the thorn pierced the hand of the Rose Maiden. It is but the familiar form which the myth is sure to receive at the hands of the common folk; but the transformation makes our task a simpler one for thousands of popular tales,

Parallelisms in the incidents of mythical tales.

---

[1] Bunsen asserts naturally, that this myth is an exact counterpart of the earliest myth of Herakles, who falls into the sleep of winter, and lies stiff and stark till Iolaos wakes him by holding a quail to his nose."—*God in History*, ii. 488.—In Hellenic mythology, Delos, the brilliant birthplace of Phoibos, is also Ortygia, the land of the quail, the bird of morning. Max Müller, *Lectures on Language*, Second Series, 506.—The German wachtel may mean, as some hold, the quacking bird; but it is not impossible that the equivocation between quacking and waking may have determined the choice of this bird in the German myth.

and we see at once that we have only Persephonê or Iduna in another form when, in the story of the Dwarfs, the maiden, having eaten a golden apple,[1] sinks a hundred fathoms in the earth, where the prince (the same, of course, who rescues Dornroschen) finds her with the nine-headed dragon resting on her lap; or, again, as we read of the House in the Wood in which lies a princess seemingly dead, and how, when presently the sides crack and the beams groan as if riven from their fastenings, the stairs fall down, and the whole roof gives way, she awakens from her death-like trance to find herself in a splendid palace, and in floods of dazzling sunlight. What have we here but the sudden overthrow of the wintry powers, when the maiden finds herself on the green couch of the life-giving mother? We may trace the same idea through the story of the Nix of the Mill Pond,[2] of Jungfrau Maleen,[3] of the Ill-tempered Princess in the Spanish Patraña, in the Hindu tale of Surya Bai, the Sun-maiden,[4] of Holda and of Frau Berchta, as well as, again, in the myth of Dêmêter and Iasiôn, and of the Latin Ceres and Saturnus.[5]

In some of these stories we have the guidance of etymology; perhaps we may be said to have them in many, if names which tell their own tale are to be taken into account. But from this point of view an etymological character may possibly be traced between the greater number of the tales which form the vast mythical inheritance of the nations. There remain many, however, between which no such links can be found. There is no etymological

Illustrations from myths in which the names do not translate each other.

---

[1] This golden apple or pomegranate, which is eaten or tasted by Persephonê just before she leaves Hades, answers to the narkissos, or stupifying plant, which the Maiden (Korê) takes before she is stolen away. For the signification of the pomegranate, see *Aryan Mythology*, ii. 298.
[2] Grimm, *Household Stories.*   [3] *Ib.*
[4] Frere, *Deccan Tales.*   [5] *Aryan Mythology*, ii. 306–8.

connexion between the Hindu story of Punchkin[1] and the Teutonic tale of the Giant who had no heart in his body;[2] yet it is impossible not to see that the death of the one, both in the mode of its infliction and in the whole train of incidents which led to it, is the precise counterpart of the catastrophe which overtakes the other.[3] The names Sisyphos and Ixion may explain themselves, although in the case of the latter this has been disputed; but apart from this can it be questioned that wealth and wisdom and a terrible punishment are the characteristics of Sisyphos, Ixion, and Tantalos, and that the stone which Sisyphos heaves to the summit of the hill, only to see it roll down again, is but the blazing four-spoked wheel on which the body of Ixion is stretched as on a rack at noonday? Can it be doubted that the presumption which marks these three mythical beings brings on Tantalos a penalty precisely similar in character, though not in outward form? Could the effects of drought be more vividly described than by the myth of the Sun, who scorches the fruits which he has quickened into life, as he puts his face down close to the earth, or makes the water flee away as he stoops to quench his thirst? We may take the Ottawa tale of Iosco, which Mr. Tylor regards as 'evidently founded on a myth of Day and Night.' 'Iosco seems to be Ioskeha, the White One, whose contest with his brother Tawiscara, the Dark One, is an early and most genuine Huron nature-myth of Day and Night.'[4] It is scarcely necessary to say that the story would suffice to determine their character, even if the names did not, as they seem to do, explain themselves. But how abundant a spring is here touched by the comparative mythologist! The counterparts of these Ottawa deities are found in the Vedic Asvins, or twin horses or horsemen; sometimes brothers, sometimes sisters, sometimes friends or enemies,

---

[1] Frere, *Deccan Tales*.   [3] Grimm, *Household Stories*.
[2] *Aryan Mythology*, i. 135–142.   [4] *Primitive Culture*, i. 314.

sometimes both brilliant, sometimes, as in the Ottawa story, one light and one dark. 'The twin pair adopt various forms,' says the Vedic poet: 'one of them shines brightly, the other is black; twin sisters are they, the one black, the other white.'[1] The rivalry, here seen in germ, becomes more prominent in the myth of the Hellenic Dioskouroi, and reaches its climax in the feuds of Theban Eteokles and Polyneikes. But whether as friends or as foes, sometimes as both in succession, whether regarded as the two Dawns (Ushasau), or the two Rudras (Rudrau), the morning and evening breezes, or as Heaven and Earth (Varuna and Mitra), or as the opposing powers of Light and Darkness, we find the idea of these correlative deities running through the myths of Eros and Anteros, of Phaethon and Helios, of Romulus and Remus, of Herakles and Iphikles, Pelias and Neleus, Eurysthenes and Prokles, Glaukos and Sarpêdôn, Peirithoös and Theseus, Achilleus and Patroklos, of Grettir and Illugi in the Icelandic Saga, of Prometheus and Epimetheus, of Rama and Luxman, of Soma and Sûrya, of Krishna and Arjuna, of Danaos and Aigyptos, Amphion and Zethos, of Phoibos and Artemis, and many more of the so-called classical deities of India, Greece, or Europe, who reappear under more familiar forms in the common stories of the people as the Two Brothers, the Two King's Children, the Two Sisters, or the Two Wanderers.[2]

Enough has been said to show that identity of idea, and similarity in a marked train of incidents, are sufficient evidence that any given stories belong to the same stock. The conclusion is one which is, of course, quite independent of the further inquiry whether the stories stand to each other as brother and sister, or father and child, or as more distant kinsfolk who have grown to manhood without having ever seen each other, or known each of the other's existence.

Classifications of popular stories.

[1] *Aryan Mythology*, i. 391. [2] Grimm, *Household Stories*.

Introduction.

The likeness may be the result of direct borrowing or importation, or it may be caused by independent growth, as of plants from seeds which once came from a single tree; but, whatever be the cause, the likeness is still there, and according to these points of likeness these stories may be grouped and classified.

Of the stories contained in this volume it must be said that such resemblances are found not only in details but in their whole structure. It is quite possible that myths may fasten upon some portion of the life of really historical men, generally upon their early or their last days. If we take the story of Cyrus as a whole, we find that there are certain parts which will not yield to the tests employed for the detection of mythical elements. The reason is obvious. We approach here the region of actual fact. But those parts which do yield to these tests are none the less mythical; and in such parts the story of Arthur, for instance, must still be regarded as mythical, even if it could be proved that other portions possess a genuine historical character. Such portions, if found at all, will assuredly be few and far between; and it may be safely said of the whole narrative, that its general outlines and its special features may be traced not only in other mediæval romances, but in the traditions of almost every Aryan tribe. Nor can it be maintained that these resemblances are such as may be traced at the will of any who choose to find them in any two or more of modern novels, if these novels profess to relate incidents belonging to real life.[1] The incidents which mark the story of King

Tests for the detection of mythical elements in popular tradition.

---

[1] It would be impossible to explain Sir Walter Scott's story of the Antiquary or his Legend of Montrose as nature-myths. As a picture of the times of which it professes to treat Ivanhoe may be worthless; but the words and acts of Prince John and his followers, of Cedric and the Templar, of De Bracy and Front-de-Bœuf, may be the words and acts of real men. It is otherwise when we come to the exploits of Locksley at the tournament, for here Scott has chosen to insert a bit of popular legend

Arthur are confessedly extraordinary, or miraculous, or impossible; and it is the recurrence of precisely these features either in different portions of the same story, or in other legends, which both shows how each romance has been brought into shape and determines its affinity with other versions of the same tale.

In the form which the Arthur myth had assumed in the time of Jeffrey of Monmouth, we are confronted at the outset with a counterpart to the story of Alkmênê and Am'phitryon in the device by which Uther Pendragon gains access to Igerne, the wife of Gorlois. The incidents which follow the birth of her child Arthur carry us to the tales which tell us of the birth and early years of the Persian Cyrus, the Latin Romulus, or the Theban Oidipous. The reasons which compel us to banish the Arthur legend from the region of history into the circle of myth would justify us in comparing the golden robe in which the new-born Arthur is wrapped with the golden robe in which Cyrus is arrayed, each as the child of a king, and both with the fair white raiment which the nymphs placed round the newly-born Phoibos, when they washed him with pure water in the morning land of Delos. All these heroes are made known by doing something which others cannot do; but the mode in which Arthur is revealed is identical with that in which Sigmund is made known in the Volsung tale. In the Arthur story the sword is firmly fixed in an iron anvil; in the Volsung legend it is thrust into the roof-tree by the one-eyed stranger who appears with a slouched hat and a spotted cloak.[1] If in the one

[margin: Birth and early years of Arthur.]

---

belonging to the story of Robin Hood or William of Cloudslee and Adam Bell; and the affinity of these stories with the myth of Tell will scarcely be disputed.—*Aryan Mythology*, ii. 99.

[1] This is the heaven-god Odin or Woden himself, 'an old man, wrapped in his wide cloak, and clouding his face with his wide hat, "os pileo ne cultu prodēretur obnubens,' as Saxo Grammaticus has it. Odin is one-

case we have the inscription that he who can pull the sword out of the stone and anvil is rightwise-born King of England; in the other the one-eyed old man says, 'Whoso draweth this sword from this stock shall have the same as a gift from me, and shall find in good sooth that never bare he better sword in hand than is this.'[1] If the weapon yields to Arthur's touch although all others strive in vain to stir it, so Sigmund when he sets hand to the sword Gram 'pulls it from the stock, even as if it lay loose before him, though it would in no wise come away howsoever others tugged at it.' It may certainly be maintained that the Arthur version is a direct copy of the Sigmund myth; but few will assert that the latter was directly suggested by the myth of Theseus, who draws from beneath the great stone the sword of his father Aigeus, the sword with which Perseus had slain the mortal Gorgon. This weapon reappears necessarily in the myths of all lands. It is the Morglay which Bevis wields, the Durandal which flashes like the sun in the hands of Roland. When Arthur draws it from its sheath, it gleams on the eyes of his enemies like the blaze of thirty torches (p. 84); when Achilleus holds it up, the splendour leaps up to heaven like the lightning.

The incidents relating to the daughter of Earl Sanam

eyed; he desired to drink from Mimir's well, but he had to leave there one of his eyes in pledge, as it is said in the Voluspa—

"All know I, Odin,
Where thou hidest thine eye
In Mimir's famous well."

'We need hardly seek this wonder in Mimir's well of wisdom, for any pool will show the lost eye of Odin, to him who gazes at the sun reflected in its waters, when the other eye of heaven, the real sun, stands high at noon.'— Tylor, *Primitive Culture*, i. 317.

So Ushas the Dawn, is spoken of in the Vedic hymn as bringing the eye of the god. So too the Kyklops, the storm-cloud through which the sun glares, is a being with one eye. With these stories may be compared the myths which profess to explain why Savitar and Tyr are one-handed.

[1] *The Story of the Volsungs and Niblungs*, Morris, p. 7.

and the wife of the King of Orkney (p. 85) are cardinal points in the myth of Arthur. As in the Theban story, the ruin of the hero or of his kingdom must be brought about by his own son or descendants; and Mordred and the wife of the King of Orkney stand to Arthur in the relation of Polyneikes and Iokastê to Oidipous. The Queen of Orkney is Arthur's sister, the daughter of Igerne, though he knows it not—as Oidipous unwittingly becomes the husband of his mother, the widow of King Laios. It is the Sun-god wedding the dawn-maiden, who is the daughter of the Darkness or Night, or may have been his bride. But in the Arthur version there is a further point on which stress must be laid. The two incidents here related clash altogether with that ideal of spotless purity and perfect constancy to which modern poetry has especially delighted to raise the lord of the peerless fellowship of the Round Table. The Arthur who is the husband of Guenevere may resemble the Herakles of the apologue of Prodikos, although the story scarcely warrants the inference; but the Arthur of earlier days falls far below the standard of Lancelot. He dallies with the Queen of Orkney, though she comes to his court with her four sons, as he dallies with the daughter of Earl Sanam, for the mere attraction of her beauty. In neither case has he any misgivings of conscience. If his relations with the mother of Mordred cause him sadness, this sadness is not awakened until he has dreams which forebode the ruin to be one day wrought. But if Arthur really belong to the same heroic company with Perseus and Theseus, with Minos and Sigurd and Herakles, and these again to the more exalted society of Indra, or Agni, or Phoibos, or Krishna, this sensuous characteristic is precisely that which we should first look for. All these are and must be lovers of the maidens, the fiery sun greeting the dawn, the dew, the moon, or the clouds. Thus Minos is the lover of Diktynna and of Prokris, the dew, who is

The loves of KingArthur.

Introduction. 19

elsewhere the bride of the Sun-god Kephalos, who unwittingly slays her. So the Vedic poet, addressing the Sun as the horse, says, 'After thee is the chariot; after thee, Arvan, the man; after thee, the cows; after thee, the host of the girls,' who all seek to be wedded to him, and who are all wedded at one and the same moment to Krishna, who at the same moment visits each in her separate mansion. 'Sixteen thousand and one hundred,' says the Vishnu Purana, ' was the number of the maidens; and into so many forms did the son of Madhu multiply himself, so that every one of the damsels thought that he had wedded her in her single person.' The impossibility of the fact as interpreted of human life reveals its exquisite truth as a picture of a common sight in the world of nature. The maidens wedded to Krishna have been rescued from the black giant Naraka. The dew is seen only when the darkness is slain; and the same sun is reflected in a million dew-drops.

Nor may we pass over the incident which closes the first portion of the Arthur-myth, and which tells us that Arthur, on hearing that his destroyer should be born on May-day, orders that all the children born on that day shall be brought to him. With these Mordred is placed in a ship which is wrecked, and, as we may suppose, Mordred is the only one saved. So in the myth of Krishna, the fears of the tyrant Kamsa are awakened by the knowledge that the child who shall supplant him is his sister's son, as Mordred is the son of Arthur's sister; and therefore he orders the slaughter of all the children newly born. *Arthur and his destroyer.*

But the sword which Arthur draws out of the stone is not the weapon by which his greatest deeds are wrought. It is snapped in conflict with the knight Pellinore. Precisely the same are the fortunes of the sword which Odin thrusts into the roof-tree of the Vol- *Arthur's sword.*

¹ *Aryan Mythology,* ii. 135.

sungs. The sword of Arthur, whether as Excalibur, or, as some versions have it, Mirandoise, is bestowed on him again by the Lady of the Lake: and the shards of the sword Gram, welded together by Regin the smith, are brought by the fair Hjordis to Sigurd her son, who now stands in place of his father Sigmund. But the Lady of the Lake and the mother of Sigurd are simply counterparts of Thetis, the nymph of the sea, who brings from the smith Hephaistos the armour which is to serve for her child Achilleus in place of that which Hektor had taken from the body of Patroklos. The parallel is complete, and its significance cannot be mistaken.

The scabbard of this sword is even more marvellous than the weapon itself: nay, the sage Merlin tells Arthur that it is worth ten of the sword, for so long as he bears the sheath about him, the sorest blow shall not cause him to lose one drop of blood: and thus Arthur is placed in the ranks of that large class of heroes who may be wounded only in one way, whether as being vulnerable in one part only of their body, like Achilleus in the heel, or only when they lack some portion of their panoply, or only by some particular weapon or instrument, as Sifrit can be slain only by Hagene, the thorn, Baldur by the mistletoe, or Ragnar Lodbrog by the viper. In all these stories a way is necessarily provided by which the catastrophe may be brought about. Arthur, invulnerable with the scabbard, must somehow or other be deprived of it; and here this is done by means of Arthur's sister, Morgan le Fay, to whom he intrusts it for safety, but who, loving Sir Accolon more than her husband Sir Uriens, gives it to him, making by inchantment a forged scabbard for her brother. In a fight which follows the king is well nigh overcome; but though he regains the sheath, yet Morgan contrives once more to get it into her hands. Excalibur she cannot take from the grasp of Arthur as he sleeps; but

[1] *Aryan Mythology*, i. 279.

[Sidenote: The scabbard of Arthur's sword.]

she hurls the scabbard into a lake, and the death of the king at some time or other is insured.

Nor is it here only, in the Arthur cycle, that this magic sword is seen. The whole story is repeated in the episode of the good Sir Galahad. When the day for filling up the Perilous Seat has come, a squire tells the king that he has seen a great stone floating down the river, and a sword fixed in it. Here again we have the inscription, by which the weapon is made to say that no man shall take it hence but he by whose side it ought to hang, and that he shall be the best knight in the world. At Arthur's bidding, Lancelot, Gawaine, and Percivale, strive to draw it forth, but it will yield only to the touch of the pure Sir Galahad, who in full assurance of winning this sword has come with a scabbard only, and who says emphatically that it is the same weapon with which the Knight Balin avenged the dolorous stroke by which Balan smote King Pelles (p. 93). *[Repetition of myths in the Arthur story.]*

The reluctance which Uther's nobles show to receive Arthur as their lord, on the ground that he is but a baseborn boy, brings before us another familiar feature in this whole class of legends. With perhaps not a single exception, these Fatal Children, as Grimm calls them, have to spend their early years in banishment, or disguise, or humiliation; and when they come to claim their rightful inheritance, they are despised or jeered at by men of meaner birth, who can never be their match in strength and wit. So it is with Cyrus and Romulus, with Oidipous, Perseus, Theseus. The wise Odysseus is mocked for his beggarly garb as he stands on the day of doom in his own hall; and this passing shame before the great victory is reflected in countless popular stories which tell us of the degradation of Boots and Cinderella, a degradation which culminates in the Gaelic lay of the Great Fool, who of course proves to be wiser and mightier than all others in the land, and who becomes *[Arthur and the fatal children.]*

the husband of Fairfine, who is but Euryphassa or Pasiphae, or any other of the beautiful maidens, whose home is in Ganzblick or Breidablick or Lykia or Delos. The whole story is repeated in the episode of Sir Tor, who is brought in by Aries the cowherd. The herdsman, supposing him to be his son, complains of his folly—the folly o Boots or the Great Fool; but the wise Merlin, who happens to be present, declares that he is the son of King Pellinore. The same imputation of weakness is seen again in the demands made to Arthur for homage to his alleged sovereigns—demands which are in each case refused, and which lead to the utter discomfiture whether of King Ryons or the Roman Cæsar.

The recurrence of precisely the same idea in the story of the poor knight Balin (p. 88), throws light on the me-

The story of Balin the poor knight. thod in which a crowd of originally independent stories have been sorted and pieced together in order to produce the Arthur story of Jeffrey of Monmouth, and still more of Sir Thomas Malory. In truth, the myth already told of Arthur is now told all over again of Balin, and Arthur becomes altogether subordinate to the new protagonist. Here, as before, the first incident is that of the drawing of a sword: but in this case the weapon is attached not to an anvil or a stone, but to the side of a maiden, who cannot be freed from it save by a true knight, guileless of treason. No knights of the court of King Ryons have been able to rid her of the grievous burden; and Arthur himself is now not more successful. Hence, when Balin, the poor-clad knight, who has but just now been let out of prison, begs that he may be suffered to try, the maiden tells him that it is in vain for him to do so when his betters have failed before him. Still he will take no refusal, and when he puts his hand on the hilt, the weapon yields as easily as those which were drawn forth at the touch of Arthur or of Galahad, or as Havelok the Dane bears away the huge stone, which others striving with all their might cannot stir.

Introduction. 23

The poor knight goes on his way, bearing the sword which is to be his bane, for with it he was to smite King Pelles with the Dolorous Stroke, and to hurt to the death his brother Balan, whom he takes to be a stranger. These two brothers in their friendship and their antagonism are but reflexions of the Asvins, or Dioskouroi, or other twin deities found in the mythology of the Aryan and non-Aryan world alike. In the fight which they wage for Arthur against the brother of King Ryons they do as wondrously as Castor and Pollux for the Romans at the battle of the lake Regillus.[1] Later on in the myth we have the counterpart of the deadly feud between Eteokles and Polyneikes in the bloody battle between the two brothers Bors and Lionel (p. 192).   *The two brothers.*

The cap of Hades which enables Perseus to make himself invisible at will appears so often as the Wishing Cap or Tarnkappe of Teutonic story, that the achievements of the invisible knight, Garlon, who plays a contemptible part in comparison with the Argive hero, are at once explained.   *The invisible knight.*

But in many cases incidents of which the meaning is easily understood in Hellenic or other traditions survive in the Arthur story as mere arbitrary customs, for which no reason is assigned. Among these is the practice (of which two instances occur), according to which a maiden coming to a certain castle must give a dishfull of her blood for the healing of the lady who lies sick within it. This penalty is inflicted first on the maiden who serves as guide to Sir Balin (p. 93), and again on the sister of Sir Percivale in the episode of the Holy Grail (p. 195). In the latter case, although Percivale and his comrades, when they hear what is wanted of the maiden, offer a fierce resistance, they are overpowered, and assured that, unless they allow the sacrifice to be made, they must do battle to the death on the morrow.   *The sacrifice of Sir Percivale's sister.*

[1] Vide sup. p. 13.

But Percivale's sister offers herself as a willing victim, and dies for loss of the blood which is shed for the saving of the lady of the castle. An incident so strange provokes a comparison with that more famous sacrifice of an Argive maiden in behalf of a fair lady who also was shut up within castle walls on the heights of windy Ilion. But even the story of Iphigeneia, as related by Æschylos, is, like that of Percivale's sister, a mutilated version of the older myth. When the Teutonic poet told of Helgi Hundingsbana, the tale which furnished Burger with the materials for his ballad of Lenore, he added at the end, that 'in old time folk trowed that men should be born again, though their troth be now deemed but an old wife's doting; and so, as folk say, Helgi and Sigrun were born again,' and lived a new life under different names. Even so was it with Iphigeneia, for she herself is not only Helen but Artemis, and thus her death at the beginning of the expedition which is to issue in the rescuing of Helen, is but the death of the evening which must fade away, like Percivale's gentle sister, before the dawn can be set free from her prison-house.[1]

With the death of the two brothers Balin and Balan the story returns to the myth of Arthur and his wedding with Guenevere, whose character approaches more nearly to that of the Helen of the Greek lyric and tragic poets than to the Helen of our Iliad and Odyssey. As Helen is with Æschylos the ruin of ships, men, and cities, so is Arthur here warned by Merlin that Guenevere is not wholesome for him; and at a later time the knights who are besought to come forward as champions in her behalf demur to the request on the ground that she is a destroyer of good knights (p. 204). Their reluctance is fully justified. The real Guenevere of the Arthur story is sensual in her love and merciless in her vengeance; nor is Lancelot the austerely-devoted

The marriage of Arthur and Guenevere.

[1] *Aryan Mythology*, ii. 145. Morris, *Story of the Volsungs*, p. 176.

knight whose purity is lauded in the pages of Mr. Tennyson. By equivocation or direct falsehood Lancelot contrives to avoid or rebut the charge brought against him by Sir Meliagrance: but when in the encounter that follows that knight goes down beneath the stroke of Sir Lancelot and yields him to his mercy, the latter is sorely vexed because he wished to destroy the evidence of his guilt; and when he looks to Guenevere, she makes a sign, which expressed the will of the Roman ladies in the amphitheatre, that the vanquished gladiator should die (p. 214). It may, of course, be maintained that the incident which furnished grounds for the accusation of Meliagrance has been interpolated into the myth; but the process is at best perilous which rejects from a legend every portion which clashes with our conceptions of the character of certain heroes. And assuredly it cannot be said that the acts which roused the angry suspicions of Meliagrance are consistent with any notion of merely Platonic affection (p. 211). Nor is it safe to impute the coarseness which characterises Lancelot and Guenevere, Tristram and Isolte, wholly to the coarseness of the mediæval story-tellers. There is everything to support, and little or nothing to invalidate, the conclusion that the harsher and more repulsive portraits are the older; and if in the original myth Lancelot had been a man such as the Poet Laureate has painted him, the quest of the Sangreal could not have been accomplished, for it is only by personating Guenevere that Elaine becomes the mother of Sir Galahad.

But Guenevere, like Helen, has her treasures as well as the rich dower of beauty; and her special gift to Arthur is the Round Table. This table Merlin is said to have made in token of the roundness of the world; but no explanation can be received as adequate which is confined merely to its shape and takes no notice of its marvellous powers. The quest of the Holy Grail

The dower of Guenevere.

may be to all appearance a narrative wholly distinct from that which tells us how the fellowship of the Round Table was formed; but in all essential characteristics the Round Table and the Sangreal do but reflect each other. Around the one Arthur and his knights hold high festival; the other makes its presence felt among the whole company of the Round Table, filling the air with exquisite fragrance, and placing before each knight the viands which he would most wish to have. They are both, in short, different forms of the same vessel of plenty which carries us at length to the Egyptian lotos and the Yoni of the Hindu. Appearing first as the sign of the Earth, the fertilised mother, this symbol assumes the form of a ship, as in the Argo or the ship of Isis, and then passes through all possible forms of boat-shaped vessels, from the great cosmic mixing bowl of the Platonists to the Luck of Edenhall. Like the table of the Ethiopians, the round table may minister to the wants of the indifferent or the bad as well as of the good,[1] while the Holy Grail may be seen by none but the purest of the pure: but the difference is not greater than that which separates the Herakles of Prodikos from the Herakles of the story of the daughters of Thestias, or the Herakles who sojourns in the house of Omphalê. The same idea, which led to the establishment of the Hierodouloi at Corinth, was presented in another aspect by the Gerairai of Athens, the Vestal Virgins of Rome, and the nuns of Eastern and Western Christendom. If the mystic vessel of the Sangreal acts as a test of righteousness and purity, the same power is possessed by the horn which Sir Lamorak sends to King Mark (p. 143); and this horn is manifestly the horn which Oberon gives to Huon of Bordeaux, and which yields the costliest wine in the hands of a good man only.[2]

[1] It should, however, be remembered that in Homer the Ethiopians are always 'blameless.' If we make this a condition of feasting at their table, we have again all the elements of the Christian myth of the Sangreal.
[2] *Aryan Mythology*, ii. 120.

It is scarcely necessary to say more. We have reached that wide region in which the symbols of reproduction produce a wonderful harvest of fancies which run riot among images of inexhaustible wealth and fertility. The high standard of action, which must be attained by those who would see the Holy Grail, stands, when we compare it with the nature of the symbolism from which it takes its rise, in precisely the relation borne by the original sensuous roots to the words which we employ to express the highest spiritual conceptions.[1] Thus the story of the Sangreal is but a reproduction of the story of the Round Table: and it is not here only that we shall find ourselves going round in the same magic circle.[2]

Symbols of wealth.

With his election as king begin the toils and the wanderings of Arthur. No sooner is one enemy overcome than another assails him from some other quarter. 'Alas!' he mournfully complains, when he hears that the King of Denmark is ravaging his northern lands, 'never have I had one month's rest since I became king of the land' (p. 99). The same doom lies on all or almost all the heroes of mediæval romance; and the plea that this may be explained by the conditions of feudalism and the practice of knight-errantry may be taken for

The toils and wanderings of Arthur.

---

[1] *Aryan Mythology*, bk. i. ch. ii.

[2] Dr. Craik (*History of English Literature*, i. 142) cites the opinion of the Abbé de la Rue (*Essais historiques*), 'that the original romances on the quest of the Saint Greal are to be considered as forming quite a distinct body of fiction from those relating to the Round Table, and that much misapprehension has arisen from confounding the two.' If the evidence of comparative mythology is to be trusted, the original independence of the two myths can scarcely be questioned.

The notion of the author of the Introduction to *Britannia after the Romans*, also cited by Dr. Craik, that greal is 'a Welsh word signifying an aggregate of principles, a magazine, 'which passed into the Latinised form *gradalis*,' may be safely dismissed as a *hysteron proteron*. The opinion that the Latin *gradalis* represents the Greek kratēr, a goblet or mixing bowl, is far more plausible; but the strange connexion of the vessel with the Holy Blood seems to justify the conjecture that to this we owe the name of the Sang-real.

what it is worth. Tristram and Lancelot are pre-eminently knights errant; but Havelok, Olger, and Beowulf can scarcely be regarded as heroes of chivalry in this sense, nor can it well be supposed that all knights errant had the adventures and underwent the misfortunes of Lancelot and Tristram. Banishment and madness, degradation and final triumph, are their common portion; and we find these to be the great features in the career of a vast number of manifestly mythical heroes. The Teutonic stories gathered by Grimm resolve themselves in great part into versions of brothers or younger sons who go to seek their fortunes, and who all become possessed of the same miraculous powers. But whether we look at the tales of the common people or those which have assumed a more permanent form in epic poetry, we find that on all the heroes of whom they speak there lies the doom of perpetual pilgrimage. Nor can we fail to see whither we are tending when we read in the Gaelic story that the spell laid by the Dame of the Fine Green Kirtle on the Fair Gruagach is, that where he takes his breakfast there he may not take his dinner, and where he takes his dinner, there he may not sup, till he finds out in what place she may be under the four brown quarters of the world.[1] Of course in the end he does win her, and her fine green kirtle is found to be a garment endowed with the magic properties of the robe which Medeia received or inherited from Helios, the sun. In short, there is but one being of whom this tale is eternally true, and that being is the sun, who can never rest until he joins in the evening the beautiful maiden from whom he was parted in the morning. The force of the evidence becomes irresistible as we ascend from the wanderers of folk lore stories to the great company of epical heroes, whether it be the Icelandic Grettir, or the Teutonic Helgis, or Sigurd, or Siegfried, the Hellenic Perseus, Bellerophon, Theseus,

[1] *Aryan Mythology*, i. 291.

Herakles, Odysseus, to the divine persons whose real nature is clearly known to those who speak of them; to Dionysos, the wine-god, and to Phoibos, who cannot rest in Delos, the morning-land, but who, having wandered far away to the west, ever comes back to his bright birthplace; to Wuotan, who is Wegtam, the pilgrim of the road, and to Indra the wonderful, who, like all the rest, is a wanderer.

Nothing can grow without a root, and the most grotesque fictions are not altogether unreasonable or absurd. Thus when in these legends we come across men whose strength increases from nine to twelve o'clock, so that towards noon they become almost irresistible, while from the moment of noon their power begins slowly but steadily to decline, we are at once driven to ask whether there be any sense in which these words may be strictly true, at least according to the impressions made by outward objects on human sense; and it becomes impossible to resist the conclusion that here again we are reading of heroes who have had transferred to them the properties which belong only to the one-eyed wanderer who daily performs his journey through the heavens. This power of growth until noon is possessed by Sir Gawaine (p. 224), while his adversary, Marhaus, who here represents the opponent of the sun-god, waxes bigger and bigger at sundown. It is shared also by the Red Knight of the Red Lawns; and the knight Prettyhands, who is here playing the part of Boots or Dummling, is specially warned not to blow the horn which hangs by the castle gate until it be noon, for until that hour the Red Knight's strength increases, till, as men say, he has the strength of seven men (p. 125). This magical power in Sir Gawaine, of which, with one of the many direct contradictions exhibited by the legends pieced together to form the Arthur story, we are told that Arthur alone was aware, is especially manifested in the last desperate struggle with

Lancelot, which ends in the death of Gawaine. And thus we have the clue which leads us through such stories as the legend of Ahmed, the Pilgrim of Love, who, like all others, is seeking the bright maiden, and whose magic horse overthrows all against whom he is borne until the noontide hour strikes, when, hurrying away from the lists, he swims the Tagus, and buries himself in the cavern from which he had been led in the morning.[1] Finally we reach the myths in which all these stories find their explanation; the myths which tell us of the punishments inflicted on beings indisputably solar, of Ixion stretched on the four-spoked wheel which blazes in the heavens at noontide, or Sisyphos, who never fails to roll his great orb to the summit of the hill, but who succeeds in doing this only to see it roll down, or Tantalos, whose glowing face scorches the fruits which he longs to taste, and dries up the waters with which he yearns to quench his thirst.

If any doubt yet remained that these otherwise inexplicable characteristics of the Knights of the Round Table or their antagonists are remnants of nature-myth, these would be removed by the transparent scene in which three fatal sisters, the Norns, the Parcæ, the Moirai, the Thriai, the Graiai, or the Gorgons, are brought before us by the stream side in the forest of Alroy.[2] The images of the Past, the Present, and the Future with its budding hope, cannot be mistaken in the three maidens, of whom the eldest wears a circlet of gold on hair white with the snows of more than threescore winters, while the second has seen thirty years, and the third, whose head is crowned with flowers, is but in her fifteenth summer. These maidens sit where the roads part, watching for errant knights, whom they may teach strange adventures. It is enough to say that Uwaine and Marhaus choose the more sober and discreet of the sisters;

The weird sisters.

[1] *Aryan Mythology,* i. 151.   [2] *Ib.* ii. 16, &c.

the youngest falls to the share of Gawaine, and by her early desertion of him illustrates the truth that the young and his hopes, like the fool and his money, are soon parted.

Already, in the Arthur legends, there have been brought before us two distinct mythical cycles, the one telling the story of Arthur himself, the other of the poor knight Balin. We now reach a third, in which are related the adventures of Lancelot du Lake. This cycle is interwoven with the Arthur myth, which is made to serve as a common framework for these and for two other cycles which are included with them. *Mythical cycles in the Arthur romance: I. Arthur; II. Balin; III. Lancelot.* The main thread in the legend of Lancelot is the love which he bears to Guenevere, and which the queen fully returns. This love the mediæval story-teller has evidently sought to exhibit in the fairest light. When Morgan le Fay, and three other queens bid him choose one of them for his lady love, Lancelot's answer is a stern refusal (p. 113); and to the daughter of King Bagdemagus, who tells him that he lacks one thing, the love of a lady, and warns him of the rumours which are busy in connecting his name with that of Guenevere, Lancelot replies that he thinks not ever to be a wedded man, but that he wishes only to keep his hands clean and his heart pure. It is enough to say that the story gives sufficient evidence that the love of Guenevere and Lancelot is not pure, and that if it had been pure, the quest of the Holy Grail would never have been accomplished.

But the narrator leaves, to be taken up hereafter, the threads which are to join the Lancelot story with the story of Arthur and Tristram. For the present he betakes himself to a fourth cycle of myth, *The fourth cycle, Gareth.* which is concerned with the adventures of Sir Gareth. The story of this knight, who is brought into Arthur's court unable to walk and leaning on the shoulders of two men, is throughout one of that vast class of solar myths which speak of weakness issuing in victory. It is, in short, only another version of the story of Boots, or Cinderella, of Havelok and Hamlet, of the Gold Child, or the Widow's Son.[1] The first thing related of him carries us at once to the other tales which tell of great heroes whose lower limbs are out of proportion with the rest of their bodies. If Gareth seems unable of himself to walk, we must remember that Odysseus standing is comparatively insignificant, but that when he sits his presence is more dignified than that of Menelaos. So, again, of the Icelandic Grettir, it is said that he is right well ribbed about the chest, but few might think he would be so small of growth below. They are all, in truth, counterparts of the Shortshanks who figures in the folk lore of northern Europe.[2] But the destiny of Gareth, who, though the goodliest youth on whom the eyes of Arthur have ever rested, yet, like Cyrus or Romulus or Odysseus, knows neither his name nor his parentage, is for the present the kitchen. Like Halvor in the story of Soria Moria Castle, he must grub among the ashes: like the lad who knew not how to shiver, he cannot be placed far away from the living embers, which are to reveal his future splendour. As he has no birth-name, Sir Kay contemptuously calls him Prettyhands, and bids him go to the kitchen and there have fat brose, that at the year's end he may be fat as a pork hog. But Gareth has in him the ambition which enables Boots to ride up the mountain of ice in the story of the Princess on the Glass Hill; and thus he hurries to see any justing of knights which may chance to be going on, while, though he cannot walk, none could cast bar or stone as he did by two yards. The time for action at length comes, when a maiden beseeches Arthur to send succour to a lady besieged in her castle by the Knight of the Red Lawns (p. 118);

[1] *Aryan Mythology*, i. 159.   [2] *Ib.* i. 325.

but even now he must drink a bitter draught of humiliation. When he entreats Arthur that he may be sent on this service, the maiden asks indignantly if she is to be put off with a kitchen-knave, and hastens away in wrath. Sir Kay, who wishes to see how the ash-boy fares, speedily receives a stroke which compels him to believe that in his case discretion is the better part of valour; and even Lancelot, who ventures to parry lances with him, is constrained to own that their quarrel is not so great but they may fairly leave off. Nevertheless, the revilings of the damsel are not stayed by his first or his second achievement. In each case she finds some method by which she may explain away his success, until at last she too is driven to confess that he deserves all praise, since, with all his strength and after so many exploits, he could listen to slander without retort.

This myth is repeated in the episode of the Knight with the ill-shapen Coat, the ubiquitous garment of humiliation worn by the wanderer who owns the Knapsack, the Hat, and the Horn in the German story, by the Gold Child when he appears before the king in the guise of a bear-hunter, and the soldier who is seen in the Boots of Buffalo-leather. *Repetition of the myth of Gareth in the episode of the Knight of the Ill-shapen Coat.* Here too the maiden reviles him (p. 146), and tells him that if he will follow her, his skin shall be as well hewn as his coat. The answer of the youth is that when he is so hewn, he will ask for no plaster wherewith to heal him. When soon after this a hundred knights assail him at once, and fighting his way through them he seizes his horse which the maiden had taken from him in order to insure his death, we deal with an incident which recurs in the Saga of Grettir, and shows that we have before us the deeds of a Herakles, a Samson, or a Rustem. The inevitable issue is that the young knight becomes lord of the castle of Pendragon and the husband of the maiden who has reviled him.

He is, in short, the successful knight who wins his way, when others can do nothing; and so here we have repeated the story already told a thousand times in forms which excite pity, terror, or disgust. Brynhild can be rescued from the dragon which encircles her only by the peerless hero who can ride through the walls of flame; but the many who essay the task are scorched to death. So is it in the story of Briar-Rose, where the youths who seek to force an entrance through the hedge of thorns are unable to release themselves and perish miserably. Sometimes the thorny hedge becomes a hedge of spears or bayonets, or a wall of ice; and he who cannot leap it, meets his death at once. More often the penalty of death is inflicted by the executioner who has to deal with those who have been warned by the king, that if they are not victors in the appointed contest of running, leaping, or whatever it be, they must lose their heads. This is the burden of the myth of Atalantê. In the same way here we have a castle, near which on great trees hang the bodies of nearly forty knights; and when Prettyhands asks why they have been slain, the answer of the damsel Linet is, 'They are the knights who sought to deliver my sister from the Knight of the Red Lawns: for all who are overcome by him die a shameful death' (p. 125). In Prettyhands we see, of course, the conqueror by whom not only the Knight of the Red Lawns but all others like him are smitten down. If again Brynhild on the glistening heath sleeps within a circle of fire, we see precisely the same idea in the story of the maiden whom, as being the fairest of all women, Morgan le Fay shuts up in a tower where she boils in scalding water, until the best knight of the world should take her by the hand (p. 164). So too, just as the prickly hedge presents no barrier to the hero who is destined to rescue Briar-Rose, the doors open of their own accord when Lancelot approaches; and the deliverance of the maiden is followed

The knights who fail, and the knight who wins.

by the destruction of the serpent who lurks in the tomb.
It is but another form of the story of Rapunzel, of the
Rose of the Alhambra, of Surya Bai, and the Argive
Danaë.

Nor is this the only mythical incident, rendered familiar
to us in the legends of many lands, which has been introduced into this story of Gareth. After the battle The snake-
before the Perilous Castle the youth thinks at leaves.
once to win the lady of his love; but she tells him that
though she will never love another, yet he must be
tested by flood and field till twelve months should have
passed by, before she can be his wife. The spirit of the
old myth is so far weakened that means are devised for
cutting short the ordeal. But he has no sooner met again
the lady of the Perilous Castle, than he becomes an
actor in a series of astonishing scenes in which the notion
lying at the root of the story of the Snake-leaves is ex-
travagantly exaggerated. In the German tale a prince,
seeing a snake approach the dead body of his wife, cuts it
in two, and presently another snake brings in three leaves
which it places upon the severed portions and restores the
snake to life. This is only another version of the story which
is related of Polyidos and Glaukos, and is told again in the
Deccan tale of Panch Phul Rance, the Queen of the Five
Flowers. Here it assumes a coarse form in the hands of
a tale-teller, to whom the story conveys not a tittle of its
original meaning. The head of the knight who, approach-
ing Gareth in the night with a drawn sword, is beheaded
by him, is made to grow on his body again by means of
salve which the damsel Linet applies to it. When the
knight, thus restored to life, again attacks Gareth on the
following night, the latter not only smites off his head, but
hews it in pieces. But Linet is not to be thus baffled,
and the murderer is again made to live.

A like exaggeration is seen in the powers of the ring
which the lady of the Perilous Castle gives to Prettyhands.

The owner of the ring of Gyges became invisible or visible according to the way in which he handles it; in the Arabian story of the Wonderful Lamp, the hand-ling of the ring brings into sight the demon who is its slave. Here the ring has this power, that that which is green it will turn to red, red to green, blue to white, and so with all other colours, while he who wears it shall lose no blood. In other words it will both disguise and guard him effectually; and this is the idea which lies at the root of the Gyges myth, in which the ring represents the circular emblem of wealth and fertility common to the mythology of the whole human race, and pre-eminent in the Arthur story both as the Round Table and the vessel of the Sangreal. Under cover of this disguise Gareth does wonders at the tournament which King Arthur holds at Pentecost; but when he wishes to go and drink, his dwarf persuades him to leave the ring with him lest he should lose it while drinking, and thus he is made known as appearing in his own yellow colours (p. 132).

The magic ring.

Having brought Gareth to the scene of his glory, the story now enters on a fifth cycle of myth, which retraces in the person of Tristram the threads of the tale which relates the adventures of Lancelot. If there be a difference between them, it is that the Tristram story is more full of incidents common to all tales, the origin and meaning of which cannot be questioned. But in their love and their madness, their bravery and their sufferings, their triumphs and their punishment, they are but shadows each of the other. So close indeed is the parallel that Guenevere herself strikes the equation which makes herself and Lancelot, on the one side, the counter-parts of Tristram and Isolte on the other.

The fifth cycle. Tristram.

By his birth Tristram belongs to the class of heroes destined to become great men. He is the child of sorrow, born in the dark forest in which his mother seeks her lord, who has been entrapped and shut up in

The child born to be great.

a dungeon. Like Macduff and Asklepios, Dionysos and Sigurd, Tristram is scarcely seen by his mother, who before she dies has only time to give him his ill-boding name; but with him as with the Persian Rustem, with Adonis, with the Danish Olger and the Teutonic Sceaf the son of Scild, the woes of his infancy are but clouds which are scattered before the splendour of his manhood.[1] This story is repeated in the episode of Sir Alisander (p. 155), whom King Mark of Cornwall, who is here represented in the darkest colours, orders Sir Sadok to slay. Like the long series of heroes who are born to be kings,[2] Alisander is really saved by Sadok who pretends to the king that he has drowned the lad. On growing up he receives from his mother the blood-stained sark of his murdered father, and swears to take vengeance on King Mark, who on hearing that his intended victim is still alive seeks again to slay him by means of Morgan le Fay. But no woman can approach him without loving him, and Morgan le Fay enables him to overthrow all antagonists, until at length he wins the love of Alice the Fair Pilgrim. The same tale we find in substance in the romance of Havelok the Dane, who is intrusted to Godard as Alisander is to Sadok, that he may be got rid of. But Godard, like Harpagos in the story of Cyrus, chooses to do the work through the agency of another, and Havelok thus falls into the hands of Grim the Fisherman, who, rising at midnight to do Godard's bidding, is astonished at seeing the child's head wrapped in the halo of glory which showed the royal destiny of the young Servius Tullius, the slave's child, in the Roman myth, and revealed to the shepherd Aristhanas the divine parentage of the desolate Asklepios.[3]

Tristram, again, is pre-eminently the huntsman, like

[1] *Aryan Mythology*, ii. 33.
[2] Morris, *Earthly Paradise*, *The Man born to be King*.
[3] *Aryan Mythology*, ii. 35.

Alpheios in the Ortygian legend, while as a harper 'passing all other harpers that ever lived,' he is the representative not only of Hermes, Orpheus, Amphion, Pan, and the Seirens, but of the piper of Hameln, of the Erl King, of Sigurd, Glenkundie, and Wäinämöinen.[1]

Tristram the hunter and musician.

[1] *Aryan Mythology*, book ii. ch. v. No apology is needed for placing before the reader two versions of the Tristram story. The Tristram of the Arthur romance is in all essential features the same as the Tristram of Thomas the Rhymer; but the points of difference, slight though they may be between the one tale and the other, are not uninstructive. In both Tristram is the child of sorrow; but in the one he is born while his father still lives, in the other the death of the father precedes the birth of the child. But the difference is only in seeming. In both the wife is left alone and forsaken, like Prokris, or still more, like Korônis (*Aryan Mythology*, ii. 34). The story of the Norwegian merchant-ship, the captain of which orders sail to be set in order to beguile Tristram who is on board playing at chess with him, points to an incident in the German tale of Faithful John (Grimm), and to the version of the myth of Io, generally taken to be a piece of euemerism, as given by Herodotos. Tristram, like the heroes of all these tales, is the slayer of worms or dragons; but, the narrative which relates Tristram's special exploit is manifestly identical with the story related in Grimm's tale of the Two Brothers. The lying steward of the Tristram myth is the lying marshal of the other, and the mode in which each is convicted is precisely the same. For the connexion of this tale with other legends see *Aryan Mythology*, i. 162 et seq.

The difference to all appearance most noteworthy between the two stories of Tristram is that which relates to the character of King Mark of Cornwall, who in the version of Thomas the Rhymer is genial and faithful, while in the other he is an embodiment of falsehood and treachery. Such contradictions, if the story be regarded as in any way a narrative of historical facts, would suffice to deprive it of all credibility; but in the old myths the beings whom the sun has to supplant are not always malignant; and the two phases of Mark's character are reproduced in the Ring of the Frithiof Saga and the Rinkrank of the popular German tale, (Grimm, *Old Rinkrank*). In all these narratives, the good and the bad King Mark, the kindly Ring and the hard Rinkrank, each deprive the young and beautiful hero of his bride; in each case the maiden is united with her lover either in life, as Penelope with Odysseus, or in death, as Iolê with Herakles, or Kleopatra with Meleagros.

Sir Henry Strachey (*Morte d'Arthur*, xiii.) regards the fact that Mark appears in his more general form in the older romance as evidence that the later romance-writer found in the king's treachery some sort of palliation for what Sir Walter Scott calls the extreme ingratitude and profligacy of

Introduction. 39

The time comes when Tristram must do deeds of arms, and he alone ventures to encounter Sir Marhaus whom the King of Ireland sends to demand tribute from King Mark of Cornwall. The combat is long and fierce, but at length Marhaus is smitten down by Tristram's sword, of which a piece is left sticking in his head. This piece is carefully stored away by the queen of Ireland, whose palace Marhaus reaches only to die there. But Tristram also is sorely wounded by the arrows of Marhaus which were poisoned. On this fact it would be difficult to lay too great stress. Whatever may be said for African savages or even for the Achaians of the Greek heroic age, it can never be maintained that the employment of poisoned weapons is a fit work for Christian chivalry, or that the fact of their being so used is credible. But what is to be said if we find this practice avowed without shame in the heroic legends of almost all

(marginal note: The poisoned weapons.)

the hero. The charge of ingratitude seems but scantily borne out, or rather, even according to Malory's story, it has no foundation at all. The truth is, that, if we judge the story from the standard of our human morality, we shall find profligacy everywhere. Tristram pledges his faith to Isolte in Ireland: but when he returns to Cornwall, he and King Mark quarrel not for her, but about the wife of the Earl Segwarides (p. 139). Rather it may be said that in the relations of Mark with Isolte, Tristram displays a singular fidelity; but the multiplication of theories is really not needed to explain variations which are common to the myths of the Aryan nations generally.

Here, as elsewhere, the method which we have employed makes it quite unnecessary to enter into controversies which can have interest only on the supposition that we are dealing with powers and persons which are in some degree historical. Hence we may leave on one side the conclusion of Mr. Price (Introduction to Warton's *History of English Poetry*, 1824), that Sir Walter Scott had wholly failed to prove any connexion between this romance and the Rhymer of Ercildoune. It might rather be doubted whether Thomas the Rhymer was a poet at all, for of the man himself we can scarcely be said to know anything, and by Sir Walter Scott's admission the name existed at the time as a proper name in the Merse, John Rymour, a freeholder of Berwickshire, being among those who did homage to Edward I. in 1296, (*Tristram*, p. 6.) But even if the poet's existence be proved, Sir Walter Scott admits further that the romance existed before him; and our present concern is with the materials on which he worked.

lands? Poisoned arrows are used by Herakles, and by him bequeathed to Philoktêtes, who with one of them inflicts the death-wound of Paris. Nay, they do not scruple to make use of poison in other forms. The poisoned robe of Medeia scorches to death the Corinthian Glaukê and her father Kreôn; the blood of Nessos seals the doom of Herakles, when he puts on the white robe sent to him by Deianeira; the messenger of Morgan le Fay is burnt to coals by the garment which she had been charged to lay at the feet of King Arthur. If we absolutely refuse to believe in the historical employment of such methods in ancient or modern Europe (and we must refuse to believe it of our own land in any Christian age), how are the legends which speak of this employment to be explained? The negation of their historical character at once supplies the solution of the problem by banishing it from the land of living men to the regions of mist and space. The poisoned spears are the piercing rays of the sun; the poisoned robes are the fiery clouds which eat out his life as he sinks at his journey's end in the west. The parallel may be carried still farther. Medeia alone can heal the mischief which she works. Oinônê alone can save the life of Paris when he is smitten with his fatal wound; and in like manner the wound of Tristram can be healed only in the land from which the venom came, and in which dwells the maiden who shall be the lady of his life-long love.

But at this point again we are confronted with a characteristic which we can scarcely regard as having belonged to any Christian Knighthood. We have already seen how far Arthur comes up to Mr. Tennyson's idea of peerless purity; and the blemish on Arthur's fair fame is seen again not only in Lancelot but in Tristram. At the very time when Tristram, who, being discovered by the hollow place in his sword to be the slayer of Sir Marhaus, is compelled to leave the land, tells Isolte that she can never fail to have all his devotion, he is really in love with the wife of Sir

Parallelisms in the myths of Arthur, Lancelot, and Tristram.

Segwarides, who at the last refuses to hold further parley with him, because when it was in his power to rescue her he failed to do so. In short, it is with Tristram as it is with Arthur and Lancelot. There may be from time to time words put into the mouths of all three, which attribute to them a strict and even ascetic severity; but it would be no hard task to bring together a formidable group of inconsistencies and contradictions in a legend which, like that of Arthur and his Knights, is the result of many accretions; and by all the analogies furnished by the popular literature of the world we are driven to the conclusion already anticipated that the higher ideal is the later conception, and that the coarser form is of the very essence of the myth. It is scarcely credible that the manifest sensuousness of many scenes in the relations of Lancelot with Guenevere can have been introduced into the story by the man who seeks to exhibit their love as absolutely Platonic and pure. But even if it be so, the fact remains that every one of these three, whose career otherwise resembles the career of the great mythical heroes of all lands, resembles them also in the multiplicity of their loves. Like Arthur and Lancelot, Tristram is φιλογύνης, and takes his place in the company of Phoibos, Theseus, Dionysos, Alpheios, Krishna, Kephalos and a host of other gods or heroes. Nay, the very relations which exist between Tristram, Isolte, and King Mark are precisely reproduced in those which are found between Sigurd, Brynhild, and Gunnar in the Volsung tale. In Isolte Tristram finds the woman to whom he can give his whole heart, while Tristram is the only man who can win the love of Isolte, as Sigurd is the only hero who can wake the heart of Brynhild. But both are under the same doom. The bride is in each case, like Helen, the most beautiful of women, as the hero is peerless among men, and she must in each case be wooed for another, and Mark of Cornwall in the Tristram story takes the place of Gunnar. We may trace the parallel even further. The naked sword which Sigurd places between himself and Brynhild, when he lies down to sleep by her side, is placed again by Tristram between himself and Isolte, and is used for the same purpose in the German story of the Two Brothers, the Norse legend of Big Bird Dan and the Arabian tale of Allah-ud-deen. These instances alone suffice to prove not only the common origin of these popular stories, but their nature, and justify the remark of Dr. Dasent which I have quoted elsewhere, and on which I again lay emphatic stress, that 'these mythical deep-rooted germs, throwing out fresh shoots from age to age in the popular literature of the race, are far more convincing proofs of the early existence of these traditions than any mere external evidence.'[1] But we need go no further than the Tristram story itself for a plain avowal of the parallelism, in the charge given by Isolte to Palamides, that he should go to King Arthur's court and tell Guenevere that ' within this land there are but four lovers, and these are Sir Lancelot of the Lake and Queen Guenevere, and Sir Tristram of Liones and Queen Isolte.' We must go further still. If, like Sigurd, Tristram and Lancelot give their love to women who are or who must be the brides of others, there yet remains in each case one whom each must wed, and as Gudrun is but a weaker reflexion of Brynhild (and how should she be otherwise, since she was a Niflung, or child of the Mist?), so is Elaine, the mother of Lancelot's child, a weakened image of Guenevere, and Isolte of the white hands a feeble likeness of Isolte the Fair.[2] So again the

[1] *Aryan Mythology*, i. 281.
[2] If Guenevere is reflected in Elaine the daughter of King Pelles, as Gudrun wears the likeness of Brynhild, so is the story of the daughter of King Pelles manifestly reproduced in the exquisite episode of the Fair Maid of Astolat, who also bears the name Elaine, the only difference being that the one would be, while the other really is, the mother of a child of Lancelot. In either case the spell which lies on the maiden is irresistible, as with Isolte the Fair it was impossible to withstand the witchery of Tristram's harping.

Introduction. 43

enmity between Gudrun and Brynhild is reproduced in the antipathy of the two Isoltes and the ill-concealed dislike of Guenevere for Elaine. If, yet more, Brynhild on learning that Sigurd has wedded her in the form of Gunnar declares that she will bring about the death of the hero to whom, as knowing no fear, she has yielded her love, so Isolte the Fair, on hearing that Tristram has married her namesake, warns him that henceforth she is his deadly foe.

If precisely the same impossibilities are attributed to the heroes of romance in different ages or lands, the likelihood is that all such tales have a common origin and a common meaning; and it is only necessary here to say that Tristram forms no exception to the heroes, who, resembling him, resemble also Herakles or Samson. Like the rest, he is able, single-handed, to slay scores or hundreds. It matters not how many may assault him, or whether they do so secretly or openly. It makes no difference to Bellerophon whether the ambush into which he falls hide twenty or fifty foes: it matters not to the Icelandic Grettir whether he finds himself surrounded by forty or eighty enemies, or to the Knight of the Misshapen Coat whether he be assailed by a hundred knights at once (p. 146), or to Tristram whether a whole troop of King Mark's men set upon him single-handed (p. 143). In each instance the same doom awaits the assailants which falls on the captains with their fifties sent to summon Elijah to the presence of King Ahaziah. All are scattered as chaff before the wind, or smitten like a tree blasted by the thunderbolt. With men these things are absurd impossibilities. If as nature-myths which tell us of the irresistible power of the sun, the lightning, or the hurricane, these stories become full of truth and meaning, what justification can we have for resisting the inevitable inference?

Physical powers of mythical heroes.

What, again, is the madness which comes upon Tristram and Lancelot in their mad career, but the madness which seizes on Herakles after a long course of beneficent action; and what is the madness of Herakles but the unrestrained force which converts the beautiful Phoibos, whom the Nymphs wrap at his birth in a spotless robe of white, into the terrible Chrysâor whom no earthly being can withstand?

The madness of Tristram and Lancelot.

We have already seen that in the stories of Sir Balin and Sir Gareth, Arthur himself becomes a subordinate personage, and that, too, in the very points in which in his own myth he is the peculiar hero. In each case a sword is to be drawn forth from a stone or an anvil; and in each case it moves lightly as a feather at the touch of the one knight who alone is destined to draw it out. This knight is necessarily the hero of each particular story. Nothing can show more clearly or convincingly the artificial process by which the romance as we have it has been brought into shape. Nor can this assertion be twisted into a charge that unity of authorship is denied for compositions which have manifestly proceeded from a single poet or storyteller. It leaves this controversy altogether on one side. The whole myth of Arthur might have been first put into its present form by Sir Thomas Malory, although we know that it was not; but it would be none the less a fact that the stories of Arthur, Balin, Lancelot, Tristram, of the Isoltes, and the Elaines, and Guenevere, repeat each other, that this likeness is inherent in the materials on which the romance-writer worked, and that he was compelled in each episode to give the supremacy to the hero of that episode. If then into this episode the heroes of other tales be introduced, it follows inevitably that they must play in it a subordinate part. For our present purpose it is a matter of not the slightest moment whether one or a hundred Homers put together our Iliad. But if the whole Trojan war be a nature-myth, exhibiting

Subordination of Arthur in the myths of Balin, Lancelot, and Tristram.

Introduction. 45

the struggle of the solar powers in the East to recover the dawn goddess who with her treasures of light and beauty had been stolen from the West, it is a fact as self-evident that Sarpêdôn, the creeping light, who comes from Lykia, the brilliant land, through which flows the golden stream of Xanthos, is a solar hero, along with his friend Glaukos, the gleaming day, which survives the death of the bright sun of the morning. But it is not the less clear that this piece of genuine solar myth is misplaced in the later structure of the Iliad, for Paris as stealing away Helen from the West represents the robber Panis, who seek to detain Saramâ in their strongholds, and that they who take part with him are defending the citadel of night against the children of the sun who are come to take away the Dawn-maiden from the East and lead her to her Western home. Hence, in mythical congruity, Sarpêdôn ought to be fighting by the side of Achilleus; but to the old storytellers such inconsistencies were matters of little moment, and not only Sarpêdôn, but Memnôn, the very child of Eôs, the dawn, are arrayed on the side of Hektor. Yet the real spirit of the myth is in no case violated, for to Sarpêdôn Ilion is a spot far to the west of his bright Lykia, and no sooner is he slain than the old phrases assert their supremacy, and Phoibos himself wraps in a pure white robe of evening mist the body which Sleep and Death bear through the still night hours to the gleaming portals of the dawn. Nay, even into the story of Paris himself a mass of solar myth has been imported, and from the Trojan point of view the false seducer becomes in his relations with Oinônê the kinsman of Achilleus, Meleagros, or Sigurd.[1] These modifications, rendered necessary by the interweaving of independent myths, precisely illustrate the changes which pass over Arthur or Lancelot in those parts of the tale which bear no immediate relation to themselves. In his own field each is supreme; but when we reach the episodes of Balin

[1] *Aryan Mythology,* ii. 75, et seq.

or Galahad, he can no longer be the peerless knight, and the sword which had yielded to his touch now remains immovable in spite of all his efforts. Nay, he undergoes even positive defeat, and Arthur is unhorsed by Tristram (p. 152). In a still more striking scene, the powers of healing, which Arthur vainly tries to exercise on Sir Urre of Hungary, are roused by the touch of Lancelot, for here we are in that portion of the tale in which Lancelot is the bravest and best knight in all the world. As such, he fights with and overcomes a terrible boar, which, before he can slay it, succeeds in gashing his thigh and inflicting a fearful wound,—an incident which we find again in the early career of Odysseus, and in the transparent myth of Adonis.[1]

In the horn of Morgan le Fay, which is said to test the fidelity of wives, we see another feature common to the myths of many ages and many lands. Except in the hands of the innocent, the liquor of the horn is spilt (p. 143), just as in the so-called Orphic poem the testing stone held in the husband's hand hurls the faithless wife from her couch. The same marvellous power of discernment belongs to the horns of Bran and Ceridwen, of Huon of Bordeaux, and of Tegan Euroron. This property is possessed also by the vessel of the Sangreal, which heals the guileless knight, while it may not be seen by Sir Lancelot (p. 180). In the story of Bevis of Hampton the stone becomes a talisman insuring the safety of the maiden who wears it (p. 279), while the purity of the maiden becomes itself in turn a power which, as in the story of Una, disarms the rage of lions (p. 283).

Talismanic tests.

Not less noteworthy is the ship or barge of the dead, which, while it carries the dead to their last home, also tells the story of their lives or proclaims their wrongs. Thus, when Hermanec the lord of the

The ship of the dead.

---

[1] *Aryan Mythology*, ii. 172.
[2] *Lithika*, 312. *Aryan Mythology*, ii. 120.

Introduction.   47

Red City is murdered, the barge in which the dead man lies with a letter in his hand is seen by Tristram and Palamides, and the latter, who hastens to avenge him, is borne on the vessel past the Red City to the Delectable Isle, where he fights with and slays the murderers (p. 160). In the touching episode of the Fair Maid of Astolat the barge which bears her body down the Thames is espied by Arthur and Guenevere, and the letter in the maiden's hand reveals to them the story of her ill-fated love for Lancelot. The same process which converted the horn of Amaltheia into a talismanic test as the horn of Oberon has derived from the barge of the dead the ship of Faith, which warns all the mistrustful against entering it, and into which Galahad enters with Percivale and his sister in the quest of the Holy Grail (p. 194). But the sister of Percivale, when, like Iphigeneia, she has yielded up her gentle life to heal the lady of the castle, is laid again in the same and yet another barge, which is to bear her to the city of Sarras, that there her body may be laid to rest in the Spiritual Place, in which the good Sir Galahad is also to take his long sleep. And once again the ship reappears in the tale, when Arthur himself is to be borne away from the sight of men, and when the three queens, who have already been seen in different guise in the early career of Gawaine and his brother, once more do their office as the Weird or Fatal Sisters. A clearer light is thrown on the nature of this ship in the story of Sceaf, the father of Scild, in the myth of Beowulf. Here Sceaf, whose name tells its own tale, comes, as he goes, in a ship, with a sheaf of corn at his head; and when his work among men is done, he bids his people lay him in the ship, and in the ship he is laid accordingly with the goodliest weapons and the most costly of ornaments, and with all things which may gladden his heart in the phantom land. Here we have in its fairer colours the picture which in many lands and ages has been realised in terrible completeness. In all these instances we see the expression of the ancient and universal animistic conviction, which ascribed to the dead all the feelings and wants of the living, and which led men to slay beasts to furnish them with food, and to slaughter their wives or comrades that they might journey to their new home with a goodly retinue.[1] For the ideal of the ship itself we must look elsewhere. All these vessels move of their own will, and though without oar, or rudder, or sail, or rigging, they never fail to reach the port for which they are making. They belong, in short, to that goodly fleet, in which the ships may assume all shapes and sizes, so that the bark which can bear all the Æsir may be folded up like a napkin. The child who is asked where he has seen such ships will assuredly say, 'In the sky:' and when this answer is given, the old animism, which, as Mr. Tylor well says, is the ultimate source of human fancy,[2] explains everything in the myths related of these mysterious barks, which grow big and become small again at their pleasure, which gleam with gold, and purple, and crimson, or sail on in sombre and gloomy majesty, which leave neither mountain, nor field, nor glen unvisited, and which carry with them wealth or poverty, health or disease,—which, in short, are living beings. As such, they know the thoughts and works of men, and can speak with those whom they carry across the seas of heaven; and thus we have the ship which bears Odysseus from the Phaiakian land to the shores of Ithaka, and carries the Argonauts to the coasts of Kolchis.

Another boat-shaped vessel is the Sangreal itself, which imparts to the Arthur myth, or rather to that of Lancelot,

The Sangreal. its peculiar character. Whatever be the beauty which the influence of Christian sentiment has thrown over this legend, all that we have to do in the first

---

[1] Tylor, *Primitive Culture*, vol. i. ch. xi.   [2] *Ib.* i. 248.
[3] *Aryan Mythology*, ii. 278.

instance is to mark closely the points of likeness between this and other myths, and these points of likeness are to be found in its shape, its healing and life-giving properties, and its inexhaustible fertility. To these are added certain talismanic powers which, as we have already seen, it shares in common with some other circular or boat-shaped symbols of wealth and plenty. But elsewhere this oval emblem is most closely associated with the rod, the pillar, or the spear, the stauros or the pole, which became the special sign of the sun as the generative or fecundating power. Hence, even if the Grail vessel were not in this Arthur or Lancelot myth connected with any spear-shaped signs, we should be fully justified in placing this mysterious dish in the class to which belong the cups of Rhea and Démétêr, of Serapis, and of the milkwoman or gardener's wife in Hindu folk-lore, the lotos of Harp-i-chruti, the jar of Aristomenes, the divining cup of Joseph, the ivory ewer of Solomon, the goblet of Taliesin, the luck of Edenhall, the horn of Amaltheia, the inexhaustible table of the Ethiopians, and the Round Table of Guenevere,—all of these being simply modifications of the Hindu Yoni, which reappears in the ships of Isis and Athénê, and the altar of Baal which supported the Semitic Ashera. But the connexion of the Grail vessel with the spear-shaped emblem, which is but a modification of the Phallos, is not only not lacking in the Lancelot story: it is put forward with a prominence which is the more significant, if we assume that the romance maker was utterly unconscious of the nature and origin of the materials on which he was working. If in other myths the upright emblem, the staff or rod of wealth and prosperity which Phoibos gives to Hermes, becomes the *arbor vitæ* or *crux salutifera*, and if in purely heathen models it is represented as shedding drops which denote the blood or the life, we have the whole framework of the myth over which the introduction of Christian sentiment has shed a colouring of marvellous beauty.[1] If, while we feel that the evidence is overwhelming, the conclusion to which we are brought should seem somewhat repulsive, we have only to remember again that precisely the same idea lies at the root of institutions to all appearance so utterly unlike each other as those of the Corinthian Hierodouloi, the Gerairai of Athens, and the vestal virgins who reappear in the Catholic and orthodox nun. But to the connexion of the two emblems it is impossible to shut our eyes, as we read how, after seeing the Sangreal in the house of King Pelles, Bors, having laid himself down to sleep in his armour, beholds a light in which he discerns a spear great and long coming straight towards him point-long. This spear is seen again in the supreme vision vouchsafed to the pure Sir Galahad and his two comrades, when, the holy Grail being manifested, four angels enter, two bearing candles, the third a towel, and the fourth a spear from which fall three drops of blood, and which is finally placed upright on the holy vessel. But it was obviously inevitable that this imagery should to Christians convey another meaning; and thus the liquor, which in the horn of Oberon is the costliest wine, becomes the blood of the Saviour which Joseph of Arimathea caught in the sacred dish in which he ate the lamb on Shrove Tuesday, while its life-giving and healing powers are not less necessarily referred to the Eucharist (p. 200). That the

[1] The author of the Introduction to *Britannia after the Romans* speaks of the Romance of the Sangreal as 'a blasphemous imposture, more extravagant and daring than any on record, in which it is endeavoured to pass off the mysteries of bardism for direct inspirations of the Holy Ghost.'—Craik, *History of English Literature*, i. 141.—Speculations on these mysteries may be safely left to those who may possess, and be satisfied with, the evidence that such mysteries ever existed. But when we see that the elements of the myth are found in traditions scattered over the world, the notion that the Grail story is an imposture of late invention becomes absurd. Doubtless the romance-maker shed his own colouring over the legend; and this colouring was necessarily Christian. Nothing further is needed to explain the whole romance in the shape which it finally assumed.

achieving of the Sangreal should be confined to the pure Galahad is, it needs scarcely to be remarked, no peculiarity in the Grail myth. We have already traced this property through a large number of legends relating to the signs or symbols of life, fertility, wealth, healing, and power.

But the myth lent itself so readily to the purposes of Christian teaching that we cease to feel surprised when in the Arthur romance it becomes the means of en- <small>Introduction of Christian sentiment.</small> forcing many doctrines of mediæval Catholicity. Thus when Galahad rescues the wounded Sir Melias from the attacks of two knights, he is told by a hermit that the punishment was inflicted because Melias had ventured on the quest of the Grail without first making a clean confession, and that the two knights who attacked him were pride and covetousness (p. 179). Thus the dalliance of the Christian with deadly sin is allegorised in the temptation of Sir Percivale by the beautiful woman whose pavilion, when he makes the sign of the cross, vanishes away in smoke and flame (p. 185). This temptation is practised with less success upon Sir Bors, but the mode in which it is repelled is the same (p. 190). In the same way the incident of the serpent and the lion, on each of which rides a woman, is explained as an allegory of the old law and the new (p. 184). The ingenuity exhibited in the framing of these allegorical visions cannot be disputed. There is a singular force and beauty in the dreams of Ector and Gawaine, who are told that the fair meadow which they had seen is humility and patience—things ever fresh and green—the black bulls which fed in it being knights of the Round Table, who set out on the Grail quest, black with sins, while the three white bulls are Galahad, Percivale, and Bors, the one spot in the last of these three being the taint of the single sin to which he is yielding. In this vision Lancelot is seen upon an ass, which denotes his humiliation; while the incident which represents the water as sinking away from him when he stoops to drink is clearly derived from the myth of Tantalos (pp. 188, 189). But if the Christian meaning attached to the myth of the Sangreal has led to the same gross and repulsive notions of transubstantiation which disfigure the lives of some saints of the Roman Church, and which make the romance-writer represent Lancelot at mass as hastening to the help of the priest whom he supposes to be burdened by the human form which two men standing on either side above him have placed between his hands (p. 198), it has also reached a higher standard and enforces a more wholesome lesson when to Lancelot's assertion that, if he be sinful, the prayers of his pure son Galahad should be of benefit to him, the priest replies, 'Be sure that thou dost fare the better for his prayers; but the son shall not bear the iniquity of the father, neither the father bear the iniquity of the son' (p. 186).

But although almost all the closing scenes of the romance are lit up with the splendour of Christian feeling, there are features in it which we can no more regard as Christian, or even as human, than we can the narratives of certain events related in the Odyssey. The high ascetic tone imparted to the close of Lancelot's relations with Guenevere may be and is probably due entirely to the force of Christian opinion; and this fact must clearly distinguish the earlier and later characters of the myth. Rather it must be said that the whole romance, as we have it, is really built up on the assumption that the love of Lancelot and Guenevere is throughout sensual. The very achievement of the Sangreal depends on the birth of a child of Lancelot; and except on such an assumption the result is rendered impossible. Lancelot is entrapped by Elaine, because he supposes that he has been summoned to Queen Guenevere. But this is not a solitary instance. The same incident is repeated when the daughter of King Pelles visits the court of Arthur;

The two Elaines and Guenevere.

nor is it possible to mistake the nature of the colloquy between Lancelot and Guenevere when the knight tears away the bars from the window that he may thus enter her chamber (p. 211). It may be urged that these are later additions which mar the ancient purity of the myth; but in favour of such a notion there is little indeed to be said. It cannot be said that the romance-maker who has drawn a perfectly consistent character in Galahad would have allowed a series of incidents which involve a monstrous contradiction between the character and the career of Lancelot and Guenevere, as he has drawn them. Galahad before his birth is destined to be the pure and spotless knight, and such he remains always. Not less earnestly are Guenevere and Lancelot made to declare that their love has never been of a kind to reflect the least dishonour on King Arthur; yet this solemn asseveration, made again and again, is contradicted by a series of incidents which they are compelled to keep out of Arthur's knowledge by a long course of equivocation and lying. In short, we have here two stories—one in which Guenevere is faithful to her husband, and Lancelot looks on her as a man may look to his guardian angel, and another in which she is faithless, and responds to a sensual love on the part of Lancelot; and all that we have to determine is, which of these stories is the earlier. It seems almost self-evident that the idea which is certainly here found in the germ, and which has been expanded by Mr. Tennyson until the result is a complete transformation of these two characters, is but a thin coating of later Christian sentiment thrown over the earlier picture in which Guenevere not only seems to play, but really plays the part of Helen as she is drawn by the great tragic poets of Athens. When first Arthur thinks of wedding her, he is warned, as we have seen, by the wise Merlin that she will not be a wholesome wife for him; and from the circumstances already noticed it is clear that according to the conception of some one or other of the romance-makers her actual faithlessness began before Lancelot had seen the future mother of his child. We may, if we please, say that the sensual fury, displayed by Guenevere when she finds that the very plan which she has laid to keep Lancelot by her side leads to his being again entrapped by Elaine while she sojourns in Arthur's court, is to be charged to the corrupt imagination of a later age: but we need only repeat that the very structure of the story which relates the career of Galahad utterly precludes this notion. Nay, Guenevere is not only a destroyer of many knights, as she might easily be on the hypothesis that though seemingly guilty she was really innocent; we have seen that she combines cruelty with her sensuality (214). Knowing perfectly well that Meliagrance was speaking the truth and is fighting in a righteous cause, she longs to see him slain; and when he is overthrown and yields to Lancelot in the ordeal of battle, she gives to her lover a private signal that he shall in no case suffer the defeated knight to live. As to Lancelot, who thus commits murder at her bidding, he avoids in this instance the utterance of a direct lie, because the partial knowledge of Meliagrance makes it possible for him to employ the tricks of a dishonest special pleader. Thus then we have falsehood and treachery on the one side, and faithlessness on the other,—in other words we have in Lancelot and Guenevere the counterparts of Saramâ and the Panis, of Paris and Helen; and the taking away of Guenevere from the court of Arthur, who had cherished him as his friend, answers to the taking away of Helen from Menelaos by the man in whom he had placed a perfect trust. Except on the one supposition, which we have seen to be untenable, the character of Lancelot precisely reflects that of Paris; and the words of Menelaos before the walls of Ilion are echoed in those of Arthur in the supreme strife before the gates of Joyous Gard, 'Fie on thy fair speech; I am now thy mortal foe, for thou hast slain my knights, and dishonoured my queen' (p. 220). In short, Lancelot is throughout a man of fair words, who disclaims all thoughts of treason (pp. 222, 223), even while he knows that he has shamefully deceived his friend. It is the picture of Paris as drawn in the Iliad; and if it be said that in that poem, as we have it, Paris does not exhibit the unfaltering courage or the invincible strength of Lancelot, we have only to remember that the portrait given to us in our Iliad is not the only mythical picture of the treacherous son of Priam.[1] But in spite of all his efforts, the Christian sentiment of the romance-maker cannot disguise the nature of the materials which he was handling. If Arthur was the man so little extreme to regard what is done amiss, as he is here represented, so little disposed

[1] The verdict of the poet of the Iliad may be summed up in the single line,

Δύσπαρι, εἶδος ἄριστε, γυναιμανὲς, ἠπεροπευτά.—*Il.* iii. 39.

But the story of the birth and the early years of Paris, his irresistible prowess at the games, his redoubtable exploits against thieves and evil-doers, are not less parts of the great myth of Paris, as it has come down to us, than those portions of it which are related in our Iliad. That the two pictures are inconsistent is unquestionable; but it is inconsistent that the invincible Arthur should be defeated by Balin, or that Sarpêdôn and Memnôn, the bright solar heroes, should be found fighting on the side of the thievish powers of darkness. But on this point it is not necessary to add to the remarks already made. The real matter to be determined is the idea which lies at the root of each mythical character—the natural inference being that that which is inconsistent with this idea in the myths, as they come before us, is of later growth, and that to this fact we must attribute the fairer colouring thrown over the career of Lancelot. Beyond all doubt, in the history of the human mind, the cruder fancy generally precedes the more polished fiction; and thus it has been well urged by Mr. Paley that the conception of Helen by the Greek lyric and tragic poets is inexplicable on the supposition that they were already familiar with the character of Helen as drawn out in our Iliad and Odyssey. The so-called answer of Aristotle is, as he contends, no answer at all, for it is a mere matter of fact that the Iliad, as we have it, abounds with dramatic scenes and incidents more striking perhaps than any which the tragedians have handled, and far more likely to make a deep impression upon an audience.

to think evil of another without due evidence, the persistence with what he follows up to the death a quarrel with his friend on a charge which, according to some portions of the story as we have it, is unproven, and even after the touching protestations of innocence which mark the restitution of Guenevere to her husband (p. 223), becomes inexplicable. But if the character of Arthur, as here drawn, is not Christian, it is because the portraits given of Achilleus and Odysseus in our Iliad and Odyssey are not human. The perplexity which we must feel, so long as we take them to be what they are not, will cease so soon as we recognise in all these heroes the chief actors in the great tragedy of nature.

The ending of this great drama we have now reached, as it is wrought out in the great Arthur myth. The victory of the snake Ahi is the victory of the great worm of darkness which slays the light of day; and in the myths of every land this worm, viper, or dragon plays its deadly part. The fair Dawn maiden treads unwittingly on the adder which stings her to death, and goes down to her cheerless sojourn in Hades till Orpheus comes to lead her back again to the land of the living. The young sun, Herakles, strangles these snakes of darkness when they assail him in his cradle. The throttling viper of the Veda becomes the Azidahaka or Zohak of Zoroastrian and modern Persian mythology, the Kalinak or black dragon slain by Krishna in later Hindu legends. And thus, after his wild but brilliant career, Ragnar Lodbrog is thrust into the dungeon where he charms the serpents with his music, until at last one creeps stealthily to his side and stings him in the heart. Hence also in the Arthur myths visions of snakes bring the foreboding of the end. The king dreams that he sits in a chair, fastened to a wheel, beneath which lies a deep black water full of serpents and noisome things, and that suddenly the wheel turns round and he is plunged into the infernal

Arthur and Mordred.

stream where the serpents seize him by all his limbs. From this terrible dream he passes into a half-waking state in which he thinks that he sees the form of the dead Gawaine, and hears his voice warning him not to fight on the morrow, but to make a month's truce with Mordred, whose name (although little can be said of the names in these later compositions) seems to betoken him as the murderer, biter, or crusher. The king follows Gawaine's advice; but his doom is not thus to be averted. It had been agreed that if during the conference between Arthur and Mordred a sword should be raised on either side, this should be the signal for mortal battle. But while they are yet speaking the snake again plays its part. An adder bites the heel of one of Arthur's knights, who raises his weapon to slay the venomous beast; and Mordred's people, taking alarm, rush upon their adversaries. The prophecy of Merlin is well nigh accomplished. The father and the son are to die, each by the other's hand. In vain Sir Lucan warns Arthur to remember his dream; but he will not hear. He sees the traitor who has done all the wrong, and betide him life, or betide him death, he is resolved to slay him. But Mordred, writhing like a snake along the spear which has passed through his body, smites Arthur on the temples with the sword which he holds in both hands, and the king falls back in a swoon. It is the old tale of the fatal children, of children born to be great, born to be kings, born to slay their parents. There is death everywhere; and the phrases which described the death of the day and the night, of the sun and the darkness, of the dawn and the dew, explain every incident of the closing scenes in the lives of the heroes or maidens who represent them in mythical stories. If it was said of the morning and the sun that the bright children had slain their dark parent, this in mythical tales would become Romulus and Remus slaying Amulius, Oidipous slaying Laios, Perseus smiting down Akrisios, and Cyrus overthrowing Astyages.[1] If the sun put the dawn to flight, this was Indra shattering the car of Dahana, or Phoibos chasing Daphnê, or Alpheios hastening after Arethousa. If the sun scorched up the dew, this was Kephalos smiting Prokris with the unerring spear in the thicket where the dewdrops glisten longest. If the shadows of night blot out the day from the heaven, this was Paris slaying Achilleus in the western gates, or the blood-red clouds of eventide eating out the life of Herakles. All this, it may be urged, has been said again and again; but we can but bring together once more the parallelisms which make the death of Arthur only another phase of the death of all solar heroes. One feature more remains. With the death of the sun his rays cease to shoot across the heaven. The great being is gone who alone could yield the unerring spear, or bow, or sword; and his weapon must go with him. Hence Arthur's sword must no more be profaned by the touch of mortal hand; and as the sun rises from the eastern waters as Phoibos springs to life on Delos, and plunges into his sleep like Endymion or Odysseus in the Western Sea, so the sword Excalibur must be restored to the waters from which it had arisen. It is the daily fate of the sun, as Kephalos falls from the Western Cape into the Leukadian Gulf, or as Aphrodite returns to the sea-foam from which she sprang, like Athênê the Triton-born.

Arthur himself, as we have seen, is borne away in the barge in which the weird sisters have long waited for him; but he departs, not to die, but only to heal him of his grievous wound in the valley of Avilion, the Latmian land in which Endymion takes his rest. Still, as the ages rolled on, and experience taught men more and more, that there is no man who shall not see death, and as the belief grew that in telling Arthur's

The departure of Arthur to the vale of Avilion.

---

[1] The name Astyages, the Persian Asdahag, is but Azidahaka, the biting snake, Zohak.—*Aryan Mythology*, ii. 83.

story they were speaking of a man who had really lived on the earth, so was the need felt more and more of saying plainly that he died. But the old myth still retained something of its old power; and the storytellers who chanted the lays of the Helgis or of Arthur were each constrained to avow that according to the older faith neither Helgi the slayer of Hunding nor Arthur the peerless knight had ever died at all, and that he who had been king should yet be king again. Arthur was now, in short, one of that goodly company which numbers in its ranks the great Karl and Barbarossa, Sebastian of Portugal, the Tells of Rutli, and the Moor Boabdil. None of these are dead; for the sun, while men see him not, is but slumbering under that spell of night, whether in her beautiful or in her awful forms, which keeps true Thomas beneath the hills of Ercildoune, or Tanhaüser in the caves of the Horselberg, or Odysseus in the grotto of Kalypso. Arthur does but sleep in the charmed slumber of the Cretan Epimenides, of Endymion the darling of Selênê, of Narkissos, and the Seven Sleepers of Ephesus; and under this spell lies not Arthur only, but the wise Merlin who had foretold his birth and destiny, had received him as a babe, and had witnessed his glory.[1]

[1] In his wisdom and his foresight, in his perfect knowledge of a coming fate which yet, to Arthur's surprise (p. 243), he makes no attempt to avoid, Merlin strongly resembles the Hellenic Odysseus. But the point of the story in its closing scenes is the besotted affection of the old sage for a damsel who, he knows, cares nought for him. But he suffers the maiden, who is a water-nymph, to entice him into a cavern in which she imprisons him beneath a great stone. This is precisely the story of Tanhaüser and the goddess of the Horselberg; with very slight modification it is the story of Thomas of Ercildoune (a name which is only another form of Horseldonne or Horselberg), and of Prince Ahmed and the Peri Banou in the Arabian Nights Tales. Here he is kept fast in an imprisonment from which none can deliver him except the woman who lured him into it; or, as the story avers, not an hundred men could lift the huge stone beneath which Merlin made great dole. This is substantially the legend of the philosopher

The analysis of detail in the story might be carried much farther; but enough probably has been said to leave little doubt of the nature of the materials on which the romance-makers had to work, and of the extent to which they unconsciously repeated themselves,—so that the same writer could in one and the

<small>Composition of the Arthur romance.</small>

Abu Ajeeb, related by Washington Irving in the Legends of the Alhambra. It is true that here it is the sage who contrives to get the Gothic princess within the inchanted gate of his paradise; but the besotted affection of the old man for the blooming maiden is precisely reproduced, and here again it is the sorceress only who can set him free. Whenever the sage shows symptoms of awakening from his charmed slumber, the tones of her magic harp speedily lull him to sleep again. As she is herself imprisoned with him, like Venus in the Tanhaüser story, this is obviously the only way in which she can prolong his captivity. In the Arthur tale, she can leave him to himself, because she has enticed him to enter in, while she stands without.

Of the Merlin legend it is scarcely necessary to say more than that the notion of his being a demon-child is the result of the same degradation which converted Odin himself and all the Æsir into devils. Neither in Teutonic nor in Hellenic lands did the Christian missionaries question the existence of the gods or heroes named in the mythologies of the tribes to whom they preached. The deities were allowed to live, but they lived on under a curse. But that these deified or supernatural beings might connect themselves with mortal women, was a belief unquestioned whether by those who framed the story of the hero Astrabakos (Herodotos, vi. 69), or of the loves of the angels in Hebrew tradition. Hence the child of a deified hero or demigod and of a mortal woman would, in the estimation of Christian teachers, be the offspring of a diabolical incubus; and thus the nature of Merlin, as of Tamlane in the Scottish ballad, would be definitely determined. The marvellous powers of the child would be the natural result of his extraordinary parentage; and the same powers which made the child Iamos acquainted with the language of birds would enable Merlin to vindicate the name of his mother, or at the least to convict her accusers of sins not less than those which were laid to her charge. Like Herakles, Perseus, Dionysos, and other mythical beings, Merlin has many enemies who are bent on taking his life; and his wisdom is specially proved by his power of revealing the reason why the walls of a castle fall down as soon as they are built,—a result due to the agency of dragons underneath a running water. This connexion of dragons with water is common to a vast number of legends; but this special revelation of Merlin may be compared with that of the griffin or the giant in the German story of the Old Griffin and the Norse tale of Rich Peter the Pedlar, and perhaps also with the problem on the solution of which depends the life of the giant or the sorcerer in the Hindu story of

Introduction. 61

same narrative present three or four versions of the same tale, believing them, nevertheless, to be different, because the names and the local colouring were more or less changed. The Argives, the Athenians, and the Thebans believed most firmly in the thorough independence of their several tribal legends; and yet the story of Perseus simply reflects that of Theseus, and is repeated in that of Oidipous. The same condition of thought rendered it possible for a mediæval composer or compiler of romance to relate the story of Arthur and Balin, of Gareth and Galahad and Lancelot and Tristram, in a connected narrative, without the consciousness that he was really weaving together five or six different versions of one single story.[1] But without going further, it may safely be maintained that no features of any importance in the whole Arthur romance have been left out of sight in these remarks, and that the whole story may therefore take its place in that large family of heroic legends which have their origin in mythical phrases describing the phenomena of the day or the year.

Romances like those of Bevis of Hampton and Guy of Warwick may be regarded as rather the arbitrary fictions of a comparatively late age, than the genuine growth of popular mythical tradition; but this very fact, if it be admitted, only makes more noteworthy the adherence of the romance-maker to the old models. When he could insert at will the fancies of his

The story of Bevis of Hampton.

Punchkin (Frere, *Deccan Tales*), and the Norse tale of the Giant who had no heart in his body (Grimm).

The Merlin story which Jeffrey introduces into the life of Arthur is found in Nennius (*History of the Britons*, 42) who, however, calls the child Ambrose, and having said that he was conceived by no mortal man, makes him assert that a Roman consul was his father. Whatever be the date of Nennius, his 'History' is probably two centuries earlier than that of Jeffrey.

[1] The Arthur story has been shown by Mr. Campbell to be in all essential features the same as the Highland legend of the history of the Feinne. —*Popular Tales of the West Highlands*, iv. 267. *Aryan Mythology*, i. 316.

own mind, it is strange that he should still keep within the
charmed circle in which we recognise the familiar imagery
of the oldest Aryan myths. Like Arthur, or Tristram, or
Lancelot, or Galahad, Bevis is born to greatness:[1] like
Tristram, and Arthur, and a host of others, he is in peril
from those who wish to take his life, and the device which
Saber hits upon to hide the fact that Bevis is not slain is
one which we find far beyond the circle of Aryan folk-
lore. The sequel of the story seems to be built on the
model of that of Bellerophon. Like him, Bevis is a
match for any number of men who may assail him: like
him, he is the victim of treacherous letters which order
his host to put him to death. Like him, he is subjected
by his host to terrible dangers; but from the noisome pit
full of reptiles, answering to the Iron Stove or the Glass
Coffin of German tales, Bevis escapes as Bellerophon escapes from the ambuscade which is placed for his destruction. With this story are interwoven incidents which are
common to the myth of Odysseus and the tale of Logedas
Rajah and other popular Hindu legends. He returns to
the home where he had left the lady of his love, clad in
palmer's raiment, and is told that of all who come in such
garb she, like Penelope, asks tidings of the man of many
griefs and wanderings who has left her mourning. As
Odysseus again is recognised by his dog Argos, so is Bevis
known at once to his trusty steed Arundel. Like almost
all other kindred heroes, he is a slayer of dragons and a
tamer of giants, and Ascapard plays the part of a Troll
who may be made to do good service but is not altogether
to be trusted. Doubtless the constant repetition of incidents proves a comparative lack of imagination on the
part of the romance-maker; but it proves still more
clearly the nature of the materials which he sought to

---

[1] There were versions which represented Bevis as a son of Olger the
Dane.—Ludlow, *Popular Epics*, ii. 303.—But the parentage of these heroes
is a matter of very secondary importance.

Introduction. 63

bring into shape. Josian, who lulls her suitor to sleep on her lap in order to be rid of his importunities and then strangles him, is simply a more active Penelopê avenging her own wrongs. In the disguise by which she makes herself like the Loathly Lady, she assumes a form which the brilliant hero or the beautiful maiden of Eastern and Western tradition can alike put on, and which, passing through the phase exhibited by the ugly frog or toad in German folk-lore, carries us to the myth of Bheki the frog-sun. Of the battle in Cheapside it is enough to say that it is as sheer an impossibility as the most marvellous exploits attributed to Grettir or to Herakles. The great strife is followed by a long period of peace and happy love, until at last Bevis, and his horse Arundel, and the devoted Josian, all pass away from earth together.

The idea which runs through the earlier portions of the story of Guy of Warwick has found expression in the Arthur story in the contempt shown by the maiden who serves as guide to Gareth in his disguise as Prettyhands, and in the ordeal to which he is subjected by the lady of the castle (p. 123). But not only is Guy a knight-errant and a slayer of dragons and noisome beasts; the doom of the wanderer presses on him still more heavily. He toils hard and achieves great glory, that he may win the maiden whom he loves: and when he has won her, forty days only pass before he feels that he must go from her side, and putting on a pilgrim's dress he wanders away to the Holy Land. But he has still mighty works to do; and the Ethiopian giant and other foes fall beneath his hands. In his later wanderings he comes across his friend Thierry, of whom an incident is recorded which is found in other legends, and illustrates the old animistic belief of the separable soul which can go out from the body and return to it again. In the story of King Gunthram the soul goes forth in the form of a snake; but the movement of the weasel which creeps

The story of Guy of Warwick.

from Thierry's throat differs not much from that of the snake.[1] The fact that in the Gunthram myth the watcher is a servant seems to show that Guy here plays really the subordinate part which Arthur plays in those portions of the romance which do not immediately concern himself. Of the incident itself Mr. Tylor says: 'This is one of those instructive legends which preserve for us, as in a museum, relics of an early intellectual condition of our Aryan race, in thoughts which to our modern minds have fallen to the level of quaint fancy, but which still remain sound and reasonable philosophy to the savage. A Karen at this day would appreciate every point of the story: the familiar notion of spirits not crossing the water, which he exemplifies in his Burmese forests by stretching threads across the brook for the ghosts to pass along; the idea of the soul going forth embodied in an animal; and the theory of the dream being a real journey of the sleeper's soul.'[2] It is possible that this idea may be faintly traced in that scene in the wanderings of Vicram Maharajah[3] in which the cobra emerges at will from his throat. But the connexion cannot go beyond the mere suggestion of the imagery; for the story of Vicram makes it evident that the cobra which enters into his throat is the snake of winter, which makes the rajah miserable until he can be freed from it; nor can he be freed from it except by Persephoné or Iduna who returns in spring from the cheerless land. If any doubt still remained as to the nature of this myth it would be set at rest by the fact that the slaying of the cobra is followed by the recovery of the treasure which he had stolen,—an incident repeated in the transparent myth of the treasure guarded by the serpent Fafnir who is slain by Sigurd. It is singular, however, that the connexion between the snake and water, or hidden treasure, should be preserved in this story of

[1] *Aryan Mythology*, i. 402-4.   [2] *Primitive Culture*, i. 397.
[3] Frere, *Deccan Tales*, 129.

Thierry, as in the myths of Kadmos, the Delphian Phoibos, the Sphinx, and many others. Of the closing scenes in the life of Guy all that needs to be noted is the slight modification which here also a Christian sentiment has introduced into a legend otherwise repeating the old tale of Achilleus and Briseis, of Herakles and Iolê, of Odysseus and Penelope. They must be united after the weary wandering and the hard strife; but like Odysseus, and Vicram, and the Old Soldier of German folk-lore, and a thousand others, he returns in the form of a pilgrim or a beggar, and the wife whom he has forsaken prays him, if he can, to give her tidings of her love. But the sight of her gentle care of the poor and needy makes him shrink from the thought of breaking in upon her works of mercy; and, like Enoch Arden, he turns away and takes up his abode in a hermit's cell. When he feels that he has but a few hours to live, he sends her a ring by a herdman; and his wife instantly knows that the poor pilgrim is her husband the great Guy of Warwick. Like Kleopatra, she clasps the hero in her arms, as he gently breathes his life away; and as Kleopatra lingers not long upon earth after Meleagros is gone, so he has been but a fortnight dead when the sorrow of Felice is ended by her union with him in the land where there is no more parting. The beautiful hues of Eôs cannot linger long in the sky, when the Sun-god has gone to his rest.

Of the legend of Roland but little remains to be said after the remarks already made on the historical residuum which may exist in the story of King Arthur. No amount of mythical analysis will enable us to assert the impossibility of any given incident which may or may not have happened. The fact that the incidents of the Trojan war as given in the Iliad are found in many other national or tribal traditions, cannot disprove the possibility that some actual struggle may have taken place on the shores of the Hellespont; but if every

The tale of Roland.

incident be untrustworthy, if we are to get rid of Achilleus and Helen and Memnon and Eòs and Sarpêdôn, the tale of Troy is gone, and our knowledge of the war, if ever there was a war on the plains of Ilion, must be got from other sources. From the Iliad we can learn nothing of it; and from the romance of Roland we can learn nothing of the catastrophe which may have befallen the army or a portion of the army of Charles the Great. According to the romance, Roland and his comrades win a victory as splendid as that of Leonidas at Thermopylai, although at the same cost. But at best this is but a popular tradition; and another popular tradition is found in the magnificent song of Attabiscar,[1] which gives a vivid picture of the utter defeat of the invaders. The one tradition is worth as much as the other, and no more: and the attempt to extract any history from them must be fruitless.[2] Of the two, the popular Basque song is the more credible. Armies may be as utterly routed as that of the great Charles is there said to have been; but the exploits of Roland and his comrades are absolute impossibilities. Nay, even when the ground is piled with the dead whom their swords have smitten down, Roland has not so much as a scratch upon his body, though his armour is pierced everywhere with spear-points; and his death is caused not by any wound but by the excessive

[1] Michel, *Le Pays Basque*, p. 236. *Edinburgh Review*, April 1864, p. 382. *Aryan Mythology*, i. 189.

[2] Mr. Ludlow, *Popular Epics of the Middle Ages*, i. 353, cites the opinion of M. Paulin Paris, that the battle fought in the Pyrenees, in which twelve Frankish chiefs are said to be killed in the time of Dagobert, is a mere reflexion of the traditional Roncesvaux, the twelve chiefs representing the twelve peers of Charles the Great. Here again we need only to fall back on our position that the process of extracting history from legend must be essentially untrustworthy. Whether a second battle of Roncesvaux in the time of Lewis the Pious was in popular tradition confused with the fight in which Roland fell, is a question with which we are not concerned. The reader will find some remarks on this subject in Mr. Ludlow's work (i. 359), as well as on the dates to be assigned to the poems which profess to relate this hero's exploits.

toil which splits his skull and lets his brain ooze out at his temples. He is, in short, one of those invulnerable heroes, whom death must nevertheless be suffered somehow or other to lay low; and his sword Durandal is one of those magic weapons of which Excalibur, and Morglay, and Mirandoise, and Gram are the fellows. If, when drawn from its sheath, it flashes like lightning and blinds the eyes of foemen, this may be put down to the license of poetical fancy; but there must surely be some method in the madness of so many poets when all describe the armour of their heroes in the like terms of hyperbole, absurd when the words are spoken of any weapons fashioned by human hands, but less than the reality when spoken of the spears of Indra or of Phoibos. Nay, Roland himself knows that it is no earthly weapon which he wields. It has been brought by angels from heaven, like the robe which came to Medeia from Helios; and when Roland feels that his death-hour has come, even he is utterly unable to break it. In vain he strives to shiver against marble, sardonyx, and adamant; and then he sinks down exhausted, but with the firm conviction that the angels who brought the sword will bear it away again, as Excalibur is drawn down beneath the waters from which it had arisen. Of the beautiful Holda, to whom Roland is betrothed, it is enough to say that she belongs to that bright array of beings to whom death brings life and gladness, and among whom are seen the glorious forms of Kleopatra and Brynhild, of Daphné and Arethousa, of Oinônê and Isolte and Felice, of Iolê and Briséis, and that with this touching myth of the dawn-maiden's death ends the lay of the hero, in whom some see the commonplace prefect of the Britannic march, named in the pages of Eginhard.

But Roland appears again in Olger the Dane.[1] The

[1] The method which we have felt bound to follow leaves but little interest for questions which turn on the country to which a hero belonged.

name may be changed, and the incidents of his career may be somewhat different; but he is the same invincible hero, whose weapons have been forged on no earthly anvil. He is the defender of the same land, a warrior in the same hosts which the mythical Roland led on to victory; and those points in which he seems to be unlike the mighty Paladin serve only to identify him with other heroes to whom both he and Roland stand in the relation of brothers. Like Arthur and Tristram and Macduff, like Telephos, Perseus, Cyrus, Romulus, Oidipous, he is one of the fatal children, whose greatness no earthly obstacles can hinder. At his birth the fairies appear to bestow on him their gifts and their blessing, as the Moirai are seen round the cradle of Meleagros. His life on earth is to be spent in defending the realm of the great Karl: but he stands to him in the relation of Herakles to Eurystheus. He is a hostage placed in the emperor's hands by his father the King of Denmark, and is sentenced to a hard punishment because his father fails in his trust. He is rescued from death only by the sudden appearance of formidable enemies against whom Karl sees that Olger may be as useful as Herakles was to his Argive master. In the cause of Karl Olger performs exploits as wonderful as those of the son of Alkmênê; but a sense of wrongs suffered at the hands of the emperor sends him forth to be, like Indra and Savitar and Woden and Phoibos, a wanderer over the wide earth. But Olger is also, like them, one whom all women love, and more especially he is the darling of

<small>It may be, as M. Barrois, cited by Mr. Ludlow (*Popular Epics*, ii. 247), asserts, that Olger's being called a Dane is the mere result of a confusion of words, inasmuch as for *Danois* we ought to read *Ardenois*, and that the Dane-marcke, Den-mark, which is Ogier's country, is simply the March of Ardennes. Mr. Ludlow doubts 'how far the Danish people, who have erected Holger Danske' into their national hero, may assent to the view which reduces him into a petty Walloon noble.' As he belongs really neither to the one nor to the other, the question is one with which we need not concern ourselves.</small>

Morgan le Fay, who at his birth had promised that when he had achieved his greatness she would take him to dwell with her in her fairy paradise of Avilion, whither Arthur went to be healed of his grievous wound. In her love for the Danish warrior we can but see a reflexion of the love of Eos for Tithonos, of the goddess of the Horselberg for Tanhaüser, of the Fairy Queen for True Thomas of Ercildoune. But in this her delicious land, where he forgets the years which have passed away, Olger may not tarry for ever. The influence of the old faith still survives, which holds that Helgi the slayer of Hunding must appear again on earth in other guise, that Arthur must once more be king, that the slumber of the Ephesian sleepers must come to an end, that Sarpedôn must once again gladden his bright Lykian home. While his days pass away in Avilion in a dream of delight, the land which he had guarded is overrun by foes; and in answer to the cry of the Franks Morgan le Fay lifts from his head the cap of forgetfulness, and instantly he is eager to hasten to the help of the people for whom he had fought in times past. But the years which have rolled by have had an effect which only the magic of Morgan has been able to counteract; and, by a singular modification of the myth of Tithonos, she gives him a ring which shall preserve his youth so long as he keeps it on his hand. If he parts with it he will be a wrinkled old man from whose fingers all strength will have passed utterly away. Thus defended, he appears again in the land of the Franks; and the scenes to which his strange questions and answers lead reflect the incidents which followed the visit of the Seven Sleepers to the Ephesus where they had spent the days of their youth. The old fortune of Olger pursues him still. Women cannot see him without loving him: and more than all others the princess of the land seeks to obtain him for a husband. But the strange rumours which had gone abroad about this redoubtable champion had reached her ears and she determines to test their truth by taking away the ring from his hand. Instantly he becomes the withered old man which Odysseus appeared to be when Athênê took away all beauty from his face and all brightness from his golden hair. When it is replaced on his finger, he is seen again in all the vigour of early manhood; and in this lusty guise he is leading the daughter of the land to the altar, when he is once more taken away by the Fay Morgan to her beautiful home, whence the popular belief still avers that, like Arthur and Helgi and Harold and Sebastian, he will return once more.[1]

The story of Havelok.

The story of Havelok is more curious and important, not so much in its own incidents, as in the strange modifications which it has undergone and the wide range of myths with which, etymologically or otherwise, it is connected. The comparatively late date at which the English story, as we have it, was put together, may be taken for granted; but although from a certain point of view this fact has its significance, it has little to do with the nature of the materials out of which the legend has been evolved. Like Arthur and Tristram and Guy and Bevis, Havelok is one of the fatal children who are born to be kings and to destroy those who keep them out of their rightful inheritance. He is, in short, another

[1] In the infinite multiplicity of details introduced into the myth by French romance-makers it is possible that some may be really borrowed from history while others are mere arbitrary fictions, as from their stupidity many of them may be fairly supposed to be. Others are as manifestly borrowed from the old familiar stories of mythical imagery. Ogier's horse Broiefort, while his master is in the underground prison, is carried away and made to serve in a limepit, where all his hair is worn off his flanks and his tail is shorn to the stump. But when Ogier, whose weight crushes all other beasts, leans against him, Broiefort, far from yielding, only strengthens himself against the weight. This is, plainly, only another version of the myths in which the sword or the cloak is useless except to the one man who is destined to draw the one or to put on the other—as in the stories of Arthur, Balin, Lancelot, and Orendil.—Ludlow, *Popular Epics*, ii. 295.— When Ogier draws his sword, we have the comparison with which the weapons of Achilleus, of Arthur, and Tristram have rendered us familiar.

peerless hero, and there is but one maiden in the world whom he may take as his wife. Into the Havelok myth the story of this maiden is introduced independently; and thus we have in Denmark Havelok and his sisters intrusted to the care of Godard, and in England Goldborough, the daughter of Æthelwald, intrusted to the care of Godric, the trust in both cases betrayed, and the treachery made to subserve the exaltation of the intended victims. Godard is resolved that he, not Havelok, shall bear rule in Denmark, and Godric that Goldborough shall not stand in his way in England. But the Moirai and the Norns do not work in vain. Godard puts Havelok into the hands of Grim the fisherman, with the strict charge that he shall put him to death: and this trust is in its turn betrayed, as it is by Harpagos and the messengers of Amulius in the stories of Cyrus and of Romulus. When at midnight Grim rises to do Godard's bidding, he sees streaming from the mouth of the child the bright light, which, incircling the head of Servius Tullius, betokened the future greatness of the son of the slave Ocresia, and as it gleamed round the head of Asklepios, warned the shepherd Aristhanas that he saw before him a divine child. Havelok is thus recognised by Grim as the son of King Birkabeyn, and the fisherman, to avoid the wrath of Godard, hastens away from Denmark, and takes up his abode in the town which bears his name in England. But what is Havelok to do in the new land? His preserver is poor, he himself is meanly clad and without friends, and so, when he reaches Lincoln in search of work, he becomes the scullion-boy in Earl Godric's kitchen. In other words, he is now the poor despised Boots, lying, like Cinderella, among the ashes, and jeered at by those who are really his inferiors, like the Prettyhands of the Arthur tale. But as in the Gaelic legend the Great Fool is still the one to whom hosts yield, and it is he alone who is destined to be the husband of the young Fairfine, so Havelok alone can win the queenly daughter of Æthelwald; and even thus it comes to pass, that at the games held by Earl Godric the kitchen boy distances all his competitors in a way which renders all thought of coping with him impossible. The will of Zeus is being accomplished. Godric sees in the victory of the scullion-lad an opportunity for humiliating Goldborough. He has promised her father that he will wed her to the strongest man, and he will keep his word. The marriage is accordingly celebrated, and Goldborough finds herself in the hovel of Havelok with a feeling of disgust equal to that of the princess who in the Norse and German stories marries King Thrushbeard or King Hacon Grizzlebeard in their disguise as beggars. But like Grim, Goldborough sees at night the flame which streams from Havelok's mouth, and she hears an angel say that she is wife of the man who is to be king of Denmark. Havelok on waking says that he too has seen a vision which assured him that he was to sit upon King Birkabeyn's throne; and with his wife and the three sons of Grim he sets sail from England to fight for and to win back his inheritance. In Denmark his might is at once proved by the destruction of sixty-one thieves, who, when they assail the house where he is sojourning, are all slain by him and the three sons of Grim. The next night Ubbe his host sees a great light streaming from his chamber, and going in, he beholds what Grim and Goldborough had beheld before him. The sequel of the story tells us of the discomfiture and death of Godard in Denmark and Godric in England, and the romance ends with a period of repose as profound as that which marks the close of the Odyssey, and thus the whole myth resolves itself into elements found throughout the wide range of all Aryan Mythology.

But the English story of Havelok does not stand by itself. In the French poem, put together probably about The loves of Argentile and Curan. the time of Henry the Second, the heroine is not Goldborough, but Argentile, a name which looks as mere a translation as the Gaelic Fairfine from the Greek Chryseis,—and Havelok has become Havelok Cuaran. Here then we have the story of the loves of Argentile and Curan, one of the narratives in Warner's poem intitled Albion's England, in which Curan, in order to win Argentile, becomes a scullion in the household of Ethil, who compels her to marry him from the same motives which led Godric to insist that Goldborough should wed Havelok. If we ask what or who is Curan, we are carried to the Danish hero whom the Angles called Anlafcwiran, and we are put on a track which ends in the identification of the name Anlaf with that of Havelok, whose story, as furnishing groundwork for the claim of the Danes through him to England, is connected with the myth of Guy of Warwick. The chronicles cited by Sir F. Madden give to the Kings of Denmark and Norway, who bring over Colbrand, the names Anelaphus and Conelaphus: in the metrical romance of Guy of Warwick these names appear in the forms Hanelocke and Conelocke, while the MS. English chronicle Harl. 63, referred to by Sir F. Madden, speaks of the Danes who 'had claimed before by the title of King Havelocke that wedded Goldesburghe, the King's daughter of Northumbr''

But Havelok further presents a link with the saga of Beowulf, as bearing a name which is only a modification of that of Higelac, one of the heroes of that myth. Whether this name is further to be identified *Havelok and Hamlet.* with the Danish Chochilaichus of Gregory of Tours, is a question which has an interest only in so far as it may tend to prove that the names of historical persons have found their way into popular legends,—a position which no comparative mythologist will be tempted to dispute, but which really adds nothing to the stock of our historical knowledge. But when we find the name Anlaf, Anelaph, Hanelocke, in the Latinized Amlethus, we are brought at once to a name familiar in all English ears; and Hamlet is seen to stand to Havelok in the relation of *cloth* to *cloak*, and we are compelled to ask what stories are told of Hamlet beside that which has been told by Shakespeare. Without venturing further into the province which Dr. Latham has made his own, and in which it is to be hoped that we may see more abundant fruits of his learning, I may here remark that on the very face of the Shakespearian play we have the same myth repeated more than once, while none will dispute the fact that other versions of the drama existed before Shakespeare took the subject in hand. This undisputed fact is all that is needed for our present purpose, for the pre-eminent genius of Shakespeare is no more questioned than that of the poets who put into their present shape our Iliad and Odyssey. If we look into the incidents of Shakespeare's play, we find, apart from the connexion of Denmark with England which marks the story of Havelok and Grim, that the method of Hamlet's death agrees precisely with that of his father. The latter is poisoned while sleeping in his orchard of an afternoon, and the ghost tells Hamlet that the false report given out to cover his uncle's guilt is that he had been stung by a serpent; but in either case, whether by accident or otherwise, we have the features common to a thousand mythical stories,—the snake which appears in the myths of Eurydike and Arthur, the poison which plays a part in many a story of Dawn-maidens, the orchard with the apples which gleam in the garden of the Hesperides, the afternoon slumber into which Endymion sinks in the land of Latmos.

Another salient feature in Shakespeare's drama is the constraint put upon Hamlet by the tyrant who has usurped his father's throne; but this state of bondage, in which the greater is made to serve the less, is the very groundwork of half the myths which tell of the toil of the Sun for the benefit of the mean thing

Hamlet and his uncle.

called man. It is the subordination of Achilleus and Agamemnon, of Herakles to Eurystheus, of Perseus to Polydektes. But still more noteworthy is the narrative of Ophelia's death, who, like the Valkyrie, sings her swan song in her last hours, and who from her melodious lay is pulled down to muddy death. To say the least, there is a strange correspondence between this tale and the Cretan myth about Helenê Dendritis, which tells us how Helen was surprised while bathing, and hung up to a tree.[1]

[1] *Aryan Mythology*, ii. 157. When we remember that Ikaros is a son of Daidalos, the cunning workman who shapes the labyrinth of the clouds in the heavens, we can scarcely fail to connect the myths of Ophelia and Helen with that of Maira, who hangs herself on a tree from grief for the loss of Ikaros who lies buried beneath it.

The pro-Shakespearian German version of Hamlet calls for special attention from those who are interested in ascertaining the nature of the materials on which Shakespeare worked. With the points of likeness in the phraseology of the two dramas we are not here concerned; but I cannot pass in silence a passage which has been pointed out to me by Dr. Latham, as evidently connected with a myth of Artemis, in which the giant 'Ephialtes, like Ixiôn, seeks to win Hêrê while Otos follows Artemis, who in the form of a stag so runs between the brothers that they, aiming at her at the same time, kill each other.'—*Aryan Mythology*, ii. 254.—In the German Hamlet, the prince lands on an island where he proposes to dine and rest, and is there told by two ruffians who have sided with him that he must die, as they have orders to put him to death. Having vainly intreated mercy, he prevails on them to let him have a few minutes for prayer, and then to aim each a pistol at his two sides,—promising to give them the signal for firing. When he does this, he falls forward, and the ruffians shoot each other. On the body of one of them he finds a letter bidding the King of England put Hamlet to death, if he should live to reach the island—a point of connexion with the story of Bellerophon. In Snorro Hamlet lives in the kitchen, like other heroes of whom the familiar model is Boots.

For these remarks on Hamlet, I am indebted to the kindness of Dr. Latham; and I acknowledge my debt with the more gratitude, inasmuch as his inquiries have been instituted for purely historical purposes. It has been his object to ascertain how far Hamlet belongs to a family which existed in history: and the result of his search is that almost every name with which he is connected is the subject of myths of which it is impossible not to see the identity with the myths of other branches of the Aryan race.

For myself I may add that I have carefully abstained from meddling with the plays of Shakespeare, feeling that the task must be left to those

When we go further back in the mythical genealogy of Hamlet, we find ourselves amongst a crowd of beings whose names are as transparent as those of Asterodia, Asteropaios, Narkissos, Aethlios, Selênê, Chryseis, or Fairfine. We need go no further than the story of his father Orendil, or Aurentil, who reappears in the lay of Gudrun as Hjarrandi, the being who like Orpheus, Amphion, Hermes, or Pan can charm all men with his sweet sounds, and whose name probably denotes nothing more than the hearing ear (ohr, auris). But Orendil is one of the three sons of Oygel, King of Treves, who with a slight change of name appears as Eigil,[1] a counterpart of Tell, the shooting god, and is possibly the same as the Higelac of Beowulf. Like his son Havelok, Orendil can wed but one woman in the world, and she is Queen of Jerusalem; but when he sets sail in search of her, the fleet is held wind-bound for three years in the Kleber-meer, another Aulis, until the Virgin hears his prayer and lets them go, as Artemis at last sent a breeze to waft the Achaians to Ilion. The sequel of the story is a strange jumble of images drawn from many myths. The fleet is wrecked when within sight of

The genealogy of Hamlet.

who care to ascertain the nature and state of the materials on which he worked. That some of his plays contain mythical elements is a proposition which few will venture to dispute. Whether Othello may hereafter be found to come within their number, is a point on which I do not speak, but for which I am prepared to weigh such evidence as may be alleged; nor can I suffer myself to be frightened from this judicial impartiality by the declaration of the Edinburgh Reviewer. (*Edinburgh Review*, October, 1870, p. 347, &c.) The fact that the reviewer has studiously kept out of sight the evidence for the conclusions reached by comparative mythologists, and has represented the few illustrations adduced in my introductory chapters as the sum total of all the evidence producible on the subject, and actually cited at length in the later chapters of the work, may perhaps justify an expression of grave regret; but I will content myself with asserting that his criticism from beginning to end has been met and summarily refuted by Mr. Tylor in the chapters on Mythology in his work on *Primitive Culture*, and that nothing has been said to shake conclusions which stand on a basis as sure as the results of comparative philology.

[1] *Aryan Mythology*, ii. 100.

the Holy Sepulchre, and none escape but Orendil, who, becoming servant to a fisherman, catches a whale in the body of which is a grey coat. Although he wishes earnestly to possess this coat and it is offered for sale at a very low price, he cannot meet the cost: but when any one else tries to put it on, the garment splits. When Orendil dons it, it not only becomes as good as new, but makes him invulnerable,—a myth which recalls not only the stories of Medeia and Nessos, but more especially those of Arthur, Balin, Lancelot, Tristram, and Galahad. The coat which will suffer only one man to put it on is but the sword which will yield only to one man's touch; and the scabbard of Excalibur possesses precisely the power of the grey coat of making its owner invulnerable. Henceforth Orendil bears the name Graurock, the man with the grey or gleaming robe.[1] In a tournament, in which he next takes part, he has to borrow a horse, and he is miraculously provided with golden spurs, and like Ahmed, the Pilgrim of Love, in the Spanish legend, he is of course the conqueror. The betrothal of Orendil with Queen Bride is followed by a war for the conquest of Jerusalem in which he outdoes Grettir or Samson or Herakles or Rustem, by slaying single-handed sixteen thousand men, and by other exploits scarcely less marvellous. At length an angel forewarns Orendil and his bride of the hour in which they must die, and when that time has come, they are borne away to heaven. The grey frock becomes, it is scarcely necessary to say, the holy coat of Treves, where Orendil's father had been king.

Through Higelac, the Wægmunding, the romance of Beowulf is connected with that of Havelok, as through the myth of Sceaf it is connected with that of Arthur.[2]

---

[1] The word denotes strictly not subdued but dazzling light. It is the Glaukos of the Sarpédon myth, and Athéné is Glaukôpis, the maiden with the flashing face.

[2] A further point of connexion is furnished by the name of King Birka-

The saga of Beowulf. The saga itself is pre-eminent among the legends which describe the struggle of light with darkness. Grendel is the gloomy demon in one of his most awful forms; and we see in him the monstrous Sphinx who strikes terror into the citizens of Thebes, the robber Cacus who breathes fire from his nostrils, the giant Ravana who steals away the beautiful Sita, or any other of the fearful beings who find their prototype in the thievish Paṇis, and in Ahi, the throttling snake, who can be slain only by the sun-god Indra. When Grendel is killed, his fearful mother, the devil's dam, comes to avenge his death, but the second struggle, in which Beowulf is conqueror, is but a reflexion of the first: and both are repeated in the later encounter with the great dragon, which, like Vritra and the Paṇis, like Fafnir and Python, keeps guard over his priceless treasures—the treasures of light and life, which he hides away greedily beneath the earth. Like Hamlet, again, like Havelok and Tristram and Herakles and Achilleus, Beowulf reaps no great harvest of his toil, although the king for whom he works is a more kindly master than Eurystheus. But in death as well as in life, Beowulf is but a counterpart of the great son of Alkmênê. The latter died by the blood of the Kentaur Nessos, whom he had smitten to death; the former dies by the blood of the fiery dragon which he has slain. The venomed drops

---

beyn, who is here the father of Havelok, and in the French poem is the father of Havelok Curan. Of the word Birkabeyn, Dr. Latham says that is 'no true proper name; neither is it Danish so much as Norwegian. It is, however, a truly historical term, the period of the Birkebeins being a well marked period in Norwegian politics.' These Berkabeyns seem to have appeared in the latter part of the twelfth century, the popular explanation being that the men to whom the name was given had to flee from their enemies into the forests, where, when their clothes were worn out, they wound the bark of the birch tree about their legs, and thus became known as Birkebeiners. See Dr. Latham's very valuable and learned paper on *Havelok the Dane*, Transactions of the Royal Society of Literature, vol. vii. new series.

which remain on his hands burn and swell, until the poison courses through his limbs, and rages fiercely in his breast. It is the same great tragedy of nature in which we see the death agonies of Herakles on his funeral pile on Oita; and as to the mighty son of Zeus there yet remained a solace in the beautiful face and glowing form of Iolê, so in the more sombre and less refined northern legend Beowulf asks to look again upon the choice treasures which he has won for the people before his eyes are closed in death, and thus, having feasted once more on the dazzling vision of golden cups and jewelled bracelets and gleaming coffers, he hastens from the land of the living to the unseen regions, whither the Wægmundings have gone before him. It may seem but a barbaric vision: yet the splendour which soothes the eye of the dying hero is but the brilliance of the golden doors and brazen stringcourses, the youths of gold holding up everlasting torches, which shed their dazzling lustre on the palace of Alkinoös. So far as the conceptions differ, the contrast is but the result of impressions made by the phenomena of sunset on the mind of the Teuton beneath his harsher sky, and of the Greek in his more genial home.[1]

Whatever be the value of the romances contained in this volume as works of art (and if some rise to high merit, none are despicable), the scrutiny to which they have now been submitted leaves, I venture to think, no room for any reasonable doubt as to the origin and nature of the materials out of which they have been shaped. The processes by which they have

General results of the inquiry.

[1] The date at which the epic of Beowulf was composed is uncertain. It exists in a single manuscript of the tenth century.—Craik, *History of English Literature*, i. 57.—But, in truth, the question of the date at which the romance assumed its present shape is one of but slight importance, when the materials of which it is composed are seen to be common elements in a wide family of traditions spread throughout the Aryan tribes, and perhaps beyond them.

been brought into their present form may seem to be somewhat monotonous: yet it may very safely be asserted that the keenness with which we may spy out repetitions, or trace the substantial identity of any given story with other tales with which, at first sight, it might seem to have little in common, will detract nothing from the charm of the tales themselves. Rather, it may be said that our knowledge of the source whence the stream flows will add indefinitely to the interest with which we trace its wanderings, until by the confluence of its tributary waters it swells into the great ocean of national epic poetry, while incidents, which, regarded as events in the lives of human beings, must appear absurd, or impossible, or disgusting, will not unfrequently be invested with a touching truth and beauty. To the most eager lover of these stories as stories I feel that I can have done no wrong by showing that, like the great epic poems of Greeks, Hindus, and Teutons, these romances are, as I have already maintained and must emphatically repeat, 'simply different versions of the same story, and that this story has its origin in the phenomena of the natural world, and the course of the day and the year.'[1]

G. W. C.

[1] *Aryan Mythology*, i. 151.

THE STORY OF KING ARTHUR AND HIS KNIGHTS.

CHAPTER I.

THE CROWNING OF ARTHUR.

UTHER PENDRAGON lay sick with love and sorrow, for the lady Igerne would not hearken to the words which he had spoken to her, and she had gone away with her husband Gorlois, the Duke of Cornwall, who placed her in the castle of Tintagil, in the Cornish land, while he shut himself up in another castle called Dimilioc. When the knight Ulfin saw that his lord Uther was sick, he asked what ailed him; and when he knew that the king longed for the love of Igerne, he went to the wise Merlin who knew the things that were to come; and Merlin promised that the king should have his heart's desire. So he brought it about that Uther went to the castle of Tintagil in the likeness of Gorlois, who had just been slain behind the battlements of Dimilioc; and Igerne welcomed Uther, thinking that in very truth her husband stood before her.

On the next day the tidings came to Igerne that her husband had been slain three hours before Uther entered the gates of Dimilioc; and she marvelled who it might be that had come to her in the guise of her lord. But soon there came messengers from Uther who told her of the love which the king bare to her, and Igerne became the queen of the land.

When the time drew near that her child should be born, Merlin the sage came to the king and asked that the babe should be given to him at the postern gate of the palace unchristened. And the king promised, and so when the child was born, it was wrapped in cloth of gold and given to Merlin, who placed it in the hands of a true and faithful man named Sir Ector: and Sir Ector's wife nourished the babe, until after a great fight at St. Albans Uther Pendragon came back to London, and there fell sick unto death. But before he died, he charged his nobles and great men that they should make Arthur king in his stead. Howbeit, when he was dead, many strove to be chosen king, and the Bishop of Canterbury bade that all the lords of the realm should come up to London at Christmas on pain of cursing. So at Christmastide, they were gathered together in the great church; and when the mass was done, there was seen in the churchyard against the high altar a great stone four square, and in the midst was like an anvil of steel, and therein was stuck a fair sword, naked by the point, and about the sword there were written letters in gold which said, 'Whoso pulleth this sword out of this stone and anvil is rightwise born King of all England.'

But of all the lords there was not one who could move the sword; and the bishop said, 'He is not here that shall draw out the sword, but doubt not God will make him known.' Then by his counsel ten knights were named to guard the stone; but though they kept watch day by day, none came who could pull out the weapon. At the last Sir Ector journeyed to London with his son Sir Kay, and with them went Arthur his foster-brother. As they went on their road, Sir Kay perceived that he had left his sword at home, and prayed Arthur to hasten back and fetch it. But when Arthur reached the house, there was none within, for all were gone to see the justing. Then in his wrath he said within himself, 'I will ride to the churchyard and take the sword that is fixed in the stone, for my brother shall not lack a sword this day.'

So Arthur hastened to the churchyard, and found no knights there, for they too were gone to the justs; and when he seized the sword, it came out of the stone lightly at his touch, and he carried it to Sir Kay, who took it to his father and said, 'Here is the sword of the stone, and I must be king of the land.' But his father took him into the church and made him say before the altar how he came by the sword; and so it was made known that Arthur had drawn it forth. Then said Ector, 'Arthur must be king of the land, if he can place the sword back again where it was and once more draw it forth.' So Arthur placed the sword again in the stone, and when Ector strove to pull it out, he could not do so, neither could Sir Kay; but whenever Arthur touched it, it came forth lightly as a feather. Then knelt Sir Ector before his foster child, and said, 'Now know I that thou art of an higher blood than I had thought; and therefore it was that Merlin brought thee to me.' But Arthur was grieved when he learnt that Sir Ector was not indeed his father nor Ector's wife his mother.

Yet for all this the lords strove that Arthur should not be king, for they held it shame to be governed by a boy of no high blood born; and thus, though all failed to pull out the sword, yet from Twelfth-day to Candlemas, from Candlemas till the high feast of Easter, and from Easter till Pentecost, they put off the crowning of Arthur; but at Pentecost, when still Arthur alone was able to draw forth the sword, the people cried out all, 'We will have Arthur for our king. It is the will of God.' So was Arthur crowned, and he sware to keep the laws and deal true justice between man and man, and he redressed all the wrongs that had been done throughout the land since the days of King Uther. Then Arthur made his foster-brother seneschal of England, and Sir Baldwin was made constable, and Sir Ulfin chamberlain: and the people loved their king, and evil-doers feared him because of his might and his righteousness.

Not long after this, Arthur held high feast at Caerleon,[1] and thither hastened chieftains from Lothian and Orkney, from Gower and Carados, and to them Arthur sent precious gifts. But the kings evil-intreated the messengers who bare them, and bade them go back and say that they would have no gifts of a beardless boy that was come of low blood, but that they were coming to give him gifts of hard blows between the shoulders. Then Arthur shut himself up with five hundred knights in a great tower, to which the kings laid siege, though Merlin the sage warned them that they could not withstand the might of Arthur. But they laughed him to scorn, and said, 'Shall we be afraid of a dream-reader?' Then Merlin vanished from among them, and came to Arthur and bade him set on fiercely, but not to use the sword which he had got by miracle, unless he should be sore pressed. So forthwith Arthur came down upon them and there was a fierce battle, until at last the Chief of Lothian smote down the king; and the king drew his sword, which flashed in the eyes of his enemies like the blaze of thirty torches, and at each stroke of the sword a man died, till the kings fled with the knights that were left alive, and Merlin counselled Arthur to follow them no further, but to send messengers to King Ban of Berwick and King Bors of

[1] Of the geography of the Arthur romance it may be said that the comparative mythologist who has ascertained that the story with which he deals has its origin in the phenomena of cloudland will be disposed to spend little time on the profitless task of inquiring whether towns and hamlets bearing historical names have been rightly placed or not. All that Sir Henry Strachey can say on this subject is that "the geography of Arthur's Roman war is very coherent; but that of the rest of the book it is often impossible to harmonise." (*Morte d'Arthur*, xi.) In all likelihood the episode of the Roman war was put together by some one familiar with the imperial tradition which English kings were pleased to maintain from the days of Ecgberht onwards.—Freeman, *Norman Conquest*, i. 158, et seq.; *Edinburgh Review*, July 1869, p. 188.

Gaul, promising that he would aid them in their wars against King Claudas if they would help him against the Kings of Lothian and Orkney and their friends. So King Ban and King Bors came; and the six kings who had fled away from Arthur got five other kings to join with them under an oath that they should not leave each other till they should have slain Arthur, who was now in the castle of Bedegraine in the forest of Sherwood. Thither hastened the eleven kings with their men, and there was fierce fighting in which King Ban and King Bors wrought mightily for the king, and Arthur himself smote on until of threescore thousand he had left but fifteen thousand alive, so that Merlin rebuked him and said, 'God is wroth with thee that thou wilt never have done, for yonder eleven kings cannot be overthrown now; but go now whither thou mayest list for they shall not lift hand against thee for three years.'

When Merlin was now gone to his master Blaise who dwelt in Northumberland, and wrote down all that befell King Arthur, there came the daughter of Earl Sanam, to do homage, as others did after the great battle; and Arthur set his love upon the damsel, and she became the mother of Borre, who was afterward a good knight of the Round Table. Then Arthur rode to Caerleon, and thither came the wife of the King of Orkney with her four sons, Gawaine, Gaheris, Agravaine and Gareth; and she was the sister of Arthur, though he knew it not, for she was the daughter of Igerne; and she was so fair that the king cast great love upon her also. But withal there came heavy dreams which made him sad at heart, and when by and by he rode long after a strange beast, and then rested by a fountain, a knight came and took away the king's horse; and while one went to fetch it back, Merlin stood before the king, like a child fourteen years old, and told him that Uther and Igerne were his father and his mother. But Arthur laughed the child to scorn, and Merlin vanished, and came again in the form of a man fourscore years old, and told him the same words. Further he said, 'God is displeased with you for the deed ye have done of late, and thy sister's child shall destroy you and all the knights of your realm.'

Then Arthur sent for Igerne, for he said, 'If she too says that I am her child, I shall believe it;' and when she came with her daughter Morgan le Fay, Ulfin charged her with treason, because she had not spoken the truth from the first, and because Arthur's lords had withstood him, not knowing whose son he was, and because they would not be ruled by a base-born boy. Then Igerne told all the story, how, when the child was born, Uther bade that it should be given to Merlin, and how she never saw the babe again, or wot what had become of him; and Ector also told how he had received the child at Merlin's hands, and nourished him by the king's command. Then Arthur took his mother in his arms and kissed her, and they wept on each other for the greatness of their joy.

After this, there came from the Emperor of Rome twelve knights who asked of Arthur homage for his realm; and the king answered that because they were messengers they should live, and bade them tell their master that he would give him homage on a fair field with a sharp spear and a sharp sword. So the messengers departed; and as Arthur rode away he came to a place where a knight stood who suffered none to pass unless they first crossed spears with him. Then was there a long and fierce fight between them, until the knight smote Arthur's sword in two pieces, and sware to slay him unless he would yield himself as conquered. 'Death is welcome,' said Arthur, 'when it comes; but as for yielding to thee, I would rather die than be so shamed;' and therewith rushing on the knight he seized him by the middle and threw him down, and took away his helmet.

Yet was not the knight overcome, albeit he was sore dismayed; and he had well nigh slain Arthur, when Merlin came and bade him stay his hand. 'This knight,' he said 'is a man of more worship than thou deemest.' 'Why, who is he?' said the knight. When Merlin said that it was King Arthur, the knight would have slain him forthwith because he feared his anger; but Merlin cast a spell upon him so that he fell to the earth in a great sleep. Then was Arthur wroth because he thought that Merlin had slain the brave knight; but the sage said, 'Fear not, he shall rise up again in three hours: and this knight, whose name is Pellinore, shall have two sons, Percivale and Lamorak, who shall be good men and true, and he shall tell you the name of your sister's son, that shall bring ruin to all this realm.'

Then with Merlin Arthur went to the abode of an hermit, who was also a great healer of men, and in three days he was healed of the wounds which Pellinore had given. But when he would go further, he said to Merlin, 'I have no sword;' and Merlin answered that he should have one by and by; and presently they came to a lake in the midst of which an arm was seen rising from the water, and bearing a sword aloft. 'Yonder,' said Merlin, 'is the sword of which I spake, and yonder is the Lady of the Lake, whose is that sword. Speak fair to her when she comes to you, that she may give it you.' Then after kindly greeting, Arthur besought her for the sword, and the maiden said, 'If thou wilt give me a gift when I ask for it, it shall be thine.' So the king sware unto her, and the maiden bade him row himself in a barge that lay near, and take the sword with its scabbard; and when Arthur laid his hand upon it, the hand that bare it up went under the water. On their way back they saw a rich pavilion, and when Arthur knew from Merlin that Pellinore lay within it, Arthur would have tried his new sword in fight with him; but Merlin said that so it must not be, and that hereafter the king would be right glad to give to Pellinore his sister for a wife. 'But which likest thou the better' asked Merlin, 'the sword or the scabbard?' And Arthur said, 'The sword.' 'Ye are unwise,' answered the sage, 'for the scabbard is worth ten of the sword, for while ye have the scabbard upon you ye shall never lose blood, though thy wounds be never so sore; wherefore see that you keep the scabbard always with you.'

Then went Arthur to Caerleon; and thither came messengers from King Ryons, who said, 'Eleven kings have done me homage, and with their beards I have trimmed a mantle. Send me now thy beard, for there lacks yet one to the finishing of my mantle.' Then answered Arthur and said, 'Go tell your master my beard is full young yet to make a trimming of it; but yet a little while, and he shall do me homage on his knees.'

Now Merlin had told the king that he who should destroy him should be born on May-day. Therefore Arthur charged that all the children born of lords and ladies on that day should be brought to him; and they were placed in a ship, and Mordred, the child of the wife of the King of Orkney, was sent with them. But the ship was driven against a castle, and broken in pieces, and all died save Mordred, whom a good man took up and nourished till he was fourteen years old.

CHAPTER II.

THE STORY OF BALIN AND BALAN.

Now it came to pass that while Arthur with his lords and knights tarried at Camelot, a damsel brought a message from the great Lady Lile of Avilion; and as she stood before the king she let fall her mantle, that was richly furred, and she was seen to be girt with a noble sword. Then the king marvelled greatly, and asked wherefore she, being a maiden, was thus girt with a sword. And the maiden said that the weapon gave her great sorrow and cumbrance, and that she could not be freed from the sword save by a good and true man without villainy and without treason. She told, moreover, how she had been at the court of King Ryons, and how no knight there was able to take the sword from her side. Then spake the king, 'I say not that I am the best knight, but I will essay to draw the sword, that at the least I may give an example to my barons.' But, though he strove mightily, the sword would not out, and the maiden said, 'Ye need not pull hard; the man that shall pull it out shall do it with little might.' But neither were any of the barons who stood round able to draw it forth; and the damsel took leave of the king to go upon her way. As she went, there stood before her a poor knight, named Balin, clad in a homely garment; and he had been prisoner half-a-year and more because he had slain a knight who was cousin to the king. But although he had been delivered out of prison, yet, for the poorness of his raiment, he would not put himself far in the throng, though, in his heart, he was sure that, if the chance were given to him, he could do as well as any knight that then was. At the first the damsel would not hearken to his prayer; but Balin bade her remember that righteousness lies not in a man's vesture, and that many a good man is not known unto all people. So she suffered him to try, and at his touch the sword came from her side, and she said, 'This is the best knight that ever I found; he shall do many good deeds.' Then she asked Balin to give her back the sword again; and when he would not yield it up, she said, 'Ye are not wise to keep the sword, for with it thou shalt slay thy best friend, and it shall be thy ruin.' So she went her way heavy and sorrowful.

Then would Balin go on his also, although the king sought to stay him because he had done him wrong; and Arthur besought him that at the least, if he went, he would not tarry away long. But while Balin was making ready to depart, the Lady of the Lake came to demand of the king the gift which he promised to her when she gave him the sword Excalibur; and when Arthur bade her say what she would have, she desired the head of the maiden who had brought the sword to Balin, or the head of Balin himself. But when the knight heard this he went up to the lady and straightway smote off her head. Then was Arthur full of wrath, nor would he be soothed, although Balin told him she had destroyed many good knights, and had caused his mother to be burnt by her lies. And the king charged Balin to go from his court. So Balin went to his squire, and bade him bear the head to Northumberland, and tell his friends there that his worst foe was dead, and that he himself was out of prison. But the squire mourned that his master had displeased the king; and Balin said that he would go forth and do battle with King Ryons, so that Arthur might be gracious to him again if he came back conqueror.

But while the king was yet wroth with him, a knight named Lanceor besought Arthur that he might go after Balin and quite him for the despite which he had done in slaying the lady. Then, at Arthur's bidding, Lanceor, the Knight of Ireland, rode hastily after Balin, and challenged him to deadly combat, though Balin would fain have journeyed on in peace. But Lanceor would not let him go; and when they fought together the Knight of Ireland was slain. Presently a maiden came riding by, and when she saw the knight lying dead, she cried aloud for her anguish, and said, 'O Balin, thou hast slain two bodies and one heart, and two hearts in one body, and two souls hast thou lost!' And with these words she took the sword from her dead lover's hand and passed it through her own heart. Great was Balin's grief when he saw the twain lie dead together; but as in his sorrow he looked towards a great forest, he saw coming towards him his brother Balan, who first rejoiced to see Balin, and then mourned for the evil plight in which he found him. 'Let us go hence,' said Balin, when he had told him all the tale. ' King Ryons lays siege to the castle Dimilioc, and by slaying him I trust to win back the king's grace.' But not far had they gone, when they met a dwarf who came from the city of Camelot, and who, on hearing what had happened, told Balin that by slaying Lanceor he had done great damage to himself. 'Trust me,' he said, 'the kin of this knight will chase you through the world till they have slain you.' 'I fear not greatly for that,' answered Balin, 'but I grieve that I have displeased the king.'

There, on the spot where the knight Lanceor died and the maiden whom he loved slew herself, King Mark of Cornwall raised a fair tomb, and placed their bodies within it; and then Merlin told King Mark that the greatest battle should be fought that ever was or shall be betwixt the truest lovers, and yet neither of the knights should slay the other, and these should be Lancelot du Lake and Tristram. And to Balin Merlin said, 'Because thou hast slain this maiden, thou shalt strike a stroke the most dolorous that ever man struck, except the stroke of our Lord, for thou shalt hurt the truest knight that now lives, and bring three kingdoms into misery for twelve years.' After these words Merlin vanished away, and King Mark said to Balin, 'Tell me thy name.' Then said Balan, 'Ye see that he beareth two swords, and the Knight of the Two Swords you may call him.' But as the brothers rode away together, Merlin again came to them, and made them lie hidden in a wood among leaves beside the highway, that so they might fall upon King Ryons as he passed by. So when at midnight he came with threescore of his best knights, they slew his horsemen, and carried Ryons away, and gave him in charge to the porters of King Arthur. But Merlin hastened on before them to tell the king that his worst foe was taken. 'By whom?' asked the king. 'By two knights whose names thou shalt know on the morrow.' And on the morrow, when Arthur learnt that it was Balin with his brother Balan who had done him this service, he said that he had ill-deserved the kindness. 'He shall do yet more for thee,' said Merlin, 'for the brother of Ryons is even now at hand with a great host to do battle with thee to the death.'

In the fight which then came off the two brothers did wondrously; and the brother of King Ryons was worsted with all his host, because Merlin held back the King of Orkney and his people with a tale of prophecy, till the battle was well nigh done. And when at length the King of Orkney came to the fight, he was slain by Sir Pellinore, on whom Sir Gawaine, the king's son, ten years afterwards avenged his father's death. Twelve kings were killed in this battle: and for them Arthur made twelve tombs, each with an image holding a waxen taper, which Merlin said should burn no more when he was dead. Then the wise man charged the king to keep heedfully the scabbard of Excalibur, because he should lose no blood while he had this scabbard about him. So for great trust he took it to his sister Morgan le Fay: but Morgan loved another knight named Accolon better than Arthur or her husband Uriens, and to him she gave the scabbard of Excalibur while she made another like it for her brother by inchantments.

Not many days after this, as Arthur lay sick in his tent, there passed by a knight in great sorrow, who gave no heed though the king strove to comfort him. Then Arthur bade Balin go and bring back the sorrowful knight; and when Balin came up to him, the knight promised to do as he desired, if Balin would be his warrant. So Balin sware to him; but for all this the knight was slain by the hand of one whom none might see; and as he fell he said, 'This is the deed of Garlon.' Then as Balin rode onward with the damsel who had loved the dead knight, and with another knight Perin of Montbeliard, the hand of Garlon unseen smote again and Perin fell dead: and Balin went on with the damsel alone, till they came to a castle, where the men seized the maiden and would not let her go till she had bled a silver dish full for the lady of the place, who was sick and who could in no other wise be healed, even as it befell afterwards the sister of Sir Percivale in the story of the Sangreal.

Yet a few days after this, Balin was lodged in the house of a man whose son had been smitten by the invisible knight, and could not be healed till he had drunk of that knight's blood. Then said Balin, 'This is Garlon, who has already slain two of my comrades, and I would rather slay him than have all the gold in the realm.' 'He shall come before thee,' said his host, 'in a feast which King Pellam will hold not many days hence.'

At that feast the invisible knight was slain; and King Pellam and his knights rose up fiercely against Balin, because he had killed their brother: and Balin put up his sword to ward off the stroke of King Pellam, but his sword was shivered in twain, and Balin ran from chamber to chamber seeking a new weapon, until he came to a chamber marvellously light, in which was a bed arrayed with cloth of gold, and by it a table of pure gold borne up by four pillars of silver, and on the table was a marvellous spear strangely wrought. Seizing this spear Balin smote Pellam; and this was the dolorous stroke: for thereon Pellam fell down in a swoon, and the castle roof and walls fell to the earth, and lay upon Pellam and

Balin three days. At the end of these days came Merlin, who lifted them up, but Pellam lay many years sore wounded, till Galahad healed him in the quest of the Sangreal. Then Balin bade farewell to Merlin and said to him, 'In this world we meet never more;' but whereever he went, the people cried, 'O Balin, thy dolorous stroke hath brought us to ruin; and doubt not but the vengeance will fall on thee at the last.' Glad was Balin to get out of these dismal lands; but when he had left them behind him, there were yet grievous things for him to see and to suffer. For first, a knight whom he had aided to find the maiden whom he loved, slew the damsel for her treachery, and then drave his sword into his own body; and next, Balin was intrapped into a fair castle, in which he saw an hundred ladies and many knights, with whom was dancing and minstrelsy and all manner of joy, and the lady of the castle told him that he must just with a knight who kept an island, and another bade him leave his own shield and take from the wall another which was larger. So Balin did even as he bade him; and when he drew near to the island, a knight hastened towards him with spear in rest, and their horses drave together with a great shock, so that both were thrown down and lay in a swoon. Presently they rose up and fought again till their breath failed, and all the place as they strove was blood red. At the last the other went away to one side and laid him down, and Balin said, 'Who art thou? for never have I found one to match me.' 'My name,' said the other, 'is Balan, and I am brother to the good knight Balin.' Then Balin swooned away again for grief and anguish. and when he awoke once more he said, 'O brother, thou hast slain me, and I thee, and all the world will speak of us both.' 'Alas!' said Balan, 'I knew thee not, for though I saw thy two swords, yet, because thou didst carry a larger shield, I thought that thou wast not the same knight.' As they thus made their moan the lady of the tower came with four knights and six ladies, and six yeomen with them, and these they besought that they might be buried within the same place where they had fought together; and so the brothers died. In the noon came Merlin and wrote on the tomb letters of gold which said, 'Here lieth Balin the Knight of the Two Swords, who smote the dolorous stroke.' And he took Balin's sword, and set on it another pommel in place of its own, and gave it to a knight to handle: but the knight could not stir it. Then said Merlin, 'None but the best knight shall handle this sword; and that shall be Sir Lancelot, or his son Galahad: and with this sword Lancelot shall slay Sir Gawaine, the man that he loved best in the world.' Then also Merlin made a bridge of iron and steel into that island, half-a-foot broad, over which those only should pass who were not guilty of fraud and falsehood;[1] and by his subtilty he caused Balin's sword to be put in a marble stone standing upright as great as a millstone, and the stone, heaved up above the water, swam down the stream for many years till it reached the city of Camelot. On that same day Galahad brought the scabbard of Balin's sword, and so got the weapon in the marble stone that floated upon the water. And when these things were done, Merlin came to King Arthur and told him of the dolorous stroke which Balin gave to King Pellam, and of all the evils which had followed it; and King Arthur mourned at the tidings, for he said, 'In the world I know not two such knights as these.'

So ends the tale of Balin and Balan, the good knights of Northumberland.

[1] This is manifestly the bridge Al-Sirat of Mohammedan tradition. With it may be compared the Teutonic Bifröst, the waving bridge which joins earth and heaven.

CHAPTER III.

THE WEDDING OF ARTHUR AND GUENEVERE.

Now the king took counsel with Merlin, because his barons would have him take a wife; and Merlin asked, 'Is there any on whom thy love is set?' 'Yes,' said the king, 'I love Guenevere, the daughter of King Leodegrance who has in his house the Round Table which he had from my father Uther.' 'In truth,' answered Merlin, 'the maiden for her beauty is right well-fitted to be a queen: but if ye loved her not so well as ye do, I might find another who should please thee not less, for Guenevere can not be a wholesome wife for thee, and she will bring great sorrow to thee and to thy realm. But when a man's heart is set, it may not easily be turned aside.' 'That is true,' said the king: and straightway he sent messengers to King Leodegrance to ask for his daughter, and Leodegrance rejoiced at the tidings. 'I would yield him rich lands with my child,' he said, 'but Arthur has lands enough. Yet will I send him a gift that shall please him more, for I will give him the Round Table which Uther Pendragon gave me, and to which there were a hundred knights and fifty. Of these fifty have been slain in my days, but the hundred shall go with Guenevere.' So they set out, and by water and land came royally to London, where the king joyously welcomed his bride and the hundred knights, and bade Merlin spy out fifty more knights throughout the land, who might be worthy to sit at that table: but only twenty-eight could Merlin find. Then the Bishop of Canterbury came and blessed the seats for the eight-and-twenty knights, who did homage to the king. And when they were gone, Merlin found in every seat letters of gold that told the names of the knights who had sat therein. But two seats were void.

Then came young Gawaine and besought the king to make him a knight on the day in which he should wed Guenevere; and the king said that so it should be, because he was his sister's son. And after him, riding upon a lean mare, came a poor man who brought with him a fair youth; and he also besought Arthur that the youth might be made a knight. 'Thou askest me a great thing,' said Arthur. 'Who art thou? and does this prayer come of thee or of thy son?' 'I am Aries the cowherd,' answered the man, 'and I desire not this of myself. Nay, to say truth, I have thirteen sons, who will ever do that which I bid them: but this one will spend his time only in folly and delights only in battles and to see knights.' Then the king bent his eyes on the youth, who was named Tor, and he saw that he was both brave and fair; and he bade that the other sons of the cowherd should be brought. But all these were shapen like the poor man, and none was in any wise like Tor. Then the youth knelt and besought the king to make him a knight of the Round Table. 'A knight I will make you,' said Arthur, 'and hereafter thou shalt be also of the Round Table, if thou art found worthy.' Then turning to Merlin, he said, 'Will Tor be a good knight?' 'Of a truth, he will,' answered Merlin, 'for he is no son of the cowherd. His father is King Pellinore.'

When on the morrow King Pellinore came to the court, the king brought Sir Tor before him and told him that he was his son; and Sir Pellinore embraced him joyfully. Then the king asked Merlin why two places were void in the seats: and Merlin said, 'No man shall sit in those places, but they that are of most worship: and on the Perilous Seat there is but one man on the earth who shall be found worthy to sit. If any who are not worthy dare to sit on it, he shall be destroyed.' Then taking Pellinore by the hand, he put him next the two seats and the Seat Perilous, and said, 'This is your place, for of all that are here you are the most worthy to sit in it.' When Sir Gawaine heard these words, he was moved with envy, that the man who had slain his father, the King of Orkney, should be thus honoured; and he would have slain him straightway, but his brother Gaheris besought him not to trouble the high feast by so doing. 'Let us wait till we have him out of the court:' and Gawaine said, 'I will.'

When now the marriage day was come, the king wedded Guenevere at Camelot in the Church of St. Stephen; and afterwards there was great feasting, and Arthur gave charge to Sir Gawaine and Gaheris his brother, to Sir Tor and his father Sir Pellinore, who went forth, and each did great deeds before they came back to the king. With Sir Pellinore came a lady, whom he had rescued, named Nimue; and as they journeyed to Camelot, and were resting under the shadow of thick trees, two knights met, as they rode by, and one asked the other what tidings there might be from Camelot; and the other told him of the fellowship of Arthur's table, and said, 'We cannot break it up; and well nigh all the world holdeth with Arthur, for there is the flower of chivalry. Wherefore with these tidings I ride to the north.' 'Nay,' said the other, 'there is no need. I have a remedy with me; for I bear a poison to a friend who is right nigh to Arthur, and with it he will poison the king.' So they went each on his way, and Sir Pellinore told all that he had seen and heard when he came to the king at Camelot, with the lady whom he had rescued.

But when Merlin set eyes on the damsel, he was besotted with her, and would let her have no rest, but always she must be with him. And she spake him fair till she had learned of him all manner of things that she sought to know. Yet the old man knew what should befall him, and he told the king that yet a little while, and he should go down into the earth alive, and he warned Arthur to keep well the sword and the scabbard, for these would be stolen by a woman whom he most trusted.

'Nay,' said the king, 'but if thou knowest what shall befall thee, why dost thou not prevent that mishap by thy craft?' 'It may not be,' said Merlin; and presently the damsel went away, and Merlin followed whithersoever she went; but she had made him swear to do no inchantment upon her, if he would have her love. So he went with her over the sea to the land of Benwick, where Merlin spake with Elaine, King Ban's wife, and there he saw young Lancelot; and Elaine mourned greatly for the fierce war which Claudas made against Ban. 'Heed it not,' said Merlin, 'for before twenty years are gone, this child shall revenge you on King Claudas, and he shall be the man of most worship in the world.' 'Shall I indeed,' asked Elaine, 'live to see my son a man of so great a prowess?' 'Yea, indeed thou shalt see it,' answered Merlin, 'and live many years after.' Soon after this, the maiden departed, and Merlin went with her till they came into Cornwall; but the damsel was weary of him, and afraid because he was a devil's son, and so it came to pass that when Merlin showed her a marvellous rock, beneath which there were great inchantments, she besought him to go under the stone and show her the marvels that were there; but when he was beneath it, she so wrought that he never came forth again; and she left him and went her way.

CHAPTER IV.

THE TREASON OF MORGAN LE FAY.

About this time, as Arthur rode to Camelot, the tidings came that the King of Denmark, with five other kings, was ravaging the land of the north. 'Alas!' said Arthur, 'when have I had one month's rest since I became king of the land?' Nevertheless, he would not tarry an hour, although his lords were wroth because he set out thus hastily. So he hastened away with Guenevere the queen (for he said that he should be the hardier if she were with him), and came into a forest beside Humber; and a knight, when he heard that Arthur was come, warned the five kings to make haste and do battle with him, for the longer they tarried they would be ever the weaker, and Arthur stronger. And the five kings hearkened to his words, and fell on Arthur in the night; but though they killed many, and there was for some while a great tumult, yet Arthur and his knights, Sir Kay, Sir Gawaine, and Sir Griflet, slew the five kings. In the morning, when their people knew that they were dead, they were struck with such fear that they fell from their horses, and Arthur and his men came upon them, and slew them to the number of thirty thousand, so that well nigh no man escaped alive; but on Arthur's side were slain only two hundred, with eight knights of the Round Table. And Arthur raised a fair church and minster on the battle-field, and called it the Abbey of Good Adventure.

Then the king took counsel with Sir Pellinore about the knights who should be chosen for the Round Table in place of those who had been slain; and Pellinore gave counsel to choose Uriens, the husband of Morgan le Fay, the king's sister, and Galagars, and Hervise, and the King of the Lake, and with these four younger knights, of whom there were Gawaine, Griflet, and Kay; and for the fourth he bade Arthur choose between Tor and Bagdemagus. And Arthur choose Tor, because he said little and did much; and Bagdemagus went away sore displeased, and swore never to come back till he should be worthy to be chosen for the Round Table. As he rode with his squire he found a branch of an holy herb which was the sign of the Sangreal, and no man of evil life could ever find it. Then he came to the rock beneath which lay Merlin, making great dole; but when he would have helped him, Merlin bade him not to spend his strength for naught, for only she could help him who had put him there. So Bagdemagus went his way, and after doing many great deeds he came back and was chosen a knight of the Round Table.

Now Arthur, with many of his knights, went hunting and chased a hart till they left their people far behind them, and at last their horses fell dead. 'Let us go on on foot,' said Uriens; and at last they came up with the hart, and they saw also a great water, and on it a ship which came straight towards them, and landed on the sands. But when they looked into it they found no earthly creature therein, and they wondered for the beauty of the ship, which was hung all over with cloth of silk. And now it was dark night, when suddenly there burst forth a great light, and twelve damsels came forth, and welcomed Arthur by his name, and led him with Uriens and Accolon of Gaul, who were with him, to a table laden with wine and costly things, and then brought them each into a fair chamber that they might rest. But in the morning Uriens found himself in Camelot with Morgan le Fay, his wife, and King Arthur found himself in a dark prison, in which he heard the moaning of many who were shut up with him. Then the king asked them how they came there, and they told him that they had all been entrapped on their way by an evil knight, named Damas, who kept back part of his heritage from his brother Sir Ontzlake, whom men loved as much as they hated Damas; but because Ontzlake was the better knight, Damas was afraid to fight with him, and sought to get a champion, but none would take spear in hand for so evil a man; and so it came to pass that they abode in the weary prison till eighteen had died. Presently there came a damsel who asked Arthur if he would fight for Damas. 'Yea, I will do so,' he said, 'for it is better to fight with a knight than to die in a dungeon—but only if all here be set free.'

Then the maiden said that so it should be, and that a horse and armour should be brought for the king. And the king said to the maiden, 'Surely I have seen thee in the court of Arthur;' and she said, 'Nay; for I am the daughter of the lord of this castle.' But she spake falsely, for she was one of the damsels of Morgan le Fay. So was it sworn between them that Damas should set all the knights free, and that Arthur should do battle for him to the death.

Thus had it fared with Arthur. But when Accolon awoke, he found himself by a dark well-side, and from that fountain through a silver pipe the water ran in a marble basin; and Accolon said, 'God help King Arthur, for these women have betrayed us.' And even as he spake there came a dwarf who brought him greetings from Morgan le Fay, and bade him be of good heart. 'In the morning,' he said, 'thou shalt fight with a knight at the hour of prime, and here is Excalibur, Arthur's sword, and the scabbard. Wherefore rise up and do battle without mercy, as ye love her.' So he sware to do as he was bidden for the love of Morgan le Fay; and presently a knight and a lady, with six squires, led him to the house of Sir Ontzlake: and a messenger came from Damas to say that he had found a knight to fight for him, and to challenge Ontzlake to the battle. But Ontzlake was sorely wounded, and besought Accolon to take his cause in hand, and thus it came to pass that Accolon fought with the king's sword against the king whom he loved, for he knew not who it was who fought for Sir Damas. Long and terrible was the fight, for the false sword which Morgan le Fay had given to Arthur bit not like Excalibur, and the blood streamed from the king's body because the scabbard which he wore was not the scabbard of Excalibur, and thus as the strife went on Arthur grew weaker, while Accolon waxed stronger. But Arthur would not yield, not even when his sword broke at the cross and fell into the grass while the pommel remained in his hands. Then Accolon stood over the king and bade him yield himself, for he was greatly loth to slay him; but Arthur said, 'I have sworn to fight to the death, and I lose not good name because I lose my weapon.' So when Accolon came against him once more, Arthur struck him with the pommel a blow so heavy that he reeled three strides backward. But the Lady of the Lake was looking on, and it was a grief to her that such a knight as Arthur should be slain. So at the next stroke she caused Excalibur to fly from the hand of Accolon, and Arthur leaping forth seized it in his hand, and said, 'Too long hast thou been from me, and much harm hast thou wrought me.' Then looking at Accolon he spied the scabbard of his own sword, and with a quick rush he seized it and threw it far away from them both. 'Now,' said Arthur to Accolon, 'thou shalt die;' and he dealt him a blow that the blood rushed from him in a torrent. 'Slay me if thou wilt,' said Accolon, 'but I have sworn not to yield me in this fight. Yet thou art the best knight that ever I have seen, and well I know that God is with you.' 'Tell me, then, who thou art,' said Arthur; and he answered, 'I am Accolon of Gaul, of King Arthur's court.' 'Nay, but I am Arthur,' said the king, in great fear because of the inchantments of Morgan le Fay; 'tell me now, how camest thou by the sword and the scabbard?' Then Accolon told him how the dwarf had brought them from Morgan le Fay, but that he knew not against whom he was using them in this fight; and he besought the king's pardon. Then said Arthur, 'Thee I can forgive; but upon my sister I will take such vengeance that all Christendom shall ring with it, for I have worshipped her more than all my kin, and trusted her more than mine own wife.' Then Arthur told the keepers of the field that there would have been no battle between them if each had known who the other was; and Accolon said,

'This knight with whom I have fought, to my great sorrow, is the man of most manhood and worship in the world, for he is our liege lord, King Arthur.' Then the people, falling on their knees, prayed for mercy. 'Mercy ye shall have,' said Arthur; 'and this is my judgment betwixt the two brethren. For thee, Sir Damas, I learn that thou art but a worthless knight, and full of villainy; thou shalt give to thy brother the whole manor to hold of thee; also thou shalt swear no more to harm knights who may be journeying on their way, and thou shalt give back to those knights who have been set free from thy dungeon all the harness of which thou hast robbed them; and if any come to me to say thou hast not done this, thou shalt die. Thee, Sir Ontzlake, I bid to my court, for thou art a brave knight, and an upright man.' Moreover, Arthur told Ontzlake how the battle between himself and Accolon had been brought about, and Ontzlake marvelled that any man or woman could be found to work treason against Arthur; and the king said, 'I shall soon reward them by the grace of God.' But the king needed rest after the fight, and they brought him to a fair abbey where in four days Sir Accolon died, for he had lost so much blood that he could not live. Then said Arthur, 'Bear his body to my sister, Morgan le Fay, and say that I send it to her as a gift, and that I have my sword and its scabbard.' So they bare the body of Accolon to Camelot.

But meantime Morgan le Fay made sure that Arthur had died, and she bade one of her maidens fetch her husband's sword, for now would she slay him. In vain the damsel besought her not to do so; and she went to Sir Uwaine and said, 'Rise up, for thy mother is about to slay thy father, and I go to fetch the sword.' Presently, as Morgan le Fay stood by the bedside with the sword in her hands, Sir Uwaine seized her and said, 'Ah, fiend, what wilt thou do? Men say that a devil was Merlin's father, and I may say that a devil is my mother.' Then

Morgan cried for mercy and besought him not to discover her; and Uwaine made her swear that she would not do the like in time to come.

At last the tidings came that it was Accolon who had died, and that Arthur had again his sword and his scabbard, and the heart of Morgan almost burst with her grief. But because she would not have it known, she suffered not her face to bewray her sorrow; and because she knew that if she tarried till Arthur came back no ransom should save her life, she besought Queen Guenevere for leave to ride into the country; and on the morrow she hastened to the abbey where Arthur lay sleeping, and lighting off her horse went straight into the chamber, where she found Arthur asleep and Excalibur naked in his right hand. So, grieving terribly that she might not take the sword without awaking him, she took the scabbard, and went her way. When Arthur awoke and saw that his scabbard was gone, he charged his knights with having watched him falsely; but they said, 'We durst not withstand your sister's bidding.' Then Arthur bid Sir Ontzlake arm and ride with him in all haste, and they hastened after Morgan, until they saw her speeding from them as fast as her horse could bear her. When at last she knew that there was no hope of escape, she swore that her brother should never have the scabbard, and taking it from her girdle she hurled it into a lake hard by, and it sunk forthwith, for it was heavy with gold and precious stones. Then riding on she came to a valley where there were many large stones, and because she saw that Arthur would soon overtake her, she turned herself and those who were with her into stones, so that when they came up, the king could not discern between his sister and her men. So he rode back to the abbey whence he had come; and when he was gone, Morgan turned herself and her men into their former likeness, and as she went on, she rescued, from a knight who was going to drown him, a cousin of Accolon named Manassen, and she bade him go tell Arthur that she had rescued him not for the love of the king but for love of Accolon, and that she feared nothing so long as she could change herself and those who were with her into stones, for she could do greater things than these when the time should come.

Not long had Manassen reached Camelot when there came a damsel, bearing the richest mantle that ever was seen, set full of precious stones, and she said, 'Your sister sends this mantle that you may take this gift from her, and if in aught she has done you wrong, she will amend it.' But the Lady of the Lake warned him in secret, 'Take heed that the garment come not nigh thee or any of thy knights, until thou hast made the bringer of it put it on.' Then said the king to the maiden, 'I would see upon you this raiment which ye have brought,' and when the damsel said that it was not seemly for her to wear a king's garment, Arthur made them put it on her, and she was burnt to coals. But the king turned to Sir Uriens and said, 'I know not what these treasons may mean. Thee I can scarcely suspect, for Accolon confessed to me that Morgan would destroy thee as well as me; for Uwaine I hold suspected, and I bid thee send him from my court.' Then said Gawaine, 'He who banishes my cousin banishes me;' so the two departed, and Gaheris said, 'We have lost two good knights for the love of one.'

As they went upon their way Uwaine and Gawaine came to a tower in a valley, where twelve maidens with two knights went to and fro near a tree on which hung a white shield, and they spit at the shield and threw mire on it as they passed: and they asked the maidens why they did so, they said, 'It is the shield of Sir Marhaus who hates all ladies.' 'It may be that he has cause,' said Gawaine; and presently came Marhaus himself, and the two knights of the tower hastened to do battle with him, but they were both slain; and after this Marhaus jousted with Gawaine and Uwaine. The fight was long and fierce, for so it was that from nine of the clock till noontide Gawaine waxed stronger and stronger; but when it was past noon and drew toward evensong, Sir Gawaine's strength waned, and Sir Marhaus grew bigger and bigger; and at last Marhaus said, 'It were a pity to do you hurt, for you are passing feeble.' So they took off their helmets and kissed each other, and swore to love henceforth as brethren: and they went together to the home of Sir Marhaus, with whom Gawaine and Uwaine tarried seven days till their wounds were well healed. Then Marhaus guided them to the forest of Alroy, in which by a fair stream of water they saw three damsels sitting. The eldest had a garland of gold upon her head, and her hair was white under her garland, for she had seen threescore winters or more. The second had on her head a circlet of gold, and she was thirty winters old. The third, whose head was crowned with flowers, had seen only fifteen summers. 'Wherefore sit ye by the fountain?' asked the knight, and the maidens answered, 'We sit here watching for errant knights, that we may teach them strange adventures: and if ye be men who seek adventures, each one of you must choose one of us, and we will lead you to three highways, and then each of you shall choose his way and his damsel shall go with him; and when twelve months have passed, ye must meet here again; and to this ye must plight your troth.' 'It is well said,' they answered; and Sir Uwaine said, 'I am the youngest and the weakest, therefore will I have the eldest damsel, for she has seen much and can help me best when I have need.' Then said Sir Marhaus, 'I will have the second damsel, for she falls best to me.' 'I thank you,' said Sir Gawaine, 'for ye have left me the youngest and fairest, and she only it is whom I would have.' When they came to the parting of the roads, they kissed and went each his way—Sir Uwaine to the west, Sir Marhaus to the south, and Sir Gawaine to the north.

Now, when he had gone some way, Gawaine came to a

lawn, and near a cross which stood there, there came by the fairest knight that they had ever seen: but he was mourning as one in great grief. Then there followed ten knights who threw their spears at the sorrowful knight, but he unhorsed them all, and afterwards suffered them to bind him and to treat him shamefully. 'Why go you not to his help?' said the damsel to Gawaine. 'I would do so,' he answered, ' but it seems he will have no help.' But now three knights came and challenged Gawaine to just with them: and while they were justing, another knight came to the damsel and asked why she abode with him who had brought her thither. 'I find it not in my heart,' she said, ' to abide with him any longer, for he helps not those who need his aid;' and she departed with the stranger. When the justing was ended, Gawaine asked who the sorrowful knight might be; and they told him that his name was Sir Pelleas, and that he loved the lady Ettard, who would not listen to his suit and even drove him from her with evil words, although in a great justing he had won the right to crown the fairest lady, and had placed the circlet upon her brow. But so was Pelleas smitten by love for Ettard, that he suffered her knights to bind him after he had conquered them in fighting, in hopes that he might thus be brought into her sight; but he hoped in vain. Then said Gawaine, 'I will go and help him, and he shall see the lady of his love.' So on the next day he made an oath with Pelleas that he would win the damsel for him, and when he came to the house of Ettard, he told her that he was a knight who had slain Sir Pelleas. At this Ettard was so full of joy that she welcomed Gawaine and made him good cheer, until he forgot the word he had plighted to Pelleas, and wooed the maiden for himself. When Pelleas knew that Gawaine was forsworn, he took horse, for he could tarry no longer for pure sorrow; and he went his way and laid him down upon his bed to die. But the Lady of the Lake whom Merlin had loved came and looked on him as he slept, and she said, 'So fair a knight shall not die;' and in two hours she came back with the lady Ettard, and threw such an inchantment upon her that Ettard loved Pelleas now as much as she had hated him in time past. But when Pelleas woke and saw her standing near, he hated her with all his soul. 'Begone, traitress,' he said, 'and never come near me more.' So Ettard went away and died of sorrow, and the Lady of the Lake led Pelleas into her own land, and they loved together while they lived.

But Marhaus with the maiden of thirty winters' age did better things, for he came first to the house of a duke who received him churlishly, and when he knew who he was, said that on the morrow he must fight with himself and his six sons, because Gawaine had slain his seven sons and now was the time for vengeance, and Marhaus must fight alone with seven against him. So on the morrow they fought, and Marhaus was so mighty that he overthrew them all, and made them swear never more to be foes to King Arthur or his knights. Then Marhaus went on with his damsel, and at a great tourney he won a rich circlet of gold worth a thousand besants, and afterwards slew a terrible giant who ravaged the lands of Earl Fergus, and delivered many ladies and knights out of the giant's dungeon. There he got great riches, so that he was never poor all the days of his life, and so went on his way with the maiden to the trysting-place.

Likewise with the damsel of sixty winters' age, Sir Uwaine bore himself as a good knight, for he avenged the Lady of the Rock against those who had robbed her of her heritage, and restored to her all her lands; and Sir Uwaine dwelt with the lady for nearly half a year, to be healed of the grievous wounds which he had received when he did battle on her behalf. Then as the year came round, he hastened with the maiden to the trysting-place: and all met there, as they had agreed; but the damsel that Gawaine had could say little good of him.

So at last they came back to the king, who was right glad to see them, and bade them tell him all that had befallen them. When the feast of Pentecost came, the Lady of the Lake brought with her Sir Pelleas, who was made a knight of the Round Table, and Sir Marhaus also, for there were two seats void, for two knights were slain that year: and Sir Pelleas was afterwards one of the four that achieved the Sangreal.

CHAPTER V.

THE CROWNING OF ARTHUR AT ROME.

Now it was that, as Arthur held a royal feast with the knights of the Round Table, and the kings and princes who were his friends and allies, there came twelve ancient men and charged him to pay truage for his realm to the emperor who was at Rome. Then some of the knights and lords were so wroth that they would have slain the messengers, but Arthur stayed their hands. 'I like not their message,' he said, 'but I must remember mine honour.'

Then Arthur took counsel, and when the King of Scotland, the Lord of West Wales, and the King of Little Britain, with many others, had sworn to help him, he sent for the Roman messengers, and said, 'Go tell your lord it is I who am emperor, not he, and I am coming to Rome with my army to make good my right and subdue those that rebel against me.' Then with large gifts and great courtesy he sent them away: and when they reached Rome, there was sore fear among the great men who were with the emperor, and one said to him, 'It may be thou hast made a rod for thyself, for Arthur is all another man than ye think for, and around him is the noblest fellowship of knights, lords, and princes that is in the world. For his courage the world is too little, and in his person he is the most manly man that lives.' Then the emperor told how he meant to pass the mountains and do battle with Arthur; and he summoned together all the kings and chiefs who were bound to do him service from Europe and from Africa, from Ind and Egypt, Galatia and Turkey, and with them fifty giants who were born of fiends to guard his person. So came the emperor to Cologne.

And Arthur held a parliament at York, and there left his queen and realm to the governance of Sir Baldwin and Sir Constantine, and then sailed away with his host from Sandwich. After they had landed at Barflete in Flanders, there came a poor man who told the king of a great giant who slew men and devoured children in Britanny, and how he had stolen away the duchess, the wife of Howell, the king's cousin. Then with Sir Kay and Sir Bedivere he rode on pilgrimage to St. Michael's Mount, but when he reached its foot, he bade them stay while he went up alone. Fearful was the fight when he found the giant gnawing the limbs of a man and challenged him to battle, for when the king had smitten him, the giant threw away his club and catching him in his arms crushed his ribs; and so they struggled and wrung together, till they rolled down the hill and reached the sea mark at the place where the king had charged Sir Kay and Sir Bedivere to await him. And now he bade Sir Kay to smite off the giant's head and bear it to Sir Howell; and the people came and thanked the king for his great exploit. 'Give the thanks to God,' he said, 'and part the goods among you.'

Then were there fearful battles between Arthur's men and the hosts of the emperor; but everywhere Arthur's men were the conquerors, and when he saw what great things his knights had done, he embraced them knight by knight in his arms and said, 'Never was there king that had knights so noble as mine.' At the last there came a day in which Arthur fought with the emperor and smote him with Excalibur that he died; and he sent the body with the bodies of many lords who had been slain, charging the men who bare them to tell the Romans that the king sent them as the tribute for which they had asked, and that if this did not suffice he would pay them more when he came himself to Rome. Thither he went by Milan and Pavia, and through Tuscany, and in the cities to which he came all the people yielded him homage and sware to be his subjects for ever; and at Rome at Christmastide he was crowned emperor by the Pope, and then he held high festival with his knights, and gave lands and realms unto his servants, in such wise that none complained whether rich or poor. So was his journey ended with honour and worship. Then said the king, 'To tempt God is no wisdom; therefore wend we again to England;' and to England they came, and Queen Guenevere hastened to meet her lord at Sandwich; and at every city and burgh the commons brought him splendid gifts to welcome home their king.

CHAPTER VI.

THE EXPLOITS OF SIR LANCELOT DU LAKE.

AMONG the knights who had fought for Arthur with the Romans none had done so great deeds as Lancelot du Lake; and for this Queen Guenevere had him in favour above all other knights, and of a truth he loved the queen above all other ladies and damsels all his life, and for her did many deeds of arms. When he was now well rested, he set out with his nephew Sir Lionel, and they rode into a deep forest and so into a deep plain; and as the sun waxed hot, the eyes of Lancelot became heavy with sleep, and Lionel said, 'See here is a great apple-tree; there rest we ourselves and our horses.' So there they alighted, and tied their horses to trees, and Lancelot sank to sleep heavily while Lionel kept watch. But as he watched, there came three knights riding, and yet another followed who smote down the three who had gone before; and Lionel thought to rescue them, and privily mounted his horse, because he sought not to awake Lancelot. But he fared no better than the three knights, for he too was taken, and carried by the knight to his castle, where he with them was beaten with thorns, and thrust into a dungeon. In like manner fared Sir Ector de Maris, who had followed Lancelot to aid him. He too was seized by Sir Turquine, and when he found Sir Lionel in the dungeon, he asked him where Sir Lancelot might be. 'I left him asleep,' he said, 'under an apple-tree, when I went from him; but what is become of him I cannot tell.' 'Alas!' said the knights who were captives in the dungeon, 'if Lancelot rescue us not, there is none other that can deliver us out of the hands of Turquine.'

Now, as Lancelot lay sleeping under the tree, there came by four queens, and as they looked on his face, they knew that it was Sir Lancelot, and they began to strive for him, for each said she would have him to be her love. 'Nay,' said Morgan le Fay, 'I will put an inchantment upon him, and when he wakes up from it, let him choose which of us four he will have.' So they bare him sleeping to the castle Chariot; and on the morn the four queens stood before him, and said, 'We know thee well that thou art Sir Lancelot, King Ban's son; and well we know that Queen Guenevere has thy love; but as now thou must lose her for ever, therefore thou must now choose one of us four. I am Morgan le Fay, and here is the Queen of North Wales, the Queen of Eastland, and the Queen of the Out Isles. Choose which thou wilt have; and if thou wilt not choose, in this prison thou shalt die.' Then said Lancelot, 'I will have none of you, for ye are all false inchantresses: and for Guenevere, I would prove, were I free, that she is the truest lady living.' Then the queens left him in great wrath; but a fair maiden rescued him from their wiles, and she was the daughter of King Bagdemagus. She it was who brought him to his armour and his horse, and bade him ride to an abbey of white monks, whither she would bring her father to him. And even so it came about; and Lancelot promised to aid Bagdemagus in a great tourney which was soon to be held. In that tourney Lancelot did great things, for he smote down the King of North Wales and Sir Mador of the Gate, and after him, Sir Mordred and Sir Gahalatine; and so was it judged that Bagdemagus should have the prize.

Then said Lancelot that he must go seek his brother Lionel; and as he journeyed, it so chanced that he came into the same forest where he was taken sleeping; and a damsel came, which asked him if he would do battle with Sir Turquine, who had in his dungeon threescore and four knights of Arthur's court. Then Lancelot sware to do as she desired; and presently he saw riding towards him a great knight, before whom an armed knight lay bound across his horse; and Lancelot knew him to be Galeris, the brother of Sir Gawaine. Then Lancelot challenged Sir Turquine to the battle; and they fought fiercely, until at length Turquine promised to free all his prisoners if Lancelot would tell him his name, because he was the bravest knight whom he had ever met, and like one knight that he hated above all other knights. 'It is well said,' answered Lancelot; 'and now tell thou me, who is this knight whom thou hatest above all other men?' 'To say sooth,' said Turquine, 'he is Lancelot du Lake, who slew my brother Carados; and if ever we meet, one of us shall remain dead upon the ground. For his sake I have slain a hundred good knights, and have scores in prison, and all these will I set free, so thou be not

Lancelot.' 'Well,' said Sir Lancelot, 'if thou wilt know it, I am Lancelot du Lake, the son of King Ban of Benwick, and very knight of the Round Table.' 'Ah!' said Turquine, 'thou art most welcome to me of all men, for we part not till one of us be dead.' But for all his large words, Turquine was smitten to death by Lancelot, who rescued Gaheris, and bade him go to Turquine's castle and give his greeting to Arthur's knights who lay in the dungeon, charging them to take such stuff as they might find, and then to go to the court and await his coming about the time of Pentecost. But this they would not do, for they said that it would be shame to them if they hastened not to his help.

And once again Lancelot did good service to the daughter of Bagdemagus by rescuing her from the hands of Sir Peris of the Forest; and after that he asked if she needed aught more at his hands. 'Nay,' she said, 'at this time. But God guard thee for the greatest knight that now lives. But one thing thou lackest—that ye will not love some maiden; and it is noised that ye love Queen Guenevere, and that she has ordained by inchantment that ye shall never love any but her; wherefore many are sad in this land, both great and small.' 'Fair maiden,' said Lancelot, 'I may not keep people from saying what it pleaseth them to say; but I think not to be a wedded man, and I would go on my way with my hands clean and my heart pure.' So they parted; and Lancelot went on to do great things. At the Castle of Tintagil, where Uther won Igerne, he slew two giants, and set free three-score ladies who had been their prisoners for seven years. And after this he rescued Sir Kay from three knights who had set upon him, and he made them yield themselves to Sir Kay, and swear to go and tell Queen Guenevere that Sir Kay sent them to be her prisoners.

In the night, as Sir Kay and he slept together, Lancelot rose quietly and put on Sir Kay's armour and shield, and so went on his way; and soon he had to fight with other two knights, who took him to be Sir Kay. These also he overcame, and he charged them to yield themselves to Queen Guenevere at Whitsuntide, and to say that Sir Kay had sent them unto her. After this, a maiden, whose brother was sore wounded, besought him to go into the Chapel Perilous, and thence bring a sword and a cloth, which should stanch his bleeding, for in no other wise could it be stanched. So Lancelot went into the chapel, and within he saw a dim lamp burning, and before the altar a corpse covered with a cloth of silk. As he stooped down to cut off a piece of this cloth, the earth quaked, so that Lancelot was afraid; but he seized the fair sword which lay by the body, and hastened out of the chapel. As he passed out, a fair damsel bade him leave the sword, if he would not die. 'It may not be,' said Lancelot. 'Thou hast done well,' answered the maiden, 'for if thou hadst left the sword, thou shouldest never see Queen Guenevere. And now, I pray thee, kiss me but once.' 'God forbid,' said Sir Lancelot. 'Well,' said the damsel, 'hadst thou kissed me, thy days had been done; but now have I lost all my labour, for I ordained this chapel for thy sake and for Sir Gawaine: and once I had Sir Gawaine within my power, when he fought with Sir Gilbert, the dead knight, whose sword thou hast taken. But know now, Sir Lancelot, that I have loved thee these seven years past; yet may no woman have thy love but Guenevere. Still, if I could not have thee alive, I should have no greater joy in this world than to have thy body dead. Then would I have embalmed and kept it all my days; and daily should I have kissed thee in spite of Guenevere.' 'God preserve me from your subtle crafts,' said Lancelot. And so he went his way; and the maiden pined away in her sorrow till, on the fourteenth night, she died; and her name was Hellawes, the sorceress, the lady of the castle Nigramous. Presently there met him the damsel who had prayed him to stanch the bleeding of her brother, Sir Meliot, and when she saw him, she clapped her hands for joy. Then they went together to the castle where the bleeding knight lay; and when Lancelot touched his wounds with Sir Gilbert's sword, and wiped them with the cloth that he took from Gilbert's body, Sir Meliot rose up hale and strong as ever he had been in his life, and Lancelot charged him to show himself at Arthur's court on the feast of Pentecost. But Lancelot himself yet went on his way, doing brave and knightly deeds; and sometimes they for whom he wrought them were worthy, but sometimes they were treacherous, and sought to trap him by his goodness and his courtesy.

At the last he journeyed back to Arthur's court, and there were all those whom he had charged to go and yield themselves at the feet of Guenevere, and there also were Gawaine and Gaheris, and all praised Lancelot for his great exploits. 'Yea,' said Sir Kay, 'Lancelot took my harness and left me his; and so I rode in peace, and none had aught to say to me, because they took me for Sir Lancelot.' And Sir Meliot also told his tale. Then was there great joy and gladness: and at that feast Sir Belleus was made a knight of the Round Table.

CHAPTER VII.

THE STORY OF SIR GARETH OF ORKNEY.

KING ARTHUR was holding high festival in the Castle of Kinkenadon upon the sands that marched nigh Wales, when there came into the hall two men on whose shoulders there leaned the fairest and goodliest youth that ever man saw, as though of himself he could not walk. When they reached the dais, the youth prayed God to bless the king and all his fair fellowship of the Round Table. 'And now I pray thee, grant me three gifts, which I seek not against reason: the one of these I will ask thee now, and the other two when twelve months have come round.' 'Ask,' said Arthur, 'and ye shall have your asking.' 'Then,' answered the youth, 'I will that ye give me meat and drink for a year.' And though the king bade him ask something better, yet would he not: and Arthur said, 'Meat and drink enough shalt thou have; for that I never stinted to friend or foe. But what is thy name?' 'That I cannot tell,' said the youth. 'Strange,' said the king, 'that thou shouldest not know thy name, and thou the goodliest youth that ever mine eyes have seen.' Then the king gave him in charge to Sir Kay, who scorned him because he had asked so mean a gift. 'Since he has no name,' said Sir Kay, 'I will call him Pretty-hands, and into the kitchen shall he go, and there have fat brose, so that at the year's end he shall be fat as a pork hog.' So the youth went to the hall door and sat down among boys and lads, and there he ate sadly. Yea though Sir Gawaine and Sir Lancelot would have him come and drink wine in their chamber, yet would he not stir from the place where Sir Kay had put him. So was it throughout the twelve months, that he displeased not man nor child by reason of his meekness and his mildness. Only when there was any justing of knights, he hastened to see it; and when they were any sports, none might cast bar nor stone, as he did, by two yards.

At Whitsuntide the king again made high festival; and a maiden came beseeching him to succour a lady who was besieged in her castle by the Red Knight of the Red Lawns. But she would not tell the lady's name: and because she would not, the king said that none of his knights that were there should go to help her with his will. Then came the youth and spake to the king. 'I have had one gift: and now I ask the other two, as thou didst promise. First, let me have this adventure: and next, bid Sir

Lancelot make me knight, for of him alone will I take knighthood.' 'All this shall be done,' said the king. 'Fie,' said the maiden, 'am I to have only your kitchen-knave?' and she took her horse and went away wroth.

At that moment came one who said to the youth that a dwarf was come with his armour and horse, and with all manner of rich things. So the youth mounted his horse, and rode after the damsel. Then said Sir Kay, 'I will go and see how the kitchen-boy fares;' but when the youth saw him coming, he turned and bade Sir Kay beware. But Sir Kay put his spear in rest; and when the youth saw this, he rushed towards him and thrusting aside the spear with his sword, smote down Sir Kay, and took his shield and his spear, and rode away. But soon Sir Lancelot overtook him, and they justed together so fiercely, till at the last Lancelot said, 'Fight not so sore: our quarrel is not so great but we may fairly leave off.' 'That is true,' answered the youth, 'but it does me good to feel your might, nor was it I who challenged the fight; and now I pray you give me the order of knighthood.' But Lancelot said that he could do so only if the youth told him his name. 'Well, then, if you swear not to discover me, I will tell thee. My name is Gareth, and I am brother to Sir Gawaine.' Then was Lancelot right glad and forthwith made him a knight: and the youth rode away. But when he overtook the damsel, she reviled him, and told him that his clothes were full of the grease and tallow of the king's kitchen, and that he was but a mover of spits and a ladle-washer. 'Say to me what thou wilt,' answered the youth, 'I go not from thee till I have done that which I sware to do.' And they had not gone far before a man, who was fleeing away with all his might, prayed him to give him aid against six thieves, who were in the wood: and the youth slew them all. But none the less the damsel reviled him, and said that he had overpowered them not by bravery but by chance, nor would she sit at the same board with him in the house of the man whom he had rescued from the thieves.

On the morrow the youth set forth again with the damsel and came to a ford where on the other side stood two knights to bar the passage. 'Wilt thou match yonder knights?' asked the maiden. 'Yea,' answered the youth, 'though they were not two but eight;' and so it came to pass that in the fight which followed one was drowned and the other cloven to the chin. But the maiden said that he had won all by chance, for the horse of the first knight stumbled, and the second knight fell by mishap. 'Say what thou wilt,' answered the youth, 'I heed it not, so I may win your lady.' Onwards thus they went, the damsel reviling, till they came to a black lawn on which a black banner hung upon a black hawthorn, and on the other side a black shield; and near it stood a black spear and a black horse covered with silk, and a black stone hard by, and by it sat, all armed, the Knight of the Black Lawn, who asked the damsel if she had brought a knight of King Arthur to be her champion. 'Nay,' she said, 'this is but a kitchen knave, of whom I cannot be rid; and I have seen him this day slay two men by mischance, and not by prowess.' Then said the black knight, 'I will but put him down on one foot, and take his horse and his harness, for it were shame to do him any more harm.' But the youth spake in few words and said, 'Sir Knight, thou art full liberal of my horse and harness; but neither shalt thou have of me, unless thou winnest them with thy hands. Let us see then what thou canst do.' 'Is it even so?' said the black knight: 'leave then thy lady, for it is not seemly that a kitchen page should ride by her side.' 'Thou liest,' said the youth, 'I am of higher lineage than thou art, and I will prove it on thy body.' Then they came together and fought fiercely till the youth was sorely hurt, but at the last the black knight fell down in a swoon and died; and the youth put on his armour and took his horse, and rode after the damsel. But still she urged him to flee away, for all that he had done had been done by chance: and still the youth sware that he would not leave her till he should see the uttermost of that journey.

Next, there came towards them a knight clad in green, who asked the maiden if she had brought with her his brother, the black knight. 'Nay,' she said, 'this kitchen-page has slain thy brother; but it was by mischance.' 'Ah! traitor,' said the green knight, 'thou shalt die for thus shamefully slaying my brother.' 'I defy thee,' answered the youth; 'and I tell thee that I slew him knightly.' So, as he had fought before with the black knight, he fought now with the green knight, until he had unhorsed him, and the green knight besought his mercy. 'No mercy will I give thee,' said the youth, 'unless the maiden who came with me pray me to save thy life.' But she would not, for she thought scorn to ask a boon of a kitchen-page; and the green knight prayed again, and sware to bring thirty knights to do the youth service. 'It will avail thee nought,' said the youth, 'if this maiden ask not for thy life;' and he made as though he were about to slay him. Then said the damsel, surlily, 'Slay him not, for if thou dost thou shalt repent it.' With this was the youth satisfied, and he released the green knight, who kneeled to him and did him homage; and all three rode to the green knight's house, where they lodged that night.

On the morn they arose, and after mass the green knight led them through the forest, and he sware that he and his thirty knights should be ever ready at the youth's bidding. 'See then,' said the youth, 'that ye go and yield yourselves to King Arthur when I call upon you.' But the maiden was churlish and sullen still, and she warned the youth that he would never be able to go through the Perilous Pass. 'Well then,' he answered, 'let him who fears flee.' Presently they saw a tower white as snow, and under the tower was a fair meadow; and when the lord of the castle saw them coming, he thought that it was his brother, the black knight. So he cried aloud, 'Brother, what do ye in these marches?' 'Nay,' said the maiden, 'it is not he. He has slain thy brother; but he did it by chance, for he is but a kitchen-knave; he has also overcome thy brother the green knight. But now thou mayest be revenged on him, for I can never be quit of him.' Then was there again a fierce strife, in which the red knight sorely wounded the youth, so that the blood came from him in streams; but at the last he, too, was struck down to the earth, and prayed for mercy. 'No mercy shalt thou have, if this damsel ask not thy life.' But when he made as though he would slay him, the maiden charged him not to do it, for he was a noble knight. And the youth bade the red knight stand up and thank the damsel for his life. Then the red knight took them into his castle, and when the night was come he ordered sixty knights to keep watch round the youth, and guard him against treason, and with these knights he sware to serve him always. And again the youth charged them to be ready to go and yield themselves to King Arthur when he should bid them.

But as they rode on, still the damsel reviled him; and she warned him that they would soon come to the lands of a knight who should pay him all his wages, for he was the man of most worship in the world except King Arthur. 'It is well,' answered the youth, 'for the more he is of worship, the more shall be my worship if I conquer him.' Soon they saw before them a beautiful city, and before the city a fair plain full of pavilions richly dight; and the maiden said, 'These are the pavilions of Sir Persant of Inde, and about him are five hundred knights and gentlemen-at-arms.' 'It may be,' answered the youth; 'but if he be a knight brave and courteous, as you say, he will not set upon me with all his men or with his five hundred knights: and if there come against me but one at a time, I shall not fail while my life lasts.' 'Fie,' said the maiden, 'that such a knave as thou shouldest boast thus.' 'It boots not to talk,' he answered; 'let him come and do his worst.' Then said the damsel, 'I marvel who thou mayest be, for never has a woman ruled a knight so fully and shamefully as I have ruled you, and yet hast thou ever treated me courteously; nor could any do this who came not of gentle blood.'

'Maiden,' said the youth, 'a knight is worth little who cannot suffer a damsel. I took no heed to thy words, but the more they angered me, the more I wreaked my wrath on those with whom I had to do. And so it is that all thy foul words have furthered me in my battles.' 'Alas!' she said, 'forgive me for all that I have said or done amiss against thee.' 'With all my heart,' he answered; 'for, to say sooth, all thy evil words pleased me.' Even so it came to pass in the battle with Sir Persant that the youth was conqueror; and the damsel was no more loth to pray for his life; and Sir Persant said, 'Well, I wot now that thou didst slay my brother, the black knight, and didst overcome my brethren, the green and the red knights. And now shalt thou have homage and service of me and of my hundred knights.' That night they lodged with Sir Persant, who asked the maiden whither she was leading her knight, and she said that he was going to the help of her sister, who was besieged in her castle. 'Ah,' said Persant, 'he who besieges her is the Knight of the Red Lawns, a man without mercy, and with the strength of seven men. God save you from that knight, for he doth great wrong to that lady, who is one of the fairest ladies of the world, and your damsel is, I think, her sister. Is not your name Linet?' 'It is,' she said, 'and my sister's name is Liones.' Then Sir Persant told the youth that the Knight of the Red Lawns might have won the lady many times, but that he kept up the siege because he wished to do battle with some great knight, such as Sir Lancelot, or Sir Tristram, or Sir Lamorak, or Sir Gawaine. 'God speed you well,' said Sir Persant; 'for if thou canst match the red knight, ye shall be called the fourth knight of the world.' Then said the youth, 'I would fain be of good fame; but my father was a noble man, and, so that ye will keep it close, I will tell you who I am.' 'Nay, we will not discover you,' said they, 'till ye bid us.' 'Truly, then, I am Gareth of Orkney, the son of King Lot and of King Arthur's sister; and my brothers are Sir Gawaine, and Sir Agravaine, and Sir Gaheris, and I am the youngest of them all. Yet neither Arthur nor Gawaine know who I am.'

Then went a dwarf to the lady who was besieged, and brought the tidings that the youth was coming to her aid, and told her all his story from the hour when he was made a knight by Lancelot; and the lady rejoiced at the news, and bade the dwarf go to an hermitage hard by, and make ready food and wine for the youth, that he might be refreshed.

As the dwarf went back from the hermitage, he met the Knight of the Red Lawns, who asked him whence he came: and the dwarf said that he had been with Dame Liones' sister, who had brought a knight with her. 'Then is her labour but lost,' said the knight; 'for were it Lancelot, Tristram, Lamorak, or Gawaine, I think myself good enough for them all. Is he, then, one of these four?' 'Nay, he is not,' said the dwarf, 'but he hath passed all the perilous passages, and conquered all with whom he has fought.' 'What is his name?' asked the red knight. 'That will I not tell you,' said the dwarf, 'but Sir Kay in scorn called him Prettyhands.' 'I care not,' answered the knight: 'whosoever he be, he shall die a shameful death.'

On the morrow, the youth and the maiden Linet rode

after mass through a fair forest, and came to a plain with a goodly castle and many pavilions and tents, and in one part were great trees on which hung the bodies of nearly forty knights. 'What means this?' asked the youth. 'These are the knights,' answered Linet, 'who sought to deliver my sister from the Knight of the Red Lawns; for all who are overcome by him die by a shameful death.' Then fast by a sycamore tree he saw a horn hanging, of elephant's bone. 'Blow not the horn,' said Linet, 'to challenge the red knight till it be noon, for till that hour his might increaseth, so that, as men say, he has the strength of seven men.' But the youth, heeding her not, blew the horn so eagerly that all the castle rang again; and the Red Knight of the Red Lawns armed him hastily, and blood red was his armour and his shield, and his men brought him a red spear and a red steed.

'Be glad and light now,' said Linet to the youth, 'for yonder is your deadly foe, and at yonder window is my sister Liones.' When the youth looked up and saw her fair face as she looked down kindly upon him, he said that he could ask for no better quarrel, and that she alone should be his lady always.

Then was fought a fight more fierce than any that had gone before. From prime to noontide, from noontide to evensong, their blows fell thick as hail, till all their bodies were gashed and men might see their bare flesh, as the blood streamed out in rivers.

Then at last they stopped to rest, for their hands were too weary to strike more; and as they bared their faces to the cool wind, the youth saw Liones looking down upon him lovingly from her window, so that his heart waxed light and merry, and he rose up to do battle again to the death. At the first the red knight had the best, but in the end the youth smote the sword out of his hand, and then he unlaced his helmet, as though he were about to slay him. Then the red knight yielded him to the youth's mercy; but Sir Gareth remembered the knights whose bodies he had seen hanging on the trees, and he said that he could show no mercy to murderers. 'Nay, but hear me,' said the red knight. 'The lady of my love had her brother slain, she said, by Lancelot or Gawaine; and she bade me promise, if I loved her, to put to a shameful death such knights as I might conquer.' Then came others also and prayed for the red knight's life; and to those Sir Gareth said, 'I am loth to slay this knight, though he has done shamefully; but he shall have his life if he will go first and yield him to the lady of the castle, begging her forgiveness, and thence go to King Arthur's court and ask mercy for all the evil that he has wrought.' Even so it came to pass; and when the red knight yielded himself to Arthur and Gawaine, they marvelled who this youth might be who had borne himself so knightly. 'Marvel not,' said Lancelot, 'he shall do more wondrous things yet than these.' 'Thou knowest then his name and whence he comes,' said Arthur. 'Yea, I do; but he charged me not to discover him until he bade me do so.'

Now after the battle Sir Gareth hastened to the castle, for he was eager to talk with Liones; but when he drew near to the gate, he found the drawbridge pulled up and the port closed; and looking up he saw Liones at a window, who said, 'Go thy way, Sir Knight, for I may not wholly give thee my love, till thou have a place among the number of the worthy knights. When twelve months have passed, thou shalt hear new tidings.' 'Alas!' said Gareth, 'I have served you well, and I weened not to be thus treated.' 'Nay,' said Liones, 'be not hasty nor wroth. Thy toil and thy love shall not be lost. Wherefore go on thy way with a merry heart, and trust me that ever I shall love thee and none other.' Then Gareth rode away, but all his strength was gone for very sorrow; and that night he was lodged in a poor man's house, and as the hours wore on, still he writhed for the love of the lady of the castle.

On the morrow he arose and rode to a broad-water, where three hours before noon he lay down to rest with his head on his shield, when he had given his horse to the dwarf, bidding him watch beside him. Meanwhile, Liones had called to her brother, Sir Gringamore, and charged him to go and bring away Sir Gareth's dwarf, for she said, 'Until I know his name and of what kindred he is come, I shall never be merry at heart.' So Sir Gringamore hasted and finding the dwarf watching by his master's side, he rode away with him as fast as he could to his own castle. But the dwarf, as he went, cried out aloud to Sir Gareth, and Gareth awaking saw Sir Gringamore hastening away. Then over hill and dale, through marshes and fields, he rode furiously after Gringamore, who had reached his castle and brought the dwarf before Liones. Then the lady asked him straightway of his master's name and kindred, and the dwarf made not much ado to tell her all, and then he prayed to be sent back to his lord again. But even as he spake, Sir Gareth came in at the gate with his drawn sword in his hand, and crying, 'Thou traitor, set free my dwarf, or I shall do thee all the harm that I can.' Then would there have been hot words and hard blows, if Liones had not stayed her brother, and told him that now she sought for nought else but to speak with the knight who had rescued her out of the hand of the Knight of the Red Lawns. So Sir Gringamore went to Gareth and cried him mercy, and led him by the hand into the hall where his own wife was: and thither presently came Liones, and the youth could not take his eyes off her as she sat before him. 'Would,' he said, 'that the lady of the Perilous Castle were so fair as she.' So ever, as the hours wore on, his love for her waxed greater and greater; and Sir Gringamore, seeing it, told his sister that even if she was better than she was she would be well bestowed upon him, and after he had talked with her awhile, he went to Sir Gareth and said, 'My sister is yours, for she loves you as well as ye do her, and better if better may be.' Then answered Gareth, 'There lives not a gladder man than I;' and he went to Liones and kissed her many times, and she promised to love him and none other all the days of her life, and told him withal that she was the lady for whom he had done battle before the Perilous Castle.

In the night, as Gareth lay down to sleep in the hall, he saw coming towards him a knight with a grim countenance, having a long battle-axe in his hand; and leaping from his couch, he rushed at him with his drawn sword, and after a short while smote off his head from his body; but he was bleeding so that he swooned away, and the cry of Liones who found him thus called forth Sir Gringamore, who asked how these things had been done. 'I know not,' said Liones, 'for it was not done by me nor by mine assent.' Likewise said her brother, and they strove to stanch his bleeding as well as they might. Then came the damsel Linet, and taking up the head that had been smitten off anointed it with an ointment; and when she placed it on the neck, the knight leaped up whole as he had been, and Linet put him in her chamber. Then said Gareth to her, 'I weened not that ye would thus deal by me;' but she said, 'Tarry yet awhile, and thou shalt see that all which I have done shall be for your honour and worship.'

On the next night Gareth saw coming to him again the man whose head he had cut off, and there was again a fierce strife between them, until Gareth smote off his head again; and this time he hewed it in pieces, and flung them out of a window into the castle ditch. But so had he strained himself that his old wound bled afresh, and he had swooned away when Liones and her brother came to him. Then as they strove to stanch the bleeding, Linet gathered the pieces of the head from the ditch of the castle, and anointed them as she had done before, and when she had put them together the knight was alive again. 'I have not deserved this at thy hands,' said Sir Gareth. 'Tarry yet a little,' answered the maiden, 'and thou shalt see that I have done all for thy honour and worship.'

At Pentecost, when Arthur made high festival, there came the green knight with fifty knights and yielded him to the king. After him came the red knight, and did homage with sixty knights, and after him the blue knight with an hundred knights; and these three told how they had been overcome by a knight named Prettyhands. 'I marvel,' said the king, 'what knight that is, and of what lineage he is come; for he was with me a year, and but poorly was he fostered, and Sir Kay called him Prettyhands in scorn.' But even as he spake, Sir Lancelot came to tell him that there stood without a goodly lord with six hundred knights, and the king went to them and asked their errand. 'Sir,' said the knight, 'I am Sir Ironside, the Red Knight of the Red Lawns, and a knight named Prettyhands has charged me to yield myself to you; and never until he came had knight been able to withstand me these thirty winters.' 'Ye are welcome,' said the king, 'for I trust to have thee now as much my friend as thou hast been my foe, and if thou wilt hold of me I will make thee a knight of the Round Table: but then thou must be no more a murderer.' 'Yea,' said Sir Ironside, 'that I have sworn already to Sir Prettyhands, and now must I pray forgiveness from Sir Lancelot and Sir Gawaine.' 'God forgive you,' said they, 'as we do; and we pray you tell us where we may find Sir Prettyhands.' 'That I cannot tell,' said Sir Ironside. Then as all spake in his praise, the king said, 'I shall do you honour for the love of Sir Prettyhands, and as soon as I meet with him, I will make you all upon one day knights of the Round Table.' Then turning to Sir Persant, the red knight, he said, 'I marvel that I hear not of the black knight, thy brother,' and they told the king how he had been slain by Sir Prettyhands.

Now while yet they kept the feast there came the Queen of Orkney, Arthur's sister; and her three sons, Gawaine, Agravaine, and Gaheris, knelt at her feet to ask her blessing. But turning to the king she asked, 'What have ye done with my youngest son, Gareth? He was amongst you for a year, and ye made him a kitchen knave, which is shame to you all.' 'Alas! mother,' said Sir Gawaine, 'I knew him not.' 'Nor I,' said the king, 'but he is now a worshipful knight as is any now living, and I shall never be glad till I may find him. But, sister, ye might have warned me of his coming, and then if I had not done well to him ye might have blamed me.' So the king told her all his story, and his sister said that she had sent him forth right well-armed and horsed, and with plenty of gold and silver. 'We saw none of this,' said Arthur, 'till the day when he went away, and then some knights told me that a dwarf had come bringing him a goodly horse and splendid armour, and we marvelled all whence those riches might come.' Then said the Queen of Orkney, 'I marvel that Sir Kay did mock and scorn him, and yet he named him more righteously than he thought, for, I dare say it, he is a man as fair-handed and well disposed as any living.' 'Sister,' said Arthur, 'let all this pass, and be merry, for he is proved to be a right true man, and that is my joy.'

Then would Gawaine and his brethren go forth to seek their brother, but Sir Lancelot stayed them and counselled the king to send messengers to the Perilous Castle, bidding Liones come to the court in all haste. When Sir Gareth heard this, he said to Liones, 'That is because of me, and I would have you now advise the king that he hold a tourney on the feast of the Assumption of our Lady, and to say that what knight there proves him best shall wed you and have your land.' Even so Liones gave this counsel to the king, and with all care they made ready for the tournament. Then at Linet's bidding Liones sent for Sir Persant of Inde, and for Sir Ironside, to come with all their knights, and through many countries far and wide was the cry made that men should come to the Perilous Castle beside the isle of Avilion, and there choose which side they should take in the tourney. So were gathered together kings and princes, barons and chiefs, and noble knights from England and from Scotland, from Brittany and Wales, and Gareth prayed Liones and her knights that there should none of them tell his name. Then said Liones to Gareth, 'I will lend you a ring which I pray you give back to me when the tournament is done, for it increaseth my beauty much more than it is of itself; and its virtue is that that which is green it will turn to red, red to green, blue to white, and white to blue, and so with all manner of colours. Moreover, he who bears this ring shall lose no blood.'

So when the day was come, and the mass was done, the heralds blew the trumpets, and the knights came together in the fight, and many knightly deeds were done on both sides. But of Sir Gareth all men marvelled who he might be that one time seemed green and another time blue or red, and before whom every knight went down. 'Truly,' said King Arthur to Lancelot, 'that knight with the many colours is a good knight. Go thou and encounter with him.' 'Nay,' said Lancelot, 'when a good knight has had so great labour, it is no good deed to rob him of his worship; and it may be that he is best beloved by the lady of the Perilous Castle among all that be here. Therefore, as for me, this day he shall have the honour, for though it lay in my power to put him from it, I would not.'

At the last, when Sir Gareth had wrought wondrously among all the knights, he rode out on the one side to drink; and his dwarf said, 'Give me your ring, that you lose it not while you drink.' So he left the ring with the dwarf, who knew now that Sir Gareth would be made known; for now, wherever he was seen, he was in yellow colours which changed not. And at Arthur's bidding the heralds came and saw written in letters of gold about his helm, 'This helm is Sir Gareth's of Orkney:' and they cried aloud, that all might hear, 'This is Sir Gareth, of Orkney, King Lot's son.' When Gareth saw that he was discovered, he doubled his strokes and smote down his brother Sir Gawaine. 'O brother,' said Gawaine, 'I thought not ye would strike me.' Then Gareth gat him out of the press, and bade the dwarf yield up the ring, that so men might know him no more. So he took it, and then they all wist not what had become of him; and afterwards he took counsel with the dwarf, who bade him send the ring back to Liones, and say that he would come when he might. With this message the dwarf hastened to the lady, while Sir Gareth rode amid thunder and rain through a dark forest until he came to a castle, and prayed the porter to let him in, for he was sore wearied. Then the porter went to tell the duchess that a knight of Arthur's court prayed for lodging, and the duchess rose up and came to Gareth and said, 'Sir Knight, the lord of this castle loves not King Arthur nor his court; and therefore it were better thou shouldest not come within this castle. If thou dost come, it must be under pledge that thou wilt yield thyself to him in whatsoever place thou mayest meet him.' So Gareth promised, and then she let the drawbridge down, and there he rested that night.

On the morrow he rode to a mountain where a knight named Bendelaine sought to bar his way, and Gareth smote him so that Bendelaine rode to his own castle and there died. But when Gareth drew near to it, there came out twenty of Bendelaine's men, who slew Gareth's horse when they saw that they could overcome him in no other way. But when he was on foot, they prevailed none the more against him. At the last, when he had well nigh slain them, he took the horse of one of them, and rode till he came to a castle where he heard great cries and moaning of women; and he asked a page, who passed by, what these sounds might mean. And the page said that there lived here a pitiless knight who had shut up thirty ladies in his dungeons. This knight Sir Gareth fought with and slew; and going into the castle, he set the ladies free. On the morrow morn, when he went to mass, he saw the thirty ladies kneeling upon divers tombs, and he knew that in those tombs lay their lords, whom the pitiless knight had slain. Then he charged them to go at the next feast of Pentecost to the court of King Arthur and say that Sir Gareth had sent them thither. After this he went his way, and met the Duke de la Rowse, the husband of the duchess in whose castle he had lodged, and would have yielded himself to him. But the duke would have him fight; and Gareth smote him, and conquered him, and charged him to go and yield himself to King Arthur; and when the duke was gone, there came another knight with whom he fought, and so fierce was the strife that the blood ran in streams upon the ground. At last there came the maiden Linet, and when she saw them, she cried aloud, 'Sir Gawaine, Sir Gawaine, leave thy fighting with thy brother Sir Gareth.' So soon as he heard these words, he threw away his sword, and running to his brother took him in his arms and craved his mercy. Then they embraced each the other, and wept a great while before they could speak: and Sir Gawaine besought Linet to go to the king, and tell him in what plight he was. And she found Arthur but two or three miles off, and the king hastened on his palfrey: but when he drew nigh to the place where Gawaine and Gareth were seated on the hill side, he sought to speak but could not, and he sank down in a swoon for gladness. So they hastened to their uncle and bade him be of good comfort; and the king was right glad, but withal he wept as he had been a child. And after him came Arthur's sister, their mother, and she too swooned away for gladness. There they tarried for eight days till the wounds of Gawaine and Gareth were healed. Then said Arthur to Linet, 'Why comes not thy sister to see a knight who hath loved her so well and wrought so much for her?' And Linet said, 'She knows not that he is here.' Then the king bade her go and charge Liones to come straightway; and when she was come, he asked Gareth whether he would have her for his wife. 'Yea,' said Gareth, 'I love her above all women living.' And of Gareth Liones said, 'He is my first love, and he shall be my last.' So was it agreed that they should be married on the coming Michaelmas at Kinkenadon by the sea; and Gareth sent his summons to all the knights and ladies whom he had conquered or rescued, that they should be on his marriage-day at Kinkenadon on the sands. So upon Michaelmas-day, they were wedded by the Bishop of Canterbury, and on the same day Gaheris wedded the damsel Linet, and Agravaine married Dame Laurel: and at the high feast which followed Arthur made Sir Persant of Inde and his two brothers, and the Red Knight of the Red Lawns, and the Duke de la Rowse, knights of the Round Table. But when the justs were done, Sir Lamorak and Sir Tristram departed suddenly, and at this the king and his fellows were sore displeased.

CHAPTER VIII.

THE HISTORY OF SIR TRISTRAM.

AMONG the kings who held their lands of Arthur was Meliodas, King of Liones, who had a meek and gentle wife named Elizabeth. But there was another lady who loved him, and one day when he was hunting she lured him to chase a hart by himself alone, till he came to a castle where she made him prisoner. Sore was the grief of Elizabeth when her lord came not back, and she went forth to search for him through the dark forest, and there was her child born, and then she knew that she must die. So as her strength failed her, she bade the woman who was with her to carry the child to the king. 'Let him call it Tristram,' she said; 'for he is the child of sorrow. Ah, my child! as thou hast brought so much woe at thy birth, thou art full likely to be a manly man in thine age.' But Merlin rescued King Meliodas from his prison, and when he came home there he found the child of sorrow, and they told him that the fair and gentle lady, his wife, was dead. For seven years the king abode lonely in his grief, and then he married the daughter of Howel, the King of Brittany, and when this queen saw her children around her she hated Tristram, and placed poison in a silver cup that the boy might drink it and die. But her eldest son spied the cup, and he drank of it and straightway fell dead. Yet she put more poison in the cup; and when King Meliodas came in and would have drunk the wine, she dashed the cup from his hand. 'Ah, traitress!' said the king, for he remembered that her son had fallen dead suddenly, 'tell me what manner of drink this is, or I will slay thee.' So she told him all, and she was judged to be burnt. But when they tied her to the stake, Tristram besought his father for a boon.

'What wouldst thou have?' asked the king. 'The life of the queen,' answered Tristram. 'Nay,' said the king, 'that is not rightly asked, and chiefly for thy sake she ought to die.' Nevertheless, Tristram prayed yet again for her life, and the king gave word that it should be as he desired, but he would no more have Tristram abide at his court. So he sent him to France for seven years, and at the end of that time the boy came back again to his home. There he learnt to be a harper passing all other harpers that ever lived; and more than all others he had skill in hunting and hawking, and all the names that are for those sports were made by him.

Now it came to pass that the King of Ireland sent a messenger to King Mark of Cornwall to ask truage for his kingdom. And King Mark said, 'I will pay truage no more: if it please your master let him send a knight to do battle for him, and I will find another to do battle for me.' Then the King of Ireland prayed Sir Marhaus, who was a knight of the Round Table, to fight for his cause; and King Mark, when he came, knew not whom he might set in array against him, for no knight of the Round Table would fight with him. So as his messengers sped throughout the land, Tristram heard the tidings, and having sought leave of his father, he hastened to King Mark and said, 'I come from King Meliodas, who wedded thy sister; make me a knight, and I will fight with Sir Marhaus.' Then King Mark welcomed him joyfully, and though he saw that he was but a youth, he made him a knight, and sent a messenger to Sir Marhaus with letters saying a knight would come forth presently to do battle with him. 'It may well be,' said Sir Marhaus, 'but go back and say I fight with none who is not of royal blood.' When King Mark heard this he said to Tristram, 'Who art thou?' and he answered, 'I am the son of King Meliodas, and the child of thy sister, who died in the forest when I was born.' Then was King Mark right glad, and he sent letters to Sir Marhaus to say that it was even the son of a king and queen who should do battle with him: and Sir Marhaus also was well pleased.

Long they fought together, until at last Sir Marhaus wounded Tristram in his side with his spear; and when they had fought for many hours more, Tristram waxed stronger and smote with his sword through the helmet of Marhaus so fiercely that the sword stuck in the helm, and when he pulled it out, a piece of the blade was left in the head of Sir Marhaus. Then Sir Marhaus fled groaning, and would turn no more to fight with Sir Tristram; and he sailed away to Ireland, but he had not been many days in the king's house when he died, and the piece of Tristram's sword was found in his head, and the queen kept it.

But Tristram also was sore wounded, for the spear of Marhaus was poisoned; and there came a wise woman who said that he might never be healed but in the land from which the venom came. So Tristram went into the ship with his harp, and came to the court of the King of Ireland, and at the gate he harped so sweetly that the king sent for him and welcomed him gladly, and gave him in trust to his daughter Isolte, to heal him. And so she did: but with the healing she gave him also her love, for he taught her to harp, and she could not withstand the spell of his sweet music. But another knight loved Isolte, and he was Sir Palamides the Saracen.

Now it came to pass that the King of Ireland proclaimed a great tourney for the lady of the lawns, who should be given to be wife of the knight who should do most valiantly. Then said Isolte to Tramtrist, (for so had he called himself since he came to her father's house,) 'Wilt thou not just in this tourney?' 'I am but a young knight,' answered Tristram, 'and in my first battle I was sore wounded: but if thou wilt keep my name secret, I will go forth to the field.' 'Do so,' she said, 'and I will bring thee a horse and armour.' When the day came for the justing to begin, Sir Palamides came with a black shield and smote down many knights of the Round Table; and on the second day too he was doing wondrously, when the fair Isolte arrayed Tramtrist in white harness and placed him on a white horse; and he came into the field as it had been a bright angel; and when he had smitten down Sir Palamides, he charged him to forsake the maiden Isolte, and to wear no harness for a twelvemonth and a day. Then was Tramtrist in great honour; but as he tarried yet in the house of the King of Ireland, it chanced that the queen saw his sword in his chamber, and when she took it up, she marked that a piece was lacking from the edge. In great wrath she hastened to fetch the piece that was found in the head of Sir Marhaus; and when she fitted it to the sword, the weapon was whole. Then fiercely griping the sword, she hurried to the bath where Tristram lay, and would have slain him, but a knight who was with him thrust her back. And when she was thus hindered, she went to the king to make her plaint against Tramtrist, saying that he was the traitor knight who had slain Sir Marhaus. 'Leave me to deal with him,' said the king. So he sent for Tristram, and said, 'Tell me all thy story, and if thou hast slain Sir Marhaus.' So he told him all and the king was well satisfied, but he said, 'I may not maintain you here, unless I displease my barons, my wife, and her kin.' Then answered Tristram, 'I go my way; but ever shall I bear in mind your kindness, and the goodness of your daughter, who healed me of my grievous wound; and of her now let me take farewell.'

So was Tristram brought unto Isolte the Fair; and there was great sorrow between them when he told her all his story, and why he had hidden his name from her, and how that he must now depart from the land. 'All the days of my life,' he said, 'I shall be your knight;' and he gave her a ring and she gave him another; and he went his way and sailed to Cornwall, and went first to his father

Meliodas and then to King Mark. But now the friendship of King Mark was changed to jealousy, for both he and Tristram loved the same lady, and she was the wife of the Earl Sir Segwarides. So it came to pass that the lady sent a dwarf to Tristram, praying him to come and help her; and King Mark heard it, and when Tristram set forth, he hastened after him, and both were wounded in the fight; and Tristram rode forth bleeding to the lady's house, and there she made him good cheer, and would have him tarry with her; but there came tidings that the earl was nigh at hand, and Tristram hastened away, and after him presently rode the earl, who was smitten as King Mark had been smitten before him.

Yet a few days, and there came a knight of the Round Table, and at his prayer King Mark promised to give him whatsoever he might ask. And the knight asked for the fairest lady in the court, 'and this is the wife of Sir Segwarides.' So he took her away, but the earl was wroth and rode after the knight, and again he was smitten; and the tidings were brought to the court of King Mark. Then was Tristram ashamed and grieved, and hurrying away he came up with the knight, who, after a sore battle, yielded him, and it was agreed between them that the lady should go with the man whom she might choose. So she stood before Tristram and said, 'Thou wast the man whom I most loved and trusted, and I weened that thou hadst loved me above all: but when this knight led me away, thou didst suffer the earl, my lord, to ride after me to rescue me, and therefore now will I love thee no more, and I pray this knight to lead me to the abbey where my lord lieth.' And even so it was done.

But so great now was the hatred of King Mark for Tristram that he sought how he might destroy him; and he charged him to go to Ireland and bring back for him the fair Isolte to be his bride. So he set off with the goodliest knights that were in the court: but the winds drove back the ship to Camelot; and at this time it chanced that the King of Ireland was summoned to Arthur's court on pain of forfeiting his lands and the king's good grace, and when he was come, Sir Blamor de Ganis charged him with having slain his brother; wherefore the King of Ireland must fight either with his own body or by his champion. When Sir Tristram heard these things from his esquire, he rejoiced that he might now requite all the kindness which he had received at the hands of the king in his own country, and he hastened to him and said that he would fight in his quarrel if he would only swear that he had not been consenting to the knight's death, and that after the battle he would give him the reward for which he might ask. So fought Tristram with Blamor de Ganis who would not yield him when he had been smitten, but desired Tristram that he should slay him forthwith. At this Tristram started back, for he thought it foul shame that so brave a knight should be slain, and he besought the judges of the field that they would take the matter into their own hands. So after much striving, they took up Sir Blamor, and he and his brother were made friends that day with the King of Ireland and Sir Tristram.

After this the king asked Tristram what boon he desired to have; and Tristram said, 'Give me Isolte the Fair, to be the wife of mine uncle King Mark, for so have I promised him.' 'Nay,' said the king, 'far rather would I that thou shouldst take her for thyself: but if thou wilt give her to thine uncle, thou mayest do so.'

So was Isolte taken to the ship; but the queen her mother had given unto her damsel Brengwaine a drink that Isolte and King Mark might drink to each other on the day of their wedding, and then must they love each other all the days of their life. But it so happened that while the ship was yet on the sea, as Isolte and Tristram sat in the cabin, they spied the little golden vessel, and Tristram said, 'Here is the best wine that ever ye drank, which Brengwaine and my esquire have kept for themselves.' Then they drank to each other, and when they had so done, they loved each other so well that never their love departed for weal or for woe. But there were hard things to be done yet, before they should come to the palace of King Mark, for the ship was driven to the Weeping Castle, which was so called because all knights who came thither had to fight with the lord of the castle, and if the ladies who came with them were less fair than the lady of the castle, they must lose their heads, but the lady of the castle must lose hers, if any stranger should come fairer than she. And so now it came to pass, for Isolte was judged fairer far, and the head of the lady of the castle was stricken off; and afterward Tristram slew Sir Brennor, her lord.

Now Sir Brennor the Savage was the father of the good knight Sir Galahad, who now fought against Tristram, aided by the king with the hundred knights; and Tristram yielded himself, more for the number of Galahad's men than for the might of his hands. Then Galahad sware friendship with him, for he hated the evil customs of his father and his mother whom Tristram had slain; and he besought Tristram to go to Sir Lancelot du Lake. Then said Tristram, 'Of all the knights in the world I most desire his fellowship.'

Then they went again to the sea, and came to the city of King Mark, and there were the king and Isolte richly wedded. But some who were moved by hate and envy took the maiden Brengwaine, and bound her hand and foot to a tree, where Sir Palamides found her and took her to a monastery, that she might regain her strength. But Isolte so grieved for the maiden's loss that she wandered into a forest, where by a well she met Sir Palamides, who promised to bring Brengwaine safe and sound, if Isolte would do the thing for which he might ask. And so glad was she of his offer, that unadvisedly she promised to grant that which he might desire. In a little while he came back with Brengwaine, and bade Isolte remember her promise, which he could not ask her to fulfil save in the presence of King Mark: and in turn Isolte bade him remember that, albeit she had promised largely, she had thought no ill, and no ill would she do.

So Palamides rode after them, and when he saw King Mark he told him all that had happened, and demanded that the queen should do as she had promised. Then said the king, 'That which she has sworn must she do,' and Palamides answered, 'I will, then, that she go with me whithersoever I may lead her.' 'Take her,' said the king in wrath, 'for, as I suppose, ye will not keep her long.' So soon as they were gone the king sent for Tristram, but when he could nowhere be found, another knight said that he would go and fight with Sir Palamides. As these two knights fought, the fair Isolte sped away and a good knight who found her by a well-side led her towards his castle, and when Palamides came up the gates were shut, and he sat down before the gate like a man that is mazed. Thither soon came Tristram, and there was a fierce strife, in which Sir Palamides was smitten down, but the queen prayed for his life; and when Tristram had granted it, she said to Palamides, 'Take thy way to the court of King Arthur, and commend me to Queen Guenevere, and tell her from me that within this land there are but four lovers; and these are Sir Lancelot of the Lake and Queen Guenevere, and Sir Tristram of Liones and Queen Isolte.'

Then was there great joy when Tristram brought the queen back; but there was a traitorous knight named Andred who sought to do a mischief to his cousin Sir Tristram, and told false tales to King Mark, who believed his lies, and would have slain Tristram. But Tristram smote him down with the flat of his sword, and then taking his horse rode into the forest, where a troop of

King Mark's men attacked him, but he killed some and wounded thirty more. Then King Mark took counsel with his barons what they should do, and they advised him to take Tristram into his grace, 'for,' said they, 'if he goes to King Arthur's court, he will get such friends there that he may well avenge himself of your malice.'

About this time it came to pass that as Sir Lamorak was riding with another knight, there came up one sent by Morgan le Fay, bringing with him for King Arthur a horn of such virtue that no women might drink of it but such as were true to their husbands, and if they were false, they would spill all the drink. 'Now,' said Lamorak to this knight, 'thou shalt bear this horn not to King Arthur but to King Mark; and if not, thou shalt die. And say to him that I sent the horn that he may make trial of his wife.' When the knight had carried this message to the king, a hundred ladies were made to drink of the horn, and the wine was spilled by all save four: and they who spilled it were adjudged to be burnt. Then the barons gathered together and said plainly that they would not suffer this, because the horn came from as false a sorceress as any living; and many vowed that if they came across Morgan le Fay, they would show her scant courtesy.

But still Sir Andred played the spy on Sir Tristram and the fair Isolte; and one day when they were together, he set upon him suddenly with twelve knights and bound him hand and foot, and they led him to a chapel upon the sea rocks, there to take his judgment. When Tristram saw that there was no help but he must die, he brake silence and bade them remember how many good deeds he had done for King Mark and for his people. But Sir Andred reviled him, and drew his sword upon him. Then suddenly Tristram pulled in his arms and got his hands free, and leaping on Sir Andred he wrested his sword from him, and when he had smitten down Andred, he slew ten other knights. But when he saw the people draw nigh to him, he shut fast the chapel door, and breaking the bars of a window threw himself out upon the crags. There his esquire and some knights that were his friends saw him and lifted him up, and when he asked where Isolte was, they told him that she had been placed in a leper's house. 'She shall not be long there,' said Tristram, and with his men he rescued her and carried her away into a forest, and there abode with her. But one day while he slept in the wood, a man whose brother he had slain shot him through the shoulder with an arrow, and Tristram leaped up and killed the man; but the wound wrought him sore mischief, for the arrow with which he was hurt was poisoned. When Isolte the Fair heard it, she sent a damsel to Tristram, saying that she might not help him, because she was strictly shut up by King Mark, but bidding him go to Brittany to King Howel, whose daughter, Isolte of the White Hands, should heal him of his wound. And even so it came to pass; and Tristram did great deeds against the enemies of the king, and there grew up great love between him and Isolte, and at last she became his wife. When the tidings of this marriage were brought to Sir Lancelot, he said, 'Of all knights in the world I loved Tristram most; but now that he is false to his first love, Isolte the Fair, the love between him and me is done for ever, and from this day forth I am his deadly foe.' And Isolte the Fair, when she heard that Tristram was wedded, wrote a letter to Queen Guenevere, telling her how she had been forsaken by the man whom most she had loved. Then wrote Guenevere, bidding her be of good cheer, 'for although by crafts of sorcery ladies might make noble knights like Tristram wed them, yet in the end it shall be thus, that he shall hate her and love you better than ever he had done before.'

Not long had Tristram been wedded when he went with his wife in a little barge; but the wind blew them away to the coast of Wales, to an island on which was Sir

Lamorak, and there the barge was broken on the shore, and Isolte of the White Hands was hurt. By a well on that island, Tristram saw Sir Segwarides and a damsel, and Segwarides said, 'I know you for the man whom I have most cause to hate, because ye took away from me the love of my wife; but I will never hate a noble knight for a false woman; wherefore I pray thee now to stand by me, for we are sore bestead. Here dwells the giant Sir Nabon, who slays all the knights that he can seize of Arthur's court; and there is one of his knights wrecked upon these rocks, and we will bid the fishers bring him hither.' When he was come, Tristram knew Lamorak, but Lamorak knew not him; but when Tristram told him his story, and that his malice had not much hurt him, they made peace together, and fought with Sir Nabon and his knights. And Tristram slew Nabon and his son; and then all the people of the land said that they would hold of Sir Tristram. 'Nay' said Tristram, 'that may not be; but here is the good knight Sir Lamorak who shall rule over you wisely and justly.' But neither would Lamorak have it, and so the land was given to Segwarides, who governed it worshipfully. And Lamorak went his way, doing many knightly deeds, to the court of King Arthur.

CHAPTER IX.

THE MADNESS OF SIR TRISTRAM.

Now there came at this time to the king a young man of a goodly form, whose coat, of rich golden cloth, sat ill across his shoulders. And when Sir Kay knew that he was named Sir Brennor the Black, he said that he should be called the Knight of the Ill-shapen Coat, for he thought scorn of him as he had done of the knight whom he called Prettyhands. But when the king asked why he wore that coat, the young man said that his father was hewn to death in it by his enemies, who fell on him when he was asleep, and that he would wear it until he had revenged that deed upon them. Then he besought King Arthur to make him a knight, and Lamorak and Gaheris prayed him likewise, for they said, 'Even such a one was Sir Lancelot when he first came to this court, and now he is proved the mightiest knight in the world.' But before the king was able to knight him, the youth had done a great deed, for as he was left behind with Queen Guenevere a lion brake loose from a stone tower, and came furiously towards her, and while others fled for fear, the knight of the ill-shapen robe clave his head asunder. Wherefore he was made knight with the more honour.

That same day came a damsel bearing a shield, and she asked whether any knight there would take up the task which the owner of it had left undone, because he was sorely wounded: and when all others stood silent, the knight of the ill-shapen coat laid his hand on the shield and said that he would go. But the damsel reviled him, like the maiden who had reviled Sir Prettyhands, and she said, 'If thou wilt follow me, thy skin shall be as well hewn as thy coat.' 'Nay,' said the youth, 'when I am so hewn, I will ask you no salve to heal me withal.' As they went on their way together, they were met by two knights, each of whom unhorsed the youth; but he said, 'I have no disworship for this, for neither would dismount and fight with me on foot.' Not long afterwards, a hundred knights assailed him at once; and he got off his horse and put himself against a chamber-wall, for he wished rather to die thus than to bear the rebukes of the damsel of the evil words: but as he stood and fought there, she came up slily and taking away the horse tied him by the bridle to the postern, and then, going to a window at his back, she called to him and said, 'Thou fightest wondrously well, Sir Knight; but nevertheless thou must die, unless thou canst win thy way to thy horse, which I have tied up to abide thy coming.' Then with a mighty effort the youth threw himself upon the throng, and, cleaving down one and then another, reached his horse and rode away. But the maiden who was talking with Sir Mordred deemed that he was either slain or taken prisoner; and when she saw the youth hastening towards her, she said that they had let him pass only as a dastard, and sent a messenger to ask how it came about that the knight of the ill-shaped coat had escaped from their hands. 'He is a fiend,' they said, 'and no man. He has slain twelve of our best knights, and neither Tristram nor Lancelot could stand before him.'

Then the youth rode with the damsel till they came unto the castle called Pendragon, where five knights set upon him with spears, and, taking him prisoner, led him into the castle. But Lancelot du Lake heard tell how he had been taken captive and placed in dungeons where were many other knights and ladies belonging to King Arthur's court, and straightway fighting with the lord of the castle, he made him yield himself and swear to deliver up all his prisoners; and so Sir Lancelot rescued the knight of the evil-shaped coat from the hands of Sir Brian of the Isles: and he charged the damsel never more to rebuke the youth. Then said the maiden, 'Think not that I rebuked him because I hated him; nay, but I have loved him always;' and so likewise had the damsel spoken who rebuked Sir Prettyhands. 'Be it so,' said Sir Lancelot; 'and now thou shalt be called no more the Damsel with the Evil Words, but the Maiden of the Good Thoughts.' Then he made the youth with the evil-shapen coat lord of the Castle of Pendragon and all its lands; and there the youth wedded the maiden that had reviled him.

Now about this time, when Isolte the Fair had heard that Tristram was wedded to Isolte of the White Hands, she sent him letters as piteous as any that ever were written, beseeching him to come over with his bride, and saying that both would be right gladly welcomed. Then with Sir Kehydius, and the maiden Brengwaine, and his esquire, Tristram went into a ship, which the winds drove on the coasts of North Wales, near the Perilous Castle. There, riding away with Kehydius, Tristram met by the side of a well a knight with whom he justed; and when he knew that it was Sir Lamorak of Wales, Tristram reproved him for the sending of the horn to King Mark's court, and he said, 'Now must one of us twain die.' Yet so knightly did Lamorak bear himself, that Tristram forgave him, and became his friend, and they sware that neither should ever hurt the other.

And now was King Arthur himself to face new perils, for the Lady Annowre, who was a great sorceress, came to him at Cardiff and by fair words made him ride with her into a forest, where she took him to a tower and sought to win his love. But the king thought only of Guenevere, and when Annowre could prevail nothing with him, she sent him forth into the forest that he might be slain. But the Lady Nimue of the Lake knew her wiles, and she rode about until she met Sir Tristram and bade him hasten to the succour of a right noble knight who was hard bestead. 'It is King Arthur himself,' she said; and Tristram was sore grieved, and putting spurs to his horse he soon reached a place where two knights had unhorsed one, and a maiden, which was Annowre, stood by with a sword drawn in her hand ready to slay him. Then like a thunderbolt Tristram dashed down on those knights and slew them, and he cried to the king, 'Let not that lady escape;' and Arthur seizing his sword smote off her head, which the Lady of the Lake bare away at her saddle-bow. Then Sir Tristram placed the king on his horse and rode with him until they met Sir Ector de Maris, with whom he left King Arthur: but he would not as at this time tell the king his name.

Then went Tristram back to his ship, and sailed away to Cornwall, and when they had landed, the maiden Brengwaine went with a knight to the court of King Mark to tell the queen that Tristram was nigh at hand. 'Let me speak with him,' said the fair Isolte, 'or my heart will break.' So the maiden went back and brought Tristram with Kehydius into a chamber which the queen had assigned. What joy there was now between Isolte the Fair and Tristram tongue cannot tell nor pen write, nor the heart think. But Kehydius too was smitten with the love of Isolte, so soon as he had seen her; and of that love afterwards he died. And he wrote letters and ballads, the goodliest that were, to the queen, who in pity of his love and sorrow sent him a letter in return. This letter Tristram found one day when King Mark was playing at chess in the window: and full of grief and rage he rebuked Isolte for her treachery to him, and would have slain Kehydius; but when Kehydius saw what Tristram would do, he leaped from a window and escaped. And Tristram also went his way from the Castle of Tintagil, heeding not whither he went. In vain the lady of a great castle sought to make him good cheer. He would neither eat nor drink, and he wandered away again into the forest, and there he played upon his harp and wept, until his sorrow drove him mad. Even so he abode for three months, lean of flesh and ragged in raiment, among herdmen and shepherds, who held him to be a fool; and the deeds of a fool he did in his madness and his misery. But a little while and there came false tidings that Tristram was dead: and Isolte the Fair would have slain herself in her frenzy, if the king had not caught her when she was going to fall upon a sword. So was Isolte placed in a strong tower and strictly guarded.

But soon after this there came a knight to the palace

of King Mark, bearing a giant's head; and he told the king how when this giant would have slain him, a naked fool who lay by a well-side came and smote off his head. 'I will see that wild man,' said King Mark, and riding to the fountain, they found the man, but knew not that it was Tristram. Nor did any know him when he was brought into the king's palace, not even Isolte the Fair, so grievously was he changed. But the little dog which he had given to the queen when first he brought her to Cornwall leaped upon him for joy, and then Isolte, knowing that Tristram was before her, swooned away for gladness. When she came to herself, she said but few words, for her heart was heavy. Only she prayed him to hasten to King Arthur's court, where he would be right welcome. 'If King Mark learns who thou art,' she said, 'he will seek to slay thee; and as for me, whenever I may, I shall send unto you, and ever to my dying day thou hast all my love.' And even as Isolte said, it came to pass, for the little dog which would not leave Tristram made him known to Sir Andred, who told the king, and the king sought to have Tristram judged to death: but because some of the barons would not suffer this, Tristram was banished out of the country for ten years. Then stood up Tristram and said, 'Ye have given me a goodly reward for all my deeds. Ye have recompensed me well for delivering this land from truage, for bringing the fair Isolte from Ireland, for rescuing the wife of Sir Segwarides, for smiting down Sir Lamorak of Wales, for doing battle with the king of the hundred knights, for saving the queen from the hands of Palamides, and for all else that I have done. Be ye sure I shall come again when I may.' And having thus said he departed; and soon he fell in with a damsel who was seeking knights to come and help Sir Lancelot, for the queen Morgan Le Fay had placed thirty knights who should set upon him as he passed by. And these knights Sir Tristram and his comrade Sir Dinadan fought with, and part of them they slew and the rest they put to flight.

But when Tristram had gone yet a little further, there met him another damsel, who told him that he should win much glory by doing battle with a knight who wrought great mischief in all that country. So he rode on with her, but after six miles Sir Gawaine met them, and he knew that the damsel was one of the maidens of Morgan le Fay, and his heart misgave him that she was leading away the knight to his hurt. So straightway drawing out his sword, he said, 'Tell me, damsel, whither thou art guiding this knight, or thou shalt die.' Then she cried for mercy, and told them how Morgan le Fay was plotting against Tristram the same treason which she had plotted against Sir Lancelot.

Thus through Sir Gawaine Tristram escaped this peril, and after this King Arthur held a great tournament. On the first day Tristram won the prize, but on the second, after he had smitten down Sir Gaheris, he went his way, and none knew whither he had gone; on the third day the prize was adjudged to Sir Lancelot, but he would not have it, for he said that by right it was Tristram's, who had done more than any other could do. But Tristram could not be found; and Lancelot with nine other knights sware that for a whole year they would not rest two nights in the same place until they had found Tristram and brought him back to the court. But Tristram was now shut up in the dungeons of Sir Darras, whose sons he had slain or wounded in the tourney; and then Tristram again became sick almost unto death, and in his knightly pity Sir Darras let him go with his fellows on this covenant, that he should be a good friend to the two sons of Sir Darras who still remained alive.

CHAPTER X.

THE TREASONS OF KING MARK AND PALAMIDES.

Now was the time come that Tristram should match himself with King Arthur, and thus it came to pass. The king seeing him with the shield which Morgan le Fay had given him, asked him to describe the arms, and to say whence he had it. Then Tristram told the king who it was that had given him the shield, but the arms he knew not how to describe. 'Then,' said he, 'tell me your name.' But when Tristram would not, the king challenged him to fight, and after a fierce struggle the king was unhorsed, and he said, 'We have that which we deserved.'

Then Tristram departed, and as he rode towards Camelot there met him a knight, clad all in white raiment, with a covered shield. And they fought together, not knowing who the other might be. At the last Sir Lancelot asked, 'Who art thou that fightest thus wondrously?' And Tristram said that he was loth to tell. 'Nay,' answered Lancelot, 'I was never loth to tell my name to any that asked it.' 'Then,' said Tristram, 'tell it to me now,' and when he knew that it was Sir Lancelot, he said, 'What have I done, for thou art the man that I love best in the world?' Then said Lancelot, 'Tell me thy name.' And when Tristram told him, Lancelot rushed down and yielded up his sword, and Tristram kneeling yielded his; and many times they kissed each other, and then went on their way to Camelot, where they met with Gawaine and Gaheris, and Lancelot said to them, 'Your quest is done, for here is Sir Tristram.'

Great was the joy of King Arthur's court that this noble knight had come back; and the king went to all the seats about the Round Table which lacked knights, and in the seat of Sir Marhaus, whom Tristram had slain, he saw the words written, 'This is the seat of the good knight Sir Tristram,' and so was Tristram made a knight of the Round Table.

But the more that his glory was spread abroad, the more King Mark of Cornwall hated him, and at last he left his own land to seek out Tristram and slay him: and strange things befell him as he went from one country to another, searching for him. For first he came to a fountain, and by it he heard Sir Lamorak of Wales making moan of his love for Arthur's sister, the wife of the King of Orkney, whom Pellinore slew: and when King Mark went to him and questioned him of his sorrow, Sir Lamorak knew him to be a Cornish knight, and rebuked him because he served the most traitorous king that ever lived. Next he came to a castle, where the lieutenant knew him to be the man who had murdered his father, and the lieutenant said, 'For the love of my lord, I will not hurt thee whilst thou art here; but when thou art beyond this lodging, I will do thee what harm I may, for thou didst slay my father treacherously.' And again another day he heard Sir Palamides as he mourned for his love of the fair Isolte, who would give no heed to his prayer. 'A fool am I to love thee,' he said, 'when thy love is given to Tristram only, and thou art the wife of a coward and a traitor. Alas! that ever so fair a lady should be matched with the most villanous knight of the world.'

Then without a word King Mark hastened away to Camelot, where the knight Amant had charged him with treason before Arthur; and the king bade him do battle with his accuser, and when they met, King Mark smote down Sir Amant, who was in the righteous quarrel.

Great was the grief of Tristram when he saw Amant stricken down for the love of himself and of the fair Isolte: and when Lancelot saw Tristram weeping, he prayed the king to let him go after King Mark. But when King Mark saw Lancelot, he would not fight. Falling straightway from his horse, he yielded himself as a recreant, and as a recreant was he brought back and shamed in King Arthur's court, and made to own himself the king's man. And the king said, 'This I bid thee, that thou shalt be a good lord to Sir Tristram, and that thou take him into Cornwall and cherish him there for my sake.' This King Mark sware to do, and as he had done many a time before, so now he sware falsely. Then said Lancelot to King Arthur, 'What hast thou done? Knowest thou not that Mark is a traitor and a murderer?' And Arthur said, 'It was Tristram's own desire. I have made them of one accord: and what could I do more?' So as they went forth, Lancelot gave King Mark solemn warning. 'See that thou break not thy faith,' he said, 'with Sir Tristram: for if thou dost, with mine own hands I will slay thee.'

At this time it was that Sir Aglavale brought to King Arthur a young man whom he prayed him to knight; and he was Sir Percivale of Wales. When all things were ready, a maiden who had ever been dumb came into the hall, and going to Sir Percivale led him by the hand to the right side of the Perilous Seat, and said, 'Take here thy seat, fair knight, for to thee it appertaineth and to no other.' And when she had so said she went away and died.

Now the sons of the Queen of Orkney knew how Sir Lamorak loved their mother, and with the intent to slay him they sent for their mother to a castle near Camelot; and there, while Sir Lamorak was with her, Sir Gaheris came in with a drawn sword and smote off his mother's head. And great again was the grief in Arthur's court, that the sister of the king should thus be slain.

But now were the tokens seen of yet greater evils; for there came letters to Arthur from King Mark, bidding him look to himself and his wife and his knights, and not to meddle with the wives of others. When he had read this letter, he mused of many things, and he thought on the words of Morgan le Fay respecting Guenevere and Lancelot; but when he remembered how his sister hated the queen and Lancelot, he put away the thought. To Lancelot also King Mark sent letters; and Lancelot took counsel respecting them with Sir Dinadan, who said, 'I will make a lay of King Mark and teach it to many harpers.' And the worst lay it was that ever harper sang to his harp.

At this time came the men of Sessoins against King Mark to claim truage, and at the king's bidding Tristram did battle for him, and slew Sir Elias their leader. At the feast which followed, a harper came named Eliot, who sang Sir Dinadan's lay, and he escaped the king's vengeance only because he was a minstrel; and he was driven forth from the king's presence. But the king added now other treasons to his old crimes, for he murdered his own brother the good knight Sir Baldwin, who had burnt the ships of the men of Sessoins by sending fire-ships among them; and Baldwin's wife, the Lady Anglides, took his bloody sark and kept it secretly. But yet more did the king seek to slay her son Alisander the orphan, and he charged Sir Sadok to do the deed. By and by, Sir Sadok came back and told the king that he had drowned the child: but he had let him go free with his mother. So passed the years away until Alisander was grown up; and on the day on which he was made a knight, his mother drew out the blood-stained doublet and placed it in his hands. 'It is the shirt which thy father wore,' she said, 'when King Mark plunged the dagger in his heart.' And the young man said, 'Thou hast given me a great charge, my mother; and I promise thee, I will be avenged on King Mark when I may.'

When these tidings were brought to King Mark, he was sore dismayed, for he weened that Alisander was long ago dead, and he sought how to slay Sir Sadok, but Sir Sadok struck fear into his heart by his stern words; and King Mark sent instead to Morgan le Fay, and prayed her to set the country on fire through her sorceries, so that in anywise Sir Alisander might be slain. So Morgan stirred against him the knight Malgrin; and Sir Alisander fought with him, and although he was sorely wounded himself, yet slew he his enemy. Then Morgan le Fay took him to her own castle, and healed him of his wounds, when she had made him promise that for a twelvemonth and a day he would not pass the compass of the castle. And thus did he keep his oath. There came to him a damsel who said, 'If thou wilt give me thy love, I will deliver thee from Morgan le Fay, who keeps thee here that she may do with you as she will.' 'Tell me how thou wilt do this,' he said, 'and thou shalt have my love.' Then she said, 'I will send to my father, the Earl of Pase, and bid him come and destroy this castle, and after that thou shalt guard the ground on which it stands that none shall pass over it for a twelvemonth and a day.' And even so was it done; and Alisander let the heralds make a cry that he would keep that spot against all knights who came. Among these knights came Ansirus the Pilgrim, who went every third year to Jerusalem: and for this cause his daughter who was with him was called Alice the Fair Pilgrim. And Alice said in the hearing of many knights, 'He that overcometh the knight who keepeth that spot of ground where stood the castle of Morgan le Fay shall have me and all my lands.' But for all she said this, she went to Sir Alisander when he had smitten all the knights who went against him for the sake of Alice the Fair Pilgrim, and taking the bridle of his horse, she said, 'Show me thy visage:' and when she saw it she said, 'Thee must I love always, and never any other.' 'Then lift thy wimple,' he said: and when he saw her face he said, 'Here have I found my love;' and in this wise kept he his troth to the maiden who rescued him from the hands of Morgan le Fay.

Meanwhile, there were fresh perils for Sir Tristram, for the counsel of certain knights, who hated Sir Lancelot

and would have slain him, was revealed to King Mark,
who thought to send forth Tristram so disguised that
these knights, taking him to be Lancelot, should follow
him and slay him. In the fight which presently came
about between them Tristram smote down the knights,
but he was sorely wounded himself, and King Mark came
to him feigning to be sorry; and saying that he would
himself be his leech, he brought him to a castle and put
him in a strong prison. But when there was a great
outcry made among all good knights against this treason,
King Mark thought how he might be rid of Tristram
after another fashion. So he caused letters to be written
in the Pope's name, bidding all good men go and fight
against the Saracens at Jerusalem : and these letters he
sent to Tristram, saying that if he would go forth on this
errand, he should be set free. 'Bid King Mark go himself,' said Tristram, ' I stir not.' Then King Mark caused
other letters to be written in which he made the Pope
name Tristram among those who should go to the Holy
City; but when Tristram looked at the letters, he knew
whence they came, and he said, ' A liar and a traitor he
hath ever been, and ever will be.' Not long after this
came Sir Percivale of Wales, and by his means was Tristram brought out of prison; but although King Mark
sware again to Percivale that he would do no more harm
to Sir Tristram, yet he shut him up in prison again, because he found him with the fair Isolte. Then from his
prison Tristram sent letters to her, saying that now, if she
would go with him, he would take her away into King
Arthur's country, since the treasons of King Mark were
no longer to be borne. So the queen devised that King
Mark should be shut up in prison, and while he was kept
in bonds, she fled away with Tristram, and came to the
court of King Arthur

Right glad was the king to welcome them; and Sir
Lancelot brought them to his own castle of Joyous Gard;

and the days for them passed by like a happy dream. Yet did Tristram achieve many great things; and on one day he joined himself to Sir Dinadan who had made the lay on King Mark, and feigning to be but a poor feeble knight he thrust Dinadan on all manner of hard tasks, so that he was sorely buffeted and wounded, and then putting forth his might, he smote down all who sought to fight with him; and much laughing and jesting there was afterward at Sir Dinadan for the toils which came upon him while he bare the helmet of Sir Tristram. So when this was told to the fair Isolte, she bade that Dinadan should be brought before her; and when she asked him about Tristram, Dinadan marvelled that he and other knights could be so besotted upon women. 'What!' said Isolte, 'art thou a knight and no lover?' 'Nay,' said Dinadan, 'the joy of love is too short and the sorrow of it too long.' 'Say not so,' answered Isolte; 'here have been knights who have fought with three at once for the love of a maiden. Will you fight for love of me with three knights who have done me great wrong?' 'Thou art a fair lady,' answered Dinadan, 'fairer than even Guenevere: yet with three at once will I not fight whether for thee or for any other.' And all who heard him laughed; and merry was the feast that day.

At another time when Tristram went forth, he met a knight with whom he justed. For a long time neither prevailed against the other, but at last Tristram threw down his enemy, and he asked his name. 'I am Sir Palamides,' he said. 'What is the man whom thou most hatest?' asked Tristram. 'It is Tristram of Liones; and if I meet with him, one of us twain shall die.' 'Do thy worst then,' said Tristram, 'for I am he.' But so was Sir Palamides astonished at these words that he prayed Tristram to forgive him all his evil will; and so was their long enmity brought to an end.

Then they went onward together for the great tournament which King Arthur would hold at the Castle of Lonazep: and as they drew nigh to Humber bank, they saw coming towards them a rich vessel covered with red silk, and it came to land close to them, and on it was a fair bed whereon lay a dead man in whose hand was a letter, saying how King Hermanec, Lord of the Red City, had been slain by two men whom he had most of all cherished and trusted, and beseeching the knights of King Arthur's court to send some one to avenge his death. 'I cannot go and avenge him,' said Tristram, 'for I have given a pledge that I will be at this tournament.' 'Then,' answered Palamides, 'I will go;' and the vessel bare him to the Red City, where the people welcomed him joyfully. But they said, 'Thou must go again in the barge, until thou shalt come to the Delectable Isle, where is the castle of the men who murdered our king.' When he was come thither and had got out upon the land, there met him a knight who claimed the task of avenging King Hermanec as his own, but when this knight knew that it was Sir Palamides who had come to fight in this quarrel, he was right glad, and said, 'There are three knights only whom I had rather have met than thee: and these are Lancelot, Tristram, and my nigh cousin Lamorak of Wales.' 'Ye say well,' said Palamides, 'and if I be slain, go ye to Sir Lancelot and Sir Tristram and bid them avenge my death, for as for Sir Lamorak, him shall ye never see again in this world.' 'Alas!' said the knight, 'how may that be?' 'He is slain,' answered Palamides, 'by Sir Gawaine and his brethren, who slew their own mother because she loved him; but Sir Gareth, the fifth brother, and the best knight of them all, was away, and had nought to do with these foul deeds.'

Now were the tidings brought to the murderers of King Hermanec that Sir Palamides had come, an unchristened knight, to avenge him. 'If he be unchristened,' they said, 'christened he never will be, if he fights with us.'

But for all their boasting, the two brothers were slain by the Saracen knight Palamides, who hastened away after this to the Castle of Lonazep, where he found not Tristram, for he had not yet come with the fair Isolte from Joyous Gard. So to Joyous Gard he went, and he saw once more the lady he had ever loved, Isolte the Fair; and so ravished was he with her beauty that he could scarcely speak or eat.

And from Joyous Gard they rode to Lonazep, as the time for the great tournament drew nigh; and there Tristram appeared before King Arthur, but he would not tell his name, although Arthur besought him much, neither would he say upon which party he would hold in the justing. But afterwards he took counsel with Sir Palamides, who said that they should be against Arthur, who would have the greatest knights on his side, 'and the greater they are, the more worship shall we win, if we be better than they.' So on the morning Tristram and Palamides with Sir Dinadan and Gaheris rode forth clad all in green, and the fair Isolte rode with them. And when King Arthur saw them, he asked who they might be: but none knew. Then he said, 'See by the names in the sieges which of the knights of the Round Table are not here with us.' And among the names of those who were not there were the names of Tristram, Palamides, Gaheris, and seven others. Then said the king, 'Some of these, I dare to say, are against us here this day.' Then in the justing were great deeds done, and Sir Lancelot first smote Tristram; but Tristram, recovering himself, hurled King Arthur from his horse. Then going away from the field, he came back presently in red armour, that none might know him, and he placed on their horses Sir Palamides and some other knights who had been smitten down. But at this moment Palamides looking up saw the fair Isolte smiling at Tristram, for she alone knew him in his red armour; and Palamides, thinking that her smile was for him, felt himself filled with new strength, and from this time he fought like a lion, longing secretly in his heart that he might do battle to the death with Sir Tristram, his friend, because he had taken from him her love. And all men marvelled at the might of his arm, and the prize of this day was given to him. On the morrow, before the justing began again, King Arthur rode forth with Sir Lancelot to greet the fair Isolte; but when she had welcomed the king, Palamides broke in with angry words, and when the king heeded not his wrath, Palamides took his spear and smote him down; and because Sir Tristram rebuked him for this deed, he determined to go over to the other side and fight with the man whom he called his friend. On this day Tristram put forth his strength, and Palamides wept that he might win no worship, for scarce any might hope to do so when Tristram used all his manhood. But when they had justed for some time, Tristram went from the field and came back clad in black armour with Sir Dinadan; and Palamides also had disguised himself with a shield and armour which he had borrowed from a knight who was resting himself by the water-side. But for all his scheming, and though he strove with all his power against Tristram, yet was Tristram adjudged to be the best knight that day.

Full of wrath was Isolte against Palamides, for she had seen all his treachery, and how he had changed armour with the knight by the water-side. But Palamides feigned that he knew not Sir Tristram in his black armour, and Tristram forgave him for all that he had done. In the evening when the justing was ended, there came two knights armed into the tent where the fair Isolte sat at meat with Sir Tristram and Palamides; but when Tristram rebuked them for coming armed, one of them said, 'We have come for no evil; I am here to see you, and this knight seeks to greet the queen.' 'Then doff your helms,' said Tristram, 'that I may see you;' and when they had done so, they knew that Arthur and Lancelot stood before them; and great was the joy and gladness between them. Then said Arthur to Isolte, 'Many a day have I longed to see thee, so highly art thou praised: and indeed thou art fair as fair may be, and well are ye beset with the good and fair knight Sir Tristram;' and his words filled the heart of Palamides with bitter grief and rage, and all that night he wept sore for envy of his friend who had won the love of King Mark's wife.

On the next day too were great things done, but because Arthur's men were far fewer than they who were against them, Tristram said that he would go over to the king's side. 'Then answered Palamides, 'Do as thou wilt. I change not.' 'Ah!' said Tristram, 'that is for my sake, I dare to say; speed you well in your journey.' But because Palamides could not bear down Tristram in the justs that day, his wrath grew more fierce, and in the evening when they came to the pavilions he called Tristram a traitor, and sware to slay him if ever he might.' 'Well,' said Tristram, 'I see not why thou wilt not have my friendship; but since thou givest me so large warning, I shall be well ware of you.' And all these things were told to Queen Guenevere, who lay sick in a castle by the sea-side. But more grievous still became the anguish of Sir Palamides, and he wandered about as one that is in a frenzy. 'Alas!' he said, 'I have lost the fellowship of Sir Tristram for ever, and for ever have I lost the love of Isolte the Fair; and now I am never like to see her more, and Tristram and I are mortal foes.' So, as he wandered along, he came to a castle where many were weeping, and when they saw Palamides they said, 'Here is the man who slew our lord at the tournament,' and for all he fought and struggled, they took him prisoner and adjudged him to death. And so it chanced that the tidings were brought to Sir Tristram, who said, 'Palamides has done me great

wrong: yet must I rescue or avenge him, for he is too
good a knight to be thus done to death.' On the morrow then he set forth with this intent: but as Sir Palamides was led forth to die Sir Lancelot met them, and
straightway did battle with them until those who had not
been wounded or hurt fled away. Then at Tristram's
prayer Lancelot and Palamides went to the castle where
the fair Isolte abode; and glad was she to welcome Sir
Lancelot; but Palamides mourned more and more, until
he faded away and all his strength departed from him.
So wandering forth again, he came to a fountain, where
he uttered all his complaint, and Tristram who chanced to
be nigh heard it. So great was Tristram's wrath at the
first that he thought to slay Palamides as he lay. But
he remembered that Palamides was unarmed, and he
checked himself, and going up to him he said, 'Thou art
a traitor to me; how wilt thou acquit thyself?' 'Thus,'
said Sir Palamides; 'from the hour when first I saw her
Isolte has been my love, and well I know that it shall befall me as it befell Kehydius who died for her love.
Through her only have I done all the deeds that I have
done, and through all I have been her knight guerdonless, for no reward or bounty have I ever had from her.
Wherefore I had as soon die as live: and for treason, I
have done none to thee, for love is free to all men, and
Isolte is my lady as well as yours, only that thou hast her
love, and this had I never, nor shall I ever have it.' 'For
all this,' said Tristram, 'I will fight with thee to the
uttermost.' 'Be it so,' answered Palamides; 'on the
fifteenth day I will be ready for thee.' 'What, art thou
turned coward, that thou needest fifteen days to make thee
ready for battle? Let us fight on the morrow?' 'It may
not be,' said Palamides; 'my strength is gone for very
grief and sorrow: but on the fifteenth day I will not fail
you.' But so it happened that when the fifteenth day was
come, it was Tristram who could not keep the tryst, for

one day in a forest an archer shooting at a hart hit Tristram, and gave him a grievous wound. At the end of a month he was whole: and then he took horse and sought everywhere for his enemy: but Sir Palamides could nowhere be found.

CHAPTER XI.

THE BIRTH OF THE GOOD KNIGHT GALAHAD.

Now one day when King Arthur sat with his knights at the Round Table, there came a hermit, who seeing the Siege Perilous empty asked wherefore it was void; and the king said that one only might sit in it and live. 'Who then is that one?' asked the hermit: and when they could not tell him, he spake again, and said, 'The man that shall sit there is yet unborn: but he shall be born this year and shall achieve the Holy Grail;' and having so said, he departed.

Soon after this, Lancelot also went his way until he came to the town of Corbin, where the folk welcomed him as their deliverer. 'What mean ye by your cries?' said the knight. Then they showed him a tower in which lay a maiden in great pain, for she boiled in scalding water, and none had been able to rescue her. She was the fairest maiden in all the land, and therefore Morgan le Fay had shut her up in the dismal tower, until the best knight of the world should take her by the hand. But as Lancelot drew near, the doors opened to him of their own will, and on the couch he beheld the maiden, whose heart the fire had entered for many a long year. So was the damsel rescued from her inchantment, and the people said to Lancelot, 'Now must thou do yet another thing, thou must free us from a serpent that is here in a tomb.' Then as Lancelot came to the tomb, he saw written on it in golden letters, 'A leopard shall come of kingly blood, and shall slay this serpent, and from the leopard shall spring a lion which shall pass all other knights.' Even so it came to pass, for Lancelot slew the grisly snake, and the fair maiden Elaine became the mother of his child Galahad. And in the house of her father King Pelles, the cousin of Joseph of Arimathie, as they sat at meat, there came in at a window a dove, in whose mouth there seemed to be a censer of gold. With it there came a savour as of all the spicery in the world; and forthwith upon the table were seen all manner of meats and drinks. Presently there came a maiden bearing in her hands a vessel of pure gold, and before it the king and his knights kneeled and prayed devoutly. 'What may this mean?' said Lancelot: and the king answered, 'This is the richest thing that any child of man may have; and when it goes about, the Round Table shall be broken, for that which thou hast seen is the Holy Grail.'

But when Sir Lancelot saw Elaine in her father's house, he weened it had been Queen Guenevere, for he was brought under inchantment, and when he knew how he had been deceived, he would have slain the maiden, who with tears prayed him for her life, because she had given him her maiden love and faith. Then was Lancelot appeased, and the time went, and the child was born and named Galahad: and after this came another knight who had loved her long and sought to make her his wife. 'Nay,' she said, 'ask me never again. My love is set on the best knight in the world, and none other will I wed:' and when that knight knew to whom her love was given, he sware with an oath that he would slay Sir Lancelot.

But Lancelot was long since gone away, and Elaine asked Sir Bors who had come thither where the knight might be, and he told her how he was shut up in a prison by Morgan le Fay, King Arthur's sister. But even as he looked on the babe in Elaine's arms, he marvelled how like it seemed to Sir Lancelot, and she said, 'Truly it is his child;' and even as she spake, once more the white dove hovered in with the golden censer. Once more came the savour of all delightsome spicery. Once more the maiden bare in the Holy Grail, and said, 'Know that this child shall sit in the Perilous Seat, and shall win the Sangreal, and he shall be a better man far than the good knight Sir Lancelot his father.' Once more they kneeled and prayed before the golden vessel; once more the dove floated away, and the maiden vanished as she came.

On that day was Sir Bors clean shriven; and as he lay down on his couch at night, with his armour on, a light flashed round him, and there came in end-long a spear, whose head burnt like a taper, and it gave him a grievous wound in the shoulder. Hard were now the toils of Sir Bors, for first he had to fight with a strong knight, and then with a huge lion; but he beat off the one and smote the other. Then going forth into the court, he beheld a dragon with golden letters on his forehead which seemed to show the name of King Arthur, and there came an old leopard which struggled with the dragon, which spit an hundred dragons out of its mouth; and the small dragons slew the great dragon and tare him in pieces. After this came an old man with two adders about his neck, and he sang on his harp an old song, how Joseph of Arimathie came into the land; and when the song was ended, he bade Sir Bors depart, for nought there remained for him to do. Then came again the dove with the golden censer, and stayed the storm which had been raging; and again the court was full of sweet odours, and four children were seen bearing fair tapers, and an old man in the midst held a censer in one hand and in the other a spear which was called the spear of vengeance.

Then said the old man to Bors, 'Go thou, and tell Sir Lancelot that because of his sins only is he hindered from seeing and doing the things which thou hast seen and done, for though in strength of arm none may be his match, yet in spiritual things there are many who are his betters.' And as he spake, four ladies in poor array passed into a gleaming chamber, where a bishop kneeled before a silver altar; and as he looked up, Sir Bors saw hanging over his head a silver sword whose brightness dazzled his eyes, and he heard a voice which said, 'Go hence, for as yet thou art not worthy to be in this place.'

On the morrow Sir Bors departed and went to Camelot, and told of the things which had happened to him in the house of King Pelles at Corbin, and it was noised abroad that Elaine was the mother of Sir Lancelot's child.

At this time King Arthur made a great feast, and to it came Elaine the Fair, and there she saw Queen Guenevere; but, though in countenance they made good cheer, neither rejoiced to see the other. But yet more grievous was the sorrow of Guenevere, when Sir Lancelot was once again taken from her by inchantment to the daughter of King Pelles; and so wroth was she that when she next set eyes on Lancelot, she bade him depart for a false and traitorous knight and never to see her more. But even as he heard these words, the strong man fell as smitten by a sword: and when he woke from his swoon, he leaped out from the window and roamed as a madman in the woods, while twenty moons went round.

Bitter was the anger and strife between Elaine and Guenevere, when Sir Lancelot could nowhere be found. 'On thee lies the blame,' said Elaine, 'for thou hast already a lord as noble as any that may be found in the earth; and were it not for thee I should have the love of him who is the father of my child;' and having so said, she went her way, and King Arthur with a hundred knights brought her on her journey. But Guenevere tarried behind mourning, and Sir Bors saw her as the tears streamed down her cheeks. 'Fie on your weeping,' he said; 'thou weepest only when thy tears will not undo thy sin. Alas! that ever Sir Lancelot or his kin saw thee.' So said also Ector de Maris and Sir Lionel, and at their words Queen Guenevere fell down in a swoon; but presently waking up from it, she knelt before those knights and with clasped hands besought them to seek Lancelot through forest and brake, by mountain and river. But though twenty knights sought him in every quarter, yet they found him not; and strange were the fortunes of many who went on the quest of Sir Lancelot. Many a day and month passed by, and still the search went on, and the bravest of them sware never to see Arthur's court again until they should have found him. And even so it came to pass that Sir Percivale, as he journeyed on, met with Sir Ector, and neither knowing the other, they fought until both were sorely wounded; but when they knew each other they grieved, because they thought that they were smitten to the death and that they should not achieve the quest of Sir Lancelot.

But even as they mourned and wept, the Holy Grail came by, bringing the savour of all spicery, and filling the chamber with dazzling light; and the pure Sir Percivale had a glimmering of that golden vessel, and his eyes could see dimly the fair maiden who bare it. Forthwith both were made whole; and they gave thanks to God, and went their way, marvelling at the strange things which had happened to them; and Percivale learnt from his comrade that in the golden vessel was a part of the blood of our Lord Jesus Christ, which none but a perfect man might ever see.

CHAPTER XII.

THE FINDING OF LANCELOT.

MEANWHILE Sir Lancelot wandered through the forests in hunger and nakedness, doing strange deeds of wild strength, and seeking to harm those who would fain have been his friends. Thus he would have slain the kindly Sir Bliant, who brought him to the White Castle, and there tended him. But though his body gained back its health, his mind was as much astray as before. Still, though Lancelot knew not himself, he yet knew when two knights pressed hard upon Sir Bliant, and breaking his bonds, he rushed to his aid, and smote them down, so that they were glad to flee away. So he tarried still with Sir Bliant, and it came to pass, one day, that as he walked in the forest, he found a horse saddled, and tied to a tree, and against the tree a spear was leaning. Seizing the weapon in his hand, he leaped lightly on the saddle, and soon he saw before him a huge boar, which, as the knight rode up to him, tare the body of the horse with his tusks, and gashed the thigh of Sir Lancelot also. Then Lancelot put forth his strength and smote off the boar's head at a stroke; but the blood ran from his thigh in streams, and he was well-nigh faint, when a hermit looked on him with pity and brought others to help, who placed him in the cart with the boar's carcase, and bare him to the hermitage, where the hermit healed him of his wound. But though he gained strength of body under the good hermit's care, yet was his mind still astray, and so it came about that one day he fled from the hermitage and ran to Corbin, the city of the fair Elaine; and as he ran along the town to the castle, the people gibed and jeered at him; but in the castle they gave him food and shelter, for they thought as they looked upon him that they had never seen a man so goodly in form.

Not long after this, a nephew of King Pelles, named Castor, was made knight, and gave away gowns to many; and he sent a scarlet robe for Lancelot the Fool; and when the mad knight was arrayed in it, he seemed the goodliest man in all the court. Wearing the robe, Lancelot strayed into the garden, and, lying down by a well-side he fell asleep: and there some maidens saw him and ran and told the fair Elaine. Then Elaine came hastily, and when she looked on him, she knew the man who was the father of her child; and she took counsel with King Pelles, and by his good-will the knight was borne into the chamber of a tower in which lay the Sangreal, and by the virtue of that holy vessel he was healed of all his sickness.

When Sir Lancelot awoke and saw King Pelles with his daughter standing near, he was sore ashamed, and besought them to tell him how he had come thither; and Elaine told him all the story, how he had been kept as a fool and how he had been made sound again. 'Let no man know it,' said Sir Lancelot, 'for I am banished from King Arthur's court for ever.' Then after a fortnight he said to Elaine, 'What travel, care, and anguish I have had for thee, thou knowest well. Wilt thou then now for thy love go to thy father, and get of him a place where I may dwell?' 'Yea,' answered Elaine, 'I will live and die with thee, and only for thy sake, and sure am I that there is nothing which my father will not give at my asking; and wherever thou art, there, doubt not, I will be also.' So at her prayer King Pelles gave him as his abode the Castle of Bliant; but before they departed thither, Sir Castor asked him his name, and Lancelot said, 'I am the knight Ill-doer.' 'Nay,' said Castor, 'thou seemest to me rather to be Sir Lancelot du Lake.' 'Sir,' answered Lancelot, 'you are no gentle knight: for were I Lancelot, and it pleased me to withhold my name, why should it grieve

you to keep my counsel, so you be not hurt thereby?'
Then Castor kneeled down and craved his pardon: and
Lancelot said, 'It is easily given;' and so they went their
way to the Castle of Bliant, which stood on a fair island
girt with iron, with fair waters all round it ; and Lancelot
called it the Joyous Isle ; but for all its joy, Lancelot's
heart well nigh burst with sorrow as each day he turned
his eyes towards the land of Arthur and Guenevere. Yet
for all his grief he was conqueror over all the knights who
came to just with him in the Joyous Isle ; and at last
came Sir Percivale of Wales with his friend Sir Ector,
and he called to a maiden who stood on the shore of the
island with a sparrowhawk on her arm, and asked her who
was in the castle. Then said the maiden, 'We have here
the mightiest knight and the fairest maiden in all the
world.' 'What is his name?' asked Sir Percivale. 'He
calls himself the knight that hath trespassed.' 'And
how came he hither?' said Percivale. 'Truly,' she said,
'he came as a madman into the city of Corbin, and there
he was healed by the Holy Grail.' Then went Percivale
to the castle gate and bade the porter tell his lord that
a knight had come who would just with him; and
straightway Lancelot hastened into the lists. Fierce was
the fight and long: and when their breath was well-nigh
spent, Sir Percivale bade Lancelot tell him his name. 'I
am the Ill-doing Knight,' he said; 'and who art thou?'
'My name,' he answered, 'is Percivale of Wales.' 'Alas!'
said Lancelot, 'that I should have fought with one of my
fellows;' and so saying, he flung away his shield and his
sword; and Percivale, marvelling much, charged him
straitly to tell him his true name. Then he said, 'I am
Lancelot du Lake, King Ban's son of Benwick.' 'Ah me!'
said Percivale, 'what have I done? Thee was I sent to
seek, and two years long have I sought thee wearily; and
on yonder bank stands thy brother Sir Ector.' And when
Sir Lancelot had a sight of him, he ran to him and took

him in his arms, and long time they wept over each other for joy; and Elaine told all the story, how Lancelot had come to Corbin and to the Joyous Isle.

So the days went on; and after a while Sir Percivale asked Lancelot whether he would journey with them to Arthur's court. 'Nay,' he answered, 'it may not be.' Then his brother besought him, telling him of the grievous sorrow of the king and the queen, and how all longed to see again the knight who was more spoken of than any other knight then living, and that never any could be more welcome at the court than he. 'Well,' said Lancelot, 'I will go with you,' and they made ready for the journey; and with a sad heart the fair Elaine saw the man depart to whom she had given her love.

Great was the joy at Camelot when Lancelot once more stood among his fellows of the Round Table; and as the queen listened to the tale of all that had befallen him, she wept as though she would have died. Then said the king, 'Truly, I marvel, Sir Lancelot, why ye went out of your mind. There be many who deem it was for the love of fair Elaine, King Pelles' daughter.' 'My lord,' answered Lancelot, 'if I have done any folly, I have had my reward:' and the king said no more; but all Sir Lancelot's kinsfolk knew for whom he went out of his mind.

Then was it published abroad that on the feast of Pentecost next coming there should be a great tourney. To Camelot therefore Tristram took his journey at the prayer of the fair Isolte, but because she would not go with him to add to his labour, he went forth alone and unarmed. On the way he came upon two knights, of whom the one had smitten the other, and the knight who had done this was Palamides. Then as Tristram stood before him, Palamides said, 'The time is come for dressing our old sores. Thou art unarmed. Put thou on this knight's harness, for our quarrel shall be this day fought out.'

And it was fought fiercely and long: but for all his striving Palamides could not master Tristram, and at the last he said, 'It may be that my offence against you is not so great but that we may be friends. Let us then bring the strife to an end: for all that I have offended is and was for the love of the fair Isolte; and against her I have done no wrong.' 'Yea,' said Tristram, 'God pardon thee as I forgive thee.' So they rode to Carlisle together, and when Sir Palamides the Saracen had been made a Christian by the bishop, they journeyed on thence to be at Arthur's court by Pentecost.

CHAPTER XIII.

THE SHRIVING OF SIR LANCELOT.

WHEN the vigil of the feast was come, there entered the great hall of Camelot a maiden who knelt before the king and prayed him to say where Sir Lancelot might be. 'Yonder he is,' answered the king. Then said the maiden to Lancelot, 'I bring thee greetings from King Pelles, and I charge thee to come with me.' 'What would ye have with me?' asked Lancelot. 'That thou shalt know,' she said, 'when we have reached our journey's end.' Then came the queen and said, 'Wilt thou leave us now?' 'Madam,' answered the damsel, 'he shall be with you again on the morrow.'

Then riding with the maiden, Sir Lancelot came to an abbey of nuns, and being led into the abbess's chamber he saw there Sir Bors and Sir Lionel; and presently twelve nuns brought in Galahad and prayed Lancelot to make him a knight, for at no worthier hands might he receive the order. And when Lancelot knew that the desire came from the youth himself, he said, 'To-morrow morn I will make thee a knight:' and so on the morn at prime it was done; and Lancelot said, 'God make thee a good man; for one that is fairer in form no man may ever see. And now wilt thou come with me to King Arthur's court?' 'Nay,' he said, 'not now.' So Lancelot went on his way with Bors and Lionel to Camelot; and there when all were gathered together, they saw in the Perilous Seat words newly written in letters of gold, which said, 'When four hundred winters and fifty-four have been accomplished since the Passion of Our Lord Jesus Christ this seat shall be filled.' 'Then,' said Lancelot, 'it should be filled this day, for this is the feast of Pentecost, and further four hundred years and fifty-four; and if it please you, I would that none may see these letters until he be come for whom this seat has been made ready.' So over them they placed a cloth of silk: and presently a squire came in, who told them of a great stone floating down the river, and of a great sword which was stuck in the stone. 'I will see this marvel,' said the king: and when they came to the river, they beheld the red marble stone and the jewelled sword, round the pommel of which the words were written, 'Never shall man take me hence but he by whose side I ought to hang, and he shall be the best knight of the world.' Then said Arthur to Lancelot, 'That art thou, and so the sword is thine.' 'Nay,' answered Lancelot soberly, 'I ween not that I am the best knight; and he who seeks to take that sword and fails shall receive from it a wound that he shall not long after remain whole.'

Then the king turned to Sir Gawaine and said, 'Make trial of the sword, I pray you, for my love:' but Sir Gawaine would not until the king charged him on his obedience. Yet though he took up the sword by the handle, he could not stir it. Then the king thanked him, but Lancelot said, 'So sorely shall this sword touch you that you shall wish you had never touched it for the best castle in the realm.' Turning then to Percivale, the king asked if he would try the sword, and Percivale said, 'Yes, gladly, to bear Gawaine fellowship,' but neither could he stir it.

When after this they sat down to the feast, and all the seats were filled except the Perilous Siege, on a sudden all the doors and windows of the place were shut of themselves, and into the darkened hall came, none knew whence, an old man clad all in white, leading a young knight who had neither sword nor shield, but only a scabbard hanging by his side. And the old man stood before the king and said, 'I bring you here one who is of kin to Joseph of Arimathie, and who shall achieve the marvels of this court and of strange realms.' Then said he to the youth, 'Follow me,' and leading him to the Perilous Seat, he lifted up the silken cloth and found beneath it the words written, 'This is the seat of Galahad the High Prince.' Then the old man placed the youth in that seat, and departed. And all the knights of the Round Table marvelled that one who was a child durst sit in the Perilous Seat: and Sir Lancelot looking earnestly at the youth, saw that he was his own son, and his heart was filled with joy. Then were these tidings brought to Queen Guenevere, and she said, 'I may well suppose he is the son of Sir Lancelot and King Pelles' daughter.' And the king went to Galahad and bade him welcome, for he should move many good knights to the quest of the Sangreal, and should bring to an end things which none other knight had ever been able to achieve. So having said, the king led Galahad to the stone in the river, and the queen went with them. And Galahad said in few words, 'For the surety of this sword I brought none with me, and here by my side hangs the scabbard.' Then laying his hand on the sword, he drew it lightly from the stone, and as he put it in its sheath, he said, 'Now have I the sword which was sometime the sword of the good knight Balin, who with it slew his brother Balan, because of the grievous stroke which Balan gave to my grandsire King Pelles, and which is not yet whole, nor shall be till I heal him.' And even as he spake, they saw a maiden riding toward them on a white palfrey, and when she came up to them, she called to Sir Lancelot and said that he had lost his ancient name. 'How so?' asked the knight. 'This morning,' she answered, 'thou wast the best man living: and now there is one better than thou.' 'Nay,' said Lancelot, 'I know well I was never the best.' 'Yea,' answered the maiden, 'that were ye, and of all sinful men on the earth thou art so still.'

That day said King Arthur to his knights of the Round Table, 'Ye will all depart, I know, to this search for the Holy Grail, and never shall I see you all together again: therefore will I now see you all in the meadow of Camelot, that, when ye are dead, men may say the good knights were all together on such a day.' So were they gathered on the field of Camelot, and among all the knights the goodliest and the mightiest was Galahad. After the justing the king made him unlace his helm that the queen might see his face: and Guenevere said, 'Well may men say that he is Lancelot's son, for never were two men more like.'

In the evening, when they had prayed in the great minster, and as the knights sat each in his own place, they heard cracking of thunder as though the hall would be riven through; and in the midst of the crashing and darkness a light entered, clearer by seven times than ever they saw day, and all were alighted of the grace of the Holy Ghost: and as each knight looked on his fellows, behold all were fairer than any on whom their eyes had ever rested yet. But all sate dumb, and in the still silence came the Holy Grail, covered with white samite, but none might see it, or the hand which bare it; and with it came all sweet odours, and each knight had such food and drink as he loved best in the world; and then the holy vessel was borne away, they knew not whither. Then were their tongues loosed, and the king gave thanks for that which they had seen. But Sir Gawaine said, 'We have had this day all that our hearts would wish, but we might not see the Holy Grail, so heedfully was it covered: and therefore now I vow with the morrow's morn to depart hence in quest of the holy vessel and never to return until I have seen it more openly; and if I may not achieve this, I shall come back as one that may not win against the will of God.' So vowed also the most part among the knights of the Round Table.

Then was the king stricken with sorrow. 'Thou hast well nigh slain me,' he said, 'with thy vow; for thou hast reft me of the fairest fellowship and the truest knighthood that ever were seen together in any realm of the world. I have loved them as well as my life: and well I know that, when we are sundered, we shall never more meet all together on this earth again.' 'Comfort yourself,' said Lancelot. 'It shall be to us a greater honour than if we died in any other place: and die we must.' 'Ah, Lancelot,' said Arthur, 'it is my love for you all which makes me speak thus; for never had Christian king so many worthy knights around him.' But greater still was the grief of Queen Guenevere; and many of the ladies would have gone with the knights whom they loved: but an old knight came among them saying, that the knights must go forth alone, or else they would never achieve the task.

On the morrow, when the service was done in the great minster, the king took account of the number of the knights who had vowed to search for the Holy Grail; and they were one hundred and fifty, all knights of the Round Table. But Guenevere was in her chamber: and thither went Lancelot to take his leave, and then they rode all through the streets of Camelot, rich and poor weeping as they went.

Thus far Sir Galahad was without a shield; but on the fourth day he came to a white abbey, where, in a chamber, he found two knights of the Round Table, King Bagdemagus and Sir Uwaine; and when he asked them why they were there, they told him how they had heard that in that place was a shield which no man might wear except to his grievous hurt; but Bagdemagus said that nevertheless he would seek to bear it away. On the morrow a monk warned him not to touch it unless he were the best man in the world; 'That I ween I am not,' said Bagdemagus, 'yet will I make trial.' So he bore it away, and a knight met him and smote him and took away the shield, and bade the squire of King Bagdemagus carry it to Sir Galahad, to whom only the shield belonged. So Galahad won his shield, and Bagdemagus escaped hard with his life. Now Sir Uwaine would fain have gone with Galahad, but Galahad would take only the squire who brought him the shield that had been made long ago for good King Evelake, and which had won him the victory against the paynim Tolleme and his people. And the squire's name was Melias, the son of the King of Denmark; and Galahad made him a knight.

Many days they rode together, until at length they came to a place where the roads forked, and on the cross which was there set up they saw letters written which said, 'He who goes to the right hand shall not go out of that way again, if he be a good man and a worthy knight: and he who goes on the left, shall have his strength soon tried.' Then Melias besought Sir Galahad to let him take the left path, and after a while Galahad suffered him to go. So on rode Melias, and passing through a forest, came to a fair meadow, in which was a lodge of boughs, and in that lodge a chair, and on the chair a golden crown, while on the earth were spread rich cloths and on these were rich and rare dainties. For these Melias cared not; but taking up the crown he rode onwards. Full soon, however, he heard a voice behind him, which bade him set down the crown which was not his, and defend himself. Short was the battle, for the knight who had overtaken Melias smote him with his spear, and taking away the crown left him well nigh dead. In this plight Sir Galahad found him, and when he had smitten the knight who had wounded him, and yet another knight who came forth against him, he took up Melias and bare him to an abbey, where an old monk said that within the term of seven weeks he would heal him. Then Galahad told the monk how they two were in quest of the Holy Grail; and the old man said, 'For this has he been thus wounded; and strange is it that any durst take on himself the order of knighthood without clean confession. For the right-hand way was the way of the good man, the other the way of sinners. Pride it was which took this knight away from Galahad, and the taking of the crown was a sin of covetousness and theft; and the two knights whom Galahad smote were the two deadly sins which had conquered the knight Sir Melias.' Then said Galahad, 'Now I go my way, and God keep you all;' and Melias answered, 'As soon as I can ride again, I will seek you.' So Galahad went on his journey, and came to a castle which was called the Castle of the Maidens, because seven knights had seized it, and sworn that never lady nor knight should pass there, but they should be shut up within it, and many maidens had they thus devoured. These Galahad rescued, and the seven knights were slain by Sir Gawaine and Gareth and Uwaine, who were riding together in search of Galahad.

But again the pure knight had gone on his way from the Maidens' Castle, and Lancelot and Percivale met him. But they knew him not, for he was in new disguise, and they ran on him with their lances. With two stout blows Galahad smote them down and passed on, while a recluse, who dwelt hard by, cried aloud, 'God be with thee, thou best knight of the world.' Then knew Lancelot and Percivale that it was Galahad: but though they hastened after him, yet they could not find him; and Lancelot, riding on, came to an old chapel, within which he found an altar arrayed in silken cloths, and a silver candlestick which bare six great candles. But there was no place by which he could enter; and unlacing his helm, he ungirded his sword and lay down upon his shield to sleep before the stony cross which stood hard by. Presently, half-asleep and half-awake, he saw two white palfreys bearing a sick knight on a litter, and as they stood before the cross, the knight prayed to God that his sorrow might leave him, since he had endured long for little trespass. Then the candlestick with the six tapers came before the cross, but Lancelot saw not the hand that bare it, and with it came the silver table, and the vessel of the Saugreal which he had seen in the house of King Pescheur. Straightway then the knight went on hands and knees until he touched the holy vessel and kissed it, and was healed of his sickness, and the vessel and the silver table vanished away. Then the sick knight's squire asked him how he did, and he said, 'Right well, I thank God; through the holy vessel I am healed; but strange it seems to me that this knight had no power to awake when the holy vessel was brought hither.' 'Doubtless,' said the squire, 'he is in some deadly sin: but here I have brought all your arms save helm and sword, and by my counsel thou wilt take the sword and helm of this knight.' And even so that knight did, and he took Lancelot's horse also.

When Lancelot waked, he doubted whether that which he had seen were dreams or not, and he heard a voice which said, 'Harder than the stone, more bitter than wood, barer than the fig-tree's leaf, go thou from this holy place.' So heavy and grievous was Sir Lancelot when these words fell on his ears, that he wept sore and cursed the day on which he was born. 'My sin has brought me into great dishonour,' he said. 'So long as I sought earthly fame, all things went well with me, and never was I discomfited in my quarrel; but now, when I am in quest of holy things, my old sin so shames me that no power to stir remained within me when the Sangreal appeared before me.' So he mourned till the day broke, and he heard the birds sing, and their song brought him some comfort. But missing his horse and harness, he went sorrowing to a high hill where was a hermitage, and then he made confession to the hermit, how for many a long year he had loved a queen beyond measure, and how all his great and good deeds had been done for her sake, or to win himself worship to cause him to be the better beloved, and not for the sake of God only. Then said the hermit, 'I will counsel you if you will promise to me not to come in that queen's fellowship, as much as you may forbear;' and Lancelot made the promise. 'See that your heart and your mouth accord,' said the hermit, 'and you shall have more worship than ever before.' Then Lancelot told him of the strange words which he had heard; and the hermit said, 'Marvel not, for God loves you well. The voice called thee harder than stone, for thou wouldest not leave thy sin for any goodness that God sent to thee, and wouldest not be softened neither by water nor by fire. But take good heed. In all the world, no knight hath received the grace that thou hast. God hath given thee fairness and wit, prowess and hardiness, and now, whether thou wilt or wilt not, He will suffer thee to go no longer alone, but He will have thee know Him. More bitter wast thou called than wood, because thou hast in thee the bitterness of sin; and barer art thou of fruit in good thought and good will than the figtree which was cursed because leaves only were found thereon.'

So, when Lancelot had confessed his sin and sought for mercy, the hermit assoiled him and prayed him to tarry with him that day. 'That will I gladly,' said the knight, 'for I have neither helm, horse, nor sword.' 'On the morn,' said the hermit, 'I will bring to you all that belongs to you.'

CHAPTER XIV.

THE TEMPTATION OF SIR PERCIVALE.

AND now the faith of the good Sir Percivale was to be tried. For a little while he tarried with the recluse who greeted Sir Galahad as the best knight of the world, and when Percivale told her his name she rejoiced greatly, for she was his mother's sister; and they talked together of many things, and she told him how Merlin had made the Round Table in token of the roundness of the world, and how they who are made its fellows forsake all other for the sake of that fellowship. 'So,' she said, 'has it been with thee, for since thou wast admitted to that company, thou hast not seen thy mother, and now her days are ended on earth. But go thy way to the Castle of Carbonek, and there shalt thou get tidings of the good knight Galahad whom thou seekest.'

So Percivale departed and came to a monastery where on the morn he heard mass, and nigh the altar, on a bed covered with cloth of silk and gold, he saw one lie with a crown of gold on his head. But when it came to the sacring, the man rose up and uncovered his head, and Percivale saw that his body was full of great wounds on the shoulders, arms, and face, and when he asked who he might be, one of the monks said, 'This is King Evelake whom Joseph of Arimathie made a Christian, and thereafter he sought to be with the Sangreal, which he followed till he was struck almost blind, and Evelake prayed that he might not die till he should have seen the good knight of his blood, of the ninth degree, who should win that holy vessel; and when he had thus prayed, a voice was heard saying, 'Thou shalt not die till he have kissed thee; and when he shall come, thine eyes shall be clear again, and thy wounds shall be healed.'

As Percivale journeyed on from the abbey, he met twenty men of arms bearing a dead knight; and when they learnt that he was come from Arthur's court, they cried, 'Slay him;' and though Sir Percivale fought stoutly, slain he would have been, had not Sir Galahad appeared on a sudden and smitten down a man at every blow, until those fled who remained alive, and Galahad departed after them. But Percivale could not keep him in sight for he had no horse; and at last being wearied, he fell asleep, and waking saw a woman standing by, who said that if he would promise to do her will she would bring him a horse. This he promised, and straightway she brought him a coal-black steed; and on its back he rode four days till he came to a great water into which the steed would have plunged: but Percivale feared whether he could overpass it, and he made the sign of the cross on his forehead. Then with a mighty leap the horse went into the water, which seemed to be set on fire, and Percivale knew that he had been set free from a demon, and he spent the night praying and thanking God. Then going on into a valley, he saw a serpent bearing a lion's cub by the neck, and a great lion went behind it roaring. Presently there was a battle between the lion and the serpent, and Percivale took part with the kindlier beast and smote the serpent with a deadly wound, and the lion in great joy fawned on the knight, who stroked him on the neck and shoulders. All that night the lion slept by the side of Sir Percivale who dreamed that two ladies came by, the younger on a lion, the elder on a serpent; and the younger, bidding him be ready on the morrow at her lord's command to fight with the strongest champion in the world, vanished away, and then the other complained that he had done her wrong by slaying her serpent when it fought with the lion. 'Why didst thou wound it?' she asked, and Percivale said, 'Because I fought for the kindlier beast.' Then she said that he must make amends for his murder by becoming her man. 'That will I not,' he said. 'Be it so,' she answered, 'then will I seize thee if I can find thee at any time unguarded:' and she too vanished away, and Percivale's dream was ended. On the morn he rose up weak and feeble, and going to the seashore he saw coming towards him a ship, at whose head stood an old man in priestly garb, and when Percivale asked him who he was, he said, 'I am of a strange country, and hither I come to comfort you.' Then Percivale told him of his dream and prayed him to expound it; and the priest said, 'She who rode on the lion is the new law of the holy Church, and she came to warn thee of the great battle that shall befall thee: and she on the serpent is the old law, and the serpent is the fiend,—and when she asked thee to become her man, it was that she might tempt thee to renounce thy baptism.'

There Percivale abode till midday with the lion; and at noon a ship came toward him, bearing a beautiful maiden clad as a queen, and she besought the knight to help her to win back her inheritance, 'For,' she said, 'I dwelt with the greatest man of the world, and I had more pride of my beauty than I ought, and I said some words that pleased him not; so he drave me away from my heritage without pity for me or for my court. If then thou art of the Round Table, it is thy part to help those who are in trouble.' So Percivale promised, and she thanked him: but the sun was hot, and she bade one of the women set up a pavilion under which the knight might sleep, and before him she placed costly food and wine, and with the wine Sir Percivale deemed he was somewhat more heated than he ought to be. As he gazed on the lady, she seemed now to grow fairer and fairer, until he proffered her his love; but she said him nay, unless he would swear never to do henceforth anything but that which she might command him. So Percivale sware the oath, but as he drew near to her, he spied his sword which lay on the ground, with the red cross in its pommel, and remembering his knighthood and the words of the good priest, he made the sign of the cross on his forehead, and straightway the pavilion changed into smoke and a black cloud, and on the sea he saw the vessel bearing away the lady who wept and wailed, and it seemed that all the water burnt after her.

And Sir Percivale too wept and mourned for his wickedness; but presently came again the ship which he had seen the day before, and in it came again the good priest, who asked him how he had fared, and Percivale told him all. 'Did'st thou not know the maiden?' the old man asked him; and he said, 'Nay, but I know now that the fiend sent her to shame me.' 'O good knight, answered the priest, 'thou art a fool, for that maiden was the master fiend himself who was beaten out of heaven for his sin, and who would have conquered thee but for the grace of God. Wherefore take good heed.' So saying, the old man vanished away, and Percivale went into the ship, which bare him thence.

CHAPTER XV.

THE VISION OF SIR LANCELOT.

AFTER three days the hermit with whom Sir Lancelot tarried gave him a horse, a helm, and a sword; and departing at noontide the knight journeyed on, until he came to a chapel where was an old man to whom he told his quest of the Holy Grail. 'Seek it ye may,' said the man, 'but there is sin on thee, and while it be there, thou shalt never see it.' Then Lancelot asked what he should do; and the old man charged him to eat no flesh and to drink no wine and to hear mass daily so long as he might search for the holy vessel. Then riding onward, he came to an old cross, as the darkness was closing in: and putting his horse to feed, he kneeled down and prayed, and then lay down to sleep. Presently in a dream he saw a man compassed with stars and with a golden crown on his head, and behind him came seven kings and two knights, and all these worshipped at the cross, holding up their hands towards heaven. Then the clouds opened and an old man came down with a company of angels, and gave unto each his blessing and called them true knights and good servants; but to one of the two knights he said, 'I have lost all that I have set in thee; for thou hast fought and warred for the pleasure of the world more than to please me; and therefore thou shalt be brought to nought, if thou yield me not my treasure.'

On the morrow Sir Lancelot rode on, pondering much the vision which he had seen. Soon he met the knight who had taken away from him his horse, his helm, and his sword; and doing battle with him, he got them back again, and left him the horse on which he rode. Going on till nightfall, he came to the abode of a hermit to whom he told his dream and asked its meaning; and the hermit said, 'The seven kings are thy forefathers, of whom the seventh is thy father King Ban: the two knights are thyself and thy son Galahad, and of thee it was said that God will not love thee if thou yield Him not up His treasure, for little thank hast thou given to God for all the virtues God hath lent thee.' Then said Lancelot, 'The good knight whom thou callest my son should pray for me that I fall not into sin again.' 'Be sure,' said the hermit, 'that thou dost fare the better for his prayers; but the son shall not bear the iniquity of the father nor the father bear the iniquity of his son.'

The next day Lancelot riding onwards came to a castle where knights clad in black armour and on black horses were being worsted by knights clad in white armour and on white horses; and Lancelot thought to increase his worship by striking in with the weaker party. Doughty as ever were his blows: but mortal man must tire at last, and Sir Lancelot at length was borne down, faint with loss of blood. 'Ah me,' he said, 'when I fought to win prowess for myself, never man had the better of me; now when I strive to aid others, I am myself overcome.'

So being left all alone he fell asleep; and there came before him in a vision an old man who said, 'Lancelot, Lancelot, why is thy mind turned lightly towards its deadly sin?' and then he vanished away. Much musing on these words, Lancelot when he woke rode on until he came to the dwelling of a recluse to whom he told all that he had seen and what had befallen him, and she said, 'The black and the white knights were the earthly knights and the spiritual knights; and thou, seeing the sinners overcome thoughtest to win glory for thyself by hastening to their aid; but the white knights saw the Sangreal which thine eyes may not see, and so gained strength for their arms, greater than the strength even of thy arm, though thou hast not thy peer among earthly sinful men.'

Then the recluse commended Lancelot to God, and he rode on till he came to a gloomy river, over which his horse bore him safely; but when he was on the other side, there came a black knight, who slew Lancelot's horse and vanished away. And Lancelot took his helm and shield, and went on his way humbly.

CHAPTER XVI.

THE TRIAL OF SIR BORS.

THERE was aching of heart not for Lancelot only. For to many a knight of the Round Table the months rolled wearily on while they sought in vain for the Sangreal. So was it with Sir Gawaine and Sir Ector de Maris, and much they complained each to the other of the weariness of their quest. At length, as they rode one day together they came to an old chapel, into which they went to pray, and after they had prayed, they fell asleep: and in his dream Gawaine saw a hundred and fifty bulls, all black save three, which were white, but of these three one had a black spot; and these three were tied with strong cords; and the other bulls went off to seek better pasture, and some came back again so lean and weak that scarcely might they stand. But to Ector, as he slept, it seemed that he was riding with Lancelot his brother in quest of that which they should not find; and another came who took Lancelot off his horse and placed him on an ass, upon which he rode till he came to a fair well, but when Lancelot stooped down to drink of it, the water sank from him, and when he saw this he rose up and departed by the way by which he had come.

When they awoke they told each his dream; and even as they spake, a hand bare to the elbow, covered with red samite, and holding a clear burning candle, came into the chapel and again vanished away, and they heard a voice which said, 'Knights of evil faith and poor belief may not come to the adventures of the Holy Grail.'

Then departing from the chapel, the two knights went on; and upon the road they met with a knight who would just with Sir Gawaine. And when they had fought awhile,

Gawaine smote him harder than he had weened, and the knight prayed Gawaine to take him to some abbey that he might make confession before he died. 'What is thy name?' said Gawaine. 'I am Uwaine les Avoutres,' he answered, 'the son of King Uriens.' 'Alas!' said Gawaine, 'that I should slay one of my fellows of the Round Table.' Yet so must it be, for when the spear-head was drawn from the wound, Uwaine died.

In sadness and sorrow Ector and Gawaine rode on to the abode of the hermit Nacien, to whom they told their dreams and all that had befallen them; and the hermit told them the meaning of their visions. To Gawaine he said, 'The fair meadow is humility and patience—things ever fresh and green. The black bulls are the company of the Round Table—knights black with sins, save three who are Sir Galahad, Sir Percivale, and Sir Bors; but the spot of one sin mars the pure whiteness in Sir Bors. The going away of the black bulls was the departure of the knights on the quest of the Sangreal without confession, and so they came back into waste countries, where many of them shall die.' And to Ector he said, 'The thing which ye shall not find is the Sangreal: but the placing of Lancelot on the ass is the humbling of the knight, and the water which sank away from him is the grace of God, in desire of which he went back by the way by which he had come.'

Great also were the griefs and sufferings of Sir Bors, when he had departed from Camelot in search of the holy vessel. As in one place he looked up to the branches of the trees over his head, he saw a great bird on an old and dry stem smiting itself that its blood might feed its young birds which were dead of hunger; and the great bird died, but the young birds lived again and were strong. Then going on, he came to a castle where the lady lodged him richly; but while he was there, there came a messenger from another woman her enemy who said to the lady of the castle, that if she found not a knight to fight in her behalf she should be driven forth and despoiled of all her goods and lands. So Bors fought and conquered in her quarrel, but he refused all recompense which the lady would have bestowed on him.

As he journeyed thence, he met first two knights who were leading his brother Lionel bound and stripped, and scourging him with thorns: but before he could rush to rescue him, there came another knight who was striving to force a maiden into the lonely parts of the forest, and the maiden besought him to deliver her out of his hand; and for a moment Bors knew not what to do: but the cries of the maiden pierced his heart, and he fought with and smote the man who was doing her wrong. But when he had placed her in safety, he went onwards to seek his brother Lionel; and there met him a man clad in dark raiment and riding on a black horse who asked him what he sought; and he said, 'I seek my brother whom two knights were beating as they drove him on the road.' 'It boots not to seek him,' said the man, 'for he is dead, and here is his body:' and it seemed to Bors that the body which he showed him was the body of Lionel. So he took it up, and placing it on his saddle bow, he brought it to an old chapel, where they placed it in a tomb of marble. 'Now leave him here,' said the other to Bors, 'and to-morrow we will come back to do him service.' 'Art thou a priest?' asked Bors: and when he said 'Yea,' Bors told him of a dream which he had, and which showed him two birds, one white as a swan, and the other swart as a raven, and each bird in its turn promised him riches and wealth if he would tend and serve it; and how again he had dreamed and had seen, as he thought, two flowers, like lilies, and the one would have taken the other's whiteness but one came and parted them that they might not touch each other, and then out of every flower came forth many flowers and fruit in plenty. Then the priest told Bors that

the white bird was a lady that loved him truly, and would
die if he refused her his love; he said too that, if Bors
said nay to her, Sir Lancelot also should die, and so he
should be the slayer of his brother Lionel and of Lancelot
du Lake, whereas he had gone about to rescue a maiden
who pertained not at all to him. Then he led Bors to a
high tower, where knights and ladies welcomed and
unarmed him, and made him such cheer that he forgot all
his sorrow and anguish and took no more thought for his
brother or for Lancelot; and as he thus lay feasting, there
came a lady fairer than all who were around him, and more
richly arrayed than even Queen Guenevere: then said they,
'This is the lady whom we serve, and she it is who loves
you and will have no other knight but you.' Then, as
they talked together, the lady straitly asked him for his
love, until Bors was sore vexed and said, 'There is none in
the world to whom I may grant it, for my brother is
lying dead whom evil men have slain.' And when she
saw that she asked in vain, she said that she would die,
and her maidens followed her to the battlements. Still
he heard their cry, and moved with pity he made the sign
of the cross; and there was a great crash as if an army of
fiends were about, and tower and chapel, priest and
maidens, all vanished away.

Thankful and glad was Sir Bors for his rescuing, as he
rode on to an abbey, where he told the abbot of his vision
of the great bird feeding her young. Then said the abbot,
that the love of the great bird was the love of Jesus Christ,
for the blood that the great fowl bled brought back the
young from death to life, and the bad tree was the world
which of itself can have no fruit. 'But all that came
after,' said the abbot, 'was to lead thee into error, and the
fiend who spake with thee in guise of a priest lied to thee
about thy brother Lionel, for he is still alive; and here is
the dream of the dry tree and the white lilies. The dry
tree is thy brother, who is without virtue and a murderer;

and the flowers are the knight and the maiden whom he sought to injure, and hadst thou left these first to help thy brother, thou wouldst have gone to the succour of a rotten tree.'

Then, parting from the abbot, Sir Bors went his way and came to a castle where they told him of a great tournament presently to be held there, and he thought to be there himself if he might have the fellowship of his brother or of some other knights of the Round Table. So thinking, he wandered to a hermitage in the forest, and there at the chapel door he found Sir Lionel all armed, and Bors went up to embrace him for joy and gladness. But his brother cried out as he drew near, 'Nay, come not nigh me, you left me to be scourged and slain, and for that misdeed thou shalt die.' In vain Sir Bors sought to soften him and win forgiveness. 'Forgive thee will I never; and if I get the upper hand, thou diest.' So madly raged Lionel that Bors wist not what to do, for it seemed shame to him and grief to fight with his brother: and when Lionel saw that Bors would not fight, he rode upon him, and then lighting off his horse took him by the helmet and would have smitten off his head, when the hermit came and strove to stay him for very shame. But Sir Lionel turned savagely and slew the good old man, and again was about to smite Sir Bors, when a knight of the Round Table rode up hastily, and seizing Lionel by the shoulders said, 'Wilt thou slay thy brother, the worthiest knight in the world?' 'Nay, if thou seek to hinder me,' said Lionel, 'I will slay thee first and him afterwards.' At these words the knight, whose name was Colgrevance, made ready for the fight; and as they strove together, the heart of Sir Bors well nigh burst with grief and shame. But at the last the good Sir Colgrevance was slain, and Lionel rushed once more to kill his brother. The meekness of Bors and his patience were sorely tried, and he was just lifting up his hand to defend his life, when he heard a voice which said, 'Flee, and touch him not;' and there came between them a flaming cloud, so that both their shields were kindled by it. And again the voice said, 'Bear thy brother fellowship no more, but go thou to the sea where Sir Percivale awaits thee.' So, going to the shore, he found a vessel into which he stepped, and the boat straightway shot through the waters, so that it seemed to him to be flying. Onwards it sped, until the darkness closed around it, and Sir Bors sank to sleep. But when he awoke in the morning, he saw a knight lying in the midst of the vessel, whom he knew to be Percivale. But Percivale was abashed until Sir Bors unlaced his helm and showed his face. Then great was the joy between them, and Percivale said, 'We lack nothing but Galahad the good knight.'

CHAPTER XVII.

THE ACHIEVING OF THE SANGREAL.

WHILE these things were happening, Sir Galahad was doing great deeds elsewhere. First, after he had rescued Percivale from the twenty knights, he came to a castle where a tournament was going on, and where Gawaine and Ector were fighting with the men without and bearing down the men within; and Sir Galahad, striking in with the weaker, dealt a blow on Gawaine which smote him to the ground. Then, having beaten back all the knights without, Galahad stole away unseen; and Gawaine said, 'Now are Lancelot's words proved true, that the sword which was stuck in the stone should give me a buffet such as I would not have for the best castle in the world, for never before had I such a stroke from any man's hand.' 'Your quest is done, it seems,' said Ector. 'Yea,' he said, 'I shall seek no more.'

But Galahad rode on towards the Castle of Carbonek, and

he was benighted at a hermitage. As he rested with the hermit there came a maiden who bade him follow her, and she led him to a great castle where the lady suffered him to rest but for a little while, and then, leading him by torchlight to the sea, brought him to the ship in which were Bors and Percivale; and right glad were they to greet Sir Galahad. Then, as the good knight stepped into the boat, the winds bore it away swiftly over the sea, till it brought them to a narrow way betwixt high rocks where they might not land; but they saw another ship and upon it they might go without danger; and to it they went by the maiden's bidding, and they found the vessel richly dight, but there was neither man nor woman therein. But in the end of the ship these words were written, 'Beware, thou who enterest this ship, that thou be stedfast in trust, for I am Faith, and if thou failest I shall not help thee.' Then said the maiden to Percivale, 'Knowest thou who I am?' and he answered, 'Nay.' 'Know then,' she said, 'that I am thy sister, the daughter of King Pellinore; and now I pray thee enter not into this ship if thou be not firm of faith, for it will suffer no sin.' Then answered Percivale, 'I shall adventure it, and if I be an untrue knight I shall perish.'

Then the maiden showed them all the treasures of the ship, the sword which King Pelles drew to his grievous hurt (for never since that day had the wound been healed with which he then was smitten), and the rich bed which Solomon's wife had caused to be made, and the three spindles made from the tree which Eve planted. Then taking the sword, she said to Galahad, 'Gird thou on this sword which hath been so long desired of all good knights;' and when she had fastened it round him with girdle made in most part of her own hair which she had loved well in her youth, she said, 'Now I reck not though I die, for I am one of the most blessed of maidens, since I have made the worthiest knight in all the world.'

Then again the wind drove them on to the Castle of Carteloise, which was held by evil knights who had wronged their sister and put their father in prison and done great harm through all the land. These knights Sir Galahad slew and rescued the old man from his dungeon; but there was little life now left in him, and he departed thanking God who suffered him to die in the arms of the good Sir Galahad.

And again they went on to another castle, from which came a band of knights who told them of the custom of the place, that every maiden who passed by must yield a dish full of her blood. 'That shall she not do,' said Galahad, 'while I live;' and fierce was the struggle that followed, and the sword of Galahad, which was the sword of King David, smote them down on every side, until those who remained alive craved peace, and bade Galahad and his fellows come into the castle for the night; 'and on the morn,' they said, 'we dare say ye will be of one accord with us when ye know the reason for our custom.' So awhile they rested, and the knights told them that in the castle lay a lady sick to death, who might never gain back her life until she should be anointed with the blood of a pure maiden who was a king's daughter. Then said Percivale's sister, 'I will yield it, and so shall I get health to my soul, and there shall be no battle on the morn.' And even so was it done; but the blood which she gave was so much that she might not live, and as her strength passed away, she said to Percivale, 'I die, brother, for the healing of this lady. And I pray you now, bury me not in this land, but place me in a boat at the next haven, and when ye be come to the city of Sarras, there to win the Holy Grail, ye shall find me under a tower, and there shall ye bury me in the Spiritual Place, and there shall Galahad be buried and ye also.' Then, as they wept, a voice was heard which said, 'To-morrow at the hour of prime, ye three shall part each to a several way, until ye shall be brought together at the house of the maimed king.' Thus was the lady of the castle healed, and the gentle maiden, King Pelles' daughter, died; and Percivale placed in his dead sister's hand a letter which told of all the help which she had given them, and laid her in a barge covered with black silk; and the wind arose and drove it away until they could see it no more.

In the meanwhile Lancelot had been brought to the water of Morloise, and there he saw a vessel without sail or oar; and as soon as he was in the ship, he felt such sweetness as he had never known before, for all the things which he thought on or desired, these he had. In this joy he laid him down to sleep, for it was yet night: and when it was day he woke and saw lying before him the body of Sir Percivale's sister with the letter in her hand. This letter Sir Lancelot read, and learnt all the things which had befallen her and the knights whom she had aided. Here he abode a month long, for he was nourished by Him who fed His people with manna in the desert. But one night, as he rested by the water-side, he heard the steps of a horse, and a knight lighted off the steed: and when Lancelot had welcomed him, the stranger asked him his name. 'I am Lancelot du Lake,' he said. 'Then art thou my father,' answered the knight. 'Ah,' said Lancelot, 'are ye Galahad?' 'Yea,' he answered; and no tongue can tell their joy, as they embraced each other, and talked afterward of many things. So dwelt they within that ship half-a-year and served God by day and night. But after this, as they arrived at the edge of a forest, a knight clad all in white, and richly horsed, came towards them leading a white horse by his right hand: and he said to Galahad, 'Thou hast been long enough with thy father; and now must thou mount this horse, and go whither thou mayest be led in the quest of the Sangreal.' Then went Galahad to Lancelot and said, 'Sweet father, I know not when I shall see you more.' Then a voice came which said, 'Take heed to do well, for the one shall not see the other again before the day of doom.' Then said Lancelot, ' Son Galahad, since we may not see each other more on earth, I pray God keep me and you both:' and Galahad went into the forest.

And the wind arose and drove Lancelot across the water to a castle, where two lions kept the entry by the postern door. Then a voice bade him go out of the ship and enter the castle where he should see most part of his desire. So arming himself, he drew near to the gate, and when he saw the lions he drew his sword; and a dwarf coming suddenly smote him so fiercely on the arm that the sword fell out of his hand; and he heard a voice say, 'O man of poor belief, why trustest thou more in thy harness than in thy Maker?' Then said Lancelot, 'I thank thee, Lord, that Thou reprovest me for my misdeed, for now I know that Thou holdest me for Thy servant.' So making the sign of the cross he passed the lions safely, although they made as though they would do him harm; and going into the castle, he found none within, until he came to a chamber which was shut. Here listening he heard a voice singing so sweetly that it seemed to come from no earthly thing, and he thought that it said, ' Joy and honour be to the Father of heaven.' Then Lancelot knelt before the chamber, for within it, he knew, lay the Sangreal, and he prayed earnestly that he might now see some of the things for which he was seeking. Then through the opened doors came a burst of light, as from all the torches in the world; but when he drew near to enter, a voice said, 'See thou come not hither;' and drawing back, he saw in the midst of the chamber a table of silver and the holy vessel covered with red samite, and round about it stood many angels, of whom one held a burning taper, and the other a cross. Before the vessel stood a priest, as at the sacring of the mass; and it seemed to Lancelot that above the priest's hands were three men, of whom two put the youngest between the priest's hands, that he might lift it up and show it to the people. Then, thinking that the priest had great need of help to lift so great a burden, Lancelot hastened toward the silver table: and straightway he felt as though there passed on him a breath of fire, and he fell to the earth as a man without life.

Four and twenty days and nights lay Lancelot still as the dead; and at the end of the days he waked up, and when he learnt all that had happened, he said, 'The four and twenty days are a penance for the four and twenty years during which I have been a sinner.' Then, rising up, he put on him first the hair shirt, and over this a shirt of linen, and on this again a scarlet robe, and then they who stood by knew him to be the good Sir Lancelot; and word was borne to King Pelles who came right gladly to greet him, though he had for him heavy tidings, for his child the fair Elaine was dead. Four days he abode with Pelles, and the Sangreal filled the tables with all manner of meats that the heart of man might desire.

Then departing from the house of King Pelles, he made his way at length to Camelot, where he found King Arthur and the queen; but of the knights of the Round Table nearly one-half had been slain and a few only had come back, and among these were Ector, Gawaine, and Lionel. Great was the joy of Arthur and Guenevere when they saw Sir Lancelot, and they asked him to tell all that had befallen him and his fellows. So he told them all the story of Galahad, Percivale, and Bors: and the king said, 'Would all three were here.' 'That shall never be,' said Lancelot, 'for only upon one of these shall thine eyes rest again.'

Now Galahad, as he went his way, came to the abbey where lay King Modrains who had been long blind; and when the king heard who it was that had come, he rose up and said, 'Galahad, the servant of Jesus Christ, for whose coming I have so long tarried, let me rest between thine arms, for thou art as the lily and the rose for purity and sweetness.' Then Galahad took the king in his arms, and the blind man's spirit passed gently away. Then Galahad placed him in the earth as a king ought to be placed: and passing on he came to a well which boiled with great waves; but so soon as he put his hand to it, it burnt no more, and became still: and ever after it was called Galahad's well.

Yet a few days later he reached the Castle of Carbonek in the company of Sir Bors and Sir Percivale; and there as they sat in the chamber, a voice said, 'Depart ye who ought not to sit at the table of Jesus Christ, for now shall the true knights be fed.' So with the three knights remained only King Pelles and Eliazar his son and a maid who was his niece. Then came in nine knights all armed, who said that they were come, three from Gaul, three from Ireland, and three from Denmark, to be with Galahad at the table where the holy meat should be parted: and presently four women bare in upon a bed a sick man wearing a golden crown, who said, 'Ye be welcome, Galahad; much have I desired your coming, so great and so long has been my pain and anguish: but now I trust the end of my pains is come.' Then said a voice again, 'There be two among you that are not in the quest of the Sangreal, and therefore depart ye;' and King Pelles and his son went their way.

Then straightway the knights deemed that four angels bare in a chair a man clothed in likeness of a bishop, and set him before the silver table whereon was the Sangreal, and on his forehead were letters which said, 'See ye here Joseph the first bishop of Christendom.' And the knights marvelled, for that bishop was dead more than three hundred years. Then they heard the chamber doors open and angels came in, two bearing waxen candles, the third a towel, and the fourth a spear which bled three drops that fell within a box which he carried in his other hand: and when the candles were set on the table, they covered the vessel with the towel, and the fourth put the spear upright upon the vessel. So there, as the bishop came to the sacring of the mass, they saw come out of the holy vessel one that had all the signs of the passion of Jesus Christ, who said, 'My servants and my true children, ye shall now see a part of my hidden things, and receive the high meat which ye have so long desired.' Then said he to Galahad, 'Knowest thou what I hold between my hands?' and Galahad said, 'Nay.' 'This,' he said, 'is the holy dish in which I ate the lamb on Shrove Tuesday; and now must thou go hence, and bear with thee this holy vessel; and by the sea-shore ye shall find your vessel ready, thou, and Sir Percivale, and Sir Bors; and two of you shall die in my service, and one shall come again, bearing tidings.' Then giving them his blessing, he vanished away; and Galahad having touched with his fingers the blood that dropped from the spear, anointed the limbs of the maimed king, who started up on his feet as a whole man, thanking God.

That same night, at midnight, a voice came among them which said, 'My sons and not my chieftains, my friends and not my warriors, go hence where ye hope best to do, and as I bade you.' So in all haste they went their way, and coming to the shore found the ship, which bare them away to the city of Sarras; and there, as they would have landed, they saw the ship in which Percivale had placed his sister. Then said Percivale, 'She has kept her covenant well.' Then with the silver table they went towards the city, but it needed a fourth man to aid in bearing it, and Galahad called to an old man who stood by the city gate. 'Truly,' said he, 'I have not gone but with crutches these ten years.' 'Care thou not,' said Galahad, 'only help us:' and as soon as he rose to help them, he was whole. Then all the city stirred for the tidings of the cripple who had been healed by the knights who were come thither; and they brought up the body of Sir Percivale's sister and buried her, as she had besought them.

But the king of the city was a tyrant; and when he heard of all that had happened, he took them and prisoned them in his dungeon, and there they lay, fed by the Sangreal, till the year was ended, when the king, having fallen sick, sent for them to crave their mercy. So when the king was dead, the people said that Galahad should be king in his stead, and they placed on his head the golden crown. On the morrow, rising early, he saw kneeling before the holy vessel a man in the likeness of a bishop, who had about him a great company of angels; and when he had ended the sacrament of the mass, he called Galahad, and said, 'Thou shalt see now that which thou long hast yearned to see.' Then the old man offered to Galahad the holy wafer, and Galahad received it gladly and meekly; and he said to him, 'I am Joseph of Arimathie, and I have been sent to thee for two things, —because thou hast seen the Sangreal, and because thou art clean and pure.'

Then Galahad went to Percivale and kissed him, and commending his soul to God, said, 'Bid Sir Lancelot, my father, take heed of this unstable world.' So saying he kneeled down and prayed, and then the angels bare away his soul to heaven; and Percivale and Bors saw a hand take up the vessel and the spear and bear them away to heaven.

Since that day, has no man been so hardy as to say that he has seen the Sangreal.

A year and two months from this time Sir Percivale dwelt in religious clothing with a hermit, and Sir Bors abode with him in his knight's dress. Then Sir Percivale passed out of this world, and Bors laid him by the side of his sister and Galahad in the Spiritual Place: and hastening thence he journeyed away until he came to Camelot, and told to King Arthur and to Sir Lancelot all the things which had happened. 'Right welcome art thou,' said Sir Lancelot, 'and all that ever I can do for thee thou shalt find my poor body ever ready to do, while the life remains in it.' 'And be thou sure,' said Bors, 'that I will never part from thee while our lives shall last.' 'I will, as thou wilt,' said Sir Lancelot.

CHAPTER XVIII.

THE STORY OF THE MAID OF ASTOLAT.

So the days went on after Sir Lancelot had come back from the quest of the Sangreal: and he forgot the words which he had spoken, and went back to his old love for Queen Guenevere, and the heart of Guenevere clave the more to him; but because other ladies and maidens sought him to be their champion and he took their parts, therefore was the queen's anger kindled, and she chid Sir Lancelot for the cooling of his love. Long he pleaded his cause, and told her how but for the love of her he might in the search for the holy vessel have done as well as his son Sir Galahad; but he spake in vain, and Guenevere bade him depart and see her face no more. Then as he was going away in heaviness, Sir Bors strove to cheer him, and Lancelot told him all the words that had come from her lips. 'Heed them not,' said Sir Bors: 'she has spoken after this sort before, and she has afterward been the first to repent of her words.' Then Lancelot prayed Sir Bors to win back for him the love of the queen; and then went his way. Sore was Guenevere's grief in her heart, but she set her face as though she heeded not his departing.

Now about this time the queen held a feast for certain of King Arthur's knights; and a knight named Pinel, who hated Sir Gawaine, placed for him on the table a poisoned apple, but another knight named Sir Patrise took it and ate of it and fell down suddenly dead among them. Great was the wrath of the knights, for they deemed it was the queen's doing, and Sir Mador, the near kinsman of the slain man, charged the queen with the treason, and prayed the king that justice might be done upon her. Then, though the king besought him not to be over hasty, yet would he insist that the great should be dealt with as the small: and the king said, 'On the fifteenth day be ready in the field before Westminster: and if then any knight appear on her behalf, do thou thy best and God speed the right: and if thou smite down her champion, then must my queen be burnt, and there shall she be ready for the judgment.'

When Arthur was alone with Guenevere, he asked her how it all came about, and she told him that she could in nowise tell. 'Were Lancelot here, he would do battle for thee. Where is he?' asked the king. And this also she could not tell him. 'What ails thee,' he said, 'that thou canst not keep Lancelot on thy side? But if thou canst not find him, pray Sir Bors to do battle on thy behalf for Lancelot's sake.'

So she made her prayer to Sir Bors: but Bors spake roughly. 'I marvel how thou canst ask me to do aught for thee, when thou hast chased out of the country the man by whom we were most borne up and honoured.' Then in great woe she kneeled down and besought him to have mercy upon her; and even as she knelt, King Arthur came in, and besought him also, because he was sure that she was untruly defamed. So Sir Bors promised, although he knew that he should make many a knight of the Round Table angry. Then departing from the court he rode to Sir Lancelot, who was right glad that he might strike a blow for the queen; and so he plighted his faith that he would be at Westminster on the judgment day. But in the mean season there was much talk, and many said plainly that for the queen they had no love because she was a destroyer of good knights; but Sir Bors said nay to these words, and that there had been treason among them. And even so it was proved at last; for when the day was come, Sir Lancelot appeared on the field and smote down Sir Mador, and the queen was assoiled of the treason; and while there was great joy with all and Guenevere sank almost to the earth for shame that Lancelot had done to her so great kindness when she had dealt by him so unkindly, suddenly there appeared among them the Lady of the Lake, and charged Sir Pinel openly before the king with the death of Sir Patrise; and Pinel fled from the land as a craven knight, and over the tomb of Sir Patrise a writing was placed which told all the story, to the fouling of Sir Pinel's name, and the assoiling of Queen Guenevere.

But other troubles were nigh at hand for her. For, when the king bade the heralds proclaim a great tournament to be held at Camelot, she would not go thither, and when Lancelot also tarried behind, the king set forth heavy and displeased, and he lodged on the way in a town called Astolat. But when he was gone, the queen spake with Lancelot, and told him that it would be ill for his name and hers if he went not to the justing; and Lancelot said, 'Thou speakest wisely; but thy wisdom is late in coming. Yet will I go at thy bidding: but at the justs I will be against the king and his company.' On the morrow, then, he rode to Astolat, and when he was come thither, the king saw him as he entered into the house of Sir Bernard. Presently Lancelot asked him for a shield that was not openly known, and Sir Bernard gave him the shield of his son, who was hurt the same day that he was made knight and was able to fight no more; and he prayed his guest to tell him his name. 'That I may not do now,' he said: 'but if I speed well at the justs, I will come again and tell you.' Then Sir Bernard prayed him to let his younger son Lavaine ride with him to the tourney, and Sir Lavaine was exceedingly eager to go with him, but the eyes of his sister, whom men called the Fair Maid of Astolat, were fixed eagerly on Sir Lancelot; and Elaine (for this was her name) prayed him to wear a red sleeve at the justs as a token of her. Then said Lancelot, 'I have done no such thing for any maiden before ; nevertheless I will wear thy token, and I leave my shield in thy keeping.'

Bravely and mightily fought the knights when the day for the justing had come ; but the bravest and mightiest of all was Lancelot, whom none knew save the king only. Wherever he bore down on his horse, all were smitten before him like corn before the wind, until Sir Bors by mischance smote him through the shield into his side, and the head of the lance was left in the wound. So great was the pain that Sir Lancelot could not tarry to receive the prize; but riding away with Lavaine, he came to a wood-side, and there bade him draw the truncheon from his side. Loth was Lavaine to do his bidding, for he feared that Lancelot might bleed to death ; and when it was done, the stream gushed forth as though his life must pass away. But Lavaine got him at last to a hermit's house, and there the wound was stanched, and slowly his strength came back to him.

Meanwhile King Arthur had returned with his fellowship to London; and Sir Gawaine, on the road, tarried at Astolat at the house of Sir Bernard, and told how the Knight of the Red Sleeve had won the prize over all. 'Now blessed be God,' said Elaine the Fair, 'that he sped so well, for he is the first man I have loved in the world, and he shall be the last.' 'Knowest thou his name?' asked Sir Gawaine. 'Nay,' she said, 'I know neither his name nor whence he comes; but well I know that I love him.' 'How had you knowledge of him at first?' said Sir Gawaine.

Then she told him all: and when Gawaine heard of the shield he prayed that she would show it to him. 'It is the shield of Sir Lancelot du Lake,' he said when the cover had been taken off it. 'Fair maiden, thy honour is great, for four and twenty years have I known this knight, and never saw I him wear token of any lady or maiden. But I fear me that ye may see him again no more.' 'How may this be?' she said. 'Is he slain?' 'Nay,' said Gawaine, 'but he is sorely wounded.' Then Elaine turned to her father, and won his leave that she might ride to Lancelot and tend him while he lay sick: and Gawaine went back to the king and told him all that he had seen and heard.

But the wrath of Queen Guenevere broke out afresh when she knew that Lancelot had borne in the tourney the red sleeve of the Maiden of Astolat, and many a hard word she spake against him to Sir Bors. And Elaine coming to Camelot met her brother Lavaine, and asked him how fared her lord Sir Lancelot. 'Who told you,' he asked, 'that his name is Lancelot?' 'Sir Gawaine knew him by his shield,' she said: and going with her brother she reached the hermitage where Lancelot lay. There, as she saw him sick and pale in his bed, she could not speak, but fell down in a swoon and lay a great while. But when her strength came back to her a little, Lancelot said to Lavaine, 'Bring her to me;' and kissing her he said, 'Thou puttest me to pain, fair maiden; wherefore weep no more. If thou hast come to cheer me, thou art right welcome, and of my wound I trust soon to be whole.' So there she tarried, watching him day and night, so that never woman did more for man than she did for Sir Lancelot.

Thither, also, after long wandering and search, came Sir Bors, for he yearned to throw himself at Lancelot's feet, and crave his forgiveness for the wound which he had unwittingly given him. And Lancelot said, 'Thou art right welcome, cousin, but of these matters let us say no more. All shall be welcome that God sendeth.' Then Bors told him of the queen's wrath and of the cause of it, and looking at Elaine, he asked, 'Is this she whom men call the Maiden of Astolat?' 'Yes,' said Lancelot, 'it is she whom I can by no means put from me.' 'Why shouldst thou put her from thee?' said Bors. 'Happier far were it for thee if thou couldst love her; but of that I cannot advise thee. Only I see well that all her love is given to thee, nor is she the first that has lost her pain upon thee.'

When three days more were past, Sir Lancelot felt himself so strong that he sought to be on his horse again; but the steed was fresh and fiery, and as he leaped, he made the knight's wound burst forth again, and once more Lancelot was well nigh dead. In sore grief Elaine knelt beside him and sought to awaken him with her kisses; but little could they do until the good hermit came and stanched the bleeding. Then Sir Bors hastened to the king, to tell him of all that had befallen Lancelot, and the king was sorry, but Guenevere said, 'I would he had not his life.' 'His life he shall have,' said Bors, 'and except thee none should wish it otherwise but we should shorten their lives. Many a time before hast thou been wroth with Sir Lancelot, and each time hath he been proved to be a true and faithful knight.'

But at length the time came when Lancelot must depart, for now was he well and strong again, and so great was the love that Elaine bare that in nowise could she withstand it. 'Have mercy on me,' she said, 'and leave me not to die.' 'What wouldst thou?' asked Lancelot. 'To be thy wife,' said the maid of Astolat. 'Nay,' answered Lancelot, 'never shall I be a wedded man.' 'Then be thou my love,' she said; but in that too he said her nay, for he would not do her wrong. 'Then must I die for my love,' said Elaine. And ever from that hour, when Sir Lancelot was gone, she pined away, until, when ten days were past, she was shriven, and the priest bade her leave such thoughts. 'Why should I leave such thoughts?' she said, 'am I not an earthly woman? Yea, while my breath is in my body, I will complain, for I do no offence though I love an earthly man, and none have I loved but Sir Lancelot, and never shall I.' Then calling her father and her brother, she bade them write for her a letter of which she gave the words. 'When I am dead,' she said, 'and while my body is yet warm, let this letter be put in my right hand, and my hand bound fast with the letter until I be cold; and let me be put in a fair bed with all the richest clothes that I have about me; and so let my bed and all my richest clothes be borne with me in a chariot to the next place where Thames is; and there let me be put within a barge, and let my barge be covered with black samite over and over. Thus, father, I beseech you, let it be done.' And when she had so said, she died; and they put her body in the barge, and sent it on the river to Westminster. And so for her love died the maid of Astolat.

Now at Westminster King Arthur was speaking with the queen near a window, when they spied a barge, and marvelled what it could mean; and going down to the river, they found in the barge, wrapped in cloth of gold, and lying as though she smiled, the body of the fair Elaine; and the queen spying the letter in her right hand told the king, who carried it away and bade the clerk read it; and the words of the letter said only this: 'Most noble Sir Lancelot, death hath made a severance between us for thy love, for I whom men called the Fair Maiden of Astolat was your lover. Pray thou for my soul, as thou art peerless.' And all wept who heard the words; but when Lancelot came, whom the king sent for, he said, 'I am heavy for the fair maiden's death. Yet was it none of my devising, for she loved me out of measure, and nought would content her but that she must be either my wife or my love, and neither of these things could I grant to her.' Many a knight came that day to look on her fair face, and on the morrow they buried her richly. And when all was done, the queen sent for Lancelot and craved his forgiveness because she had been wroth with him without cause. 'It is not the first time that thou hast been thus wroth with me,' said Sir Lancelot.

CHAPTER XIX.

THE JUDGMENT OF QUEEN GUENEVERE.

THEN awhile they abode joyously together; and when the merry month of May came round, Queen Guenevere rode into the forest with her knights of the Round Table, all clad in green, and ten ladies with her. But even while they were sporting among the trees and flowers, an evil knight watched them named Meliagrance, the son of King Bagdemagus, who had long loved the queen and sought to steal her away when Sir Lancelot might not be with her; and now when he saw that she had but ten knights with her, he came with eightscore men well harnessed, and bade the queen and her knights stand still. 'Thou shamest all knighthood and thyself,' said the queen. 'Be that as it may,' said Sir Meliagrance, 'I have loved you many a year, and now I will take you as I find you.' Stoutly the ten knights fought for Queen Guenevere, until of the men of Sir Meliagrance forty lay dead upon the field. But they were sore bestead; and Guenevere cried out for pity and sorrow, 'Sir Knight, I will go with you upon this covenant, that thou wilt save these knights, and that they be led with me whithersoever thou mayst take me.'

So they rode together, and Sir Meliagrance was sorely afraid lest the queen might send tidings of her durance to Sir Lancelot. But though he kept close watch, yet was Guenevere able to speak for a moment with a child of her chamber, and she charged him to bear a ring to Sir Lancelot and bid him come to rescue her. 'Spare not thy horse,' said she, 'either for water or for land.' So when the child spied his time he rode swiftly away, and although Sir Meliagrance sent men after him their quest was vain. Then said he to Guenevere, 'I see that thou wouldst betray me, but I shall make ready for Sir Lancelot's coming.'

Swiftly rode the child to Westminster, and more swiftly sped Sir Lancelot back, leaving charge to Sir Lavaine that he should hasten after him with all his might, to rescue the queen, her knights, and her ladies, from her traitorous enemies. And many a peril had he to pass on the road, for Sir Meliagrance placed men who shot his horse; and at last a cart came by for gathering wood, but when he prayed the woodman to let him ride on it, the woodman said nay, not once or twice; and straightway the knight slew him. Then his fellow was afraid, and brought Sir Lancelot in his cart to the castle where the queen lay, and thrusting back the gate, Lancelot smote the porter under the ear with his gauntlet so that his neck brake.

Then was the traitor heart of Meliagrance bowed down with fear, and hastening into the presence of Queen Guenevere he threw himself at her feet and craved mercy, and put all things in the castle at her will. 'Better is peace than war,' said Guenevere, and she went to greet Sir Lancelot, who, standing in the inner court, bade the traitor come forth and do battle. 'Why art thou so moved, Sir Lancelot?' asked the queen. 'Why dost thou put this question to me?' answered Lancelot; 'thou oughtest to be more wroth than I, for thou hast the hurt and the dishonour.' 'Thou sayest true,' said the queen, 'and I thank thee. Yet must thou come in peaceably, for all things here are put into my hands, and the knight is sorely ashamed for his wrong doing.' 'That may well be,' said Sir Lancelot, 'yet are there none upon earth save thee and my lord King Arthur, who should stay me from leaving the heart of Sir Meliagrance full cold before I depart hence.' Then she took him by his bare hand, for he had taken off his gauntlet, and she brought him into her chamber, where her ladies unarmed him, and the ten wounded knights rejoiced exceedingly when they beheld him; and for many a day after he was called the Knight of the Cart.

Now Lancelot and the queen talked together, and she made him promise that the same night he should come to a window barred with iron towards a garden when all folk were asleep. All that day the queen tended the wounded knights; and when at night Sir Lancelot was in the chamber set apart for him, he told Sir Lavaine that he must go and speak with the queen. 'Let me go with you,' said Sir Lavaine, 'for sorely do I fear the treachery of Sir Meliagrance.' 'I thank ye,' said Lancelot, 'but I will have no one with me.' Then sword in hand he went to a place where he had spied a ladder, which he carried to the window, and then he spake of many things with the queen. 'Would I were by thy side,' said he at length. 'I will, as thou wilt,' answered Guenevere. 'Now shall I prove my might,' he said, and seizing the bars he wrested them clean out from the wall, but one of the bars wounded his head to the bone; and when he could tarry there no longer, he went out again at the window, putting the bars in their place as well as he could.

But in the morning Sir Meliagrance espied the blood of Sir Lancelot in the queen's chamber, and he deemed that it was the blood of one of the wounded knights, and that the queen was false to King Arthur. Therewith he charged her with the wrong doing, and the ten knights in hot anger told him that he said falsely and that they would make good their word upon their bodies; and the tidings of these things were brought to Sir Lancelot, and coming forth he met Sir Meliagrance, who told him again of that which had befallen. 'Beware what thou doest,' said Sir Lancelot. 'And beware thou too,' said Meliagrance, 'for peerless though thou mayest be, yet if thou sidest with them, thou wilt take part in a wrong quarrel, for God will have a stroke in every battle.' 'God is to be feared,' answered Lancelot; 'but I tell you plainly that none of these knights was here with my lady Queen Guenevere, and that will I prove by my hands.' So they exchanged gloves, and gaged to do battle on the eighth day in the field beside Westminster. 'In the mean season,' said Sir Meliagrance, 'plot thou no treason against me.' 'Never have I plotted treason against any,' answered Lancelot, 'and that thou very well knowest.' Then after dinner Meliagrance asked Lancelot if he would see the passages of the castle; and Lancelot followed him in all knightly faith and trust, until he trod on a trap and the board rolled, and he fell ten fathom down into a dungeon full of straw.

Great was the marvelling when Sir Lancelot could nowhere be seen; but at last they deemed that he had gone his way as he was wont to do suddenly. Then Sir Lavaine got together litters for the wounded knights, and he journeyed with them all and with the queen and her ladies to Westminster, and told the king all that had happened, and how Meliagrance had gaged to do battle on the eighth day with Lancelot. 'He has taken upon him a great thing,' said the king: 'but where is Sir Lancelot?' 'We wot not where he is,' answered Lavaine, 'but we deem he has ridden forth upon some errand.' 'Let him be,' said Arthur; 'he will meet his pledge, if he be not trapped with some treason.'

Meanwhile Sir Lancelot lay in the dungeon, where every day a maiden brought him food and drink, and wooed him to love her. 'Ye are not wise,' she said, when he would not grant her prayer, 'for but by my will thou canst not go forth, and if thou be not at Westminster on the day of battle, the queen will die in the flames.' 'God forbid,' he said, 'that she should be burnt for my default: but be thou sure they will deem, if I come not, that I am in prison or sick or dead; and sure I am that some knight of my kinsfolk will take up my quarrel.' At last on the day of battle she said to him, 'Thou art over-hard of heart; and if thou wilt but kiss me, I should set thee free with thy armour and with the best horse in the castle stables.' 'Nay,' said Lancelot, 'I know not if there be any wrong in kissing thee:' so he kissed her and went his way on a white horse which she gave him: and as he left her he said, 'Thou hast done a good deed, and for it I will do thee a service if ever it be in my power.'

The lists were made ready at Westminster, and the queen stood by the pile of wood, and Meliagrance looked for judgment against her because Sir Lancelot came not, and all were ashamed that the queen should be burnt for this cause. Then said Sir Lavaine to the king, 'Sure am I that Lancelot would be here, if he were not sick or in prison or dead; and therefore, I pray you, suffer me to do battle in his stead to save my lady the queen.' 'Be it as thou wilt,' said the king, 'for I dare to say that this knight's charge is false, seeing there is not one of the wounded knights but says that it is untrue, and that if they could stand they would prove their words with their bodies.' But even as the heralds were going to cry the onset, Sir Lancelot was seen speeding on with all the strength of his white steed. 'Ho! and abide,' cried the king: and Lancelot coming up told how Meliagrance had dealt with him from first to last, so that all who heard him felt shame of the traitor. So in the battle Sir Lancelot bare down on him and smote him with the first blow, and Meliagrance said, 'I yield me as overcome; save my life.' Then was Lancelot sore vexed, for he longed greatly to slay Sir Meliagrance, and he looked to the queen to see what she would have; and she made a sign that Sir Meliagrance should die. 'Rise up,' said Lancelot, 'and do battle to the uttermost.' 'Nay, I rise not,' he answered, 'until ye take me as recreant and overcome.' 'That will I not,' said Lancelot: 'but I will make thee a large proffer. I will leave unarmed my head and the left quarter of my body, and my left hand shall be bound behind me; and so will we fight together.' 'So be it,' said Meliagrance; and so was it done; but in spite of his vantage his head was smitten in twain by the first blow from Sir Lancelot's sword; and more was Lancelot cherished of the king and queen than ever he had been before.

After this King Arthur held his court at Carlisle; and thither was brought in a litter Sir Urre of Hungary, whose mother had borne him for seven years from land to land in quest of some one who might stanch the bleeding wounds which he had received at the hands of a knight whom he had slain in Spain; and this knight's mother was a sorceress, who said that Sir Urre's wounds should ever remain open until they were searched by the best knight in the world.

Then Sir Urre's mother told the king all the story; and Arthur said, 'I will handle his wounds, not that I think myself worthy to heal your son, but because I would encourage other good knights to do as I will do.' So the king softly handled him, and a hundred and ten knights after him; but still the wounds bled on. 'Where is Sir Lancelot,' cried the king, 'that he is not here at this time?' and as they spoke of many things, Lancelot was seen riding towards them; and when Sir Urre's sister saw him, she ran to her brother and said, 'Brother, here is a knight come to whom my heart greatly turns.' 'Yea,' said Urre, 'and so doth mine more than to all others that have searched me; and now I hope to be healed.' Then said the king to Lancelot that he must now essay what they had sought to do: but he answered that he dared not to thrust himself forward when so many noble knights and the king had tried in vain before him. 'Nay, then, thou shalt not choose,' said Arthur, 'for I will charge thee to do as we have done.' And not only did the knights pray him so to do, but Sir Urre besought him earnestly to heal him, 'for,' he said, 'since thou camest my wounds seem as though they hurt me not.' Then Lancelot kneeled down by the wounded knight, and prayed that God might give him grace to do that which of himself he might never do; and after this, each wound, as he laid his hand upon it, healed up and left the flesh as fair as it had been before Sir Urre was hurt. Then all knelt down and gave thanks to God, and Lancelot wept as a child. So came Sir Urre of Hungary into Carlisle lusty and strong, and there were justings in which he and Sir Lavaine wrought best, and after this Lavaine was married to Sir Urre's sister.

CHAPTER XX.

THE SIEGE OF JOYOUS GARD.

In merry May, when Summer comes to gladden men with fresh flowers, the flower of knighthood was crushed; and this evil was wrought by two unhappy knights, Agravaine and Mordred. For these two hated Guenevere, and daily and nightly they watched for Sir Lancelot; and at last Agravaine said openly that they must tell the king of the falsehood of the queen. 'Speak not of such matters to me,' said Gawaine to his brothers, 'for I will not be of your counsel:' and so said Sir Gaheris and Sir Gareth. 'Then will I be with you,' said Mordred. 'I would that ye left all this,' answered Gawaine, 'for I know what will fall of it.' 'Fall of it what may,' said Agravaine, 'I will show all unto the king.' And even so, in spite of all that Gawaine and Gaheris and Gareth might say, to the king they came and charged the queen and Sir Lancelot of treason. 'If it be so,' said Arthur, 'I would that Lancelot be taken in the deed, for I know no knight that is able to match him, and I should be loth to begin such a thing unless I might have proofs upon it.' Then Agravaine counselled the king to send word to the queen that he should be away one night, that so Guenevere might send for Lancelot or Lancelot go to Guenevere, and thus they should be entrapped. So the next day the king went hunting, and sent this message to the queen: and in the evening Sir Lancelot told Bors that he would go and speak with Guenevere. 'Nay, do not thus,' said Bors, 'for I fear sorely that Agravaine is on the watch to do you shame.' 'Fear not,' answered Lancelot; 'the queen has sent for me, and I will not be so much a coward but she shall see me.'

So Lancelot passed into the queen's chamber; and while he was yet there, Sir Agravaine and Mordred came with twelve knights, and cried out to him, 'Now, traitor, thou art taken:' and all fourteen were armed as for a battle. Then said Lancelot to Guenevere, 'Let me have but some armour, and I shall soon stint their malice.' 'Alas!' she said, 'I have none here, and much I fear that our long love is coming to its end, and against so many armed men thou canst not stand.' Louder yet shouted the knights outside, until Lancelot said that death were better than to endure all this pain. Then taking the queen in his arms, he kissed her and said, 'Most noble Christian queen, pray for my soul if I be here slain, and trouble not thyself; for well I know that Sir Urre and Sir Bors, and other my kinsfolk will rescue thee and will carry thee away to my lands where thou mayest live like a queen.' 'Nay,' she said, 'that may not be, for if thou art slain I shall not care to live, and I will take my death as meekly as ever did any Christian queen.'

Then Lancelot made ready for the fight, and opening the door he gave space for one man only to come; and in strode a stalwart knight, named Colgrevance of Gore; and before he could strike, Lancelot smote him dead with a buffet upon the helmet; and drawing the body within the door, he donned the dead man's armour, and so harnessed he slew Agravaine and the twelve knights, and Mordred alone remained alive, and he fled away wounded. Then turning to the queen he said, 'I fear me all our true love is brought to an end, for now will King Arthur be my foe. But if it please thee to abide with me, I will save you from all dangers so far as I may.' So Lancelot kissed Guenevere, and either gave other a ring, and the knight went to his own lodging.

After this Lancelot took counsel with Sir Bors, who said that they must take the woe with the weal, and that they should be able to do as much harm to their enemies as their enemies could do to them. So they summoned all who would take their side, and there were reckoned of them one hundred and forty knights.

'And now say what I shall do,' asked Lancelot, 'if the king adjudge the queen to the flames?' With one voice they cried, 'Rescue her. As many times ye have done for other men's quarrels, so do now for your own.' 'But even this grieves me,' he answered, 'for in rescuing her I must do much harm, and it may be that I shall destroy some of my best friends to my great grief; and if I rescue her, where shall I keep her?' 'That shall be the least care of all,' said Sir Bors. 'Did not Tristram by your will keep Isolte the Fair for three years in Joyous Gard? There may ye keep her, and afterward bring her back to the king, and it may be ye shall have love and thank where others shall have none.' 'Nay,' said Sir Lancelot, 'but have I not a warning in what befel Sir Tristram, for when he had brought the fair Isolte from Joyous Gard into Cornwall, did not the traitor King Mark slay him, as he sat harping before her, by thrusting a glaive into his heart?' 'Yea, so it was,' answered Bors; 'but Mark was ever false, and Arthur is ever true.'

Wounded and covered with blood Mordred came before King Arthur, and told him how he alone of the fourteen knights remained alive, and how Lancelot in the queen's chamber had slain them all. 'Alas!' said the king, 'he is a peerless man, and alas! that ever he should be against me; for now is the noble fellowship of the Round Table broken for ever; and now the queen must die.' Then Gawaine besought the king to tarry yet awhile before he suffered the judgment to be done, 'for,' he said, 'it may be that Lancelot was with the queen for no ill intent, and many a time has he rescued her and rescued thee; and I dare to say that the queen is both good and true, and that Sir Lancelot will prove this upon his body.' 'In good sooth I doubt not he will,' said the king, 'for so mighty is he that none may withstand him, and therefore for her he shall fight no more: and she shall have the law. Yea, if I may get Sir Lancelot, he too shall die shamefully.' 'May I never see it,' answered Gawaine. 'Why say ye so?' cried Arthur; 'has he not slain your brother Sir Agravaine, and well-nigh killed your brother Sir Mordred?' 'In truth he has,' said Gawaine, 'but I gave them warning what would befall in the end; but they would not hearken to me, and I will not lay their deaths to his charge.' Then said the king, 'Make ready, thou and thy brothers Gaheris and Gareth, to bring the queen to the fire.' 'That will I never do,' answered Gawaine, 'and never shall it be said that I had part or lot in her death.' 'Then,' said the king, 'suffer your brothers to be there.'

'They are young,' answered Gawaine, 'and cannot say you nay.' Then spake the two brothers, 'Sir, thou mayest command us, but it is sorely against our will; but if we be there we will come unarmed and in no harness of war.' And even so they did, and they went forth with the queen to the place where the fire should be kindled; but one whom Lancelot sent to see what should happen had gone back with the tidings, and like a whirlwind came Lancelot with his men, and smote on the right hand and on the left all who stood in harness round the queen; and there was a great thronging and crushing, and in the tumult the sword of Sir Lancelot smote down the good knights Gaheris and Gareth, and their bodies were found in the thickest of the press. So, having rescued the queen, he rode with her to his castle of Joyous Gard.

'Alas! that ever I wore a crown,' said the king when he heard the tidings, 'for now have I lost the fairest fellowship that ever Christian king held together. And now I charge you all, tell not Sir Gawaine of the death of his brothers, for if he hears the news it will well nigh drive him mad. Ah me! that Lancelot should slay Gareth, who loved him above all earthly men.' 'That is truth,' said some knights, 'but Lancelot knew them not in the bustling of the fight, and he willed not to slay either.' 'It may be,' said the king: 'but their death will cause the greatest war that ever was. Alas! Agravaine, for thine evil will, that thou and Mordred should cause all this sorrow.'

Then there came one to Gawaine and told how Lancelot had rescued the queen. 'In that,' said Gawaine, 'he has done a knightly deed; but where are my brethren?' 'They are slain,' answered the messenger, 'and it is noised that Lancelot slew them.' 'That may I not believe,' said Sir Gawaine, 'for Gareth loved him better than all other men.' 'Nevertheless,' said the man, 'it is noised that Lancelot slew him.' Then Gawaine swooned away for his sorrow; and when he arose, he ran hastily to the king his uncle, and told him how his brothers had been slain; and the king said that their deaths must be avenged, 'I make you now a promise,' answered Gawaine, 'that I will never fail Lancelot until he or I be slain. Get you then our friends together; and I shall seek him, if it be through seven kingdoms.' 'Ye need not seek him so far,' said the king, 'for Lancelot will abide us in Joyous Gard.'

So writs were sent to summon all who would fight for the king, and a mighty host was gathered to lay siege to Joyous Gard: but Lancelot was loth to fight against the man who had made him a knight, and he kept all his people within the castle wall. But one day in harvest time he looked over the walls, and spake with the king and Sir Gawaine, and the king challenged him to come forth and fight. 'God forbid,' said Lancelot, 'that I should encounter the noble king who made me a knight.' 'Fie on thy fair speech,' answered the king. 'I am now thy mortal foe, for thou hast slain my knights and dishonoured my queen.' 'Say what thou wilt,' said Lancelot; 'with you I will not strive; nor is there any knight under heaven that dare make it good upon my person that ever I have dealt traitorously by you. Many a time have I done battle for the queen in other men's quarrels; I have more right to do so now in my own. Take her then into your grace, for she is both true and good.' 'Yea,' cried Gawaine, 'the king shall have both his queen and thee, and shall slay you both as it may please him. What cause hadst thou to slay my brothers who loved thee more than all other men?' 'Well thou knowest,' said Lancelot, 'that it was done unwittingly, and that of free will I had as soon have slain my nephew Sir Bors.' 'Thou liest,' said Sir Gawaine; 'and while I live, I will make war upon thee.' 'Little hope then is there of peace,' said Lancelot, 'if thy mind be thus set; but if it were not so, I should not doubt soon to have the good grace of the king.'

In this Sir Lancelot spake truth; and by Sir Gawaine only was Arthur withheld from accord with Lancelot.

Then at Gawaine's bidding all Arthur's knights called on Lancelot to come forth as a false and recreant knight; and Lancelot's people would no more tarry within the castle walls, and he led them forth to the battle, charging all in any wise to save the king and Sir Gawaine. In this fight Sir Gawaine smote down Sir Lionel, who was borne away into the castle, but Sir Bors encountered with King Arthur and bare him to the ground. 'Shall I make an end to this war?' he said to Sir Lancelot, meaning that he would slay the king. 'Lay not thy hands on him,' cried Sir Lancelot, and lighting down he placed the king on his horse again, and said, 'for God's love stint this strife. Always I forbear you, but you and yours forbear not me: and call to mind also the things that I have done in times past.' Then the tears streamed from Arthur's eyes, as he thought on the courtesy which was in Lancelot more than in any other man; and the King could look on him no more, and riding away he said, 'Alas! that ever this war began.' But presently Gawaine and Bors fought together, and both were sorely wounded; and after this Arthur's men were not so eager for the fray as they had been.

The tidings of this war were borne through all Christendom; and at last they were brought to the pope, who wrote bulls charging the king straightly to accord with Sir Lancelot and to take his queen back again to him. And when the Bishop of Carlisle showed the king these bulls, he knew not what to do, for Gawaine would not suffer him to go back to the old friendship with Sir Lancelot. So it was covenanted that the king should take back the queen, and that Sir Lancelot should have the king's word and seal that he should bring the queen and go back safely. So went the bishop to Joyous Gard, and told Lancelot of the pope's will.

Then said Lancelot, 'More shall I rejoice to take her back than I rejoiced to bring her here; but I go not unless it be made sure to me that she will be free and that henceforth no words shall be cast against her.' 'Have no fear,' said the bishop, 'the pope must be obeyed;' and then he showed the pope's writing and King Arthur's; and Lancelot said, 'This is sure enough, for never Arthur brake a promise.'

So all was made ready, and Queen Guenevere went forth with Lancelot from Joyous Gard, clad both in white cloth of gold tissue, and with them a hundred knights in green velvet, each with a branch of olive in his hand in token of peace; and when they reached the Castle of Carlisle, Lancelot stood before the king and said, 'At the pope's will I have brought the queen; and ready I am as ever to prove upon my body that she is both good and true; but thou hast given heed to lying men, and this has caused debate between us. And once more would I say that, had not the right been on my side, I might not alone have had power to withstand and slay so many knights when they called me recreant and traitor as I stood in the queen's chamber.' 'They called thee right,' said Gawaine. 'Nay,' answered Lancelot, 'in their quarrel they proved themselves not right; but ye ought to remember what I have done for you in times past, for if I could have your good-will, I should trust to have the king's good grace.' 'The king may do as he will,' said Gawaine, 'but betwixt thee and me there can be no peace, for thou hast slain my brothers traitorously, and without pity.' 'Have not I said,' answered Lancelot, 'that their death is my great grief? And now am I ready to walk the land barefoot, and at every ten miles to found a house where they may pray always for their souls; and this were fairer and holier than to make war upon me, and this to no purpose.' Then was every eye that looked on Lancelot filled with tears, saving only Gawaine, who said, 'I have heard thy words and thy proffers, and the king may do as he wills; but if he accords with thee, he shall lose my service; for thou art false to the king and to me.' 'Nay,' said Lancelot, 'if thou chargest me with this, I must answer thee.' 'We are past that at this time,' said Gawaine; 'for the pope's charge and the king's pledge thou art safe to go back now; but in fifteen days thou art safe no more.' Then Lancelot sighed, and as the tears fell on his cheek, he said, 'Alas! most noble Christian realm, whom I have loved above all other realms, now must I leave thee, banished and in shame. Well is it said that in man's life there is no sure abiding.' And to the queen he said, 'Madam, now must I depart from you and from this noble fellowship for ever; but if ever ye be hard bestead by false tongues, send me word, I pray you, and if it be in the power of man, I will deliver you.' Then he kissed the queen, and before all he said, 'Let me see now who will dare to say that the queen is not true to her lord.'

So, while all wept for sorrow, Lancelot departed from the court for ever, and took his way to Joyous Gard, which ever after he called Dolorous Gard. Thence, having taken counsel with his knights, he passed over the sea and sailed to Benwick, and made his knights kings and princes in the land; and thither came also Arthur and Gawaine with threescore thousand men to make war upon him. But even as before, Lancelot was loth to fight against the king, and he sent forth a damsel who should speak with King Arthur, if so be he might make peace. And when she was brought before him and told him of the large proffers of Sir Lancelot the king was eager to bear accord with him, and all the lords prayed him to go back to the old friendship; but still Sir Gawaine said, 'Now that thou art thus far on thy journey, wilt thou turn again?' 'Nay,' answered Arthur, 'I will follow thy counsel; but speak thou to the maiden, for I cannot speak for pity.'

Then said Gawaine, 'Damsel, tell Sir Lancelot that it is wasted labour to sue to mine uncle now; and say to him from me that I shall never leave him until he be slain or I.' So she went her way weeping; and when Sir Lancelot had this answer the tears ran down his cheeks. But his knights came round him and said, 'Why weep? can we not match these in the field?' 'Yea, that we may,' said Lancelot; 'yet was I never so loth to do battle, for I cannot strike at the man who made me knight.'

So came Arthur and his men to Benwick and sat down before it, and day by day there was fighting and slaying of men; but when six months were past, one day Sir Gawaine called to Sir Lancelot to come forth as a coward and a craven; and when he heard these words Lancelot put on his harness and came forth for the battle. But none knew save King Arthur only that every day from the ninth hour until noon Gawaine's strength increased threefold, once for each hour, and after that he became as he had been before. So for those three hours Lancelot struggled hard against him, marvelling that he could do no more than shield himself against the strokes of his enemy, but when he felt that Gawaine had gone back to his own strength he said, 'Ye have done your part, and now must I do mine;' and soon Sir Gawaine was smitten down. But his hate and his rage were not conquered, and he charged Lancelot to slay him, or he would fight with him again to the death as soon as he might. 'Nay,' said Lancelot, 'I cannot slay a fallen knight, but I will withstand thee as I may.'

In a few days Gawaine was healed of his wound, and again he charged Lancelot to come forth as a recreant and craven knight. But it came to pass, as in the former fight, that Lancelot stood on his guard while Gawaine's strength increased, and once more smote him down after noontide. Then as he lay struggling on the ground he said to Sir Lancelot, 'I am not yet slain: come near me and do this battle to the uttermost.' 'Nay,' answered Lancelot, 'when I see thee on thy feet I will withstand thee, but I cannot smite a wounded man.' 'Be sure then,' answered Gawaine, 'that when I am whole I will do battle with thee again.'

For a month Gawaine lay sick; but when he was now well nigh ready for the fight, there came tidings which made Arthur hasten with his host to his own country.

CHAPTER XXI.

THE LAST DAYS OF ARTHUR, GUENEVERE, AND LANCELOT.

When King Arthur sailed with his people for Benwick, he left Mordred his sister's son to be ruler over his land, and placed Queen Guenevere under his governance. But when Arthur was gone, Mordred caused false letters to be written which said that the king was dead, and he made the people choose him king and got himself crowned at Canterbury. Then going to Camelot he told the queen plainly that she must become his wife, and he named a day on which they should be wedded. But Guenevere asked only that he would suffer her to go to London to get ready what might be needed for the marriage; and Mordred trusted her for her fair speech and suffered her to depart. But Guenevere, when she came to London, shut herself in the Tower and kept it with many knights and men, and Mordred in great wrath came and laid siege to the Tower in vain. Then came the Bishop of Canterbury to him and said, 'Wilt thou shame thyself and all knighthood? How mayest thou wed thy father's wife? Leave this wish, or I will curse thee with bell, book, and candle.' 'I defy thee,' said Mordred, 'do thy worst.' So the bishop went away and cursed him; but when Mordred sought to slay him, he went to

Glastonbury and served as priest hermit in a chapel. And soon word came to Mordred that Arthur was coming back to his own land; and he summoned folk to his standard, and many came, for they said that with Arthur was nought but war and strife, and with Mordred was much joy and bliss. So with a great host he came towards Dover, and there waited on the shore to hinder his father from landing in his own realm. But his people could not withstand Arthur and his hosts, and Mordred fled away with those that remained alive.

When the battle was over, Sir Gawaine was found in a boat half-dead; and the heart of King Arthur was well-nigh broken for sorrow, for in Lancelot and in Gawaine he had ever most joy. 'My death-day is come,' said Gawaine, 'but it is through my own wilfulness and hastiness, for I am smitten upon the old wound which Sir Lancelot gave me. But give me now pen, ink, and paper that I may write to him with my own hands.' So Gawaine wrote to Lancelot, telling him how he had come by his death, and praying him to come and see his tomb, for the great love which there had been between them, and to remember the old days before this evil war began. So at the hour of noon Sir Gawaine died; and it was told to the king that Sir Mordred lay with a new host on Barham Down. And the king went thither, and there was another battle, and Mordred fled away to Canterbury.

But yet the war went on, and at the last it was agreed that King Arthur should on a set day meet Mordred on a down beside Salisbury. On the eve of that day Arthur dreamed that he was sitting in a chair which was fast to a wheel, and far beneath lay a deep black water in which were all manner of serpents and noisome things, and suddenly he thought that the wheel turned round and he fell among the serpents, and each seized him by a limb. Then he waked up in great dread, and after a while he slumbered again, not sleeping nor thoroughly waking,

and he thought that Sir Gawaine came to him and many
fair ladies with him; and he said, 'Welcome my sister's
son; I deemed thou hadst been dead, and I thank God to
see thee now alive; but who be these who have come with
thee?' 'These,' said Gawaine, 'are ladies for whom I
fought in righteous quarrel while I was a living man, and
therefore God hath suffered them to bring me hither to
you, to warn you of your death; for if thou fight with
Mordred on the morn, ye must both be slain and most of
the folk on both sides. I bid thee then not to fight, but
to make a treaty for a month, for in that time shall Lancelot come with all his knights, who shall rescue you and
slay Mordred and all that hold with him.'

Then the king waking called for his people and told
them of his dream, and sent Sir Lucan and Sir Bedivere
with others to Mordred, and a treaty was made that
Mordred should have Cornwall and Kent for King Arthur's
days, and all the land when the king should be dead.
Then was it agreed that Arthur should meet Mordred on
the plain. But before the king went, he warned his host
if they should see any sword drawn, to strike in fiercely,
for he in nowise trusted Mordred; and Mordred gave the
like charge to his own people. So they met and drank
wine together, and all went well until an adder came out
of a little heath-bush and stung a knight on the foot;
and when the knight felt the sting and saw the snake he
drew his sword to slay the adder. But the hosts, seeing
that sword drawn, blew the trumpets and shouted, and
there was a fiercer battle than ever had been seen in any
Christian land. All day they fought, and when the sun
sank in the west there lay on the down dead an hundred
thousand men. Then looking around him, Arthur saw
that two knights only, Sir Lucan and Sir Bedivere, were
left, and these were sore wounded. 'Now,' said the king,
'I am come to mine end; but I would that I knew where
were that traitor Mordred who hath caused all this mis-

chief.' And at that moment he espied Mordred leaning on his sword among a great heap of dead men. 'Give me my spear,' said the king to Sir Lucan, 'for I see the traitor who hath done all this wrong.' 'Let him be,' said Sir Lucan; 'remember thy dream.' 'Betide me death, betide me life,' answered the king, 'he shall not escape my hands.' Then running with his spear toward Mordred, he cried, 'Traitor, thy death-day is come,' and therewith he smote him so that the spear ran out through his body. Then Mordred, knowing that he had his death-wound, thrust himself up with all his might up to the ring of the king's spear, and with his sword held in both hands he smote his father on the side of the head that the weapon pierced the helmet and the brain pan: and having so done he fell back dead. But King Arthur lay in a heavy swoon, and Lucan and Bedivere raised him up as they could, and led him betwixt them to a little chapel not far from the sea-side, and after a while they thought it best to bring him to some town. So they raised him up again, but Sir Lucan's strength failed him in the effort, and he sank upon the earth and died. Then as Sir Bedivere wept, the king said, 'Mourn not now. My time hies fast. Take therefore my good sword Excalibur, and throw it into yonder water, and bring me word again of that which thou mayest see.' But as he went to the water-side, the jewels gleaming on the pommel and haft seemed to him too goodly to be thrown away. So he hid Excalibur under a tree. 'What sawest thou?' said the king, when he came back. 'Nought but the waves driven by the wind,' answered Bedivere. 'That is untruly spoken,' said the king; 'go again and do my bidding.' But it seemed to him still a sin to cast away that noble sword, and again he hid it away. 'What sawest thou?' said Arthur. 'Nought but the waves as they plashed upon the shore.' 'Nay, that is not truly spoken,' said the king; 'and now go again, and on the

faith of a true knight do my bidding. Who would ween
that thou who hast been to me so loved and dear wouldst
betray me for the riches of the sword?' Then Bedivere
went the third time to the water-side, and binding the
girdle about the hilt, he threw the sword as far into the
water as he might, and there came a hand and an arm
above the water and caught it, and brandishing it thrice
vanished away. So Bedivere hastened back to the king
and told him what he had seen. 'Help me hence,' said
Arthur, 'for I fear me I have tarried here over long.'
So Bedivere bare him to the water-side, and when they
reached it they saw before them a barge with many fair
ladies in it. 'Now put me into the barge,' he said, and
Bedivere did so softly. And there received him three
queens, and he laid his head in one of their laps, and
that queen said, 'Ah, dear brother, why hast thou tarried
so long from me?' Then cried Bedivere, 'Ah, my lord
Arthur, what shall become of me now that thou goest
away and leavest me here among my enemies?' 'Comfort thyself,' said the king, 'and do as well as thou mayest,
for in me is no strength to trust in. And as for me, I go to
the vale of Avilion to heal me of my grievous wound, and
if thou never hear more of me, pray for my soul.' And
ever the queens wept and wailed as the barge floated away.

Now some of the old tales tell that when he could see
it no more, Sir Bedivere went weeping into the forest,
and, wandering all the night, came in the morning to a
chapel and an hermitage; and the hermit there was he
who had been Bishop of Canterbury, and he prayed now
by a new-made grave. And Bedivere asked whose body
was there laid, and the hermit said, 'I cannot tell you of
any surety, but this night, at midnight, came a number
of ladies bearing a corpse, and offered a hundred tapers
and a hundred bezants.' 'Then it is my lord King
Arthur,' said Bedivere, 'that here lies buried,' and therewith he swooned away for sorrow. But when he woke, he

would no more go from that place, and there he abode with the hermit, serving God night and day.

And some there are who say that of the three queens one was King Arthur's sister Morgan le Fay, the second the Queen of North Wales, and the third was the Queen of the Waste Lands: and with them was the Lady of the Lake, Nimue, who wedded Pelleas the good knight, and kept him to the uttermost of his days with her in great rest, and had done much good to King Arthur.

And some again there are who say that Arthur is not dead, but that he shall come again and win the holy Cross. And yet others say that on his tomb were these words graven:—

Hic jacet Arthurus rex quondam rexque futurus.

And so the faith lived on that he who had been king long ago will yet be king again.

When the tidings were brought to the queen that King Arthur was slain and all his noble knights, she became a nun at Almesbury, and there lived in fasting, prayers, and almsdeeds.

To Lancelot also came the news that Arthur was sore bestead, and in all haste he gathered his hosts, and crossed the sea to Dover. There when he asked the people of the king, they told him that the king was slain, and Lancelot wept for the heaviest tidings that had ever come to him. Then, having prayed long at Gawaine's tomb, he hastened to Almesbury to see the queen: and there, as he drew near, she swooned for sorrow and joy. But presently she said, 'Call yonder knight hither to me;' and when he was come, she said, before all that stood by, 'Through this man and me has all this war been wrought, and through our love which we have loved together is my most noble lord slain. And now am I set to get my soul in health; and so I pray you, by our old love, that thou see me again in this life no more. Go then to thy realm, and there take thee a wife and live with her in joy and bliss, and withal pray for me.' 'Nay,' answered Lancelot, 'that can I never do; but the lot which thou hast chosen for thyself, that will I choose for me also, and for thee will I pray always. That which thou doest, I must do, for in thee has been my earthly joy: but if I had found thee so minded, I had taken thee now to my own realm; but since this may not be, I go my way, as thou hast bidden me. Wherefore, I pray you, kiss me, and never again more.' 'Nay,' said the queen; and so they parted, but their grief was as though they had been stung with spears, and many times they swooned. Then her ladies bare Guenevere away to her chamber, and Sir Lancelot rode weeping all night through the forest, until he came to a hermitage between high cliffs; and there he found Sir Bedivere with the hermit who had been Bishop of Canterbury; and when he learnt from Bedivere the tale of all that had happened, he threw his arms abroad and said, 'Alas! who may trust this world?' Then he kneeled down and prayed, and besought the bishop that he might become his brother, and there he abode with Sir Bedivere.

Meanwhile Sir Bors sought Lancelot throughout the land, until at last he chanced to come to the chapel, where he found him with the bishop and Sir Bedivere; and he too prayed that he might be suffered to put on the habit and to tarry with them. And yet seven other knights of the Round Table came thither and joined with them. So six years passed away, and then Lancelot took the habit of priesthood, and for a twelvemonth he sang mass. But as the year drew to its end, he saw a vision which bade him go to Almesbury where he should find Guenevere dead, and fetch away her body that it might lie by the side of her lord King Arthur. Even so it came to pass: for queen Guenevere died half-an-hour before Lancelot reached the nunnery, for she had prayed that she might not have power to see him again with her worldly eyes.

Then Sir Lancelot looked upon her face as she lay dead, and he wept not greatly but sighed. On the morrow, when he had sung mass, they placed the body on a bier and took it away to Glastonbury. Then was the mass of requiem offered: but when the coffin was put in the earth, Sir Lancelot swooned and lay long still, and the hermit came and waked him, saying, 'Thou art to blame, if thou displease God with such sorrow.' 'Nay,' said Lancelot gently, 'I trust I do not displease God, for He knows my intent. For when I remember the beauty and nobleness which was in her and in the king, and when I remember how by my fault and pride they were laid full low who were peerless among Christian people, my sorrow may never have an end.'

From that hour the body of Sir Lancelot wasted away; and after six weeks he fell sick and lay in his bed, and sending for the bishop, he prayed him to make him ready for his last journey. 'Ye need it not now,' he said, 'by God's grace ye shall be well amended in the morn.' 'Nay,' he said, 'my body is near its death, I know well. I pray you therefore shrive me, and let my body be borne to Joyous Gard.'

In the night the bishop woke with great joy of heart, for in his sleep he had seen Lancelot standing before him with a great company of angels, who bare him up to heaven and carried him through the opened gates. Then said Sir Bors that it was but the vexing of dreams; but when they went to his couch, they found him dead, and he lay as though he smiled.

So, as he had desired, his body was borne to Joyous Gard, and laid in the fair choir, with the face bare that all might see him. And thither came, as the mass was sung, his brother Sir Ector, and when he knew that it was Lancelot who lay before him dead, he burst into bitter weeping. 'Ah, Lancelot,' he said, 'thou wast head of all Christian knights, never matched of earthly hand, the courtliest that ever bare shield, the truest lover, the firmest friend, the kindest man.'

All his days thereafter Sir Bedivere abode in the hermitage. But Sir Bors and Sir Ector with the seven other knights who had tarried with Bedivere and Lancelot, went to the Holy Land, and there, when they had done many battles upon the miscreants, on a Good Friday they died.

MERLIN.

WHEN CONSTAUNCE, King of Britain, who had freed the people from their enemies round about, was dead, his eldest son, Moyne the Monk was taken from the cloister at Winchester to sit upon the throne. And seeing him to be an unwarlike prince, Angys the Dane gathered together an army of Danes and Saxons and sailed for Britain with many high-banked ships full of kings and earls. Then King Moyne looked that Sir Fortager, which was his father's steward and captain of the host, should lead the Britons out to fight against Angys. But Fortager feigned sickness and would not go out to battle. Wherefore King Moyne went himself, and being unskilled in fight, he was defeated with great slaughter; so that Angys took many British towns and castles, and fortified himself therein. Now twelve British kings which fought under King Moyne being much displeased at his losing this battle, said, 'If Fortager had been our leader this had not been so;' and again, 'As for this Moyne, a gabbling monk, he is no king for us;' so these went to Fortager to ask his counsel; but Fortager replied, 'Seek counsel of your king; it is time enough to ask for mine when Moyne is king no longer.' Wherefore the twelve went straight to King Moyne and slew him as he sat at meat within his hall. Then they returned and greeted Fortager and made him king. Yet there were many who loved still the race of old King Constaunce, and some faithful barons took the two young princes, brothers of King Moyne, Aurilisbrosias and Uther-Pendragon, and sent them into Brittany lest Fortager should slay them also.

Now Fortager gathered together all the British kings, and fought a great battle against Angys, and drave him to his ships, and would have killed him on the strand; but Angys sued for peace and made a treaty with King Fortager to make war on him no more. So Angys sailed away with all the remnant of his host, and Fortager marched home in triumph. And while he made a feast there came to him the twelve kings which slew King Moyne, seeking reward, saying, 'O King Fortager, behold we have placed thee on high and made thee king; wherefore give us now our meed.' Fortager answered, 'Being king, in sooth I will show how kings do punish treason:' and he had wild horses brought and tare the traitors limb from limb upon his castle pavement and nailed their mangled bodies on his walls.

Howbeit Fortager thereby kindled against himself the wrath of all which helped him to the throne, and these rose up and joined with them which spake of bringing back Aurilisbrosias and Uther-Pendragon, and very few held still to Fortager; so he was hunted through his kingdom, and ofttimes beaten sore, barely escaping with his life. Then he bethought to send to Angys into Denmark, and promised half the kingdom if he would come and help him in this strait. And Angys came over again with many men and ships, and helped Fortager to fight against the Britons till the people were subdued, kept down by force of sword and spear. So the war ceased, but peace never came. Fortager went in daily fear of his life from the Britons whom he had betrayed; nor could he now rid himself of Angys whom he feared almost as much lest with his great army he should seize the whole kingdom; and yet again he feared lest the Normans should come over and fight for Aurilisbrosias and Uther-Pendragon to bring them back to the throne of their father Constaunce.

Then Fortager thought with himself to build a huge castle made of well-hewn stone and timber,—a mighty fortress with a lofty tower and battlements, deep ditch and heavy drawbridge,—the like for strength and bigness the world had never seen: and he would build it on the bleak waste of Salisbury Plain, and so dwell safe among his enemies.

Three thousand men began the work at break of day, hewers of wood and carpenters and masons and such as wrought in carven stone. So they began to dig out the foundations and lay the mighty blocks of stone well clamped with iron bonds; and when night came they left the ponderous wall reared up breast high. Next morning, coming to their task, they marvelled much to find the great stones scattered up and down upon the ground, and all their work destroyed. They wrought another day and built the wall up as before, digging the foundations deeper still, and taking greater care to mix the mortar well and fit each stone and clamp it tight. But in the night the wall was overthrown, by what power none could tell.

So Fortager called ten wise and learned clerks and shut them in a chamber open to the sky, to read the stars and find why no man might build up this castle wall. And after nine days the wise men came to the king and said, 'Sir, we have seen signs in the firmament how an elf-child has been born in Britain, knowing things past and things to come. Find the child and slay him on the plain, and mix the mortar with his blood; so shall the wall stand fast.' Then Fortager sent men to journey three and three into all parts of the country, and seek the child. After wandering many days and weeks, one of these parties of messengers lighted on a town, where, in the market-place, some children at play were quarrelling in their game. 'Thou black elf's son,' the urchins said to one young playmate five years old, 'we will not play with thee, for what thou art we cannot tell.' The messengers hearing these words thought this must surely be the child they sought, but

Merlin (for it was he) did not leave them long in doubt. 'Welcome, O messengers,' said he—'behold him whom you seek. Yet my blood will never make Fortager's castle wall stand firm for all the wise men say—blind fools, who grope among the stars for secrets and blunder past the portents at their feet.' Hearing this the men wondered greatly, saying, 'How wottest thou of our errand or of the king's intent?' Merlin answered, 'Pictures pass before my mind of all the things that be and shall be. I will go with you to Fortager and show what hinders building up his fortress on the plain.' So he set out with the messengers, they on their horses, he upon a palfrey.

Now as they journeyed through a town they saw a man buy strong new shoes and clout leather wherewith to mend them when worn out: and Merlin laughed. 'Why do you laugh?' the messengers asked. He answered, 'Because the man will never wear the shoes.' And sure enough he fell dead at his wicket gate. Next day they met a bier whereon was a child being carried to burial, and a priest sang at the head, and an old man followed behind and wept; and Merlin laughed again, for he said, 'Did these but know whose son lies there, the priest would weep and the man would sing:'—and this they found true, for the lad was not the mourner's son but the priest's. And on the third day as they rode, Merlin laughed again, and being asked why, he answered, 'King Fortager in his palace is jealous of his wife's good-looking chamberlain and threatens to take his life; forsooth he wots not that this good-looking wight is but a woman in disguise.' Then when they came to the palace they found it even as the child had said; and Merlin revealed the truth to the king, so the chamberlain was spared. Fortager marvelled much at the wisdom of this child of five years old, and talked with him about the mystery of his castle wall and why it was destroyed each night; and Merlin said, 'The fiends deceived your wise men, showing false signs among the stars; for all my kindred in the air are wroth with me because I am baptized into Christendom, and so they fain would trick me out of life. They care not for your castle wall, but only for my death. But send men now to dig a yard beneath the wall's foundation; they shall find a swift running water, and, underneath, two mighty stones which keep two dragons down. Every night at sundown these two dragons wake and do battle underground, so that the earth quakes and trembles and the wall is shaken down.'

Then straightway Fortager set his men to dig and find if this were true. And soon they came to the stream, which ran both deep and furiously; so they made a channel lined with masonry and led the water off by another way. And in the river-bed were two heavy slabs of stone which it took many men to rear up: and there beneath them lay the dragons. One was red as flame, with eyes that sparkled like the glint from off a brazen helm, his body a rood long and his tail very great and supple. The other one, milk-white and stern of look, had two fierce grisly heads which darted fire white as levin forks. And as the dragons waked from slumber, all the men fled away quickly in a panic, save only Merlin. Then rising from their dens the two monsters closed in such a deadly combat that the air was full of the fire which they belched forth from their throats; and the very clouds lightened to the thunder of the battle, and the earth shook. Thus they fought all that long summer night with fang and claw and tail; they fell and rose again and rose and fell, nor flagged either till the day dawned. Then the red dragon drave the white into a valley where for a little space he stood at bay, until recovering breath he made a fierce onset, hunting back the red dragon into the plain again, where, fixing him by the gullet, he tare him down and with his white hot flames scorched the red dragon to a heap of ashes on the heath. Then the white dragon flew away through the air.

Now after this, Merlin grew in great favour with King Fortager, and was his counsellor in all things that he undertook. Moreover when the masons next began to build, the wall no longer fell down as before. So in due time they built the fortress on the plain, a mighty castle high and strong of timber and of stone, ramparted about on every hand, a fair white castle the like whereof the world had never seen.

When it was done, men came to Fortager and prayed him ask of Merlin what the battle of the dragons should mean. So Fortager called Merlin, asking whether this strife betokened aught which should hereafter come to pass. But Merlin held his peace. Then waxing wroth King Fortager threatened to slay him. Merlin smiled in scorn, saying, 'You will never see my death-day; nay, if you bound me fast and drew your sword to strike, you would only fight with air.' Then Fortager intreated him, and sware upon the holy books that no harm should come to him, whatever the interpretation of the mystery might be. Then said Merlin, 'Hearken to the reading of the portent. The red dragon so strong to fight betokens Fortager and all the power he has gained through killing Moyne the king; the white dragon with two heads, the rightful heirs Aurilisbrosias and Uther-Pendragon, whose kingdom you withhold from them. And as the white dragon, hunted to the valley, there regained his strength and drove the red dragon back to the plain, it means that these heirs whom you have driven to Brittany have there found help and succour, and even now sail hitherward with many thousand men, who will come and hunt you through the land till you are driven to your fortress on the plain, shut up therein, and with your wife and child there burnt to ashes. This is the reading of the portent.'

Then Fortager had great sadness of heart, and prayed Merlin to tell him how to avoid the fate he had foretold, or at least how he might save his own life. But Merlin only answered sternly, 'What will be, will be.' And Fortager's anger being kindled, he started up and put forth his hand to seize the seer, but Merlin vanished suddenly from his sight. And while they sought him still within the palace, Merlin was far away in the cell of Blaise the holy hermit. There he remained long time, and wrote a book of prophecies of all the things to happen yet in Britain.

But as for Fortager it all fell out as Merlin had foretold, for Uther-Pendragon with his brother Aurilisbrosias landed with an army and marched to Winchester, and the citizens seeing the old banner of their own British kings, overpowered the Danish garrison and threw the gates wide open for the sons of King Constaunce. And when Fortager and Angys came against them with a host of Danes and Britons, the Britons of their army would not fight against their brethren, but rose into revolt. So Aurilisbrosias and Uther-Pendragon won an easy victory and pursued Fortager as far as Salisbury Plain, where he took refuge in the castle, and the Britons threw wildfire upon the walls and burned him there, together with his wife and child, and levelled the fortress with the ground.

But Angys fled into a citadel whither Uther-Pendragon followed, besieging him therein, but he could not take the place since it was strongly bulwarked on a hill. Then hearing some barons that had been with Fortager speak oftentimes of Merlin and his exceeding subtlety, Uther-Pendragon sent out men to search for him. And on a day these messengers being at dinner, an old beggar-man with a long white beard and ragged shoes, and a staff within his hand, came in and asked for alms. They jeered at him, bidding him begone. 'Wise messengers are ye,' the old man said, 'that seek child Merlin, for he hath often met you by the road to-day, and yet you knew him not. Go home to Uther-Pendragon and say that Merlin waits him in the wood hard by; for truly ye will never find him.' And as he spake these words the old man vanished suddenly.

Scarce knowing if it were a dream, the messengers returned to Uther-Pendragon, who, hearing this, left Aurilisbrosias to maintain the siege while he went to the wood to seek for Merlin. And first a swineherd met him, next a chapman with his pack, each of whom spake of Merlin; and last there came a comely swain who bade him still wait on, since Merlin would be sure to keep the tryst, but he had first some work to do. So the prince waited until far into the night and then he saw the swain again, who greeted him, saying, 'I am Merlin; I will go with you to the camp.' When they got there Aurilisbrosias said, 'Brother, there came a swain in the night and waked me, saying, "Behold Angys is come out from his citadel and has stolen past your sentinels, seeking to take your life." Then I leapt up, and seeing Angys at the tent door I fell on him and slew him easily, for while the swain stood by I seemed to have the strength of ten, and my sword cut through the brass and iron mail as though they were naught. As for the swain I missed him when the fight was done.' Uther-Pendragon answered, 'Brother, the swain was Merlin, who is here with me.' Then was Aurilisbrosias very glad, and both the princes thanked Merlin for his help. In the morning, when they knew that their leader had been slain, the Danes and Saxons yielded up the citadel, asking only for their lives and for leave to sail away in peace to their own country. Thus the land was free again, and all the people took the elder of the brothers, Uther-Pendragon, and made him king in Winchester, and held a seven nights feast of coronation.

After this, Merlin told the brothers that one of them would fall in a battle with a very great host of Northmen that would come to avenge the death of Angys, yet would he not say which of them it should be. And in a little time the sea about the Bristol Channel was blackened with a multitude of crested ships, and Danes and Saxons swarmed upon the beach in numbers like the sand. Then Merlin divided the Britons into two companies, so that with one Uther-Pendragon might give battle from the front and draw them inland, whilst Aurilisbrosias with the other stole round between the Northmen and the sea and fought them in the rear. The fight was fierce and bloody before the Britons drove their foes to their ships. Of thirty thousand Danes and Saxons five thousand only went back, and Aurilisbrosias lay dead upon the sea-beach and with him fourteen thousand Britons, while on the battle-ground for a space three miles by two no man might walk without stepping upon the dead. Then Merlin made a tomb for Aurilisbrosias with huge stones which he brought from Ireland through the air by magic, and all the people mourned for him.

For seven years after this Uther-Pendragon reigned and prospered, and conquered lands in Normandy and Brittany and Gaul, and Merlin counselled him in all things which he did. Merlin also made for him the famed Round Table whereat the best and bravest knights might sit in equal seat. One place alone was kept vacant, wherein none might sit till he came who should fulfil the marvel of the Holy Grail.

And all came to pass as the spirit of Merlin had foreseen, for, when Uther-Pendragon was dead, his son Arthur was chosen king when he had drawn the great sword which was fixed into the stone; and Merlin aided Arthur against all his enemies, and saved him from many perils which threatened his life. But at length the time drew nigh when Merlin should no more sojourn among men.

And so it came to pass that Merlin made a wondrous tomb in the Church of Saint Stephen at Camelot over twelve kings which Arthur slew. He made twelve images of copper bronze overlaid with gold, and a figure of King Arthur raised above with his sword drawn in his hand. Each image bare a waxen taper which burned day and night. And Merlin told the king, 'By these you shall be shown when I pass from the world of living men. That day the tapers will go out and never after be re-kindled. For you there remains a life of glory; the Sangreal shall be achieved, and you shall pass almost within its presence, yet not see it with your eyes, since they have looked too much upon the blood and dust of war to read the marvel of that holy thing. Fightings will never cease in your day, but you shall gain the victory and be king of Christendom, and at last die nobly in battle as a king should die. For me, alas! I must be prisoned in the air alive, and wait through ages for the Judge, awake through weary years, whilst others sleep beneath the quiet ground.'

Then Arthur counselled him, since he knew his fate, to guard himself against it by his subtile arts. But the seer answered, 'That which shall be, is: unchangeable as that which was.'

Now the spirits of the air, being very wroth at the discomfiture of all their plans, sought means, all through his life, to entrap Merlin, and snatch him from the world, but he being wistful of their schemes defeated them; nor could they in any wise have power on him until his work was done. But as he waxed in years he was beguiled by a beautiful damsel of the Lake, called Niniame, so that he fell into a dotage for love of her and would follow her whithersoever she went. But Niniame being passing weary of his love, made sport of him, and did but endure him for the sake of the wonders which he showed her. And it befell that one day as they sat together in a wood at Broceliande, she intreated Merlin to teach her a certain powerful spell, whereby a man might be shut up for ever in a narrow space about the earth, walled in by air, invisible to all for evermore. And this she begged with tears and promised him her love if he would show it her. And when she wearied him with asking, and beguiled him with many sweet words, he showed her all she asked. Then Niniame lulled him to sleep upon her lap, and, rising softly, wrought the spell in the air; and so shut Merlin up for ever in a blackthorn tree within the lonesome wood at Broceliande, where his spirit, tangled in a hopeless maze among the weird black twigs, the more inweaves itself in trying to be free.

SIR TRISTREM.

ROLAND RISE, Lord of Ermonie, was fighting for home and lands against Duke Morgan the invader; and the noise of the battle reached even to the tower where his wife, Lady Blanche-Flor, lay in her chamber. Many times the lady sent by Rohand, her faithful messenger, for tidings how the battle went; many times came back the answer, 'The fighting is furious, but neither army yields a yard of ground;' and again, 'The sword of Roland Rise, your lord, is reddened with the blood of full three hundred of his foes.' Presently there came a clatter at the castle gate, and a faithful steed bore home his master's body, not slain in fight, but foully smitten by a traitor's dagger. And when the lady knew her lord was dead, and all the land was conquered, she swooned away, and then her child was born. She named him Tristrem; for she said, 'Thy welcoming is sad, my son.' Then, calling Rohand, she charged him to bring up the child as his own; and drawing from her finger a golden ring, said, 'Keep it for my boy till he is grown, then let him take it to my brother Mark, the King of Cornwall—he will know the ring he gave me, and thereby that Tristrem is his sister Blanche-Flor's son.' Soon after that she drooped and died, and Rohand took the child home to his wife to bring up with his own babes secretly, for fear of the usurper.

Duke Morgan sent commandment to all the nobles of Ermonie to yield up burgh and city, and come to his council to pay homage. Cruel and haughty was he to his enemies; yet none gave brooch and ring, and shared rewards among his friends so freely as Duke Morgan. Rohand came to the council, rendering homage with his lips for sake of peace and Tristrem his dead master's son; but his heart burned hot against the usurper all the fifteen years he bowed beneath his yoke.

Now when Tristrem was grown a tall and comely youth, well skilled in knightly games, in books and minstrelsy, and practised in the customs of the chase, there came from Norway a merchant ship, freighted with hawks and treasure; and the captain challenged anyone to play at chess with him, staking twenty shillings a game against a white hawk. Tristrem went on board and played six games, and won six hawks; still they played on, for higher stakes each time, till he had won a hundred pounds. Then the captain, since he could not win the money back, determined to beguile Tristrem of it, and so gave orders to get up anchor and let the ship drift out of haven with the ebbing tide. Meanwhile they played and played and took no note of time. Presently, rising from the table, Tristrem looked about and saw only the gray sea and the fast waning shores, and wept, thinking of Rohand and his home; but the mariners laughed at his distress, and, having bent the sail and manned the oar-banks, they stood for the open sea. Contrary winds and storms beset them ceaselessly nine weeks. Wild waves shattered their oars, their anchor brake, and the tempest tare their sail to ribands and snapped their cordage. Then the mariners feared and said, ''Tis for the boy's sake the sea rages at us, since we have defrauded him.' So they set him ashore at the first land they sighted, and paid his winnings, giving him, besides, food and rich presents, to appease the waves, and sailed away.

It was a land of hill and forest, with black, bare, spray-beaten cliffs rising from out a rock-strewn sea. As the vessel sailed away and grew into a speck against the sky, Tristrem's heart began to sink for loneliness; but having kneeled upon the beach, and made his prayer to God, he rose more cheerfully and climbed the cliffs. A-top he found a pathway, and learning from two palmers that he was in Cornwall, promised them ten shillings to bring him to the king's court, where he thought perchance to get employment. Turning aside through a large forest they shortly came upon a party of hunters resting from the chase, whilst men brake up in quarters the stags that had been slain. The hunters took note of Tristrem from the handsome robe of blue and brown wherein the mariners had clothed him, and began to talk; while he, on his part, mocked at their ignorance of venery and the bungling way they mangled the tall game. Then said the hunters, 'We and our fathers have always so cut up the deer, but yonder lies a beast unflayed; show us a better way; we are not loth to learn.'

Tristrem thereupon took the buck, and carved it in true hunting fashion; apportioning to the forester his share, giving the hounds their due, and feeding the raven on the tree. Then he took the huntsman's horn and blew the mort.

Much wondering at his skill, the hunters brought him straightway to Castle Tintagel, to King Mark, who hearing of his cunning made him ruler of his hunt. And Tristrem sat at meat with the king, and being asked his parentage said he was Rohand's son of Ermonie (as he in truth believed). After the feast ale and mead were served in cups and horns, and the king's harper came and played a lay, whereat Tristrem found much fault, so that the harper grew angry and said, 'Show me the man will play it better.' 'Truly,' answered Tristrem, 'it would not otherwise be just to blame your playing.' Then taking the harp he played so wondrous sweet thereon that even the king's harper was constrained to own he never heard the like before, and all that sat by marvelled at his music. Thereupon King Mark, being greatly astonished and pleased, caused Tristrem to be clad in a sumptuous dress and appointed to have him always at court to harp in the king's chamber morn and night to charm away his care.

Now Rohand wandered over land and sea to find his foster-son, and after searching through seven kingdoms till his garments were in tatters, he at length fell in with one of the same palmers which had guided Tristrem to King Mark, and so found his way to Tintagel. But the porter and the usher, deeming him a mere beggar, would not let him pass, until, when Rohand had given to each a fair ring of gold, they changed their minds, and taking him for at least a prince, brought him to Tristrem. Not knowing Rohand in his rags, Tristrem at first spake harshly, but finding who it was, he kneeled, and having asked forgiveness brought him joyfully to King Mark, and claimed the beggar-man as his father before all the nobles, who tittered and made sport of him. Then Rohand was taken to a bath, and his great rough beard having been trimmed, and his tangled white hair combed smoothly out in locks, Tristrem arrayed him in a knight's scarlet robe, fur-broidered; and as he walked into the hall and took his seat beside the king at the banquet table, all they which before jeered at the ill-clad beggar were ashamed before his lordly presence.

After the feast Rohand told the story of Tristrem's birth, showing Blanche-Flor's ring in token, whereat King Mark was exceeding glad and received Tristrem as his nephew. Moreover all the knights and ladies of the court kissed him and paid him obeisance. But when Tristrem heard how his father Roland Rise had met his death through treachery, he prayed King Mark for leave to go to Ermonie to avenge his death. Though loth to part with him, and fearful of the enterprise, the king dubbed Tristrem knight, and gave him a thousand men and many ships, wherewith he sailed away with his foster-father, and after seven days voyage they came to Rohand's castle in Ermonie, and garrisoned themselves there. But fretting to remain within the walls, Sir Tristrem said, 'I will disguise myself and go and speak with Morgan, for I cannot rest longer idle in the castle.' So he took fifteen knights, each bearing a boar's head for a present, and came to Duke Morgan as he sat at meat. Howbeit Rohand determined to follow him with his army, 'For,' thought he, 'the youth is vengeful, and may be will provoke Duke Morgan and be slain.'

Sir Tristrem laid his present down before the Duke and spake thus:—

'God requite thee, Sir King, as thou hast dealt to me and mine.' Duke Morgan answered, 'Whether thou bless or curse I seek not, but thine errand?'

'Recompense,' said Tristrem, 'for my father's death and for my heritage of Ermonie.'

Then Duke Morgan called him beggar's brat and smote him in the face with his fist, whereat Sir Tristrem drew his sword and all the knights at table rose up to seize him; but at that moment Rohand and his men came up, and so began a battle which spread over all the land, for many barons joined to put down the usurper and restore the kingdom to the son of Roland Rise. With his own hand Tristrem slew Duke Morgan, and then, Rohand helping him, he routed all the army and drave them out of Ermonie. So having regained his land, he bestowed it upon Rohand to hold in vassalage, and taking ship sailed back again to Cornwall.

Now the King of England sent Moraunt, a noble knight, the Queen of Ireland's brother, demanding tribute of King Mark, to wit, of gold and silver and of tin three hundred pounds by the year, and every fourth year three hundred children. Then up and spake Sir Tristrem how no tribute was due, since Cornwall was ever a free kingdom, offering with his body to make good the truth in single combat.

Moraunt told him that he lied, and drawing a ring from off his finger gave it to Sir Tristrem for a gage of battle.

Next day they sailed to an island to fight; but when Tristrem came to land he turned his boat adrift, saying, that one boat would be enough to bring home the conqueror. Furiously they rode together and drave their spears through each other's shield, the lion on Sir Tristrem's and the dragon on Moraunt's being pierced; then they wheeled about and met again with a ringing clash of arms and armour, till Moraunt's horse brake his back with the shock of his master's spear against Tristrem's hauberk. Then as they fought on foot, fast and fiercely with their swords, Tristrem, being sorely wounded in the thigh, grew well-nigh mad with pain, and with one swift-handed heavy stroke cleft Moraunt's helmet to his skull, breaking the sword-point in his brain. So Moraunt fell dead.

Then Sir Tristrem returned to Tintagel amid great welcomings, and going to the church kneeled down before the altar and offered up his sword in thanksgiving; and King Mark appointed him heir of Cornwall to rule the country after him. But Moraunt's folk bare his body back to Ireland to the queen, with Tristrem's sword-point still sticking in the skull. Leeches came from far with salve and drink to heal the wound in Tristrem's thigh, but for all that they could do it festered and grew worse, and a canker broke out which would not be stayed, for Moraunt's sword was poisoned. So loathsome grew the wound that none would abide to be in the chamber where Tristrem lay, save only Gouvernayl his faithful servant; for the decaying flesh fouled all the air. Forsaken of his friends and thus become a pest to everyone, Sir Tristrem entered into a little ship alone with Gouvernayl and his harp for company, and let the vessel drift whither it would. Nine weeks he lay in pain, and thought to die within the boat, but his harp solaced him when nothing else could; then the wind driving the vessel into Dublin haven, he crawled ashore.

It was a summer evening and the wind had ceased. Sea and sky scarce seemed to move, but floated in a smooth, still dream; and Tristrem, resting on the beach, tuned his harp to a sweet melody while the whispering waves lapped softly on the shore. The Queen of Ireland and her daughter, fair Ysonde, sat at their palace window overlooking the sea, and hearing such tender music, came down to see the harper, whom they found surrounded by a crowd of wondering folk hushed into silence at his skill. When they asked his name and country Tristrem put himself upon his guard, for he knew the queen was sister to Moraunt whom he had slain. So he gave his name as Tramtris, a foreign merchant, who had been robbed and wounded sore by pirates. Then the queen, who had marvellous skill in medicine, undertook his cure, and having caused him to be carried to the palace, got ready a potent bath of herbs wherein he bathed from day to day and the wound began to heal. Till he regained his strength, Tramtris remained within the palace and became tutor to the beautiful Ysonde, whom he taught in minstrelsy and chess and poetry till she became as skilful as her master. But when he got well, vainly they besought the learned merchant Tramtris to abide in Ireland at the court. Not even the rare beauty of his pupil, the fair Ysonde, could make him stay. For Tristrem, off the battle-field, was a grave and quiet man, whose soul was in his book and harp, who had no thought nor care for love, to whom fair women were fair pictures and no more —Ysonde, perchance, the fairest—but a lay upon his harp was worth them all.

So being healed, he sailed back to Cornwall, where he told the story of his cure, with a grim pleasure at having beguiled the Queen of Ireland to heal unwittingly the slayer of her brother; and as he spake often of the loveliness and skill of fair Ysonde, how bright and beautiful she was, King Mark became enamoured of the picture Tristrem drew. Then the barons, jealous of Tristrem's power with the king, persuaded Mark to send him to demand the princess in marriage; thinking, when the knight returned to Ireland as ambassador from Cornwall and bearing his proper name, the queen would surely slay him to avenge the death of Moraunt. Tristrem, though he liked not the errand, was forced to go, since, as he was heir to the throne, the barons, if he had said nay, would have accused him of selfish ends in wishing the king not to marry.

Wherefore he came again to Ireland in a richly laden vessel, and sent messengers ashore with costly presents to the queen and princess, craving an audience. But the messengers returned, saying that the people of Dublin were hasting from the city in panic-stricken crowds because of a monstrous fiery dragon which had come upon the land and ravaged it. They told, moreover, how the king proclaimed the hand of fair Ysonde as the prize of the man who should rid the country of this fearful pest. Then Sir Tristrem took his spear and shield and girt on his sword, and being come to land, gat him to horse and rode till he encountered the fiery dragon.

The good spear shattered against the monster's flinty hide; the brave steed staggered and fell dead before the dragon's fiery breath; but Tristrem, leaping to his feet, fought all day long against the scaly beast, and though the flames which it belched forth burnt the armour from his body and scorched his flesh, yet Tristrem rested not until he hewed its neck-bone in twain and cleft its rocky skull. Then having cut out the dragon's tongue he placed it in his hose and set out to return; but his hot skin drew the poison of the tongue into his body, whereby being overcome with faintness, he sank down nigh the carcase and lay there senseless. Now the king's steward passing by, thought both the monster and Sir Tristrem dead, and so cut off the dragon's head, and taking it to the palace demanded of the king his daughter. Howbeit the queen, doubting his tale, would first go with Ysonde to see the battle-field. There they found a dead steed, and pieces of armour partly melted, and shreds of a rich robe that had been torn. Ysonde said, 'This is not the steward's steed nor yet his armour, nor his robe;' and when they came to a man lying on the ground and found the tongue within his hose, they said, 'Verily this is he that slew the dragon.' So kneeling at his side they gave him a cordial, whereon Tristrem, opening his eyes, claimed the victory, and offered to make good his story on the steward's body in single combat for the wager of his merchant ship and cargo. 'A merchant?' Ysonde whispered to her mother—'pity he were not a knight.' But they knew him not. They helped Sir Tristrem to the palace and led him to a bath, and while the queen went to make ready a healing drink, Ysonde remained alone with her champion. She thought within herself, 'I know his face and his long arms and broad shoulders—surely it cannot be Tramtris my old tutor!' Then searching for something to confirm her thought, she picked up Tristrem's sword, but when she saw that the point was broken, her mind went off upon another track, for she knew the broken sword-point they had found in Moraunt's skull was carefully preserved in a chest within the palace. So she ran and fetched the piece, when lo! it fitted Tristrem's sword. Thereby being well assured that this was the slayer of her uncle, she called loudly for the queen, and these two between them would have slain Tristrem in the bath with his own sword, but that the king, entering at the moment, would first hear the truth of the matter. Wherefore Tristrem pleaded that he had indeed slain the queen's brother, but in fair and open battle, though Moraunt had treacherously used a venomed sword. Then he called to mind how as Tramtris he had rendered service as tutor to Ysonde, whilst since that time he had so highly praised her that he was even now come over as ambassador to seek her hand in marriage on behalf of Mark the King of Cornwall. By this being pacified towards Tristrem, and learning moreover how he slew the dragon, the king commanded to cast the steward into prison; but to Tristrem he paid great honour, and having set him by his side arrayed in the richest apparel, he caused Ysonde to be led forth and gave her hand to him in presence of the court. 'Yet,' said the king, 'I had far rather that you should wed her yourself.' 'Sire,' he answered, 'if I did I should be shamed for ever in this world as false to the promise I have made to King Mark.' So Tristrem made ready to depart to England with his uncle's bride.

Now the Queen thought, 'King Mark has never seen Ysonde, and may not care for her, nor she perchance for him. What if they do not love each other when they wed?' Wherefore she mixed a powerful love-potion, that the pair drinking together of the cup upon their marriage night should thereafter love each other so dearly all their lives that nothing in the world might ever come between those two. And this she gave to Brengwain, Ysonde's maid, charging her to be discreet and careful.

Soon after the ship put out to sea, the wind veered round, blowing dead against the prow, so the mariners were forced to take in sail and bend to the oars to make headway in the teeth of wind and sea. Tristrem sat on the oar-bank and with his sinewy arms pulled single-handed a great stern-oar meant for two, till, thirsting at his labour, towards twilight he called for a drink. Brengwain went for it, but by misadventure in the dark she brought the cup wherein the love-potion was and gave it to Ysonde to bear to Tristrem. So he drank of it unwittingly and gave it to Ysonde, and she drank also, and they drained it to the dregs. Then love sprang up within their hearts which nothing while they lived should ever quench again. All through that fortnight's voyage their time passed like a musing dream; for they were drunken with the cup and knew not what they did, nor how the days slipped by, what sky was overhead, what foaming hills of sea their labouring vessel climbed, nor how the rowers toiled: they only knew they loved and ever thirsted for more love. Long did Tristrem battle against the new love that sprang up in his breast, sore tempted to put the vessel's head about and make for another land where he might wed Ysonde and live in happiness. But dearer than self or love to Tristrem was the honour of a knight on ambassage. He had often borne his life in his hand for knighthood's sake and for King Mark, but now after a mighty conflict he did more. For being come to land, he took Ysonde whom he loved so dear, and with a stern, set face led her forth to Mark to be his bride, whilst all the man was broken in an agony of soul. Merrily went the marriage feast with games and minstrelsy; but Tristrem's harp wailed piteously: his faith he had not broken but well-nigh his heart.

But King Mark held lightly by the gift which Tristrem gave so painfully. For there came a minstrel earl seeking a boon before he would play, and Mark having pledged his kingly word to give whatsoever he should ask, the minstrel played his lay and claimed the queen for guerdon, when, rather than forfeit his oath, King Mark suffered him to lead away the Lady Ysonde —the price of a song.

When Tristrem learnt this after he came back from hunting, his whole soul brake out in bitterness against the king. Then seizing his harp he hasted to the beach, and seeing the earl sail away upon the sea with the queen, he played a wild, sweet song which Ysonde heard afar off, and being taken with a great love-longing she made the earl put back, saying that she was sick and that nothing could comfort her but the sound of Tristrem's harp. They being come to shore, Sir Tristrem laid aside his harp and drawing his sword fought with the earl. But Ysonde, seeing neither got the advantage, and fearing for her lover, ran between their swords, craving a boon of the earl. When he promised to grant it she said, 'Go, journey to King Arthur's court and tell Queen Guenevere there are but two knights and ladies in the whole wide world henceforth, and these are Guenevere and Lancelot, and Tristrem and Ysonde.' So being caught in his own trap the earl was forced to depart upon his errand. But Tristrem brought Ysonde to the palace and restored her to King Mark, saying bitterly, 'Sir King, give gleemen other gifts in time to come.' Yet Sir Tristrem and the fair Ysonde loved ever together.

A knight there was of King Mark's court named Meriadok, who seeing Tristrem watch the queen and worship her with all his eyes whenever she passed through the hall to court or banquet, set himself to spy if ever they met or talked together; for he thought to curry favour with the king. One winter evening he found that a man had walked across the snow towards the palace with sieves upon his feet to hide the tracks; he also picked from a nail by the Queen's door a morsel of a green doublet such as Tristrem wore, and he gave it to the king. So Mark went to his wife and pretending to be about to journey to the Holy Land, asked in whose charge she would be left the while. Without a thought she answered, 'Tristrem's;' but Brengwain her maid having whispered to her to be on her guard, she added—'that is because he is your kinsman; but otherwise leave me rather to the care of Meriadok or any other knight.' So for that time the king thought no more of it; but afterward Meriadok persuaded him to send Tristrem away to a neighbouring city.

There Tristrem grieved since he could no more see the queen; for the love that was between them twain no tongue can tell, nor heart think it, nor pen write it. But at last bethinking him that the river of the city flowed past Ysonde's garden bower at Tintagel, he cut down a hazel branch, and having smoothed it with his knife cast it in the river with these words written thereon:—' A honey-suckle grew around this hazel branch and twined it closely in its arms; but the hazel being cut down the honeysuckle withered and died, and thus made its moan: " Sweet friend, I cannot live without you, nor you without me."' And Ysonde found the branch floating in the stream, and knew it was from her lover; and after that, sometimes by linden chips, at other times by twigs or flowers, the river bore messages to her from Tristrem, so she always knew his mind. But Meriadok set a dwarf to watch in the forest for their trysting-place, and having found it, came and told the king. So the king went, and waiting till he spied the pair, crept softly up to listen to their discourse. But Tristrem saw the king's shadow on the grass, and immediately raising his voice in angry words he began loudly to upbraid Ysonde for setting his uncle's mind against him, and bitterly reproached her as the cause of his banishment. Ysonde replied in the same strain, saying she would never be satisfied till he was driven from the land, for the scandal he had brought on her fair fame; to which Tristrem answered that he would gladly escape from her malice and go to Wales if she would only obtain for him a small bounty from the king with his dismissal. On this King Mark, convinced that his jealousy was unfounded, came out of his hiding-place quite overcome with joy and tenderness, and having embraced the pair restored Tristrem to favour, and so far from consenting to his departure besought him to return to Tintagel as high constable of the kingdom, to make amends for the injustice done to him.

Three years dwelt Tristrem at the court, going to and fro about his business at the palace, and all that while he strove vainly against the passion that consumed him. The cup's sweet poison rested on his lips and in his heart: and on her lips and in her heart; and for their very lives they could not help but love. What time, the banquet tables being cleared, the knights and dames sate round to hear his lays, Sir Tristrem sang for her alone and played for her, and saw none other in the listening throng; whilst for Ysonde Sir Tristrem was the one knight in all the world. And all men knew of their love and spake of it save the king, who would not know and would not see; for he felt that Ysonde had never been his wife except in outward show, nor ever, spite of all her strivings, could belong to him: and being awed at the great love of Tristrem and Ysonde, he would fain have kept them near to him and one another, thinking thus with his love to keep theirs in bounds. He sorrowed for himself because he knew that Ysonde's love was not his, and could never be; but he was a man of gentle mind, and most he sorrowed for the lovers, blaming himself for wedding her; and sometimes, for the pure love he bare to both, he wished that death might take him, and so leave them free, for he was greatly touched to see them strive so hard to do their duty and be nought to one another.

But one day, across a flour-sprinkled floor, Meriadok tracked Tristrem on a visit to the queen. Then being discovered, Tristrem fled; but King Mark for his honour's sake must needs take Ysonde to Westminster to prove her innocence by public ordeal of red-hot iron.

Disguised as a ragged peasant, Tristrem followed her and came and stood upon the Thames bank with the crowd. Ysonde looked round for one to bear her from the shore to her ship, and her eyes fell upon the peasant, and knowing him for Tristrem, she said that he and no other should carry her. Whereupon the ragged peasant took her in his arms; and when he had carried her into the midst of the water he kissed the queen, in sight of king and court and all that stood upon the shore and in the ship. The queen's servants would have drowned the peasant for the dire insult, but Ysonde pleaded for him, that being an uncouth man and ignorant of courtesy, perchance he meant no harm—so they let him go. Then being brought to her oath the Queen declared herself a guiltless woman, saying that no man save the king and that rough beggar which carried her across the water had ever kissed her lips. So when the red-hot irons were brought, the king would not suffer her to touch them, but being contented with her oath he caused her innocence to be proclaimed.

Then Sir Tristrem journeyed into Wales and offered his services to King Triamour, who being besieged by a certain giant prince named Urgan, welcomed him gladly. This Urgan, brother to Duke Morgan whom Tristrem slew in Ermonie, no sooner saw his enemy than he challenged him to mortal combat. The giant fought with a twelve-foot staff which he swung with mighty force; but Tristrem, nothing daunted by the crashing blows against his armour, with a deft stroke cut off Giant Urgan's right hand by the wrist, and while the giant fled to his castle for a cunning salve Tristrem picked up the bloody hand and rode off therewith to the city; but Urgan galloping back overtook him on the city bridge, where they fought fiercely together, till the giant, being thrust through the body, in his pain leaped over the bridge-side and was drowned. Then King Triamour offered to give up his kingdom to Sir Tristrem, who nevertheless would take no gift except a beautiful dog named Peticrewe, a present for Ysonde.

The fame of Tristrem's new exploit being noised abroad

reached King Mark, who prayed him to return to Tintagel. So Tristrem came, and was received joyfully by Mark, who made him grand steward of the realm and loaded him with honours.

But it was still as it had been before, and still Tristrem and Ysonde thirsted each for the other. Their love departed not, neither for weal nor woe, through all their lives. Together they were banished, after much long-suffering from the king. They fled, Tristrem and Ysonde, into a wood, where, dwelling in a rocky cavern and living on venison which Tristrem took in the chase, the two abode a twelvemonth save three weeks.

At length King Mark came hunting to the forest, and peering in at a cranny of the rock saw the face of golden-tressed Ysonde, lit by a ray of sunshine as she slept, and by her side a naked sword betwixt her and Sir Tristrem. Then from the token of the sword deeming them yet loyal to him, he stopped the cranny with his glove and waited. Presently Tristrem rose up and left Ysonde sleeping in the cave. Then King Mark spake kindly and tenderly to him, and would again have been reconciled, and would have brought him back to Tintagel. But Tristrem could not bear Mark's gentle words; and knowing all, dared no more go back to wrong the man that trusted him; but rather, being touched by Mark's great faith, sought how to tear himself away from Ysonde's sweet love, and so repay by sacrifice the undeserved confidence of the king. Wherefore Tristrem held his peace, and went away alone among the old familiar trees where he and Ysonde long had walked and loved. Bitterly he walked and crushed the withered leaves beneath his heel, communing with himself until he wrenched his mind round into this resolve—not to go back, never to see her more, not to return to take one last farewell, lest all his strength should fail him, but to leave her sleeping and pass out into the world with no other keepsake than

Ysonde's gold ring which rested on his finger. And lest, in spite of him, his very feet should rise up in rebellion and carry him to her presence, he would cross the sea and never any more come back. So resolved, he quickened his pace until he ran. Each footstep seemed as cruel as though his heart were under foot: yet he sped on. So when Ysonde awoke, her knight was far away. Mark took her home to Tintagel; but Tristrem with a firm set purpose, self-banished, took ship and came to Spain. Long he wandered there, a grave and silent man, communing only with his harp, and plaining on its strings the woe that made his heart to bleed. And in those days Sir Tristrem made three lays, 'The Lay of Death,' 'The Song of Ysonde,' and 'The Lay of Love which dieth not.' Then, as a knight should do, he shut his grief within his heart and sought in battle for a refuge from his care.

In Spain he slew three giants; then, passing through Ermonie where Rohand's sons ruled as his vassals, he abode with them a little space and afterward came to Brittany. There he fought the battles of Duke Florentin until he rid him of his enemies, and so having gained favour with the duke, he was brought to the palace, where he dwelt for many months.

Duke Florentin had a daughter, passing fair and gentle, whom men called Ysonde of the White Hand. And as she sat in the palace, hearing Tristrem sing with wild passion the 'Song of Ysonde'—Ysonde the beautiful, Ysonde the fair—she thought that the song was in her praise, and that the music which woke love within her own breast was meant for her. So she went to the duke her father and besought to be given in marriage unto Tristrem. Wherefore the duke spake often with Tristrem about his daughter, praying him to wed with her and promising half the kingdom as a dower. But Tristrem long held his peace, or made excuse that he should never wed, until wearying of the duke's importunity, and feeling something of compassion for Ysonde of the White Hand who seemed to pine for him as he did for Ysonde of Cornwall, and smitten moreover a little with her name, the name so dear to him, he yielded listlessly, and they were wed. But as they passed out from the church, now man and wife, the ring, the keepsake of the Queen Ysonde, slipped from his finger to the pavement. Then his heart reproaching him with treachery, he thought on all she had suffered for his love, and was suffering now, away in Cornwall; wherefore he led his wife to his castle gate, and having appointed her a retinue and maintenance, he turned his horse and went away and dwelt in another part of the land, leaving Ysonde of the White Hand a maiden wife.

Near Tristrem's solitary home dwelt a savage giant, Beliagog, on whose lands none dared hunt; but Tristrem hunted there and defied the giant to come out and fight. Vainly did Beliagog hurl his long barbed darts at his strong foeman, for Tristrem closing with him cut off his foot, and made him go upon his knees and beg for mercy. Sir Tristrem bound him, as the price of sparing his life, to build a lordly castle in honour of the Queen Ysonde. So he made Beliagog to labour at carrying great stones and heavy timber trunks. Then sent he to all parts for skilful workmen to rear the walls, and cunning carvers who could work in stone the image of all things that be. In the castle was a hall of traceried work wherein the life of Tristrem was portrayed in imagery. There one might see Ysonde and Brengwain, Mark and Meriadok, Rohand and Duke Morgan, Moraunt and Urgan—all so like that they seemed to breathe—with Tristrem harping to Ysonde, in court, in hall, in bower; and everywhere was Ysonde, with Tristrem ever at her side. There Tristrem long dwelt, a lonely man, gazing upon the imagery and harping on his harp.

One day Ysonde of the White Hand, in speaking with her brother Ganhardin, betrayed by an unwitting word that her husband never came to visit her; for, partly from shame and partly from a patient hope to win him yet, she had kept silence heretofore. Thereupon Ganhardin rode angrily off to Tristrem and demanded the reason of his neglect. Then spake Tristrem haughtily, 'Since your sister has betrayed the only secret that there was or ever could be betwixt us, I will never look upon her face again.' For he fretted at the empty marriage-bond and gladly caught at an excuse to sunder it more widely. His own suffering made him cruel; so he neither knew nor pitied the patient love which his wife bore to him. Then he led Ganhardin to his castle hall and showed the picture of Ysonde taking the cup from Brengwain's hand. 'See,' said he, 'how fair she is; thrice fairer than your sister. Fair Ysonde, who art and must be while I live my only love!' And Ganhardin, seeing her beauty only in marble, had not another word to say, but speechless sat regarding the imagery, whilst Tristrem, musing, let his fingers stray upon the harp and played the 'Lay of Love which dieth not.'

Ganhardin sat as it were in a trance before the pictured image of Ysonde, until at last so greatly did he desire to gaze on her in life that he entreated Tristrem to take him to Cornwall so that he might see with his own eyes that her beauty was not overdrawn. Then Tristrem told the story of his love to Ganhardin, who the more entreated him to go to Britain, till, wavering with persuasion from his old resolve, he sailed with Ganhardin to Cornwall.

Now Ysonde was in great distress and trouble that Canados, the king's high constable, ever since Tristrem's absence had importuned her with love, and now sought to carry her off by force of arms. Glad was the fair Ysonde when Ganhardin brought her Sir Tristrem's ring. And she and Brengwain went blithely back with him to the wood and told Tristrem all their strait. But Canados, being apprised of their meeting, came with a great army, and Tristrem and Ganhardin finding it hopeless to do battle against so many, and not wishing Mark to hear of their arrival, fled, whilst the queen and Brengwain sought to escape to the palace. Canados overtook the queen at the palace gates, but fearing then to carry her off, came straight to the king and told how Tristrem was come back. Brengwain was very angry to think that Tristrem fled, nevertheless she told King Mark the reason why Canados was so hot against him, whereat the king being enraged at the presumption of his constable banished him straightway from the palace.

After this, that he might look upon Ysonde's dear face again, Sir Tristrem stained his cheeks and dyed his hair, and came to the palace dressed in a cap and bells, with a fool's wand in his hand, and went daily in and out as jester to the court. But Brengwain, who alone beside the queen knew him in this disguise, upbraided him continually with his flight from before his enemies. Then Tristrem openly in the court threw off his jester's dress, and desired a tournament to be proclaimed that he might clear the queen. Meriadok and Canados were challengers, and Tristrem and Ganhardin rode against them in the tourney, and after a bloody combat slew them both and put to rout the rest of the talebearers.

Then Tristrem sailed again for Brittany to the castle which Beliagog had made for him. And Ganhardin came and told his sister all that he had seen. Ysonde of the White Hand had long sought patiently to win her husband to her side, but when her brother told of the Belle Ysonde of Cornwall, hope died out from her breast and in its place there came a steadfast jealousy, as patient as her love. The colour faded from her face till that grew white like the fair hands wherefrom she took her name.

Now on a day, as Tristrem rode alone in the wood, he met

a young knight named Tristrem like himself, who begged his help against a band of fifteen knights which had carried off his lady. Sir Tristrem rode after the party and attacked them on a lea beside the forest. His namesake fell in the fray; but Tristrem conquered all those knights and slew them without mercy to avenge his death. Nevertheless after the victory he lay down on the ground and fainted, for a poisoned arrow had smitten him on the old wound which he had received in battle with Moraunt. Men found him senseless in the wood, and bore him, not to his own castle but to the castle of Ysonde of the White Hand, which happened to be near. Glad was she to get her lord, though wounded, underneath her roof. Day and night she watched him with a jealous tenderness, hungering for his love and seeking but a smile in payment of her care. It came not. In his pain he dreamed but of the Fair Ysonde, and in his wanderings raved her name.

The wound grew worse and cankered, and the poison spread. Tristrem lay near death's door. No leech could cure his wound. Only one living soul could save his life, and that was she for whom alone he thought it worth the saving—Ysonde of Cornwall, who knew her mother's art. Then he called Ganhardin secretly, and giving him Ysonde's ring to bear for a token, said, 'Take ship and hasten to her. Bid her come for her love's sake and heal me. Tell her, lest I see her not, that I have loved her always and her only.' Then his heart sank as he thought, 'Will she come, and will she be in time?' So he whispered to Ganhardin again, 'Death presses heavily upon me. Yet I crave to last till you come back. If only I could know that Ysonde came with you, though I lay at the very point of death and the ship were far away, so sweet would be the tidings I could not die till she were here. I pray you take two sails, one black, one white; and as you voyage homeward, if Ysonde be with you in the vessel hoist the white sail for a sign; if not, the black. So, as I lie here wearying for the ship, I may know the quicker if sweet Ysonde perchance has not forsaken me.' Then Ganhardin sped away to do his bidding.

But Ysonde of the White Hand had overheard every word that Tristrem spake to Ganhardin; and her heart grew very cold and pitiless. Gloomily she sat watching at the window for the ship to come. A little speck, far off upon the wide gray sea, grew nearer, and the vessel hove in sight,—with a glittering white sail filled full in the fair breeze, the rowers straining their sinewy arms to gain the shore in time, and a woman standing in the prow impatient of their utmost speed. Well knew Ysonde of the White Hand who it was. One little hour and she must give her husband, not yet hers, into another's arms to tend, and suffer lips more dear to press his cheek and soothe his pain, as hers had vainly hungered to do so long.

Tristrem lay in light slumber, the breath coming fast and faint, but the murmurings of his wife roused him; and looking on her face he knew that the vessel was in sight. Painfully he lifted himself upon his bed and strove to move where he might see, but he had not strength.

'What sail, what sail?' he cried, all hoarse and flushed, and trembling betwixt hope and fear.

'Black, black!' she answered from her stone-cold lips.

Then shuddering with despair unspeakable to know himself forsaken of Ysonde, Tristrem covered up his face and fell back dead.

But the ship came to land and Ysonde, springing to shore, scarce heeded them which told her of her lover's death, but came running to the castle, and up into the chamber where he lay, and where his wife mourned loudly for him.

'Away, woman,' cried the Fair Ysonde in a hushed, soft voice, with a grief too terrible for tears,—'away, and

let me weep for him, for he is mine.' And none dared
hinder her, for fear fell on them all for the greatness
of her woe. Then falling on Tristrem's body she gathered
it in her arms, crying, 'He is mine—he loved me, he
is mine.'

So, like a wearied child, she sobbed herself to sleep
upon her lover's breast. Neither did any disturb her
more, for they knew how fast her slumber was.

King Mark sent and fetched their bodies to Cornwall.
A letter tied to the hilt of Tristrem's sword told the king
the story of the love-potion and of the loves of Tristrem
and Ysonde. Long mused he thereupon; and he wept,
seeing the writing of his nephew and the sword that had
set Cornwall free; and knowing all, King Mark forgave
them freely. Together he laid them in a fair tomb
within a chapel, tall, and rich in carven work; and above
he set a statue of the fair Ysonde, wrought skilfully in
her very likeness as she lived. And from Sir Tristrem's
grave there grew an eglantine which twined about the
statue, a marvel for all men to see, and though three
times they cut it down, it grew again, and ever wound its
arms about the image of the fair Ysonde.

BEVIS OF HAMTOUN.

SIR GUY, Earl of Hamtoun, took a young wife in his old age, the King of Scotland's daughter, by whom he had a son named Bevis. But his wife never loved him though he doted on her even to foolishness; nor did she wed Sir Guy of her own accord, but of her father's will, for she had long before given her heart to Divoun, Emperor of Almaine. Eight years she wearied of the earl's caresses, praying he might die; but life ran strong within the old man's veins. At last, tired of waiting longer for his death, she inveigled Sir Guy to go a-hunting in Hare Forest by the sea, and sent secretly to Divoun to come with a band of men and lie in ambush to slay him there.

Divoun, in his armour of proof, had pricked on before all his knights in Hare Forest, and so met Sir Guy alone, without either shield or armour, clad only in hunting dress and by his side a sword.

'Yield now, old greybeard,' said Divoun, 'and let it make death bitter to thee to know that I shall slay thy brat also, and take thy wife to be my leman.'

'Though I be old,' answered Sir Guy, 'and have no armour and no weapon but my sword, God helping me, I yet can fight for wife and child.' Furiously he rode against Divoun and turned his spear aside, grappled the man by great strength from his saddle, and flung him to the ground; then got off his steed, but scorned to smite the cowering emperor whining at his feet for pity. 'Fool,' said Sir Guy, 'you held an old man's strength too cheap.' Just then from out the brushwood came galloping a thousand knights to the succour of Divoun, and these hemmed in Sir Guy on either hand. Like some old lion at bay, he shook himself and something of the old might came back into his limbs, and all the old courage to his heart. He broke their ranks on every side, and reaped among the men as does a reaper with his sickle; so they fell and bowed before his sword like ears of corn at harvest-time. So he reaped on, until he cut three hundred of them down, till his arm waxed weary of the slaughter, and he was overcome with faintness. Then only dared his enemies rush in on him to bear him to the earth, and that same craven Emperor Divoun with his own hand smote off the noble white-haired head which never harboured an unkindly thought of knight or dame, nor plotted treachery.

Then Divoun wedded with the lady of Sir Guy, who brought him all the earl's possession for a dower. But the child Bevis, who was five years old, continually reproached his mother with her wickedness, charging her with his father's murder, insomuch that her very life became burdensome. Wherefore she sent to Saber, good knight and vassal of Sir Guy's, saying, 'Take away this brat and send me proof that he is dead, so I may live in peace.' Saber promised with a heavy heart, but had pity on the child for old Sir Guy's sake, who had been good to him; wherefore on getting home he took a boar and killed it, and having sprinkled the boy's garments with the blood, sent them to his mother; but Bevis he dressed in ragged clothes and sent him to the fields to tend the sheep.

One night, while herding the sheep upon the down, Bevis looked out towards his father's towers and saw the castle lighted up and heard the sound of tabours and of minstrelsy, and he was angry. He said within himself, 'I, the earl's son, in rags keep sheep—houseless in the bleak night, whilst the earl's murderers make merry with feasting and dances.' Then, taking his shepherd's crook in hand, he went to the castle, forced his way past the porter at the gate and marched gravely up the hall through all the dancing and the revelry, till he came to the bench where sat Divoun and his mother in state. 'What do you here, Divoun,' he cried, 'upon my lands and in my castle without leave? Base murderer and coward!' Then in sight of all he smote the emperor thrice with his crook upon the crown. But Divoun and his wife feared the boy, scarce knowing if it were not in truth his spirit, for they believed him dead. Neither did any that were in the hall lay hands on him, for many were his father's vassals, and the rest were struck with wonder seeing the grave demeanour of the child. So he passed out and came to Saber, telling what he had done. But Saber was very sorry, since now it was known that Bevis was alive it would be no longer easy to protect him from his mother's wrath. And so it fell out, for Saber had barely time to hide the boy behind the arras when his mother entered the house, demanding her son, and threatening Saber with loss of all his possessions if he failed to give him up. But Saber refused, since he feared for the boy's life. Then Bevis came out of his own accord from behind the arras, and stood before her. 'Mother,' said he, 'Saber must not suffer for me, he has done you no wrong. I am here; do with me as you will.' Then she called without, and four knights entered. 'Take this child,' she said, 'and carry him down to the seashore—seek there for heathen merchants that sail far east, who will sell him for a slave among the Paynim:' and these men did her bidding.

The merchants who bought Bevis sailed to a distant country called Ermony, and because Bevis was a handsome and stalwart lad they made him a present to the king. The king's name was Ermyn, and his wife Morage had died, leaving him a little daughter, Josian, his only

child; and she was very beautiful: her hair like sunshine
dappling on a stream, eyes tender as forget-me-nots upon
its brink, her snow-pure skin warm with the colour
of her quick young blood. Now King Ermyn soon came
to love Bevis as a son, for he was a handsome boy, and
bold and free of speech; so he made him his page to
have about him always in the palace; and he was Josian's
playmate, till as the two grew on in years she waxed
more shy, and Bevis awkward, and confused in his boy's
love for her; whilst Ermyn, not ill-pleased, looked on and
smiled at the pair. And when Bevis was fifteen years of
age, and well grown in strength and beauty, the king
said, 'Bevis, stay with me in Ermony; I have no heir
but Josian, and when you both are grown I will give her
you to wife, and you shall rule the country after me; only
forsake the God of Christendom and bow before my lord
Apollyon.' Then Bevis answered stoutly, 'Neither for
gold nor silver, nor even for sweet Josian's love, will I
forsake Christ that bought my soul so dear.' But Ermyn,
himself a bold king, liked Bevis none the less for his
steadfastness, so instead of flying into a rage he made
the lad his chamberlain, and promised in due time to
dub him knight.

One day, as Bevis rode out with fifteen Saracens, they
began to rebuke him for taking pleasure on a day kept
holy by the Christians, it being Christmas Day. But
Bevis answered that dwelling for ten years among the heathen he had lost all count of time, and knew not what day
it was. Then they reviled both him and his holy faith,
whereon Bevis told them angrily that if he were but a
knight and had a sword and lance he would just with their
whole company one by one for the honour of his God. At
this the Saracens set on him all at once, pricking him with
their swords, now here, now there, in savage sport as men
bait a bull, till Bevis, smarting with the torment of his
many wounds, rushed on them in a fury, and breaking

a sword from out the first man's hand, struck down the Saracens to right and left, cleaving some in their saddles, beheading some, and running others through hauberk and shirt of mail to the heart, until he found himself alone beside a heap of slain ; and fifteen stray horses ran riderless back to their stables. Then Bevis rode home in great pain from his wounds and gat him to his chamber, where he lay down and swooned.

When King Ermyn heard of the slaughter of his knights he was very angry, and swore that Bevis should pay for it with his life. But Josian spake up for him, and prayed her father first to hear what Bevis had to say for himself. So Josian sent two knights to Bevis saying, 'Come to the palace and fear nothing, for I will make thy peace with the king.' Yet Bevis would not rise to speak with the knights. 'Away!' said he, 'you heathen dogs, before I slay you as I did your brother hounds ; and tell your pagan mistress I have no message for her save that she is a heatheness and accursed of God and Christian men.' Howbeit Josian meekly received this hard message, saying only to the knights, 'Go back again and take me with you.' So she came to Bevis in his chamber and lifting up his head into her lap, kissed him on the lips and forehead, speaking gentle words; and so comforted and solaced him that all his care fled away. Then with ointments which she brought she anointed his wounds so that the blood staunched and the pain left them, and afterward she brought him with her to King Ermyn. There in the court Bevis showed the wounds he had received, and told how the affray began ; whereon King Ermyn prayed Josian to prepare the best chamber in the palace, and to nurse and tend him till he was well, for he said, 'I had rather lose all my treasure than such a doughty knight.' Now Josian being a skilful leech and cunning in herbs and physic, Bevis soon got well of his wounds, and became eager for some fresh battle.

In the king's forest was a great wild boar, so terrible and strong he tore both men and dogs to pieces, and had slain many knights. But Bevis went against him with a spear and sword, and got the mastery of the flinty-hided swine, and cut off his head. He finished this battle about the time of evensong; then blowing on his horn the tokening, he walked back through the wood alone, bearing the boar's head aloft on the broken truncheon of his spear; but his sword he left in the swine's carcase. Now King Ermyn's steward, being jealous of his favour with the king, lay in wait for Bevis in the wood, with four and twenty knights and ten foresters, for he thought that if he should now kill Bevis his death would be accounted to the boar. But Bevis fought with his truncheon and the boar's head for shield, and quickly beat down the steward, whom he dragged from his horse and so gat his sword, the trustiest that ever man yet bare—its name, Morglay. And not one could stand against Bevis and Morglay, nor did he give them time to flee but slew them there, all four-and-thirty men. And Josian from her tower afar off saw the mighty deeds which Bevis did.

Three years after came King Brademond the Saracen with a great army to demand Josian in marriage, having heard the fame of her beauty. King Ermyn was in a great strait how to defend himself, for his army was much smaller than Brademond's. But Josian told how Bevis single-handed slew the thirty-four men that came against him in the wood, and said, 'Make him a knight, that he may be my champion to defend my cause against King Brademond, for I wish no better man; and fear you not the number of the Saracen host, for Bevis is an army in himself.' So King Ermyn made Bevis kneel, and having dubbed him knight, appointed him to bear his banner into battle. Then the king gave him a shield, blazoned with three eagles azure and five silver sables on a golden field. Josian embroidered him the banner he should bear, and gave him also a hauberk of rare and curious work, worth many a town, and for a steed she gave him Arundel, the best and most faithful horse in all the world. With her own fair hands she armoured him and girt his good sword Morglay at his side. So he rode forth to lead King Ermyn's little host of five-and-forty-thousand men to battle.

Then as Brademond came against him, with a giant for his standard-bearer called Redesoun leading the way, Sir Bevis smote Arundel with his golden spurs, and riding out before all the army, came down upon this grimly giant like a whirlwind, drave his spear through shield, hauberk, and mail, and smote his great carcase dead to earth. Then the armies closed. King Ermyn's knights did valiantly, but Bevis slew more than all the rest together, for the Saracens went down before his sword Morglay like grass before the scythe—so that by nightfall there was cause of mourning at Damascus for three-score-thousand men that never would return. As for Brademond, him Bevis overthrew, but spared his life on his promise to do homage every year to King Ermyn and pay him tribute; so gathering the remnant of his host together, the Saracen king went home again, too thankful to carry back his life to sadden after Josian any more.

Then Sir Bevis returned victorious to the palace of King Ermyn, who straightway commanded Josian to disarm her knight, clothe him in a rich robe, and wait on him herself at table. So they made a great feast, and the king set Sir Bevis on high above all the lords of his court. And afterward, as Josian sat by Bevis on a bench, he moody and silent, she said: 'Hast thou not a word for me, Bevis? I have been very patient. I have waited for thy love till I am heart-sick, and I needs must speak. Not one little word? O! Bevis, if thou lov'st me not I needs must die: my heart will parch and wither in the drought like flowers that die for rain.' But he, though loving her as his life, yet feared to mate with one that served Mahound. 'Nay, Josian,' he answered bitterly, the while he rocked himself for very trouble of heart, 'nay, I have nought to speak. You have many wealthy suitors of your faith—there is Brademond. For me, I shall not wed.' 'O love,' cried Josian, 'I had rather have thee to my spouse though thou wert poor and evil spoken of by all mankind, than take a mate, less rich to me, who called the world his own. Sure thou dost love me, Bevis?' But he locked his hands together on his knees, and, without looking at her, said, ''Fore God I cannot love thee, Josian.' Then in sore distress she fell down at his feet and wept bitterly; but presently she stood up with scorn and anger in her tearful eyes: 'Go, you unmannered churl,' she said, 'go dig the ground and clip the hedges as a churl should do. I was a fool to waste my love on such as you, while princes, emperors, and kings would gladly bend to call me theirs. Despised, disdained of a churl, a common low-born churl!' 'Lady,' said Bevis, very cold and quiet, 'I am no churl! My father was both earl and knight of Britain, and Knight of Britain is a nobler rank than king of a few paltry heathen here in Ermony. I will go to my country. There is the horse you gave me, take it back; and your tawdry banner. I will have nothing that is yours. A churl! a churl!' So he rose and left her, that word rankling in his mind, and rode off into the town.

But when he was gone, Josian repented bitterly of having so becalled the fairest knight in all the land, and she sent Boniface, her own chamberlain, to hasten after him with this message;—Josian says, 'I am to blame, and I repent me sore of all I said, and humbly pray a word of kindness from my lord.'

But Bevis, fuming yet within his chamber, only said, 'There is no answer, tell your lady. Yet you may say the churl has paid you wages for your errand;' and he gave Boniface a mantle of white samite, gold-broidered; a present worthy of a king.

Thereupon Josian, very sad at heart, came herself to Bevis, and entered the chamber where he lay feigning to sleep, and fell upon his neck, and kissed him, saying, 'O love, I come myself to make my peace, for I am all to blame. But speak a word to me.' Then he said, 'I am weary, let me lie, but go thou home.' 'Nay,' answered Josian, 'not until thou dost forgive me,' and she wept upon his breast. 'Bevis, for thee will I forsake my gods, and take thy God for mine, and thee for ever for my lord, so I may only follow thee throughout the world.' Then said Bevis, 'Now I can love thee without stint, dear Josian;' and he kissed her tenderly. So she departed with a blithe and happy heart.

There were two knights whom Bevis had rescued from beneath Brademond's sword in the battle, and these dwelt with him in the house, his guests; but they were envious of him and of his favour with the king, even as saith the old saw, 'Deliver a thief from the gallows, and he will never rest till he has hanged thee thereon.' So these two thankless fellows went privily to King Ermyn, and falsely swore that Sir Bevis had been guilty of foul wrong against his daughter Josian, when she visited him in his chamber; and cunningly prayed him to keep the matter secret for Josian's sake and her fair fame. King Ermyn was very wroth and very sad, yet said he, 'I cannot spill this traitor's blood myself, since he saved my life and lands and child from Brademond.' Then the two knights counselled him to write a letter to his vassal Brademond at Damascus, bidding him avenge the fault, which he would gladly do as the conquered rival of Sir Bevis, and to send the letter by the hand of Bevis himself. Wherefore the king sent for Bevis, and gave him a sealed letter to King Brademond, charging the knight on no account to break

the seal or give the missive into other hands than
Brademond's. Neither would he let him take his good
horse Arundel nor his sword Morglay, saying that it befitted
not a peaceful messenger to go upon his errand like a
warrior. So Bevis rode off upon a common hack, unarmed, and all unknowing that he bare in his breast a
letter warranting his death.

Now as he drew nigh Damascus, a palmer that sat
beneath a tamarisk tree asked Bevis to partake his meal,
and Bevis, nothing loth, consented, little witting that
this palmer was no other than Saber's own son Terry,
whom Saber had sent out to travel through all lands and
find what had become of Bevis. After their meal the
men began to talk. Terry told who he was, and how
he sought a knight named Bevis who was sold among
the Paynim when a child. 'For,' said he, 'my father
Saber dwells now in a castle in the Isle of Wight, and
every year claims this boy's heritage from Divoun, and
fain would find Bevis to help him gain his earldom
from the usurper.'

But while Bevis mused whether he should reveal
himself or no, the palmer espied the silken strings
of a letter in Bevis's breast. 'Come,' said he, 'let me
read your tidings, for I am a clerk, and many a man
ere now has carried his own death-warrant for want of
clerkship.' 'Aye,' Bevis answered, 'I was warned of
this, lest any man should ask to read the message
which I bear. But I have sworn that none save he
to whom it is written shall break the seal, and I will
answer for my promise with my life. As for this Bevis
of whom you speak, I knew him some time since; he went
among the Saracens and I rather think they hanged him
to a tree, for he has not come back. It is vain to seek
him further, for being his friend I certainly should have
heard of him were he alive.' Then Terry returned to his
father in the Isle of Wight, and told him that Bevis must

have died among the Paynim; and Saber mourned much at the tidings.

When Bevis came into Damascus to King Bradcmond's palace, he was well nigh dazzled with its splendour. The doors and pillars were of shining brass, and many burnished pinnacles and minarets pierced the blue sky. The windows were of bronze and set with glass, the halls inlaid with gold and carven work. There was a deep moat round the palace, and a broad high bridge across the ditch with sixty bells which rang whenever man or beast passed across, and by the bridge end, a gold and azure tower whereon a golden eagle with big jewelled eyes gleamed and sparkled night and day. So Bevis came into the palace where Bradcmond sat at a banquet with twenty kings, and gave the letter into his hands, charging him strnitly to obey King Ermyn's commands. When Brademond had read it, he said to the kings which sate at meat with him, 'This is Sir Bevis who made me vassal to his master; rise up therefore and greet him as is seemly.' And when they had arisen, Bradcmond took Bevis by both hands as though to welcome him, but in truth to hold him fast so that he should not draw his sword, and then cried to the kings, 'Quick, fall on him, and get him down.' So before Bevis knew of their treachery, they bore him to the pavement, and having bound him fast they cast him into a loathesome dungeon deep down underground, and full of noisome reptiles. There they loaded him with chains, and gave him bread and water for food. The snakes and serpents would soon have been his death, but that he found a broken staff in his dungeon, wherewith, chained as he was, he slew them. For seven years Bevis remained a captive in this dark and dreadful prison-house, till his beard grew to his feet, and he lost the look of human kind.

Meanwhile, Josian, who mourned the sudden departure of her lover from Ermony, was told by her father that

Bevis had returned to England to marry a wife of great
estate. Yet did this true maid refuse to believe that Bevis
had forsaken her, being sure in her mind that some secret
treason was at work to keep him from her. Then came
Ynor, King of Mombraunt, to seek her hand in marriage,
and her father urged his suit; but Josian hated Ynor,
loving Bevis only in her heart. Nevertheless, after two
years' delay, King Ermyn insisted that she should wed at
once with Ynor, and her tears and prayers being of no avail,
she was married to him, and the wedding feast was held in
Ermyn's palace. Now Josian had a ring of curious make
(her mother gave it to her, and she got it from Merlin),
and in this ring was a certain stone of such rare virtue
that no man might have power upon the maid which
wore it, save she willed. King Ynor rode off with his
bride to Mombraunt, and men led Arundel beside him by
the bridle-rein. But as he drew near home, Ynor
thought to mount this horse and ride him in sight of
Josian. No sooner did Arundel find a strange rider on
his back instead of his own dear master, than he shook
himself and tossed his head, and with a sudden quiver at
his flanks, set off, swift as the wind, past city, over plain,
through wood and field and river, over dyke and fence,
and at the last threw Ynor down, and trampled the
life near out of him, so that for a whole year thereafter
Ynor lay sick and like to die. But Arundel with a
mighty neigh of triumph cantered off to his stable at
Mombraunt, where for five full years no man dared approach him, he was so fierce, and they had to lower his
corn and water down by a rope from overhead.

Now after seven years, Sir Bevis in his dungeon on a
day thus made his prayer aloud: 'O Heavenly King,
which dwellest in the light, have pity on me buried here
in this dark hole beneath the ground, knowing not night
from day, and bring me out to see Thy sunshine once
again, else shorten suddenly my days and let me die.'

His jailors hearing him complain, bade him be quiet, for it was night, and they would sleep; and when he would not, but so much the more called out upon his God, one of them let himself down by a rope into the dungeon with a lamp and sword, and sought to strike him. But Bevis lifted his two chained hands and at one blow brake the man's skull. Then he cried to the jailor's fellow above, 'Come down quickly, for this man has a fit here with the foul air.' So the other came down by the rope, and Bevis slew him also. His jailors being dead, he had no longer any food, and so for three days could do nothing but cry mightily to God: and on the third day, Jesus of his mercy brake his fetters and he stood up free, and joyfully gave thanks. Then climbing by the rope whereby the jailors had come down, Bevis reached the surface of the earth at midnight. He went into the castle, and the knights that guarded it being fast asleep, he took a spear and sword and coat of mail, then chose the best horse in the castle stable, saddled him and rode out to the castle gate. 'Awake!' he cried, to the porter, 'down with the drawbridge quickly, for Bevis has escaped and I am sent to take him.' So the sleepy porter let him pass, and Bevis rode five miles across the plain, till, stiff and sore with long captivity, he lay down on the grass to rest.

Early in the morning Bevis was missed at Damascus, and a great host of knights went out to search for him. Foremost of all came Sir Grander on a very fleet and famous horse called Trinchesis, for which he had paid its weight in silver. He far outrode the others and came upon Sir Bevis alone. But after a long battle Bevis, weak though he was with his long fasting, overcame Sir Grander and having cut off his head, leaped upon Trinchesis just as the rest of the Saracen knights came within sight, and rode until he came down to a rocky strand and saw the wild sea breaking on the beach. There, at his wit's end, with the sea before him and an army of pursuers behind, Sir Bevis lifted up his heart to Christ. 'O most sweet Jesu, Shepherd of the earth, within whose fold are all Thy works, it is a little thing for Thee, who makest creatures go upon the air and in the sea with wings and fins, to help me now.' So saying he leapt his horse into the brine and the waves upbore him bravely, and Trinchesis swam the whole day and half the night, and at length brought Bevis safe to land.

Almost starved with hunger Bevis went straight to the first castle he saw to ask a meal. But a giant lived there, brother to Sir Grauder, who seeing a knight ride on his brother's steed Trinchesis, at once did battle with him, wounding Bevis on the shoulder with a javelin and killing Trinchesis with his club. Howbeit Sir Bevis brought the giant to his knees and smote his sword into his neck. Then, entering the castle, he appeased his hunger with a plentiful banquet which was in waiting for the dead giant, and having taken a horse from the giant's stable, rode off refreshed and strengthened. He soon met a knight from Ermony who told him all that had befallen Josian, how she was King Ynor's wife and Queen of Mombraunt, and how Arundel had served King Ynor. 'Would to God,' said Bevis, 'that Josian were as true to me as Arundel!' and so rode off to Mombraunt.

On his way, meeting a palmer he changed clothes with him, and gave the palmer his horse, thinking in this disguise more certainly to learn about Josian. There were many palmers about King Ynor's castle-gate, and Bevis being dressed as one of them, with scrip and wallet by his side and a crucifix at his girdle, asked what they did. They answered: 'The queen is good to palmers and gives them audience and entertainment every day at noon, if peradventure she may learn tidings of a good knight called Sir Bevis of South Hamtoun by the Sea.'

It was yet early in the day, and the king was gone a

hunting; and as Bevis walked about the castle barbican he heard from a turret above the sound of weeping and complaint: 'O Bevis, dearly loved Knight of Hamtoun, how long must I pine before I hear of thee, only a little message or a word! Is thy God harder than Mahound, or can it be that thou art false, and must I die bewailing thee, my love?' When the queen came to the gate to talk with the palmers, Bevis waited till the last, and after the others were gone away the queen said, 'Palmer, in all your wanderings have you heard any speak of Bevis, a bold true knight who came from Hamtoun?' 'Yes,' answered Bevis, 'I have heard of him; in sooth I know him well. He had a good and faithful horse named Arundel, but lost it seven years since and sent me to travel and seek it. I am told you have it in your stable. Let me see the steed.' Josian marvelled much as she looked at the palmer, but did not know that it was Sir Bevis; so she called Boniface her chamberlain and took the palmer to the stable where Arundel was. But no sooner did Arundel hear his master's voice than he knew instantly who it was, and broke the seven-fold chain that bound him, tore down the stable with his hoofs, and leaping into the courtyard came and arched his neck in pride beneath his master's hand and neighed for very joy. Then he stood still, nor moved a foot while Bevis saddled him and bridled him and mounted on his back. Then Josian knew also that it was Sir Bevis, and wept for joy, crying, 'Take not thy horse alone, dear knight, but take thy true and faithful love.' Bevis answered, 'Thou hast been five years a queen, and it is not fit that a Christian knight should take for wife any but an unwed maiden.' But Josian said, 'Love, take me with thee. Ask of all my maids, who have not left me since my marriage-day, if ever I was wife to Ynor save in name. If it be not so, brand me with falsehood and turn me out upon the waste to die.'

Just then Boniface warned Sir Bevis that King Ynor

was come back from hunting with a great retinue. So Boniface made Sir Bevis lead Arundel back to the stable and then go and place himself again at the castle gate in his palmer's weeds to wait for the king, and Boniface told him what to say.

So when the king, riding up to his gate, saw a palmer there, he asked what tidings there might be from foreign countries. Then said the palmer, 'I have travelled far in Tyre and Egypt and in Sicily, and been through many lands. And there is peace on all hands, sire, save where Syrak wars with Bradwin King of Dabilent and presses him hard within his last redoubt, a castle on a cliff, the which he cannot hold for many days.'

'Bradwin King of Dabilent is my own brother,' said Ynor, 'and I must go and succour him.' So he gathered together his army and his knights and straightway set off for Dabilent.

As soon as the king was fairly gone, Bevis threw off his palmer's dress, and having armed himself in mail and girded Morglay once more at his side, mounted his good steed Arundel and set off at night with Josian on her palfrey, Boniface also going with them, to make the best speed they could out of Mombraunt. And by journeying through forests and by-ways they managed to avoid pursuit, until, nightfall coming on, the queen took refuge in a rocky cave with Boniface for her protector, whilst Bevis went in search of food. But this cave was a lion's den, and soon the lions came home and quickly overmatched Boniface, whom they struck down, tore to pieces, and devoured. Yet after this the lions came to Josian and laid their heads down in her lap; for there is no ravenous beast will harm a maiden. Thus when Sir Bevis returned with some venison and saw the lions nestled against Josian he knew that she had spoken truth and had been true to him, and this made him so glad and valiant that he set upon the lions and cut off both their heads at one stroke of his sword Morglay, and so avenged the death of Boniface.

Next morning as they went on their way they fell in with a huge and mighty giant thirty feet in height, whose countenance was fierce and terrible. His eyebrows were a foot apart, his lips hung like a mastiff's from his great grim mouth, his body was bristled like a boar's, and he bare for a club the knotty trunk of an oak-tree. And this giant said his name was Ascapard, and that he came out from Mombraunt to bring back Josian.

Then Sir Bevis dressed his shield and rode furiously against the giant, and being more agile and nimble in his strokes wounded him many times and yet avoided all the giant's blows. And as Sir Bevis galloped by after driving his lance to the head in Ascapard's shoulder, the giant turned after him in the retreat with such a swinging stroke of his club, that, missing his aim, he was brought to ground with the force of it;—so Bevis leaped off his horse and was about to cut off the giant's head, when Josian interceded for him, saying, 'Spare his life, dear lord Sir Bevis—for since Boniface is dead we have no page; take him therefore for your squire and I will be bond for his faithfulness.' Then Ascapard sware homage and fealty to Bevis and Josian and became their squire.

Presently the three came to the sea-coast where was a vessel full of Saracens who refused to take Bevis on board. But Ascapard waded into the water, and having turned them all out of the ship, carried Bevis and Josian on board on their horses, one under each arm, and then drew up the heavy sail and steered the great paddle with one hand till he brought them safely to the harbour of Cologne. There Bevis found out Bishop Florentine, brother to Saber in the Isle of Wight, who made great joy at his arrival, and christened Josian at her wish in holy church. The good man would have christened Ascapard likewise and had a wine tun brought on purpose, but the giant leaped out again, saying it was only deep enough to christen half of him, and that he was of too ungodly size ever to make a Christian.

Now there was in a forest near Cologne a foul and fearsome dragon which killed much people. Whole companies of men that went against him were destroyed by the venom which this monster sweltered forth, so that it was said none but Saint Michael himself could contend against him. His front was hard as steel, eight tusks stood out from his mouth and he was maned like a steed. He was four-and-twenty feet from his shoulder to his tail, and his tail was sixteen feet long. His body was covered with scales hard as adamant, and his wings glistened like glass. The way in which the dragon came to Cologne was on this wise. Two kings fought in Cola and Calabria four-and-twenty years, and laid all the country waste, so that neither corn nor reapers were left in the land; nor would they ever make peace between themselves. And when these died in mortal sin they were still such fierce enemies that the Devil feared to have them in the fiery pit; so they became two fearful dragons which still ravaged Cola and Calabria till a holy hermit prayed both day and night to Christ to drive the dragons out and give the people peace. Then the dragons took their flight. One fled to Rome, but waxing sick and helpless, as he hovered over the city, from the prayers which go up thence, fell into the river, where he still abides. The other fled through Tuscany and Provence to Cologne.

Then Sir Bevis determining to rid the country of this dreadful pest, Ascapard said he would gladly go too, and all the way spake of what he would do to the dragon with his club so soon as they should hap upon him. Yet no sooner did this great giant hear the dragon roar like thunder in his den than he trembled and shook, and ran away as fast as he could into Cologne. But Bevis, with lion-like courage, rode against the dragon alone. All day long and through the night the champion fought, and oftentimes the dragon got him down, lashed him with his tail, and spouted rankling venom on him, or with his claws tare the good knight's shield and brake his armour. Bevis would have died from the poison of his wounds, but by good fortune there was hard by a Holy Well, blessed by a wandering virgin saint for cure of mortal sickness. Therein the dragon hurled him with a blow of his tail, so Bevis was made whole, and drinking of the water was refreshed, and assailed the dragon with such new vigour that he made the monster flee. But Bevis followed him and hacked his tail till the dragon turned on him again, and then he cut the apple of his throat in twain, whereon the dragon lay upon his side roaring mightily till Bevis, with three great strokes of Morglay, smote him to the heart. It took four-score blows and more to cut the dragon's head off. But Sir Bevis carved out the tongue, which was as much as he could carry on the truncheon of his spear, and set off to Cologne, where he found the people all at mass singing his dirge, for since he had been two days gone they gave him up for dead.

After this, Bevis took ship for England to avenge his father's death upon Divoun, Emperor of Almaine. Bishop Florentine gave him a hundred knights to go with him, whilst Josian remained at Cologne in charge of Ascapard. Sir Bevis, having cast anchor within a mile of South Hamtoun, went on shore to Divoun's castle, and gave his name as Sir Gerard, a French knight, saying he had come over with a hundred companions in quest of service. Divoun said that he should be very glad of their service, since he had an enemy named Saber dwelling in a castle in the Isle of Wight, who continually annoyed him by sending to claim the heritage of a young scapegrace named Bevis, an idle spendthrift, whose inheritance he had bought, whilst the good-for-nothing pickthank had squandered the money and gone abroad. Bevis answered that he saw there was good cause for a quarrel, and therefore would willingly undertake it, provided Divoun would furnish his men with horses and armour, victual his ship, and send a hundred knights to go with him. 'Indeed,' said Bevis, 'we will promise not to lose sight of Saber till we have settled your quarrel.' Divoun readily agreed to these terms.

Now the ship being stored with provisions, and the horses and armour taken on board, Divoun's hundred knights set off to embark with Bevis and his company, going two and two, one of Bevis's men with one of Divoun's. But when they reached the ship's side each one of Bevis's men took his fellow and cast him overboard. Then they sailed off merrily with their shipload of the enemy's goods to Saber in the Wight. Saber welcomed Bevis with right goodwill, and at once began to prepare for battle. But Bevis sent a knight to Divoun with this message, 'I, that called myself Gerard, am no French knight, but Sir Bevis, Earl of South Hamtoun, and I claim my lands and heritage of thee, Divoun, and will wreak my father's murder on thy head.' Divoun was so angry at these words that he snatched the great knife from the banquet table and flung it at the messenger— him it passed by, but it smote Divoun's only son through the body that he died.

But while these things happened in England, Josian was in sore trouble at Cologne. For a certain earl Sir Milo plotted how he might carry her off, and since he could do nothing against her whilst Ascapard was by, he got a letter writ as though from Bevis, charging Ascapard to come quickly to his help, whereby the giant was beguiled to accompany some false messengers to a castle on an island far away, where they locked him in and left him. Then Sir Milo with a band of knights carried Josian off to his fortress, yet not before she had secretly sent a messenger to Sir Bevis to come to her aid. Howbeit, no sooner was Josian alone in a chamber with Sir Milo than she bespake him gently, and lulled him on her lap the while she made a slip-knot in her girdle. Therewith she strangled him and hanged him to the curtain rail. But Milo's knights, when late next day they found that the earl did not arise, brake down the chamber door, and seeing what was done, dragged Josian off into the market-place, tied her to a stake, and heaping faggots round about made a great fire, while she could only weep and pray in wanhope of ever seeing her dear lord again. But suddenly came galloping up on Arundel that good knight Sir Bevis. Right blithely Arundel leapt through the fire, while Bevis cut the bonds that fastened his dear wife, and set her free. Then turning on the multitude in a fury that was terrible, Sir Bevis hewed them down with Morglay as a woodcutter lops the green wood, whilst Ascapard, having broken out from the castle and swum to shore, came striding up in the midst of the fray, and he with his club and Bevis with his sword swept all the marketplace till not another man remained to be slain. Then Bevis sailed again for Wight with Ascapard and Josian.

The Emperor of Almaine came and besieged Saber and Bevis in their castle in the Wight, his wife's father, the King of Scotland, also bringing his host to help him, with catapults and mangonels and arbalests. And when the stones and iron darts of these great engines shook the castle walls and bid fair to make a breach, Saber said to Bevis, 'We will divide our knights into companies, and make three sallies. I will head the first, you lead the second, and Ascapard shall bring out the third. Truly this host at present is too big to be fought with until we thin them down to fairer odds.'

Then Saber rode out and bore down first Sir Maurice of Mountclere, and afterward made great havoc of the enemy, for despite his age and his white hairs he was a brave and valiant man. Next, Bevis with his company came forth, but he would fight with none save Divoun, and cutting his way to where he was he bore him from his horse with a mighty shock, and would have smitten off his head with Morglay; but the host, ten thousand strong, closed round him, and having dragged the emperor from beneath his hand, beset him and his knights so furiously they were hard put to it for their lives. But Ascapard, with his ragly club, came beating down horse and man on all sides, and so cleared a passage for his company through the host to come and rescue Bevis, and there was no armour that could stand against Ascapard's great tree-trunk. He smote the King of Scotland dead at a blow, and this was the only time he killed but one man at a stroke, for he swung his club round in a sweep full sixty feet and mowed down everything within it, knight and steed alike. Then Bevis said to his squire: 'Mark well the Emperor Divoun,—him that rides yonder on the white horse. Take him alive and I shall well reward you.' Thereupon Ascapard strode through the host, and lifting Divoun out from his saddle carried him bodily into the castle. Meantime Sir Bevis and Saber fought the discomfited host till they scarce left a soul alive to tell the tale of that defeat. After this they returned to the castle and threw Divoun into a cauldron of boiling pitch and brimstone; and Divoun's wife, hearing of her husband's shameful death, cast herself down headlong from her castle tower and brake her neck.

Then Sir Bevis went to Hamtoun and took possession of his heritage, and made a great feast in Hamtoun Castle, whereat all the lords of the shire came and did him homage as the rightful Earl of Hamtoun, their true ruler. And from that time he displayed upon his shield the three roses of Hamtoun in place of the five silver sables. After this Sir Bevis went to London to King Edgar and paid his fealty. And Edgar made him marshal of his army. And about Whitsuntide when a great race was run before the king for a thousand pieces of gold, Sir Bevis came on Arundel, late to the course, long after the rest had started ; but he shook the bridle loose, saying, ' Speed thee, Arundel, and win the prize, and I will rear a lordly castle to thy praise,' and Arundel, for his master's sake, urged to the utmost, put forth all his strength, and sped past all the rest and won the race. With the treasure Bevis, in honour of his noble steed, built Arundel Castle, which stands unto this day. But the king's son coveted the horse, and after vainly teasing Bevis to give it him, came one night to the stable where Arundel was, to steal him away; but Arundel with one hind hoof dashed out his brains. Wherefore, for this, King Edgar would have had the horse slain, only Sir Bevis, rather than lose his faithful steed, chose to leave the country; so having made Terry, Saber's son, his squire, he again took ship with Josian and sailed for Ermony.

Now Ascapard was a poor man and gat but little reward of Bevis. He was also jealous that Terry should be made squire in his stead. Wherefore when Bevis was gone he set off to King Ynor at Mombraunt, and said, ' Make me a prince and ruler in your country, and I will slay Bevis and deliver Josian into your hand.' Ynor, very glad to think of getting back his queen again, agreed joyfully, and gave him forty knights clad in iron mail ; for the giant said plainly that he would not undertake the matter by himself.

Now Sir Bevis and Terry rode with Josian through a lonely forest in Normandy; and in this forest, while they were gone for a little while, she gave birth to two boys, and almost directly afterwards Ascapard and his forty Saracens came and carried her off. Bevis on his return was so much overcome by grief when he could not find his wife, that he swooned away. On his recovery he took the two babes, and dividing with his sword Josian's ermine mantle whereon they lay, wrapped them in it, and rode on till he met a forester, to whom he gave ten marks to bring up one of the children and call it Guy. Shortly meeting a fisher, he gave him the other child and ten marks, after christening the boy Miles over against the church stile, before the handle of his sword for crucifix.

But Josian was carried off to King Ynor, who, when he saw her, marvelled greatly, saying, 'This is not Josian that was my queen'—for she had eaten secretly of a certain herb whereby her countenance was changed into loathliness. So he said, 'Take her away, for I cannot abide so foul a visaged dame.' And he made Ascapard take her to a castle on a plain five miles away, where Josian dwelt for half-a-year alone with Ascapard for warder.

Now Saber had a dream in his castle in the Wight. He dreamed he saw Sir Bevis wounded to the heart, and waking, asked his wife to read the dream. Then said she, 'How should Sir Bevis seem stricken to the heart save he had lost his wife or child?' Saber therefore chose twelve trusty and valiant men, and having armed them well in mail of proof and clad them over all in palmer's weeds, took ship and sailed through the Greek Sea till he came by good fortune to the very land where Josian was held in captivity by Ascapard. And the lady looked out from her tower and besought his help. So Saber called the giant out to fight. Now Saber and his men, having seen Ascapard in battle, knew well how to assail him. So they ran close in upon the giant where he could not use his club upon them, and hewed off his feet until they brought him down and slew him with their swords. Nevertheless Ascapard, after he was on the ground, slew all the men that went with Saber, so that he alone escaped. Thus Saber brought Josian out of her captivity in the castle, and she made a cunning ointment which brought back her beauty, and having dressed herself in poor attire, set out on foot with Saber to seek Bevis. But Saber, being old, fell sick in Greece, and for a year lay ill upon his bed, whilst Josian tended him and earned the food for both by singing and playing on a cittern, for she was skilled in minstrelsy.

Sir Bevis meantime came to a country where a great tournament was held for the hand of a princess, the king's daughter, and this he won for knighthood's sake, and after him Terry was the most valiant knight. But the princess fell in love with Bevis, until, hearing he was already wed, she prayed him to be her bachelor for seven years, then if his wife returned she would wed Terry; if not, she would take Bevis for her husband. So Bevis dwelt in a castle in that country and fought the battles of the king, and Terry was made steward of the realm.

After seven years' wanderings Saber and Josian came into the land where Bevis was; and footsore and weary Saber left her at an inn while he went to the castle to beg a bit of bread. Terry came down to the castle gate but did not know his father in his beggar's dress, all travel-worn, and very greatly aged by sickness. But Saber knew his son. 'Good steward,' said he, 'for love of the dear Rood, give me a little piece of bread.' 'Aye, palmer,' answered Terry, 'that I will, for my dear father's sake, who may be wandering as you are now. I know not where he is. Pray God be kind to him.' 'Son,' Saber said, 'thy father it is that blesses thee. Son Terry, my dear son.' Then Terry knew him, and reverently kissed his long white beard, and brought him in and served him joyfully and humbly at the table. As for Josian, she was clothed in fair apparel, and brought to Sir Bevis decked as a queen; nor were ever lovers more glad to be wed than were these two to meet again. And while they smiled and wept for joy together, the fisher and the forester came in and brought her children, hale, comely boys, who rode in mimic justs to show their mother how strong they were.

So the princess, the lady of the tournament which Bevis won, wedded with Terry. And all made great joy, for it would be hard to say which was the happier, Terry with his fair new bride and his father restored to him, or Bevis at finding his dearly-loved Josian again; yet do they say, that love grows riper after age and storm, like old wine that has passed the seas.

Soon afterwards Sir Bevis went with his retinue of knights to Ermony. King Ynor, hearing this, gathered together the greatest army he could muster, and came against him to demand Josian his queen. But after a parley they agreed to determine the matter by single combat, the victor to be king both of Ermony and Mombraunt.

They fought on an island in view of both armies, where none could interfere. From prime till undern the air resounded with the ringing of their armour and the clashing of their swords. At high noon Ynor hewed off crest and circle and the visor bars from Sir Bevis's helmet; furious whereat Sir Bevis cleft King Ynor's shoulder half a foot through mail and breast-plate, forcing him to ground upon his knee; then, mad to see his blood upon the sword blade of his enemy, Ynor started up, and rushing on Bevis like a lion, clave his shield in two and raised his right arm for a fearful stroke which Bevis, shieldless, could not ward; but he, wielding Morglay in both hands, lopped off the arm before it could deal the blow, so it fell helpless to the earth, with fingers still clenched on the weapon. Then Bevis threw him to the ground, unlaced the Paynim's helm and smote his head off. The Saracens, seeing their champion fallen, took flight; but Bevis, with his sons Sir Miles and Guy, and Saber and Terry with King Ermyn's army, pursued and slew great numbers in the way, until they came to Mombraunt. There Sir Bevis was crowned king and Josian for the second time made queen of that city.

But there came messengers from England with tidings how King Edgar had taken the estates both of Bevis and Saber, and bestowed them on Sir Bryant of Cornwall, his steward. Wherefore, Bevis sailed for Hamtoun with a great array of knights and men-at-arms, and marched to Potenhithe, where he encamped. Then with twelve knights he came to the king at Westminster and asked that his estates might be restored. King Edgar, who dreaded nothing so much as war, consented; so Bevis went away with his knights to a tavern in London City to refresh himself. Yet no sooner was he gone than the steward, to whom the lands and castles had been given, reminded the king how Bevis was an outlaw, and how his horse Arundel had killed the prince. So it befell that proclamation was made in London to close the city gates, and stretch chains across all narrow streets, while all good citizens were called upon to arm themselves and take the outlaw alive or dead.

Now when Sir Bevis in the tavern found himself beset, he armed himself, girt on Morglay, and having mounted Arundel, rode out with his knights into the crowd, and first seeing Sir Bryant the king's steward urging on the people, he spurred against him, and with his lance bore down the backbiter dead upon the roadway. But the street was narrow, and Bevis, being beleaguered by a very great armed multitude, turned his horse down God's Lane, thinking to come out in Chepe, where he would have more space to fight. Now this lane was so narrow that he could not turn his horse therein, and when he came down to the end he found huge chains across which barred his way, whilst all the crowd swarmed in and quickly chained up the other end, so there was no escape. Thus were they caught in a trap, and the people with their swords, and stones, and bludgeons, slew all his twelve knights; and Bevis was hard put to it to hold his life but for a short space longer, since he could not turn, nor scarcely swing his sword within that narrow lane. Almost despairing, he prayed Christ to bring him out of this great peril so he might see his wife and children once again. Then with Morglay he smote the chains and they fell in pieces on the pavement, so he came out in Chepe, the people shouting after him, 'Yield thee, Sir Bevis, yield thee, for we shall quickly have thee down.' But he answered proudly, 'Yea, I yield to God that sits above in Trinity, but to none else.'

New crowds poured into Chepe on all hands, and with pikes and javelins assailed this valiant knight through half the day; yet none could take him, for Arundel fought with a leal heart, and cleared the ground for forty foot to front and rear with his hoofs, the while his master cut down men on either hand far quicker than a parson and his clerk could shrive. By eventide he slew five thousand of the folk, until his arm waxed weary and he faint for need of food and parched with thirst. Then came a Lombard with a heavy mansel and smote him on the helm a blow that nearly stunned him, so that Sir Bevis leaned forward on his saddle-bow and seemed like to fall. Just then a cry was made, for lo, Sir Guy and Sir Miles with all their army, having burned the city gates, came riding into Chepe. Sir Guy cut down the Lombard, whilst Sir Bevis, gaining fresh nerve and vigour from this welcome succour, turned again and headed his army in battle against the Londoners, fighting far on into the night, until the Thames ran red with blood past Westminster, and sixty thousand Londoners were slain. Thus Sir Bevis took the city, and brought Josian to the Leden Hall, where they held feasting fourteen nights, keeping open court for all folk that would come.

Then King Edgar, earnestly desiring peace, made a treaty with Sir Bevis, and gave his only daughter to Sir Miles to be his wife; and these were wed at Nottingham amid great rejoicing as at the crowning of a king.

Sir Bevis then gave his earldom of South Hamtoun to Saber, and came by ship with Guy and Terry to Ermony. King Ermyn, being very old and near to death, took the crown from off his head and placed it on Sir Guy's. So leaving his son King of Ermony, Sir Bevis made Terry King of Ambersh, and then returned with Josian his queen to his own kingdom of Mombraunt. There they dwelt together in love for three-and-thirty years, and made all the land Christian.

Now at the last Josian the queen fell sick of a mortal sickness, and knowing her end was near, she sent for Sir Guy to bid him farewell. And while she talked alone with her son, Bevis walked sorrowing about the castle till he came to the stable where Arundel was kept. There going in, he stroked and smoothed his old and faithful steed, and Arundel arched himself for the last time beneath his master's hand, then looked up in his face and fell down dead. Then with a heavy heart Sir Bevis came back again to the chamber where Josian lay a-dying, and falling down beside her, took her in his arms and held her to him till she died; and before her body had grown cold, his soul went to her. So they passed together from the noise of the world and were nevermore divided.

But Sir Guy would not in anywise suffer them to be buried in the earth; wherefore he reared a noble church to Saint Lawrence, and made therein a fair chapel of white marble adorned with heraldry and carven work, all pictured with great deeds of knighthood for the Holy Cross and faithful love of wedded folk. There he made the bier, of marble and of gold, beneath a golden canopy, high-cornered, wrought with curious device, and laid them there: and built withal a house where pious monks sang masses morn and eve for the rest of good Sir Bevis and fair Josian. God's pity on their souls! Aye, and also upon Arundel, if indeed it be not unlawful to pray for a horse more faithful than most men, and truer than most friends.

GUY OF WARWICK.

Of all the nobles of Britain none was so strong as Rohand, Earl of Warwick, Rockingham, and Oxford. He made just laws, and made them be obeyed; nor king nor baron in the land could buy his favour with fine words or gold, or shield the wrong-doer from his punishment. Passing fair was Felice, his daughter, like some stately marble shaft of perfect mould; haughty was she as the great gerfalcon which spurns the earth and towers up into the noon to look the burning sun in the face. Wise masters, hoar with learning, came out from Thoulouse to teach her the seven arts and sciences, until there was not her like for wisdom anywhere.

Earl Rohand had a favourite page, named Guy, son of his just and upright steward, Segard of Wallingford; a brave and fearless youth, of strong and well-knit frame, whom Heraud of Ardenne, his tutor, taught betimes to just with lance and sword, and how to hunt with hawk and hound by wood and river side.

It was the feast of Pentecost, when by old custom every maiden chose her love and every knight his leman. Guy, clad in a new silken dress, being made cup-bearer at the banquet table, saw for the first time the beautiful Felice, as, kneeling, he offered the golden ewer and basin and damask napkin to wash her finger-tips before the banquet. Thenceforward he became so love-stricken with her beauty that he heard not the music of the glee-men, saw neither games nor tourneys, but dured in a dream, liked one crazed, all through the fourteen days festival. Knights and fair dames praised his handsome figure and well-grown sinewy limbs; he heeded not—but once Felice gave him a courteous word as he offered her the wine-cup; he blushed and stammered and spilled the wine, and was rebuked for awkwardness.

The feast being over, Guy went away to his chamber, and there fell into a great love-sickness. Hopeless it seemed for a vassal to love one so far above him as his sovereign's daughter; so he gave himself up to despair, and his disease grew so sore that the most skilful leeches of Earl Rohand's court were unable to cure his complaint. In vain they let him of blood or gave him salve or potion. 'There is no medicine of any avail,' the leeches said. Guy murmured, 'Felice: if one might find and bring Felice to me, I yet might live.' 'Felice?' the leeches said among themselves, and shook their heads, 'it is not in the herbal. Felice? Felix? No, there is no plant of that name.'

'No herb is Felice,' sighing answered Guy, 'but a flower—the fairest flower that grows.'

'He is light-headed,' they said. 'The flower Felice? He seeks perchance the flower of happiness, growing in the garden of the blessed, away in Paradise. He is surely near his end.'

'It is truly Paradise where Felice is,' Guy answered.

'You hear? You see?' the leeches whispered one to another. 'Come, let us go; for we can be of no more good.'

Night came, and being left alone Guy thought to rise up from his bed and drag himself into the presence of his mistress, there to die at her feet. So weak was he become, he scarce could stand, but fainted many times upon the way.

Now Felice had heard many whisperings how Guy was dying for love of her, since her handmaidens had compassion on the youth, and sought to turn her heart towards him; but Felice was in no mind to have a page for a lover. Howbeit on this very night she had a dream, wherein being straitly enjoined to entreat the youth with kindness as the only way to save a life which would hereafter be of great service to the world, she arose and came to a bower in the garden where Guy lay swooning on the floor. Felice would not stoop to help him, but her maids having restored him to his senses, Guy fell at her feet and poured out all his love before her. Never a word answered Felice, but stood calmly regarding him with haughty coldness. Then said one of her maids, 'O lady! were I the richest king's daughter in the land, I could not turn away from love so strong and true.' Felice rebuked her, saying, 'Could not? Silly child, see that your soft heart do not prove your shame.' So with a tingling cheek the maid withdrew abashed. Then said Felice to Guy, 'Why kneel there weeping like a girl? Get up, and show if there is the making of a man in you. Hear what I have to say. The swan mates not with the swallow, and I will never wed beneath me. Prove that your love is not presumption. Show yourself my peer. For I could love a brave and valiant knight before whose spear men bowed as to a king, nor would I ask his parentage, prouder far to know that my children took their nobleness from a self-made nobleman. But a weeping, love-sick page! No! Go, fight and battle—show me something that you do that I can love. Meantime I look for such a lover, and I care not if his name be Guy the page.'

Then Guy took heart and said, 'Lady, I ask no better boon than to have you for witness of what love for you can do.'

Felice answered, 'Deeds, not words. Be strong and valiant. I will watch and I will wait.'

Then Guy took leave of his mistress and in the course of a few days regained his health, to the surprise of all the court, but more especially of the leeches who had given him over for dead, and coming to Earl Rohand, intreated him to make him a knight. To this Earl Roband having agreed, Guy was knighted at the next feast of Holy Trinity with a dubbing worthy a king's son; and they brought him rich armour, and a good sword and spear and shield, and a noble steed with costly trappings, together with rich silken cloaks and mantles fur-trimmed, and of great price. Then bidding farewell to Segard his father, Sir Guy left Warwick with Heraud his tutor, and Sir Thorold and Sir Urry for company, and having reached the nearest seaport, set sail for Normandy in search of adventures wherein to prove his valour.

They came to Rouen, and whilst they tarried at an inn a tournament was proclaimed in honour of the fair Blancheflor, daughter to Regnier, Emperor of Germany, and the prize was the hand of the princess, a white horse, two white hounds, and a white falcon. So Sir Guy and his companions rode into the lists, where was a great company of proven knights and champions. Three days they tourneyed, but none could withstand Sir Guy's strong arm. He overthrew Otho Duke of Pavia, Sir Garie the Emperor's son, Reignier Duke of Sessoyne, the Duke of Lowayne, and many more, till not a man was left who dared encounter him; and being master of the field, he was adjudged the prize. The horse and hounds and falcon he sent by two messengers to Felice in England as trophies of his valour. Then he knelt before the beautiful princess Blancheflor and said, 'Lady, I battle in honour of my mistress, the peerless Felice, and am her servant,' whereat the emperor and his daughter, admiring his constancy, loaded him with rich presents and allowed him to depart.

Sir Guy then travelled through Spain, Lombardy, and Almayne, into far lands; and wheresoever a tournament was held, there he went and justed, coming out victor from them all; till the fame of his exploits spread over Christendom. So a year passed, and he returned to England unconquered, and renowned as the most valiant knight of his time. A while he sojourned in London with King Athelstan, who rejoiced to do him honour: then he came to Warwick, where he received from Earl Rohand a princely welcome. Then Sir Guy hastened to Felice.

'Fair mistress,' said he, 'have I now won your love? You have heard my deeds, how I have travelled all through Christendom, and have yet found no man stand against my spear. I have been faithful in my love, Felice, as well as strong in fight. I might have wedded with the best. Kings' daughters and princesses were prizes in the tournaments; but I had no mind for any prize but thee. Say, is it mine, sweet mistress?'

Then Felice kissed her knight and answered, 'Right nobly have you won my love and worship, brave Sir Guy. You are more than my peer; you are become my sovereign; and my love pays willing homage to its lord. But for this same cause I will not wed you yet. I will not have men point at me and say, "There is a woman who, for selfish love's sake, wedded the knight of most renown in Christendom ere yet he did his bravest deeds—drew him from his level to her own—made him lay by his sword and spear for the slothful pleasures of a wedded life, and dwarfed a brave man down to a soft gentleman.' Nay, dear one, I can wait, and very proudly, knowing myself your chiefest prize. But seek not to possess the prize too soon, lest your strivings for renown, being aimless, should wax feeble. It is because I love you that I hold your fame far dearer than my love. Go rather forth again, travel through heathen lands, defend the weak against the strong; go, battle for the right, show yourself the matchless knight you are; and God and my love go with thee.'

Then Sir Guy gat him ready for his new quest. Earl Rohand tried to persuade him to remain at home, as likewise did his father Segard; and his mother, weeping, prayed him stay. She said, 'Another year it may not fare so well with thee, my son. Leave well alone. Felice is cold and proud and cares not for thee, else she would not risk thy life again. What is it to her? If thou wert slain she would get another lover; we have no more sons.'

Yet would not Sir Guy be turned from his purpose, but embarked with his companions, Sir Heraud, Sir Thorold, and Sir Urry, for Flanders. Thence he rode through Spain, Germany, and Lombardy, and bore away the prize at every tournament. But coming into Italy, he got a bad wound justing at Beneventum, which greatly weakened him.

Duke Otho of Pavia, whom Sir Guy overthrew in his first tournament at Rouen, thought now to be avenged on him. So he set a chosen knight, Earl Lombard, with fifteen other knights to lie in ambush in a wood and slay Sir Guy; and as Sir Guy, with his three companions, came ambling slowly through the wood, he smarting and well-nigh faint with his wound, the men in ambush broke out from their concealment and called on him to yield. The danger made him forget his pain, and straightway he dressed his shield and spurred among them.

Sir Heraud, Sir Thorold, and Sir Urry killed the three first knights they rode against. Then Earl Lombard slew Sir Urry; and at the same time Hugo, nephew to Duke Otho, laid Sir Thorold dead at his horse's feet. Then only Sir Guy and Sir Heraud being left to fight, Sir Guy attacked Earl Lombard and smote him to the heart, whilst Sir Heraud chased Hugo, fleeing like a hound, and drave his spear throughout his body. Thus were Sir Urry and Sir Thorold avenged. But one of the felon knights, called Sir Gunter, smote Sir Heraud a mighty stroke when he was off his guard, and hewed his shield and coat of mail in pieces, and Sir Heraud fell to the earth covered with blood and lay as dead.

Thereupon Sir Guy's anger waxed furious at his

master's death; and he spurred his horse so that fire rose from under its feet, and with one blow of his sword cleft Sir Gunter from his helmet to the pummel of his saddle. As for the other knights he slew them all except Sir Guichard, who fled on his swift steed to Pavia, and got back to Duke Otho.

Heavily Sir Guy grieved for the loss of his three friends, but most of all for his dear master Sir Heraud. He sought about the wood until he found a hermit. To him he gave a good steed, charging him to bury the bodies of Sir Urry and Sir Thorold. From Sir Heraud's body he would not part. Lifting the old knight in his arms, he laid him across his horse, and led the steed by the bridle-rein till they came to an abbey, where he left the body with the abbot, promising rich presents in return for giving it sumptuous burial with masses and chants. But Sir Guy departed and hid himself in a hermit's cave away from the malice of Duke Otho, until his wound should be healed.

Now there was in the abbey whither Heraud's body was taken, a monk well skilled in leech-craft, who knew the virtues of all manner of grasses and herbs. And this monk, finding by his craft that life still flickered in the body, nursed and tended it; and after a long while Sir Heraud was well enough to travel. Disguised as a palmer he came into Burgundy, and there, to his great joy, found Sir Guy, who had come thither meaning to take his way back to England. But they lingered still, till Heraud should grow stronger, and so it fell out that they came to St. Omers. There they heard how the Emperor Regnier had come up against Segwin, Duke of Lavayne, laid waste his land, and besieged him in his strong city Seysone, because he had slain Sadoc, the emperor's cousin, in a tournament. But when Sir Guy learned that Sadoc had first provoked Duke Segwin, and brought his death upon himself, he determined to help Segwin against his sovereign the Emperor Regnier. He therefore gathered fifty knights together with Heraud, and coming secretly at night to the city of Seysone, was let in at a postern gate without the enemy being aware. In the morning after mass they made a sally against their foes, which numbered thirty thousand strong, and routed them, taking many noble prisoners. Three times the emperor came against the Greeks, each time with a new army larger than before. Twice did Sir Guy vanquish the host, and drive them from the walls. The third time he took Sir Gaire, the emperor's son, prisoner, and carried him into the city. Then the Emperor Regnier determined, since he could not take the place by assault, to beleaguer it, and starve the town into surrender. And it was so that, while his army was set down before the walls, the emperor hunted alone in a wood hard by, and Sir Guy, meeting him there, gathered a branch of olive tree, and came bending to the emperor, saying, 'God save you, gentle sire. Duke Segwin sendeth me to make his peace with you. He will yield you all his lands and castles in burg and city, and hold them of you henceforth in vassalage, but he now would have your presence in the city to a feast.' So the emperor was forced to go with him into the city as a prisoner, albeit he was served with the humility due to a sovereign both by Sir Guy and Duke Segwin's knights. Sir Gaire and the other captive nobles came also and prayed for peace with Duke Segwin, for they had been so well treated that they felt nothing but the truest friendship for their captor. So it befell when the emperor found himself feasting in the enemy's castle, surrounded by the flower of his own knights and nobles, and Duke Segwin and his band serving them humbly at table as though they had been servants in place of masters, he was touched by their generosity, and willingly agreed to a free and friendly peace. And this was celebrated by the emperor giving Duke Segwin his niece to wife, whilst the

Duke of Saxony wedded Duke Segwin's sister amid great rejoicings.

Now after this, learning that Ernis, Emperor of Greece, was besieged in Constantinople his capital by the Saracens, Sir Guy levied an army of a thousand knights and went to his assistance. Well pleased was Ernis at so timely a succour, and he promised to reward Sir Guy by making him heir to the throne and giving him the hand of his only daughter the beautiful Loret. Then Sir Guy led the army forth from the city against the Soudan and his host, and defeated them so badly that for some days they were unable to rally their men for another encounter.

In the meantime one of Sir Guy's knights named Sir Morgadour fell in love with the Princess Loret, and being envious of Sir Guy's achievements as well as jealous of such a rival, he sought how to embroil him with the emperor and compass his disgrace. Wherefore one day when the Emperor Ernis was gone a-rivering with his hawks, Sir Morgadour challenged Sir Guy to play a game of chess in the Princess Loret's chamber. They played there, Sir Guy not thinking of treachery. But by-and-by the princess entered, and Sir Morgadour after greeting her took his leave quickly and came to the Emperor Ernis, telling him how Sir Guy was alone in the chamber with his daughter. Ernis, however, paid little heed to the tale, for he said—'Well, and what of it? Loret is his promised bride, and Sir Guy is a good true knight. Away with your tales!' But Sir Morgadour was not to be baffled, so he went to Sir Guy and said—'Behold how little trust is to be placed in a king! Here is the Emperor Ernis mad wroth to hear you were alone with the Princess Loret, and swears he will have your life.' Then Sir Guy in great anger summoned his knights, and was going over to the Saracens, when, on his way, he met the emperor, who told him of the malice of Sir Morgadour and all was made plain.

x

But now the Saracens coming anew against the city, Sir Guy went forth to meet them with many engines upon wheels which threw great stones quarried from a hill. Sir Guy and his army again defeated the Saracens, insomuch that a space of fifteen acres was covered so thick with dead that a man might not walk between, whilst the pile of slain around Sir Guy reached breast high. So the Soudan and his host withdrew to their camps.

Then Sir Morgadour bethought him of another wile. The Soudan had sworn to kill every Christian found in his camp, without regard to flag of truce or ambassage. So Sir Morgadour persuaded Ernis to send Sir Guy to the Soudan saying, that, since the war seemed likely to come to no speedy issue, it should be settled by single combat between two champions chosen from the Christian and the Saracen hosts. The counsel seemed good to Ernis, but yet he liked not to risk his son-in-law's life; wherefore he called his Parliament together and asked for some bold knight to go and bear this message. When all the others held their peace, Sir Guy demanded to be sent upon the business, neither could the prayers and entreaties of Ernis cause him to forego the enterprise. He clad himself in iron hose and a trusty hauberk, set a helm of steel, gold-circled, on his head, and having girt his sword about him, leapt on his steed without so much as touching stirrup, and rode up to the Soudan's pavilion. He well knew it from the rest, since on the top thereof flashed a great carbuncle stone.

There were feasting the Soudan, ten kings, and many barons, when Sir Guy walked into the pavilion and delivered his message with great roughness of speech. 'Seize him and slay him!' cried the Soudan. But Sir Guy cut his way through his assailants and rushing on the Soudan cut off his head; and while he stooped to pick up the trophy with his left hand, with his right he slew six Saracens, then fought his passage past them all to the tent door, and leapt upon his horse. But the whole Saracen host being roused he never would have got back for all his bravery, but that Heraud within the city saw in a dream the danger he was in, and assembling the Greek army and Sir Guy's knights, came to his rescue and put the Saracens to flight. Then after the battle Sir Guy came in triumph to Constantinople and laid the Soudan's head at the feet of the Emperor Ernis.

Ernis, now being at peace from his enemies, would take Sir Guy through his realms. On their way they saw a dragon fighting with a lion, and the lion having much the worst of the combat, Sir Guy must needs go and fight the dragon. After a hard battle he laid the monster dead at his feet, and the lion came and licked the hands of his deliverer, and would in no wise depart from his side.

Soon afterwards the Emperor Ernis gathered a great company of princes, dukes, earls, barons, bishops, abbots, and priors to the wedding feast, and in presence of them all he gave Sir Guy to be ruler over half the kingdom, and led forth the Princess Loret to be his bride.

But when Sir Guy saw the wedding-ring, his old love came to his mind, and he bethought him of Felice. 'Alas!' he cried, 'Felice the bright and beautiful, my heart misgives me of forgetting thee. None other maid shall ever have my love.' Then he fell into a swoon, and when he came to himself he pleaded sudden sickness. So the marriage was put off, to the great distress of Ernis and his daughter Loret, and Sir Guy gat him to an inn. Heraud tended him there, and learned how it was for the sake of Felice that Guy renounced so fair a bride, dowered with so rich a kingdom. But after a fortnight, when he could no longer feign illness because of the watchfulness of the emperor and the princess after his health, he was forced to return to court, and delay his marriage from day to day by one excuse and another, until at length fortune delivered him from the strait. The lion which Sir Guy had

tamed was used to roam about the palace, and grew so
gentle that none feared him and none sought him harm.
But Sir Morgadour, being sore vexed to think that all his
plans against Sir Guy had failed, determined to wreak his
spite upon the lion. He therefore watched until he found
the lion asleep within an arbour, and then wounded him to
death with his sword. The faithful beast dragged himself
so far as Sir Guy's chamber, licked his master's hands, and
fell dead at his feet. But a little maid which had espied
Sir Morgadour told Sir Guy who had slain his lion. Then
Sir Guy went forth in quest of Sir Morgadour, and fought
with him and slew him. He had forgiven the wrongs
against himself, since he outwitted them; but he was fain
to avenge his faithful favourite. Now Sir Morgadour was
steward to the German Emperor Regnier. So Sir Guy
showed Ernis that if he remained longer at his court,
Regnier would surely make war on Greece to avenge his
steward's death. Wherefore with this excuse he took his
departure and set sail with Heraud in the first ship he
could find. They landed in Germany, and visited the
Emperor Regnier without telling anything about his
steward's death. Then they came to Lorraine.

As Sir Guy took his way alone through a forest, having
sent his servants on to prepare a place for him at an inn,
he heard the groaning of a man in pain, and turning his
horse that way, found a knight sore wounded, and like to
die. This knight was named Sir Thierry, and served the
Duke of Lorraine. He told how he was riding through
the wood with his lady, Osile, when fifteen armed men
beset him, and forcibly carried off the lady to take her to
Duke Otho of Pavia, his rival. Then said Sir Guy, 'I also
have a score to settle with Otho, the felon duke.' Then
he took Sir Thierry's arms and armour, and went in pursuit of the ravishers whom he soon overtook, and having
slain every one, he set the lady on his steed and returned
to the place where he had left the wounded knight. But

now Sir Thierry was gone; for four knights of Duke
Otho's band had come and carried him off. So Sir Guy
set down the lady, and started to find the four knights.
Having fought and vanquished them, he set Sir Thierry
on his horse and returned. But now Osile was gone. He
searched for many hours to find her, but in vain. So as
nightfall drew on he took Sir Thierry to the inn. There
by good fortune they found the lady, Sir Guy's servants
having met her in the wood and brought her with them
to await his coming. A leech soon came and dressed Sir
Thierry's wounds, and by the careful tending of Osile and
Sir Guy, he got well. Then Sir Guy and Sir Thierry
swore brotherhood in arms.

Soon there came a messenger, saying that Duke Otho,
hotly wrath at losing the fair Osile, had gone to lay waste
the lands of Aubry, Sir Thierry's father; the Duke of
Lorraine was likewise helping him. Thereupon Sir Guy
equipped five hundred knights and came with Sir Thierry
to the city of Gurmoise where Aubry dwelt. It was a
well ramparted city, and after being beaten in two battles
with Sir Guy, Duke Otho found, despite the larger numbers of his host, that he could not stand against the courage
of the little army and the valour of its leader. Thinking
therefore to gain Osile by treachery, he sent an archbishop
to Aubry, offering peace and pledging himself to confirm
the marriage of Sir Thierry and Osile, provided only that
the lovers would go and kneel in homage to their sovereign
Duke of Lorraine. Thereon Sir Thierry and his bride, together with Sir Guy and Sir Heraud, set out unarmed,
and after wending a day's journey out of Gurmoise, they
met the Duke of Lorraine, who embraced and kissed them
in token of peace. But Otho coming forward as if to do
the like, made a sign to a band of men whom he had in
waiting to seize them. These quickly surrounded Sir
Heraud and Sir Thierry and carried them off; but Sir Guy
with only his fists slew many of his assailants, and broke

away to where a countryman stood with a staff in his hand. Snatching this for a weapon, Sir Guy beat down the quickest of his pursuers, and made his escape. Duke Otho cast Sir Thierry into a deep dungeon in Pavia, and meanwhile gave Osile a respite of forty days wherein to consent to be his bride. But the Duke of Lorraine carried off Sir Heraud.

Weary and hungered, and vexed at the loss of his friends, Sir Guy came to a castle where he sought harbour for the night. Sir Amys of the Mountain, who dwelt there, welcomed him with a good will, and hearing his adventures, offered to raise an army of fifteen hundred men to help him against Duke Otho. But to this Sir Guy said nay, because it would take too long. So, after a day or two, having hit upon a plan, he disguised himself by staining his face and darkening his hair and beard and eyebrows; and setting out alone, came to Duke Otho with a present of a war-horse of great price, and said, 'You have in your keeping a dastard knight, by name Sir Thierry, who has done me much despite, and I would fain be avenged upon him.' Then Duke Otho, falling into the trap, appointed him jailor to Sir Thierry.

The dungeon wherein Sir Thierry was prisoned was a pit of forty fathoms deep, and very soon Sir Guy spake from the pit's mouth bidding him be of good cheer, for he would certainly deliver him. But a false Lombard overheard these words, and thereby knowing that it was Sir Guy, ran off straightway to tell Duke Otho. Sir Guy followed quickly and sought to bribe the man with money to hold his peace, but without avail, for he would go into the palace where the duke was, and opened his mouth to tell the tale. Then with one blow Sir Guy slew him at Duke Otho's feet. But Otho, very wroth, would have killed Sir Guy then and there, only that he averred that this was a certain traitor whom he found carrying food to the prisoner. Thus having appeased the duke's anger, he gat away secretly to Osile, and bade her change her manner to Duke Otho, and make as though she were willing to have his love. The night before the day fixed for the wedding, Sir Guy let down a rope to Thierry in his pit, and having drawn him up, the two made all speed to the castle of Sir Amys. There, getting equipped with arms and armour, they leaped to horse on the morrow, and riding back to Pavia, met the wedding procession. Rushing into the midst Sir Guy slew Otho and Sir Thierry carried off Osile, whereupon they returned to Sir Amys with light hearts. And when the Duke of Lorraine had tidings of what had befallen Otho he had great fear of Sir Guy, and sent Sir Heraud back with costly gifts to make his peace. So Sir Thierry and Osile were wed, and a sumptuous banquet was held in their honour, with games, and hunting, and hawking, and justing, and singing of glee-men, more than can be told.

Now as Sir Guy went a-hunting one day, he rode away from his party to pursue a boar of great size. And this boar, being very nimble and fleet of foot, led him a long chase till he came into Flanders. And when he killed the boar he blew upon his horn the prize. Florentine, King of Flanders, hearing it in his palace, said, 'Who is this that slays the tall game on my lands?' And he bade his son go forth and bring him in. The young prince coming with a haughty message to Sir Guy, the knight struck him with his hunting-horn, meaning no more than chastisement for his discourtesy. But by misadventure the prince fell dead at his feet. Thinking no more of the mishap, and knowing not who it was whom he had slain, Sir Guy rode on to the palace, and was received with good cheer at the king's table. But presently the prince's body being brought in, and Guy owning that he had done this deed, King Florentine took up an axe, and aimed a mighty blow at the slayer of his son. This Sir Guy quickly avoided, and when all arose to seize him, he smote them down on either hand, and fought his way through the hall till he reached his steed, whereon lightly leaping he hasted back to Sir Thierry.

Then after a short while he took leave of Sir Thierry, and came with Sir Heraud to England, to the court of King Athelstan at York. Scarce had he arrived there when tidings came that a great black and winged dragon was ravaging Northumberland, and had destroyed whole troops of men which went against him. Sir Guy at once armed himself in his best proven armour, and rode off in quest of the monster. He battled with the dragon from prime till undern, and on from undern until evensong, but for all the dragon was so strong and his hide so flinty Sir Guy overcame him, and thrust his sword down the dragon's throat, and having cut off his head brought it to King Athelstan. Then while all England rang with this great exploit, he took his journey to Wallingford to see his parents. But they were dead; so after grieving many days for them he gave his inheritance to Sir Heraud, and hasted to Felice at Warwick.

Proudly she welcomed her true knight, and listened to the story of his deeds. Then laughingly Sir Guy asked, should he go another quest before they two were wed?

'Nay, dear one,' said Felice, 'my heart misgives me I was wrong to peril your life so long for fame's sake and my pride in you. A great love-longing I have borne to have you home beside me. But now you shall go no more forth. My pride it was that made me wish you great and famous, and for that I bade you go; but now, beside your greatness and your fame, I am become so little and so unworthy that I grow jealous lest you seek a worthier mate. We will not part again, dear lord Sir Guy.' Then he kissed her tenderly and said, 'Felice, whatever of fame and renown I may have gained, I owe it all to you. It was won for you, and but for you it had not been—and so I lay it at your feet in loving homage, owning that I hold it all of you.'

So they were wed amid the joy of all the town of Warwick; for the spousings were of right royal sort, and Earl Roband held a great tournament, and kept open court to all Warwick, Rockingham, and Oxford for fourteen days.

Forty days they had been wed, when it happened that as Sir Guy lay by a window of his tower, looking out upon the landscape, he fell to musing on his life. He thought, 'How many men I have slain, how many battles I have fought, how many lands I have taken and destroyed! All for a woman's love; and not one single deed done for my God!' Then he thought 'I will go a pilgrimage for the sake of Holy Cross.' And when Felice knew what he meditated she wept, and with many bitter tears besought him not to leave her. But he sighed and said, 'Not yet one single deed for God above!' and held fast to his intent. So he clad himself in palmer's dress, and having taken a gold ring from his wife's hand and placed upon his own, he set out without any companion for the Holy Land.

But Felice fell into a great wan-hope at his departure, and grieved continually, neither would be comforted; for she said, 'I have brought this on myself by sending him such perilous journeys heretofore, and now I cannot bear to part from him.' But that she bore his child she would have taken her own life for very trouble of heart: only for that child's sake she was fain to live and nurture it when it should be born.

Now after Sir Guy had made his toilsome pilgrimage to Jerusalem, and shrived him of his life, and done his prayers and penances about the holy places, he took his way to Antioch.

Beside a well he met a certain Earl Jonas, whose fifteen sons were held in prison till he should find a champion to deliver the Saracen Sir Triamour from the hands of a fierce and terrible Ethiopian giant named Amiraunt. So Sir Guy took arms again, and rode into the lists, and fought with Amiraunt and slew him; thus both Sir Triamour was delivered from his enemy, and the sons of Earl Jonas were restored to him. After this, Sir Guy travelled many years as a pilgrim of the Cross, till in his wanderings, chancing to come into Almayne, he there fell in with Sir Thierry, who, dressed in palmer's weeds, made sorry complaint. Sir Thierry told how a knight named Barnard inherited Pavia in the room of his cousin Duke Otho; and how Barnard, being at enmity with him because of the slaying of Duke Otho, had never rested from doing him mischief with his sovereign, until the Duke of Lorraine dispossessed him from his lands and brought him into poverty. Howbeit Sir Guy would not reveal himself, and Sir Thierry being faint and weary, laid his head upon Sir Guy's knees, and so great a heaviness came over him that he fell asleep. As he slept, Sir Guy, watching him, saw a small white weasel creep out from the mouth of the sleeping man, and run to a little rivulet that was hard by, going to and fro beside the bank, not seeming wistful how to get across. Then Sir Guy rose gently and laid his sword athwart the stream from bank to bank; so the weasel passed over the sword, as it had been a bridge, and having made his way to a hole at the foot of the hill on the other side, went in thereat. But presently the weasel came out, and crossing the stream in the same manner as before jumped into the sleeper's mouth again. Then Sir Thierry woke and told his dream. 'I dreamed,' said he, ' that I came beside a mighty torrent which I knew not how to pass, until I found a bridge of shining steel, over which I went, and came into a cavern underground, and therein I found a palace full of gold and jewels. I pray thee, brother palmer, read to me this dream.'

Then Sir Guy said that without doubt it betokened a

fair treasure hid by a waterside, and with that showed him the hole under the hill whereat he had seen the weasel go in. There they digged and found the treasure, which was very great; yet Sir Guy would have no share therein, but took leave of Sir Thierry without ever making himself known, and came to Lorraine to the duke that was Sir Thierry's sovereign.

Seeing a palmer the Duke of Lorraine asked tidings of his travels. 'Sir,' said the palmer, 'men in all lands speak of Sir Thierry, and much do blame you for taking away his heritage at the bidding of so false a knight as Sir Barnard. And palmer though I be, I yet will prove Sir Barnard recreant and traitor upon his body, and thereto I cast down my glove.' Then Sir Barnard took up the glove, and Sir Guy being furnished with armour and a sword and shield and spear, they did battle together. And in the end Sir Guy overcame and slew Sir Barnard, and demanded of the duke to restore Sir Thierry to his possessions, which being granted, he went in search of the banished man, and having found him in a church making his prayer, brought him straightway to the duke, and thus they were made friends. And when Sir Thierry found who his deliverer was he was exceeding glad and would willingly have divided all his inheritance with him. But Sir Guy would receive neither fee nor reward, and after he had abode some time with him at the court, he took his way to England.

Now Athelstan was besieged in Winchester by Anlaf King of Denmark, and could not come out of the city for the great host that was arrayed against him, whilst all the folk within the city walls were famishing for want of food and thought of nothing but surrender. Moreover King Anlaf had proclaimed a challenge, giving them seven days' grace wherein either to deliver up the city keys, or to find a champion who should fight against the great and terrible Danish giant Colbrand; and every day for seven days the giant came before the walls and cried for a man to fight with him. But there was found no man so hardy as to do battle with Colbrand. Then King Athelstan, as he walked to and fro in his city and saw the distress of his people, was suddenly aware of a light that shone about him very brightly, and he heard a voice which charged him to intrust his cause to the first poor palmer he should meet. Soon after he met a palmer in the city, and weening not that it was Sir Guy, kneeled humbly to him, in sure faith in the heavenly voice, and asked his help. 'I am an old man,' said the palmer, 'with little strength except what Heaven might give me for a people's need beset by enemies. But yet for England's sake and with Heaven's help I will undertake this battle.'

They then clothed him in the richest armour that the city could furnish, with a good hauberk of steel, and a helmet whose gold circle sparkled with precious stones, and on the top whereof stood a flower wrought of divers colours in rare gems. Gloves of mail he wore, and greaves upon his legs, and a shirt of ring-mail upon his body, with a quilted gambeson beneath: sharp was the sword, and richly carved the heavy spear he bare; his threefold shield was overlaid with gold. They led forth to him a swift steed; but before he mounted he went down upon his knees and meekly told his beads, praying God to succour him that day. And the two kings held a parley for an hour, Anlaf promising on his part that if his champion fell he would go back with all his host to Denmark and nevermore make war on Britain, whilst Athelstan agreed, if his knight were vanquished, to make Anlaf King of England, and henceforth to be his vassal and pay tribute both of gold and silver money.

Then Colbrand strode forth to the battle. So great was he of stature that no horse could bear him, nor indeed could any man make a cart wherein to carry him. He was armed with black armour of so great weight that a score of men could scarce bear up his hauberk only, and it took three to carry his helm. He bare a great dart within his hand, and slung around his body were swords and battle-axes more than two hundred in number.

Sir Guy rode boldly at him, but his spear shivered into pieces against the giant's armour. Then Colbrand threw three darts. The first two passed wide, but the third crashed through Sir Guy's shield, and glided betwixt his arm and side, nor fell to ground till it had sped over a good acre of the field. Then a blow from the giant's sword just missed the knight, but lighting on his saddle at the back of him hewed horse and saddle clean in two; so Sir Guy was brought to ground. Yet lightly sprang he to his feet, and though seemingly but a child beside the monster man, he laid on hotly with his sword upon the giant's armour, until the sword brake in his hands. Then Colbrand called on him to yield, since he had no longer a weapon wherewith to fight. 'Nay,' answered Sir Guy, ' but I will have one of thine,' and with that ran deftly to the giant's side and wrenched away a battle-axe wherewith he maintained the combat. Right well Sir Guy endured while Colbrand's mighty strokes shattered his armour all about him, until his shield being broke in pieces it seemed he could no longer make defence, and the Danes raised a great shout at their champion's triumph. Then Colbrand aimed a last stroke at the knight to lay him low, but Sir Guy lightly avoiding it, the giant's sword smote into the earth a foot and more, and before he could withdraw it or free his hand, Sir Guy hewed off the arm with his battle-axe; and since Colbrand's weight leaned on that arm, he fell to ground. So Sir Guy cut off his head, and triumphed over the giant Colbrand, and the Danes withdrew to their own country.

Then without so much as telling who he was, Sir Guy doffed his armour and put on his palmer's weeds again, and secretly withdrawing himself from all the feasts and games they held in honour of him in the city of Winchester, passed out alone and took his journey toward Warwick on foot.

Many a year had gone since he had left his wife and home. The boy whom Felice had borne him, named Raynburn, he had never seen; nor, as it befell, did he ever see his son. For Raynburn in his childhood had been stolen away by Saracens and carried to a far heathen country, where King Aragus brought him up and made him first his page, then chamberlain, and as he grew to manhood, knighted him. And now he fought the battles of King Aragus with a strong arm like his father Guy's, neither could any endure against his spear. But all these years Felice had passed in prayer and charity, entertaining pilgrims and tired wayfarers, and comforting the sick and the distressed. And it was so that Sir Guy, all travel-worn and with his pilgrim's staff in hand, came to her house and craved an alms. She took him in and washed his feet and ministered to him, asking oftentimes if in his travels he had seen her lord Sir Guy. But when he watched her gentleness to the poor and to the children at her gate, he feared to break in upon her holy life, and so refrained himself before her and would not reveal himself, but with a heavy heart came out from the lady's door and gat him to a hermit's cell. There he abode in fasting and in penitence many weeks, till feeling his end draw near, he took the ring from his finger and sent it by a herdsman to Felice. 'Where got you this token?' cried Felice, all trembling with her wonderment and fear. 'From a poor beggar-man that lives in yonder cell,' the herdsman answered. 'From a beggar? Nay, but from a kingly man,' said Felice, 'for he is my husband, Guy of Warwick!' and gave the herdsman a hundred marks. Then she hasted and came to Sir Guy in his hermit's cell, and for a long space they wept in each other's arms and neither spake a word.

Weaker and fainter waxed Sir Guy. In a little while he died, and Felice closed his tired eyes. Fifteen weary days she lingered sore in grief, and then God's angel came and closed her own.

ROLAND.

CHARLES the great king had tarried with his host seven years in Spain, until he conquered all the land down to the sea, and his banners were riddled through with battle-marks. There remained neither burg nor castle the walls whereof he brake not down, save only Zaragoz, a fortress on a rugged mountain top, so steep and strong that he could not take it. There dwelt the pagan King Marsilius, who feared not God but served Apollyon and Mahound.

King Marsilius caused his throne to be set in his garden beneath an olive tree, and thither he summoned his lords and nobles to council. Twenty thousand of his warriors being gathered about him, he spake to his dukes and counts saying, 'What shall we do? Lo! these seven years the great Charles has been winning all our lands till only Zaragoz remains to us. We are too few to give him battle, and, were it not so, man for man we are no match for his warriors. What shall we do to save our lands?'

Then up and spake Blancandrin, wily counsellor—'It is plain we must be rid of this proud Charles; Spain must be rid of him. And since he is too strong to drive out with the sword, let us try what promises will do. Send an ambassage and say we will give him great treasure in gold and cattle, hawk and hound; say we will be his vassals, do him service at his call; say we will be baptized, forsake our gods and call upon his God: say anything, so long as it will persuade him to rise up with his host and quit our land. Fear nothing, promises cost little; only promise large enough and we shall gain our ends. Wherefore let us choose out messengers to go to Charles and say after this manner: "Marsilius sends greeting to the mighty Charles. Thy servant Marsilius owns thy power, and that it is vain to strive against thee. But he would make a league with thee. Marsilius will renounce his gods, be baptized into Christendom, do thee homage and henceforth be thy vassal. Only make not war upon him, but depart in peace to thine own land and go to Aachen, and there keep the feast of Saint Michael. Thither thy servant Marsilius will haste to meet thee to perform all his covenant; and with him he will bring tribute, many lions and hounds, seven hundred camels, and a thousand moulted falcons; four hundred harnessed mules, and fifty chariots laden with gold and silver." By my right hand and beard, I swear we shall be rid of him. He will gather his warriors together and go back to his own people. He will want hostages, perchance, for the fulfilment of our covenant. Let him have them. Let him have ten or twenty of our sons; he shall have mine for one. What matters so we save our land? Charles will go back to Aachen and hold the feast, and when the day comes round, will find we have beguiled him. Then he will wax furiously wroth and slay our hostages. What then? Verily, it is better that a score of lads should lose their heads than that we should lose fair Spain. Better a score of us go childless than that all should come to beggary.'

And all the pagans said, 'It is well spoken.'

Now Charles and his host were pitched before Cordova, besieging it. And King Marsilius chose out Blancandrin, and with him nine of the cruellest of his peers who likewise would give their sons to be hostages, to go upon this errand. At the king's command men led forth ten white mules with golden bridles, and saddles trapped about with silver; and he gave olive-branches to the messengers to bear in their hands withal in token of peace and friendship, and sent them on their journey to go and make to Charles all the fair promises which Blancandrin had counselled.

Charles the Emperor held festival before Cordova, and rejoiced, he and his host, because they had taken the city. They had overthrown its walls; they had gotten much booty, both of gold and silver and rich raiment; they had put cables round about its towers and dragged them down. Not a pagan remained in the city; for they were all either slain or turned Christian. The emperor sat among his knights in a green pleasance. Round about him were Roland his nephew, captain of his host, and Oliver, and Duke Samson; proud Anseis, Geoffrey of Anjou the king's standard-bearer, and fifteen thousand of the noblest born of gentle France. Some lounged upon the white cloth of damask spread upon the grass; wise warriors of sober years sate round the chess-tables, wrapt in the plotting of their game; the younger and more agile tilted on the green. Beneath a pine tree where a rose-briar twined, sat Charles the Great, ruler of France, upon a chair of gold. White and long was his beard; huge of limb and hale of body was the king, and of noble countenance. It needed not that any man should ask his fellow, saying, 'Which is the king?' for all might plainly know him for the ruler of his people. So when the messengers of King Marsilius came into his presence, they knew him straightway, and lighted quickly down from their mules and came meekly bending at his feet. Then said Blancandrin, 'God save the king, the glorious king whom all men ought to worship. My master King Marsilius sends greeting to the great Charles whose power no man can withstand, and he prays thee make peace with him. Marsilius offers gifts of bears and lions and leashed hounds, seven hundred camels and a thousand moulted falcons, of gold and silver so much as four hundred mules harnessed to fifty chariots can draw, with all his treasure of jewels. Only make the peace and get thee to Aachen, and my master will meet thee there at the feast of St. Michael; and he will be thy man henceforth in service and worship, and hold Spain of thee; in sooth, all that he hath will he hold of thee; thou shalt be his lord, and thy God shall be his God.'

The emperor bowed his head the while he thought upon the purport of the message; for he never spake a hasty word, and never went back from a word once spoken. Having mused awhile he raised his head and answered, 'The King Marsilius is greatly my enemy. In what manner shall I be assured that he will keep his covenant?' The messengers said, 'Great king, we offer hostages of good faith, the children of our noblest. Take ten or twenty as it seemeth good to thee; but treat them tenderly, for verily at the feast of St. Michael our king will redeem his pledge, and come to Aachen to be baptized and pay his homage and his tribute.'

Then the king commanded a pavilion to be spread wherein to lodge them for the night. And on the morrow, after they had taken their journey home, and the king had heard mass and matins, he called his barons to him. There came Duke Olger and Turpin the Archbishop, Tedbald of Rheims, Gerard and Gerin, Count Roland, and Oliver his companion who was ever at his side, and with them many thousand noble warriors. Ganelon came also, he that wrought the treason and betrayed the Franks. Then the king showed them after what manner the messengers had spoken and asked their counsel. With one voice the Franks answered, 'Beware of King Marsilius.'

Then spake Roland and said, 'Parley not with him, trust him not. Remember how he took and slew Count Basant and Count Basil, the messengers whom we sent to him aforetime on a peaceful errand. Seven years have

we been in Spain, and now only Zaragoz holds out against
us. Be not slack to finish what has been so long a-doing
and is well-nigh done. Gather the host; lay siege to
Zaragoz with all thy might and avenge the blood of
Basant and Basil; conquer the last stronghold of the
pagans: so win Spain and end this long and weary war.'

But Ganelon drew near to the king and spake: 'Heed
not the counsel of any babbler, unless it be to thine own
profit. What has Marsilius promised? Will he not give
up his gods, himself, his service and his treasure? Could
man ask more? Could we get more by fighting him?
How glorious would it be to go to war with a beaten man
who offers thee his all! How wise to wage a war to win
what one can get without! Roland is wholly puffed up
with the pride of fools. He counsels battle for his glory's
sake. What careth he how many of us be slain in a
causeless fight, if he can win renown? Roland is a brave
man; brave enough and strong enough to save his skin,
and so is reckless of our lives.'

Then said Duke Naymes (a better vassal never stood
before a king), 'Ganelon has spoken well, albeit bitterly.
Marsilius is altogether vanquished, and there is no more
glory in fighting him. Spurn not him who sues at thy
feet for pity. Make peace, and let this long war end.'
And all the Franks answered, 'The counsel is good.'

So Charles said, 'Who will go up to Zaragoz to King
Marsilius, and bear my glove and staff and make the
covenant with him?'

Duke Naymes said straightway, 'I will go;' but the king
answered, 'Nay, thou shalt not go. Thou art my right
hand in counsel and I cannot spare thee.' Then said
Roland, 'Send me.' But Count Oliver, his dear companion said, 'What! send thee upon a peaceful errand?
Hot-blooded as thou art, impatient of all parleying?
Nay, good Roland, thou would'st spoil any truce. Let the
king send me.'

Charles stroked his long white beard and said, 'Hold your peace, both of you; neither shall go.'

Then arose Archbishop Turpin and said, 'Let me go. I am eager to see this pagan Marsilius and his heathen band. I long to baptize them all, and make their everlasting peace.'

The king answered, 'All in good time, zealous Turpin; but first let them make their peace with me: take thy seat. Noble Franks, choose me a right worthy man to bear my message to Marsilius.'

Roland answered, 'Send Ganelon, my step-father.' And the Franks said, 'Ganelon is the man, for there is none more cunning of speech than he.'

Now when the coward Ganelon heard these words, he feared greatly, well-knowing the fate of them which had gone aforetime as messengers to Marsilius; and his anger was kindled against Roland insomuch that the fashion of his countenance changed in sight of all. Then he arose from the ground, and throwing the mantle of sable fur from his neck, said fiercely to Roland, 'Men know full well that I am thy step-father, and that there is no love between us; but thou art a fool thus openly to show thy malice. If God but give me to return alive, I will requite thee.'

Roland answered, 'I hear thy words and despise them. These men well know I had no thought of malice. The errand is honourable, and needs a man both skilful and complaisant of speech. Be proud if the king adjudges it to thee.'

Then spake Ganelon, 'I should not go at thy bidding: thou hast never gone or come at mine. Thou art not my son nor am I thy sire. Let Charles command me, I will do his service. But thou shalt repent of this.' Thereat Roland laughed aloud. And Ganelon, when he heard him laugh, turned in a rage and said, 'You shall repent of this!' Then he came bending to King Charles, 'Rightful emperor, I am ready to go up to Zaragoz, albeit no messenger ever returned thence alive. But I pray thee for my boy Baldwin, who is yet young, that thou wilt care for him. Is he not the son of thy sister whom I wedded? Let him have my lands and honours, and train him up among thy knights if I return no more.'

Charles answered, 'Be not so faint-hearted; take the glove and baton, since the Franks have awarded it to thee, and go, do my bidding.' Ganelon said, 'Sire, this is Roland's doing. All my life have I hated him; and I like no better his companion, Oliver. And as for the twelve champion peers of France, who stand by him in all he does, and in whose eyes Roland can do no wrong, I defy them all, here and now.'

Charles smoothed his snowy beard and said, 'Verily Count Ganelon thou hast an ill humour. Wert thou as valiant of fight as thou art of speech, the twelve peers perchance might tremble. But they laugh. Let them. Thy tongue may prove of better service to us upon this mission than their swords.' Then the king drew off the glove from his right hand, and held it forth; but Ganelon, when he went to take it, let it fall upon the ground. Thereat the Franks murmured, and said one to another, 'This is an evil omen, and bodes ill for the message.' But Ganelon picked it up quickly, saying, 'Fear not: you shall all hear tidings of it.' And Ganelon said to the king, 'Dismiss me, I pray thee.' So the king gave him a letter signed with his hand and seal, and delivered to him the staff, saying, 'Go, in God's name and mine.'

Many of his good vassals would fain have accompanied him upon his journey, but Ganelon answered, 'Nay. 'Tis better one should die than many. Stay here, and if I am slain, like Basil and Basant, be true liegemen to my son Baldwin, and see you get him my lands.' Then Ganelon leapt to horse, and rode on until he overtook the pagan messengers who had halted beneath an olive tree to rest.

There Blancandrin talked with Ganelon of the great
Charles, and of the countries he had conquered, and of his
riches and the splendour of his court. Ganelon also spake
bitterly of Roland and his eagerness for war, and how he
continually drave the king to battle, and was the fiercest
of all the Franks against the pagans. Then after they
had rested, they gat to horse again, and Ganelon rode with
Blancandrin a little apart from the rest. And Blancandrin said to Ganelon, 'Shall we have peace?' Ganelon
said, ' He that sueth for peace often desireth to gain opportunity for war.' Blancandrin answered, 'He that
beareth peace to his master's enemies often desireth to be
avenged of his own.' Then each of the two men knew the
other to be a rogue; and they made friends, and opened
their hearts to each other, and each spake of what was in
his mind, and they laid their plans. So it befell that when
they came to Zaragoz, Blancandrin took Ganelon by the
hand, and led him to King Marsilius, saying, ' O King!
who holdest thy power of Mohammed and Apollyon, we
have borne thy message to the haughty Charles, but he
answered never a word. He only raised his hands on high
to his God, and held his peace; but he has sent the noble
Count Ganelon, at whose mouth we shall hear whether we
may have peace or no.'

Then Ganelon, who had well considered beforehand
what he should say, began, 'God save the worthy King
Marsilius. Thus saith the mighty Charles through me
his messenger: "So thou wilt become a Christian, I will
give thee the half of Spain to hold of me in feof, and thou
shalt pay me tribute and be my servant. Otherwise
I will come suddenly and take the land away by force,
and will bring thee to Aachen, to my court, and will there
put thee to death."'

When King Marsilius heard this, the colour went from
his face, and he snatched a javelin by the shaft, and
poised it in his hand. Ganelon watched him, his fingers

playing the while with the sword hilt underneath his
mantle, and he said, 'Great king, I have given my message and have freed me of my burden. Let the bearer of
such a message die if so it seemeth good to thee. But I
dared not leave this land, for all the gold God made,
without delivering my master's message. What shall it
profit thee to slay the messenger? Will that wipe out
the message, or bring a gentler one? Or thinkest thou
Charles careth not for his barons? Read now the writing
of King Charles the Great.' Therewith he gave into the
king's hand a parchment he had made ready in the likeness of his master's writing. And Marsilius brake the
seal, and read the letter: 'I, King Charles, remember how
thou slewest Basant and his brother Basil; and before I
will make the peace, I command thee send hither to me
thine uncle, the Caliph, that sitteth next thee on the
throne, that I may do with him as I will.' Then the King's
son drew his scimitar and ran on Ganelon, saying, 'Give
him to me; it is not fit this man should live!' But
Ganelon turned, brandished his sword and set his back
against a pine-trunk. Then cried Blancandrin, 'Do
the Frank no harm; for he has pledged himself to
be our spy, and work for our profit.' So Blancandrin
went and fetched Ganelon, and led him by the hand and
brought him against the king. And the king said, 'Good
Sir Ganelon, I was wrong to be angry; but I will make
amends. I will give thee five hundred pieces of gold in
token of my favour.' Ganelon answered, 'He that taketh
not counsel to his own profit is a fool. God forbid I
should so ill requite thy bounty as to say thee nay.'

Marsilius said, 'Charles is very old. For years and
years he has fought and conquered, and put down kings
and taken their lands, and heaped up riches more than
can be counted. Is he not yet weary of war, nor tired of
conquest, nor satisfied with his riches?' Ganelon answered—'Charles has long been tired of war; but Roland,

his captain, is a covetous man, and greedy of possessions. He and his companion Oliver, and the twelve peers of France, continually do stir up the king to war. These lead the king to do whatsoever it listeth them; but he is become old and feeble, and is aweary of them, and fain would rest. Were these but slain, the world would be at peace. But they have under them full twenty thousand men, the pick of all the host of France, and they are very terrible in war.'

Marsilius spake to him again saying, 'Tell me; I have four hundred thousand warriors, better men were never seen: would not these suffice to fight with Charles?'

Ganelon answered, 'Nay; what folly is this! Heed wiser counsel. Send back the hostages to Charles with me. Then will Charles gather his host together, and depart out of Spain, and go to Aachen, there to await the fulfilment of thy covenant. But he will leave his rearguard of twenty thousand, together with Roland and Oliver and the Twelve, to follow after him. Fall thou on these with all thy warriors; let not one escape. So shall the pride of Charles be broken; for the strength of his army is not in his host, but in these, and in Roland his right arm. Destroy them, and thou mayest choose thy terms of peace, for Charles will fight no more. The rearguard will take their journey by the pass of Siza, along the narrow Valley of Roncesvalles. Wherefore surround the valley with thy host, and lie in wait for them. They will fight hard, but in vain.'

Then Marsilius made him swear upon the book of the law of Mohammed, and upon his sword-handle, that all should happen as he had said. Thus Ganelon did the treason. And Marsilius gave Ganelon rich presents of gold and precious stones, and bracelets of great worth. He gave him also the keys of his city of Zaragoz, that he should rule it after these things were come to pass, and promised him ten mules' burden of fine gold of Arabia.

So he sent Ganelon again to Charles, and with him twenty hostages of good faith.

When Ganelon came before Charles, he told him King Marsilius would perform all the oath which he sware, and was even now set out upon his journey to do his fealty, and pay the price of peace, and be baptized. Then Charles lifted up his hands towards Heaven and thanked God for the prosperous ending of the war in Spain.

Night fell and the king lay down to sleep. And as he slept he dreamed he was in the pass of Siza with no weapon in his hand save an ashen spear; and Count Ganelon came and snatched it from his hand and brake it into splinters. After that he dreamed he was in his royal city, and a viper came and fastened on his hand; and while he tried to shake it off, and could not, a leopard sprang on him and gat him down and would have slain him, but that a faithful hound leaped straightway on the leopard and gripped him by the ear. Then the dog and the leopard fought a terrible combat; but which of the twain overcame the other he could not tell. For the king tossed upon his bed in a sweat with the anguish of his dream; and he awaked and saw the sun shine brightly all about, and knew it was a dream.

But the king arose and gathered to him his host to go away to keep the feast of Saint Michael at Aachen, and to meet Marsilius there. And Olger the Dane made he captain of the vanguard of his army which should go with him. Then said the king to Ganelon, 'Whom shall I make captain of the rear-guard which I leave behind?' Ganelon answered, 'Roland; for there is none like him in all the host.' Then Roland said to his uncle the king, 'Give me the bow that is in thy hand; I will not let it fall as Ganelon did the glove and staff. Trust me.' So Charles made Roland captain of the rear-guard, and gave the bow into his hand. With Roland there remained behind, Oliver his dear comrade, and the twelve peers, and Turpin the

Archbishop who for love of Roland would fain go with him, and twenty-thousand proven warriors. Then said the king to his nephew, 'Good Roland, behold, the half of my army have I given thee in charge. See thou keep them safely.' Roland answered, 'Fear nothing. I shall render good account of them.'

So they took leave of one another, and the king and his host marched forward till they reached the borders of Spain. They had to travel along steep and dangerous mountain ways, and down through silent valleys made gloomy with toppling crags. And ever as the king thought upon his nephew whom he left behind, his heart grew heavy with an ill foreboding. So they came into Gascoigny and saw their own lands again. But Charles would not be comforted, for being come into France he would sit with his face wrapped in his mantle, thinking of his dreams; and he often spake to Duke Naymes, saying he feared that Ganelon had wrought some treason.

Now Marsilius had sent in haste to all his emirs and his barons to assemble a mighty army, and in three days he gathered four hundred thousand men to Roncesvalles, and there lay in wait for the rear-guard of King Charles. And a great number of the most valiant pagan kings banded themselves together by a league to assail Roland in a body, and to fight with none other till he was slain.

Now when the rear-guard had toiled up the rocky pass and climbed the mountain-ridge, way-wearied, they looked down on Roncesvalles, whither their journey lay. And behold! all the valley bristled with spears, and the valley-sides were overspread with them, for multitude like blades of grass upon a pasture; and the murmur of the pagan host rose to them on the mountain as the murmur of a sea. Then when they saw that Ganelon had played them false Oliver spake to Roland, 'What shall we now do because of this treason? For this is a greater multitude of pagans than has ever been gathered together in the world before.

And they will certainly give us battle.' Roland answered, 'God grant it; for sweet it is to do our duty for our king. This will we do: when we have rested we will go forward.' Then said Oliver, 'We are but a handful. These are in number as the sands of the sea. Be wise; take now your horn, good comrade, and sound it; peradventure Charles may hear, and come back with his host to succour us.' But Roland answered, 'The greater the number the more glory. God forbid I should sound my horn and bring Charles back with his barons, and lose my good name, and bring disgrace upon us all. Fear not the numbers of the host; I promise you they shall repent of coming here; they are as good as dead already in my mind.' Three times Oliver urged him to sound his horn, but Roland would not, for he said, 'God and His angels are on our side; through Him we shall do great wonders, and He will not see us put to shame before His enemies.' Yet again Oliver pleaded, for he had mounted up into a pine tree and seen more of the multitude that came against them; far as the eye could see they reached; and he prayed Roland to come and see also. But he would not; 'Time enough,' he said, 'to know their numbers when we come to count the slain. We will make ready for battle.'

Then Archbishop Turpin gathered the band of warriors about him and said, 'It is a right good thing to die for king and faith; and verily this day we all shall do it. But have no fear of death. For we shall meet to-night in Paradise, and wear the martyr's crown. Kneel now, confess your sins, and pray God's mercy.' Then the Franks kneeled on the ground while the archbishop shrived them clean and blessed them in the name of God. And after that he bade them rise, and, for penance, go scourge the pagans.

Roland ranged his trusty warriors and went to and fro among them riding upon his battle-horse Veillantif; by his side his good sword Durendal. Small need had he to exhort them in extremity; there was not a man but loved him unto death and cheerfully would follow where he led. He looked upon the pagan host, and his countenance waxed fierce and terrible; he looked upon his band, and his face was mild and gentle. He said, 'Good comrades, lords, and barons, let no man grudge his life to-day; but only see he sells it dear. A score of pagans is a poor price for one of us. I have promised to render good account of you. I have no fear. The battle-field will tell, if we cannot. God knows the issue of the fight, but we know that much glory and worship await us upon earth and crowns in Paradise.' Then he gave the word, 'Go forward!' and with his golden spurs pricked Veillantif. So, foremost, he led the rear-guard down the mountain-side, down through the pass of Siza into the Valley of Death called Roncesvalles. Close following came Oliver, Archbishop Turpin, and the valiant Twelve; the guard pressing forward with the shout 'Montjoy!' and bearing the snow-white banner of their king aloft.

Marvellous and fierce was the battle. That was a good spear Roland bare; for it crashed through fifteen pagan bodies, through brass and hide and bone, before the trusty ash brake in his hand, or ever he was fain to draw Durendal from its sheath. The Twelve did wondrously; nay, every man of the twenty thousand fought with lion-like courage; neither counted any man his life dear to him. Archbishop Turpin, resting for a moment to get fresh breath, cried out, 'Thank God to see the rear-guard fight to-day!' then spurred in again among them. Roland saw Oliver still fighting with the truncheon of his spear and said, 'Comrade, draw thy sword,' but he answered, 'Not while a handful of the stump remains. Weapons are precious to-day.'

For hours they fought, and not a Frank gave way. Wheresoever a man planted his foot, he kept the ground or died. The guard hewed down the pagans by crowds, till the earth was heaped with full two hundred thousand heathen dead. Of those kings which banded together by oath to fight him, Roland gave good account, for he laid them all dead about him in a ring, and Durendal to its hilt reeked blood. But many thousands of the Franks were slain, and of the Twelve there now remained but two.

Marsilius looked upon his shattered host and saw them fall back in panic, for they were dismayed because of the Franks. But Marsilius heard the sound of trumpets from the mountain top and a glad man was he; for twenty strong battalions of Saracens were come to his help, and these poured down the valley-side. Seeing this, the rest of the pagans took heart again, and they all massed about the remnant of the guard, and shut them in on every hand. Nevertheless Roland and his fast lessening band were not dismayed. So marvellously they fought, so many thousand pagans hurled they down, making grim jests the while as though they played at war for sport, that their enemies were in mortal fear and doubted greatly if numbers would suffice to overwhelm these men, for it misgave them whether God's angels were come down to battle. But the brave rear-guard dwindled away, and Roland scarce dared turn his eyes to see the handful that remained. Dead were the Twelve, dead was Duke Samson, dead Engeler of Gascoigny, and proud Duke Anseis, Gerin, and his companion Gerard, Guise, and Berenger, with all the flower of the guard.

Then Roland spake to Oliver, 'Comrade, I will sound my horn, if peradventure Charles may hear and come to us.' But Oliver was angry, and answered, 'It is now too late. Had'st thou but heeded me in time, much weeping might have been spared the women of France, Charles should not have lost his guard, nor France her valiant Roland.' 'Talk not of what might have been,' said Archbishop Turpin, 'but blow thy horn. Charles cannot come in time to save our lives, but he will certainly come and avenge them.'

Then Roland put the horn to his mouth and blew a great blast. Far up the valley went the sound and smote against the mountain tops; these flapped it on from ridge to ridge for thirty leagues. Charles heard it in his hall and said, 'Listen! what is that? Surely our men do fight to-day.' But Ganelon answered the king: 'What folly is this! It is only the sighing of the wind among the trees.'

Weary with battle Roland took the horn again and winded it with all his strength. So long and mighty was the blast, the veins stood out upon his forehead in great cords; he blew on till with the strain his brain-pan brake asunder at the temples. Charles heard it in his palace and cried, 'Hark! I hear Roland's horn. He is in battle or he would not sound it.' Ganelon answered, 'Too proud is he to sound it in battle. My lord the king groweth old and childish in his fears. What if it be Roland's horn? He hunteth perchance in the woods. Forsooth a merry jest it would be for him were the king to make ready for war and gather his thousands, and find Roland at his sport, hunting a little hare!'

The blood ran fast down Roland's face, and in sore pain and heaviness he lifted the horn to his mouth and feebly winded it again. Charles heard it in his palace, and started from his seat; the salt tears gathered in his eyes and dropped upon his snowy beard; and he said, 'O Roland, my brave captain, too long have I delayed! Thou art in evil need. I know it by the wailing of the horn! Quick, now, to arms! Make ready, every man! For straightway we will go and help him.' Then he thrust Ganelon away, and said to his servants, 'Take this man, and bind him fast with chains; keep him in ward till I return in peace and know if he have wrought us treason.' So they bound Ganelon and flung him into a dungeon; and Charles the Great and his host set out with all speed to come to Roland.

Fierce with the cruel throbbing of his naked brain, and well-nigh blinded with the blood that trickled down his face, Roland fought on, and with his good sword Durendal slew the pagan prince Faldrun and three and twenty redoubtable champions. The little company that was left of the brave rear-guard cut down great masses of the pagans, and reaped among them as the reapers reap at harvest time; but one by one the reapers fell ere yet the harvest could be gathered in. Yet where each Frank lay, beside him there lay for a sheaf his pile of slain, so any man might see how dear he had sold his life. Marganices, the pagan king, espied where Oliver was fighting seven abreast, and spurred his horse and rode and smote him through the back a mortal wound. But Oliver turned and swung his sword Haltclere, and before he could triumph clave him through the helmet to his teeth. Yet even when the pains of death gat hold on Oliver so that his eyes grew dim and he knew no man, he never ceased striking out on every side with his sword and calling 'Montjoy!' Then Roland hasted to his help, and cutting the pagans down for a wide space about, came to his old companion to lift him from his horse. But Oliver struck him a blow that brake the helm to shivers on his throbbing head. Nevertheless Roland for all his pain took him tenderly down and spake with much gentleness, saying, 'Dear comrade, I fear me thou art in an evil case.' Oliver said, 'Thy voice is like Roland's voice; but I cannot see thee.' Roland answered, 'It is I, thy comrade.' Then he said, 'Forgive me, that I smote thee. It is so dark I cannot see thy face; give me thy hand; God bless thee, Roland; God bless Charles, and France!' So saying he fell upon his face and died.

A heavy-hearted man was Roland; little recked he for his life since Oliver his good comrade was parted from him. Then he turned and looked for the famous rear-guard of King Charles the Great.

Only two men were left beside himself.

Turpin the Archbishop, Count Gaulter, and Roland set themselves together with the fixed intent to sell their lives as dearly as they might; and when the pagans ran upon them in a multitude with shouts and cries, Roland slew twenty, Count Gaulter six, and Turpin five. Then the pagans drew back and gathered together all the remnant of their army, forty thousand horsemen and a thousand footmen with spears and javelins, and charged upon the three. Count Gaulter fell at the first shock. The archbishop's horse was killed, and he being brought to earth, lay there a-dying, with four wounds in his forehead, and four in his breast. Yet gat Roland never a wound in all that fight, albeit the brain was parting asunder in his broken temples, and his pain was very sore.

Then Roland took the horn and sought to wind it yet again. Very feeble was the sound, yet Charles heard it away beyond the mountains, where he marched fast to help his guard. And the king said, 'Good barons, great is Roland's distress; I know it by the sighing of the horn. Spare neither spur nor steed for Roland's sake.' Then he commanded to sound all the clarions long and loud: and the mountains tossed the sound from peak to peak, so that it was plainly heard down in the Valley of Roncesvalles.

The pagans heard the clarions ringing behind the mountains, and they said, 'These are the clarions of Charles the Great. Behold Charles cometh upon us with his host, and we shall have to fight the battle again if we remain. Let us rise up and depart quickly. There is but one man more to slay.' Then four hundred of the bravest rode at Roland; and he, spurring his weary horse against them, strove still to shout 'Montjoy!' but could not, for voice failed him. And when he was come within spear-cast, every pagan flung a spear at him, for they feared to go nigh him, and said, 'There is none born of woman can slay this man.' Stricken with twenty spears, the faithful steed, Veillantif, dropped down dead. Roland fell under him, his armour pierced everywhere with spear-points, yet not so much as a scratch upon his body. Stunned with the fall he lay there in a swoon. The pagans came and looked on him, and gave him up for dead. Then they left him and made all speed to flee before Charles should come. In haste they gat them up the mountain sides, and left the gloomy valley piled with dead, and fled away towards Spain.

Roland lifted his eyes and beheld the pagans filing up the mountain passes; and he was left alone among the dead. Then in great pain he drew his limbs from underneath his horse, and gat upon his feet, but scarce could stand for the anguish of his brain beating against his temples. He dragged himself about the valley, and looked upon his dead friends and comrades. Round about each one there lay a full score of pagan corpses, and Roland said, 'Charles will see that the guard has done its duty.' He came to where Oliver lay, and he lifted the body tenderly in his arms, saying, 'Dear comrade, thou wast ever a good and gentle friend to me; better warrior brake never a spear, nor wielded sword; wise wert thou of counsel, and I repent me that once only I hearkened not to thy voice. God rest thy soul! A sweeter friend and truer comrade no man ever had than thou.' Then Roland heard a feeble voice, and turned and was ware of Archbishop Turpin. Upon the ground he lay a-dying, a piteous sight to see; his face all marred with wounds, his body well-nigh hewed in twain, insomuch that his bowels came forth before his eyes; howbeit, he raised his trembling hands and blessed the brave dead about him in the dear name of God. And when Turpin beheld Roland, his eyes were satisfied. He said, 'Dear Roland, thank God the field is thine and mine. We have fought a good fight.' Then joined he his hands as though he fain would pray, and Roland, seeing the archbishop like to faint for the sharpness of his distress, took and dragged himself to a running stream that he espied pass through the valley; and he dipped up water in his horn to bring to him, but could not, for he fell upon the bank and swooned. And when he came to himself, and crawled to where the archbishop lay, he found him with his hands still clasped, but having neither thirst nor any pain, for he was at rest. A lonesome man in the Valley of Death, Roland wept for the last of his friends.

But the brain began to ooze out from his temples, and his pain grew very grievous to be borne. And Roland, when he found death coming on him, took his sword Durendal in one hand, and his horn in the other, and crawled away about a bowshot to a green hillock whereupon four diverse marble steps were built beneath the trees. There he lay down in his agony. A certain Saracen was plundering there among the dead, and watched till Roland ceased to moan in his pain; then, thinking there was no more breath in him, the thief stole softly up, and seeing the glitter of the hilt of Durendal, put forth his hand and drew it from its sheath. Roland lifted his eyes and saw the thief bend over him with the sword in his hand. He seized the horn from beside him, and dealt the man a blow upon the crown that brake his skull.

Then he took Durendal into his hands, and prayed that it might not fall into the power of his enemies. He said, 'O Durendal, how keen of edge, how bright of blade thou art! God sent thee by his angel to King Charles, to be his captain's sword. Charles girt thee at my side. How many countries thou hast conquered for him in my hands! O Durendal though it grieves me sore, I had rather break thee than that pagan hands should wield thee against France.' Then he besought that God would now eke out his strength to break the sword; and lifting it in his hands he smote mightily upon the topmost marble step. The grey stone chipped and splintered, but the good blade brake not, neither was its edge turned. He smote the second step, which was of sardonyx; the blade bit it, and leaped back, but blunted not, nor brake. The third step was of grey adamant; he smote it with all his might; the adamant powdered where he struck, but the sword brake not, nor lost its edge. And when he could no more lift the sword, his heart smote him that he had tried to break the holy blade; and he said, 'O Durendal, I am to blame; the angels gave thee; they will keep thee safe for Charles and France!'

Then Roland, when he felt death creep upon him, lay down and set his face toward Spain and toward his enemies, that men should plainly see he fell a conqueror. Beneath him he put the sword and horn; then having made his peace with God, he lay a-thinking. He thought of his master Charles who had nurtured him from a little child, and his face was all a-glow with pride. 'He will see that I have rendered good account.' He thought of sweet France and his home that was so dear. He thought of his dear maid, Hilda, who would weep and cry for him. Very sad and tender grew his heart. Then lifted he his weary hands to Heaven and closed his eyes; and whilst he mused God sent His swift archangels, Gabriel and Michael, to bear his soul to Paradise.

Gloom fell; the mists went up, and there was only death and silence in the valley. The low red sun was setting in the west.

Charles and his host rode hard, and drew not rein until they reached the mountain top, and looked down on the valley of Roncesvalles. They blew the clarions, but there was no sound, neither any that answered save the ringing mountain sides. Then down through gloom and mist they rode, and saw the field; saw Roland dead, and Oliver; the archbishop and the twelve valiant peers, and every man of the twenty thousand chosen guard; saw how fiercely they had fought, how hard they died.

There was not one in all the king's host but lifted up his voice and wept for pity at the sight they saw.

But Charles the King is fallen on his face on Roland's body, with a great and exceeding bitter cry. No word he spake, but only lay and moaned upon the dead that was so passing dear to him.

Charles was an old man when he took the babe Roland from his mother's arms. He had brought him up and nourished him, had taught him war, and watched him grow the bravest knight, the staunchest captain of his host. Right gladly would he have given Spain and the fruits of all the seven years' war to have Roland back again. Tears came, but brought no words; and God sent sleep to comfort him from his heaviness. And while the king slumbered, the angel Gabriel came and strengthened him, and showed what should shortly come to pass, and bade him rise and follow after the pagans. The king arose and saw that the low red sun was not yet set; for God made a miracle in the firmament, so that the sun stood still in the heavens, and went not down till he was avenged of his enemies. Duke Naymes said, 'Coming down the pass I saw a cloud of dust across the mountains on the other side. That was the pagan host fleeing to Zaragoz.' Then having watered and pastured their horses, the king left four good knights in Roncesvalles to guard the dead from birds and beasts of prey, and set out in chase of the pagans.

In the Vale of Tenebrus the Franks overtook them, hard by the broad, swift river Ebro. There being hemmed in, the river in front and the fierce Franks behind, the pagans were cut to pieces; not one escaped, save Marsilius and a little band who had taken another way and got safe to Zaragoz. Thence Marsilius sent letters to Baligant, King of Babylon, who ruled forty kingdoms, praying him to come over and help him. And Baligant gathered a mighty great army and put off to sea to come to Marsilius.

But King Charles went straightway back to Roncesvalles to bury the dead. He summoned thither his bishops and abbots and canons to say mass for the souls of his guard and to burn incense of myrrh and antimony round about. But he would by no means lay Roland and Oliver and Turpin in the earth. Wherefore he caused their bodies to be embalmed and washed with wine and piment, that he might have them ever before his eyes; and he arrayed them in stuffs of great price and laid them in three coffins of white marble, and chose out the three richest chariots that he had and placed the coffins in them, that they might go with him whithersoever he went.

Now after this Marsilius and Baligant came out to battle with King Charles before the walls of Zaragoz. But the king utterly destroyed the pagans there and slew King Baligant and King Marsilius, and brake down the gates of Zaragoz and took the city. So he conquered Spain and avenged himself for Roland and his guard.

But when King Charles would go back again to France his heart grew exceeding heavy. He said, 'O Roland, my good friend, I have no more pleasure in this land which we have conquered. When I come again to Laon, to my palace, and men ask tidings, they will hear how many cities and kingdoms we have taken; but no man will rejoice. They will say, Count Roland our good captain is dead, and great sadness will fall on all the realm. O Roland, my friend, when I come again to Aachen, to my chapel, and men ask tidings, they will hear that we have won a land and lost the best captain in all France; and they will weep and mourn, and say the war has been in vain. O Roland, my friend, would God that I had died for thee!'

Now when the people of France heard how King Charles the Great returned victorious, they gathered together in great multitudes to welcome him. And when Hilda, the fair maid whom Roland loved, heard it, she arrayed herself in her richest apparel and tired her hair with eager pains, and proudly decked herself with her jewels. For she said, 'I would be pleasing in the eyes of my brave true captain who comes home to wed with me. To-day I am his bride! There is no gladder heart in France than mine. Who will not envy me, the bride of the brave captain whose name will be on every lip to-day?' Then she hasted and came merrily to the palace. And the king's guards all drew back for fear and let her pass, for they dared not speak a word to her. Right proudly walked she through them, for she thought, 'This honour is all for Roland's sake;' and proudly came she to the king, saying—'Roland, the captain of the host, where is he? Seven long years have I waited, so patiently, while he fought the battles of the king. I never murmured; no, I am too proud of him and of France and of the king. But to-day he is mine. The king will give him to me to-day.'

And Charles feared exceedingly and scarce could see for tears. He said, 'Dear sister, sweet friend, am I God that I can bring the dead back? Roland my nephew is dead; Roland my captain and my friend is dead. Nay; take time and mourn with us all, and when thy heart is healed I will give thee Ludwig mine own son, who will sit after me upon the throne. Take Ludwig in his stead.'

But God is kind: He takes the broken-hearted home.

Hilda cried not, nor uttered sound. The colour faded from her face, and straightway she fell dead at the king's feet.

Charles and his barons wept for pity at her doleful case: and the king came down from his throne and lifted the maiden in his arms and laid her head upon his shoulder. And when he found of a truth that death had taken the gentle maid, he called four countesses and bade them see that she was interred right worshipfully. They made a noble bier and lifted Hilda thereupon and bore her to a nunnery. They set it in the midst of the chancel, that so she might lie there in her robes and jewels as she died; and all that night they sang sweet masses for her soul's good rest. At prime they buried her beneath the altar pavement.

It is written in the old chronicle, that after these things Charles sent and summoned many men from many lands to come and try if Ganelon had done him a treason or no; for the twenty thousand who were betrayed being dead and the pagans utterly destroyed, there was none left to bear witness against him. So the king sent and fetched Ganelon up out of prison and set him on his trial. Howbeit Ganelon contrived to get thirty of his kinsfolk chosen among his judges, and chief of them Pinabel, a man of great stature and strength of limb. Moreover Pinabel was a ready man to pick a quarrel with any; a man cunning of tongue and very rich and powerful, so that people feared him greatly. These thirty Ganelon bribed, with part of the price he took from King Marsilius for the treason, to give judgment for him. Then Pinabel and the others went to and fro among the judges and persuaded them, saying—'We have no witnesses, only Ganelon himself, and what saith he? He owns he hated Roland, and for that cause he challenged Roland, in presence of the king and all his court, to fight when he returned from his mission. The open challenger is not the betrayer in secret. Moreover, had he done this thing, would Ganelon have come back again to King Charles? Besides, would any man betray an army of his friends to rid himself of a single enemy? Blood enough has been shed. Slaying Ganelon will not bring Roland back. The Franks are angry since they have lost their captain, and blindly clamour for a victim. Heed not their foolish cry, for Ganelon has done no treason.' To this the others all agreed, save Tierry, the son of Duke Geoffrey; and he would not.

The judges came to King Charles and said, 'We find

that Ganelon has done nothing worthy of death. Let him live and take anew the oath of fealty to France and the king.' Then the king was grieved, and said, 'It misgives me you have played me false.' In my esteem the judgment is not just. Nevertheless, it is judgment: only God can alter it.'

Then stepped forth the youth Tierry, Geoffrey's son. He was but a lad, very little and slender of body and slight of limb. And he said, 'Let not the king be sad. I Tierry do impeach Ganelon as a felon and a traitor who betrayed Roland and the rear-guard to the pagans, and I also say that thirty of Ganelon's kinsfolk have wrought treason and corrupted judgment. And this will I maintain with my sword and prove upon the body of any man who will come to defend him or them.' Thereto to pledge himself he drew off his right glove and gave it to the king for a gage.

Pinabel strode forward, a giant among the throng. He looked down upon the lad Tierry and despised him; he came to the king and gave his glove, saying, 'I will fight this battle to the death.' The Franks pitied Tierry and feared for him, for they had hoped Naymes or Olger or some mighty champion would have undertaken the cause, and not a stripling. But Charles the King said, 'God will show the right.' So they made ready the lists for the wager of battle; and the king commanded Ganelon and his thirty kinsmen to be held in pledge against the issue.

The battle was done in a green meadow near to Aachen in presence of the king and his barons and a great multitude of people. First the men rode together and tilted till their spears brake and the saddle-girths gave way; then they left their steeds and fought on foot. Tierry was wondrous quick and agile, and wearied Pinabel at the outset by his swift sword-play; but Tierry's hand was weak against his sturdy adversary, and his sword point pierced not mail nor shield. Pinabel clave his helm and hewed great pieces off his mail, but could not slay him. Then said Pinabel, 'Fool, why should I kill thee? Give up the battle and the cause, and I will be thy man henceforth in faith and fealty. It shall prove greatly for thy profit to reconcile Ganelon and the king.'

Tierry answered, 'I will not parley; God will surely show whether of us twain be right! Guard thyself.' So they fell to again and all men saw that nothing would now part them till one was dead; and straightway they gave the lad Tierry up for lost. Pinabel's sword was heavy, and great the strength of his arm. He smote Tierry a blow upon the helm that sliced off visor and ventailles and with it the youth's right cheek. But while his blood ran down upon the grass, Tierry lifted up his sword and struck the brown steel helm of Pinabel. God put His might into the young man's arm, for the blade cleft steel and skull, and entered Pinabel's brain, so that he reeled and dropped down dead. Then all the people shouted, 'God hath spoken! Away with Ganelon and his fellows!'

Then King Charles raised up his hands to heaven and gave thanks, and taking Tierry in his arms embraced him for joy, and with his own hands took off his armour, and he set the noblest in the land to tend his wounds.

King Charles sat in judgment in his palace at Aachen. He said, 'Take the thirty kinsmen of Ganelon, perverters of justice, let not one escape, and hang them.' Blithely the Franks obeyed his word.

Then the king commanded four horses to be brought. And they tied ropes round Ganelon's wrists and ankles, and harnessed the horses to them. The traitor lay and whined and begged for life with tears and promises and cries. But the very steeds arched up their necks in pride to do a pleasant work. No whip they needed, but only to be loosed, and quick they tare the traitor limb from limb upon the grass. So died Ganelon as he lived, a coward. Thus Charles the King made an end of his vengeance for his guard.

Now after these things were accomplished, and when Charles was grown very old and decrepit and the years fell heavy on him, the angel Gabriel came to the king as he slept, saying, 'Arise and go into Syria to succour King Vivian, for the pagans do hard beset him!' Charles sat up in his bed and sighed, 'Have pity on thy servant! So weary is my life; and I would fain go home to God.'

The old king wept and feebly plucked his snowy beard.

This is the gest which Turold used to sing.

When William the Norman fought at Hastings, Taillefer his minstrel, who sang full well, rode on before the Norman host and sang of Roland and great Charles—of Oliver and the brave rear-guard which fell in Roncesvalles.

OLGER THE DANE.

THERE was weeping in the palace of Godfrey King of Denmark; for the queen whom he dearly loved had died in giving birth to a son; and all the people mourned, both high and low; for she was a good queen, beautiful and royal among the noble ladies of the court and kind and tender to the poor. They took the babe from his dead mother's arms at midnight, and having named him Olger, carried him into another chamber and laid him on a richly quilted bed of down. Presently there was a gentle rustling in the room, and lo! there appeared about the bed six shining fairies whose beauty was so awful and so wonderful that none but a child might gaze upon them without fear. One of the fairies, named Glorian, drawing near took the boy in her arms and kissed him, saying, ' I give you to be the strongest and bravest knight of all your time.' Another, called Palestina, said, ' And I will always give you battles to fight.' Faramond, the third fairy, said, ' No man shall ever conquer him.' And Meliora gave him ' to be always sweet and gentle;' and Pristina, ' that he should be dear to all women, and happy in his love.' Then Morgan le Fay, which was queen of them all, took the child and held him long against her breast for the great love she bare him. She said, ' Sweet one, there scarce remains a gift for me to give you after all my sisters have promised, yet I give you this: that you shall never die, but after you have lived a life of glory on the earth you shall be mine, and I will bring you home to dwell with me for ever in Avalon, the land of Faery.' And the lady having kissed him many times put the child back upon the bed; and all the fairies fled away into the air and the room was dark again.

Olger grew up a brave child, tall, and strong in his limbs and very comely, so that when he was ten years old there was none like him for beauty and strength, for Nature seemed to have lavished all her treasures on him.

Now Godfrey King of Denmark was a bold and haughty prince who stood in fear of no man, and it befell when messengers came from France summoning him to do homage to the emperor Charles the Great for his lands, that Godfrey returned for answer, 'Tell Charles I hold my lands of God and my good sword, and if he doubt it let him come and see. I will not do him homage.' Wherefore Charles came up against him with a mighty army, and after a long and stout resistance King Godfrey being defeated was obliged to promise to appear before the emperor every Easter and pay his allegiance. As a pledge that he would keep his word, the emperor required him to give up Olger his son for a hostage. To this Godfrey having agreed, Olger was carried away to the emperor's court, where he was instructed in all the arts of the time; and the emperor was very glad to have so fearless and handsome a youth in his retinue.

For three years the King of Denmark came faithfully to pay his court as he had promised, but in the fourth year Eastertide went by and Godfrey did not come; the truth being that he was married again and had another son, and the new queen wrought upon her husband's pride, persuading him not to humble himself any more before King Charles; for she thought, 'When the emperor finds he no longer pays homage Olger surely will be put to death, and so my son shall inherit the throne of Denmark.' As his father did not redeem his word Olger was committed to prison in the castle of Saint Omer to wait while messengers went to Godfrey to find the reason of his breaking faith. But Olger was kindly treated by the castle-keeper, for he found favour in the eyes of his wife, and especially in those of Bellisande, his fair daughter, who loved him from the moment that she saw him. So instead of being cast into the dungeon, Olger was placed in the best apartments of the castle, richly hung with tapestry; and was waited upon like a prince; and Bellisande could no more keep her eyes from regarding him or her heart from going out towards him than the lily can help holding its cups out to get their fill of sunshine.

But Godfrey of Denmark entreated the messengers shamefully. He slit their ears and noses, shaved their heads, and sent them home disgraced. Wherefore these men returned to their master, and coming before him all marred and disfigured as they were, cried loudly for vengeance against Godfrey and against his son Olger that was held as hostage. The emperor then sent orders to the castle to slay Olger instantly; but the kind-hearted castle-keeper begged that at least the lad might first be brought before him and told why, innocent, he yet must suffer death. So, being brought to the emperor at a time when he feasted among his nobles, Olger came with much gentleness and kneeled meekly at his feet. Seeing the lad thus abase himself for his father's pride, the emperor was moved with pity, and would fain have spared his life; but the messengers cried out for vengeance, and would have fallen on him themselves had not Duke Naymes of Bayiere pleaded for the boy and kept them back. Then Olger said, 'Sire, you know that I am innocent of blame, having always rendered you obedience. Let me not suffer for my father's fault; but seeing I am his true heir, deign to receive from me the vassalage and homage he denies,—that by a life of service in your cause I may atone for him. As for your noble messengers, so cruelly ill-used, I will seek from this hour to repair their disgrace and take upon me to atone for all my father's misdeeds against them and you, if you but spare my life and use it in your service.'

Now while the barons interceded for the lad, a knight rode up the hall in haste. 'Tidings, King Charles!' he cried,—'evil tidings, alas! The Soudan and the Grand Turk Corsuble, and Dannemont his son, with King Caraheu have taken Rome by assault. Ovand the Pope, the cardinals and legates, all have fled; the churches are destroyed; the holy relics lost, all save the body of St. Peter; and the Christians put to the sword. Wherefore the Holy Father charges you as Christian king and pillar of the faith to march to succour of the Church!'

Then Duke Naymes of Bayiere prayed to take Olger as his squire into the battle, offering to go bail for him in all his lands and hold himself a prisoner in his stead, if the lad should flee. Thereto the emperor having consented, straightway prepared his army for battle, swearing by his sceptre that he would never return till Rome should be restored to the Christians. But Olger first went back to the castle and wedded the beautiful Bellisande. When she wept at his departure Olger said, 'Leave these tears, for God has given me life and you have given me love; gifts that will strengthen me to do great deeds of arms.' So he rode off with the host, with Naymes and his two brothers Geoffrey and Gautier; and they journeyed till they came to Rome and encamped upon a hill before the city-walls with an army of two hundred thousand men.

Now the Paynim host came out from Rome to fight the Franks upon the plain. Olger, bewildered and amazed to see the great crowds of knights in glittering armour, and the banners, and to hear for the first time the din of war, would fain have gone with Naymes and his brothers into the fight; but they forbade him, charging him to remain among the tents.

Looking down upon the battle from the hill, Olger

watched the hosts and tracked the standard of King
Charles as it moved to the front. He saw the armies
come together with a shout and join in battle with a
noise that rent the air. But in a little while the standard
wavered; then it fell, then rose again; and then he saw
King Charles's own company of knights repulsed, while Sir
Alory that bare the standard turned and fled for very life
upon his horse. Seizing a battle-axe Olger ran down into
the plain, caught the bridle of Alory's horse, and smote down
the standard-bearer in his flight, saying, 'Coward, go home
with all the speed you may! Live among monks and
women there. But leave the noble banner, Refuge of
France, with me!' Olger quickly disarmed the frightened
and trembling Alory, got a squire to dress him in the
standard-bearer's armour, leapt on a horse, and sword at
breast, banner in hand, galloped to the battle with the
fierceness of a lion, hewed his way through the Paynim
to the thickest of the fight, and finding Naymes and
many nobles held prisoners behind the pagan ranks, cut his
way through to them, loosed their bonds, and cut a road
back again for him and them. Wherever he went about
the field Olger reaped among the enemy till he ramparted
himself within a wall of slain. Hearing the king cry out
for help, he leapt his steed out from a wall of dead and
spurred to where he was. The king was down, Dannemont
had killed his horse under him and pressed him sore on every
side. But Olger, though he had but one fighting hand,
since he bare the standard in the other, rode upon the
Paynim and quickly carved out a clear space about the
king while he mounted a fresh horse. And in like
manner three times he saved the life of Charles. Then
with Olger and the standard at their head the king and all
his host shouting their battle-cry, 'Montjoy!' charged on
the Paynim, routed them, and drove them to the city gates.

After this King Charles commanded the standard-
bearer to be brought before him; but he wist not it was

Olger in Alory's armour, for his visor was down. Then said the emperor, 'Alory, I thank you heartily for this day's work, and though I know not what should have made you flee at the outset, you have redeemed your honour nobly. I cannot tell how to reward you. Choose any province in my kingdom and I will make you ruler of it; and you shall be my lieutenant to do battle for me in all disputes touching the crown of France, O brave and fearless Alory!' And he wept for joy that God had sent him such a champion. But a squire that stood by, being surprised to hear the king speak thus of Alory, said, 'Sire, he is not on the field. Alory bowed the colours and fled at the first to save his skin, whilst as for this knight, who seized the standard from Alory's hands, I helped to dress him in Alory's armour, but I wot not who he is.' Then Olger lifted his helmet, and kneeling to the king said, 'Have pity, sire, on Godfrey King of Denmark, and let his son atone for his offence and be your faithful vassal in his stead.' And the king answered, 'You have altogether turned into love the anger which I bare against you and your father. I give you your request. Wherefore rise Sir Olger, Champion for France and Charles, and God be with you.' Thus Olger received the accolade upon the battle-field, and all the peers of France came to salute him and to render thanks for their deliverance. Then, flushed with his new-made knighthood, Sir Olger sped like an arrow against the foe and fought with a courage surmounting mortal fear. Bearing the standard aloft he made it terrible to the enemy, insomuch that the Paynim withdrew the length of a bowshot before the wind of his sword and the tramping of his steed. And wheresoever the Franks fell in disorder, or wavering turned to flee, a knight upon a great horse would surely ride into their midst and do such mighty deeds that they turned to see for very wonderment, and scarce believed him mortal, till, knowing their brave champion, they would cry with a great shout, 'Olger the Dane!' and fearless in his company, charge mightily upon the foe.

Sadonne rode from the Paynim camp to bid Dannemont hold the field, since Caraheu, Emperor of India, with thirty kings, was coming to his help. He met the Paynim army coming towards him in full flight, crying out in panic—'Save yourselves, for Michael the Archangel fights against us!'

And he saw the terrible knight on the tall horse, and threw down his arms and begged for life.

'Who are you, that I should grant it?' said Sir Olger.

He answered, 'My master is Caraheu, Emperor of Upper India, and I am Sadonne, his admiral, cousin to King Corsuble.'

Then said Sir Olger, 'I grant your life on one condition: bear Caraheu my challenge to fight with me in single combat, and so determine all the issue of the war.'

Next day came Caraheu with a stately retinue to the pavilion of King Charles, bearing in his train the beauteous Gloriande, Corsuble's daughter, the fairest woman of the East. Her hair flowed in a golden shower to her feet, and a jewelled circle of rare workmanship bound it about her temples. She wore a dress of pure white damask sewn with pearls, a wonder of the weaver's art which took nine years to weave.

Then said Caraheu the Emperor—'I seek Olger the Dane, who has demanded single combat. I accept his challenge, and I bring fair Gloriande, my promised bride, a noble prize for victory.'

But the son of King Charles, Charlot, being envious of Sir Olger, said, 'It is not meet, great Caraheu, that you should battle with my father's bondsman, but rather with me.'

Caraheu answered, 'I fight not braggarts, but men. Sir Olger is a king of men, far nobler than a mere king of land.'

'Noble enemy,' answered Olger, 'your words make me grieve to fight against you rather than at your side. Yet Charlot is the emperor's son, and worthy to just with the bravest.'

'He shall tourney with Sadonne, my admiral,' said Caraheu, 'but I will fight with you alone.'

Thus a double combat was arranged, and they went to an isle to fight, and Gloriande with them, that her eyes might strengthen them to battle for such a prize. But Dannemont the Paynim treacherously hid three hundred men among the bushes to lie in wait. Caraheu's shield bore, on a field argent, four bands azure with the figure of Mahound upon a scutcheon gules. Sir Olger's shield was white with a black eagle thereupon. Bravely they fought for half a day, and long the victory seemed to waver between these two redoubtable champions. Meanwhile Sadonne killed Charlot's horse, and then honourably dismounted from his own to fight on equal terms; but Charlot made a feint of fighting till he brought himself to where Sadonne's steed was; then leaping on it, basely fled.

Caraheu's good sword, Courtain, of marvellous temper, cut through Olger's shield and armour. Nevertheless at last the Dane by great strength bore Caraheu to the ground, and got him at his mercy; but still he admired the Indian monarch's courtesy and courage so much that he would not slay him. Then Dannemont with Corsuble and his men seeing their champion down, rushed from their hiding place and assailed Sir Olger; whereat Caraheu, being very wroth at their treachery, fought beside Sir Olger, crying, 'Traitors, better death than shame like this!' So the enemies of an hour before became brothers in arms for honour's sake, and between them slew a hundred of their common foes. Howbeit they were overpowered by numbers, and Sir Olger owed his life to Gloriande's pleading. He was led away to prison loaded with chains. In vain did Dannemont and Corsuble seek to reconcile

Caraheu, their great ally, to their treasonable act. Caraheu, though he had to leave Gloriande whom he loved, went over with all his host to King Charles, and joined with him to gain redress from the Paynim for Olger's seizure.

But Gloriande came secretly to Olger in his prison, loosed his chains, and set him free. So he escaped to King Charles and Caraheu. After that together they fought the Paynim till they discomfited them; and Rome being freed, the Pope returned to the city with his cardinals and legates, and Holy Church was stablished firm again. Olger with his own hand rescued Gloriande, and gave her into Caraheu's hands to be his wife. So they were wed and baptised in Rome; and the Indian emperor returned to his empire a Christian, with a Christian wife. But first he gave Sir Olger the famed Damascus sword, Courtain, saying, 'You conquered me in fight and won my life and also my bride, and yet you gave both back to me. Take therefore this sword, offered in friendly homage, as a pledge that I owe you all.'

Then Olger came to France with King Charles, and found his wife had died in giving birth to a son named Baldwin. And Baldwin was dear to Olger, and the child's prattle very grateful to his ears for Bellisande's sweet sake.

Now the Paynim had come down on Denmark, seizing on all the land save only Mayence, where King Godfrey was besieged and suffered famine. And the queen said, 'Surely this misery is come on us for Olger's sake whom we abandoned.' And being brought very low with hunger and distress, at last they wrote a letter to King Charles, praying him to overlook the past, and in pity send them succour lest they die. But Charles said coldly, 'Nay—since Godfrey holds his lands of God and his good sword, let him hold them. I will not raise a finger for his help;' and straitly forbade that any knight about his court should go to succour them on pain of death. Then turning to Olger he said—' You would not wish to aid a traitor who has thrown off my yoke, insulted me, and who, moreover, left you selfishly to suffer for his crimes?' But Olger bending before Charles the King, answered—' Sire, I kneel as vassal to my king, but Godfrey is my father and I go. The king will not forbid a son his duty.'

Then said Charles, ' Go—but go alone, saving your own servants. Mine shall not fight in a rebel's cause.'

So Olger hastened to Mayence with only thirty of his servants. And when he reached the city walls he found a battle raging; for King Godfrey had made a desperate sally against his enemies and thrown them into disorder, but was fallen in the fray pierced with many wounds, and the Danes were fighting for his lifeless body. Olger with his little band rode into the battle with his sword Courtain, and where he passed he left a lane hedged up with bodies upon either side, whilst the Danes, rejoicing at so good a succour, with his help put the Paynims to the rout, nor ceased pursuit till all their enemies were either slain or driven from the land. So Olger was made King of Denmark in his father's stead, and remained five years in that country till he had founded a wise government and made good laws for the people. Then he returned to France and came kneeling to the emperor at Eastertide, saying, ' Godfrey's son, of his own free will, thus pays his homage to King Charles for all the land of Denmark.' So he grew in greater favour than ever with the emperor.

One day Baldwin, his son, now grown a pretty, fair-haired boy and general favourite, played chess with Charlot, whom, having fool's-mated, he bantered on the game. The prince, ever jealous of the father, and now stung by the son's playful triumph, flew in a passion, and with the heavy chess-board beat out his brains.

Bitterly Olger wept when he returned from hunting, to find the son he left so full of life and frolic but an hour before, struck down by a murderer's hand. Taking the body in his arms, and covering it with tears and kisses, he came to King Charles and laid it at his feet.

'Sire,' said he, 'look upon your son's foul work.'

'Truly,' answered the emperor, 'I grieve for you, Sir Olger, and would give half my kingdom to blot out the deed. But there is no repayment for so great a loss.' Said Olger, 'There is no repayment, but there is punishment; and I demand to fight with your son to avenge my poor boy's death.'

'Nay, Olger, have pity;' said the emperor, 'spare my son. How could he fight with you and have a bare chance of his life?'

'What of that?' returned the knight bitterly. 'Would he have more chance with the headsman if he met his rightful doom upon the public block? What is your son more than mine? Deliver him to me.'

'I cannot,' answered the king.

'Then, sire, till you learn justice we will part'—and Olger turned upon his heel and left the court, and came to Didier, King of Lombardy, who made war against King Charles, and fought for him.

It was in Lombardy that Olger got his faithful squire Benoist, a steadfast knight, who held his life cheap in his master's cause. Followed only by Benoist, Sir Olger battled long upon the Lombard side against King Charles and his host. Where men would send a troop to re-inforce a flagging portion of the army, Sir Olger and his squire rode forth alone. Wherever went the black eagle on the argent shield, the Lombards rallied, and the Franks fell back in terror; for a line of slain was the war-track of the Dane, and where men massed the thickest there he rode and made them fall like ripened sheaves before his sword Courtain. All the Franks feared to see their champion thus arrayed against them, and murmured loudly against the king for letting him depart.

It was a long warfare, wherein the Lombards fought their way on from place to place; and the Franks, being always worsted before the mighty Dane, schemed how they might take him by subtlety. Archbishop Turpin with a little band of men came on him by a fountain lying wearily asleep after a battle, his arms flung here and there upon the grass. One seized his helm, another his sword Courtain, while others bare away his lance and shield, and bound him while he still slept heavily from great fatigue.

King Charles would have slain Olger, both because he fought against him, beating down the flower of his chivalry, and because he feared his vengeance against Charlot his son. But Archbishop Turpin said, 'Nay—it was for the sake of France and Christendom I lent myself to surprise in bonds the noblest knight that ever wielded sword; but for the sake of France and Christendom his life must not be lost. Howbeit since I took him, let me guard him safe in prison so he may do no further hurt against the cause, and I will be his bond.' Then Turpin took Olger to his castle, where he treated him with great kindness, holding him prisoner only on parole.

Now Achar, King of England, landed in France with Clarice his daughter to do homage for his crown to the emperor; but Bruhier, a Saracen giant, with a mighty army coming to make war on France, seized them before they could reach the court, and marched to battle against Charles.

Long time they fought, but Charles's army was put to the worse and fled before the giant and his host, till fearing any more to go against the Saracens, the Franks called on the emperor to send for Olger the Dane from his prison. So he sent and intreated him to come to their succour. But Olger would not until the emperor should first deliver up his son Charlot into his hand. This for a long time he would not do, but at last his army clamoured at him, saying, 'Have you no care nor thought for us that we die in thousands in a hopeless fight? What is one life to thousands?' So Charles was fain to give up his son. Charlot begged in vain for mercy, for Olger remembered but his fair-haired child and how his life was cruelly beaten out. So taking the prince by the hair he drew Courtain and raised his arm to strike. Then a voice fell from the sky, and the place was lightened round about, 'Olger, stay thy hand! Slay not the son of the king!' All heard the voice and feared greatly, and Olger's hand fell to his side without striking. Then Charles embraced him and rendered thanks to Olger. 'Thank heaven, not me,' said the Dane. 'I do but bow to its will.' So they were made friends.

Then Olger went to battle against Bruhier, and with him for their champion the Franks had no fear. Victory followed where he led. Sometimes, amazed, both friends and foes paused in the midst of conflict, wonderstruck to see his valiant deeds. He routed the Saracens and slew the giant Bruhier, and rescued the Princess Clarice, whom her father gave to Olger for his wife. So they were wed and went to England, where Achar gave up his crown to his deliverer and made him King of Britain. Olger reigned in Britain many years with his wife Clarice, till, being tired of peace, he went and fought the battles of the Cross in Palestine. There Caraheu the emperor joined him, and they overthrew King Moysant, and the Soudan Moradin and his brother Branquemond; none could stand against the spear of the knight on the great horse who bore the black-eagle shield. There Olger fought till he grew old and grey; yet waxed not his arm feeble, nor wearied he in fight; men still fell thick before his sword Courtain, and where he went still panic spread among his foes, and fearless courage filled the breasts of all his friends. He took Acre, Babylon, and Jerusalem, of all which cities he was made king; but he gave them to his kinsmen to rule in his stead, for he would fain see Charles the Great and his court again. So with a mighty retinue and accompanied by Carahen and a fleet of vessels he set sail for France.

But a storm came down upon the sea and drave the ships hither and thither, at mercy of wind and wave, till they were parted one from another; and Olger's vessel, mast, oars, and sail being carried away, was driven far out of its course into strange seas, where an unseen current drew it swiftly through the billowy foam and crashed the ship at last against a reef of loadstone rock. The mariners all leaped overboard, seeking in vain to climb the slippery rocks: the angry surf whirled the strong swimmers up and beat them lifeless on the reef. Sir Olger stood alone at night upon the sinking ship, looking out on the black tempest and the hurtling sea. He bared his head and drew his sword Courtain, which having kissed upon the hilt, he offered thanks to heaven for the might and courage granted him through life; then with an unblenched cheek awaited death.

Presently he heard a voice in the air cry, 'Olger, I wait for thee. Fear not the waves, but come!' Then he cast himself into the sea, and a great wave bore him on its crest high up in air and placed him safely on the rocks. A strange light showed a narrow pathway among the crags, which Olger followed, walking towards the brightness till he reached a shining palace, invisible by day, but which at night glows into mortal ken—a palace of ivory and gold and ebony, glorious to behold, its halls made fair with imagery—and therein was set a banquet of most rare and dainty meats. None dwelt within this palace save a fairy horse, named Papillon, who motioned Olger to the banquet, and having brought water in a golden ewer that he might cleanse his hands, served humbly beside the knight at table till he had finished his repast. Then Papillon carried him to a bed whose pillars held golden candlesticks wherein tall tapers burned through the night. There Olger slept. But in the morning when he woke the palace had waned away in the dawn, and he was lying in a garden where the trees are always green, and the flowers fade not, and the summer never dies; where the sun goes not down, and the soft sweet sky is never darkened with storm; a garden in the Vale of Avalon, the land of Faery. And whilst his eyes were yet dazzled in wonderment, there stood suddenly at his side Morgan le Fay, queen of the faeries, clothed in a shining white kirtle, who said, " Welcome, dear knight, to Avalon. A weary time have I longed and waited for thy coming. Now thou art mine; my lord, my love. So let the restless ages roll, and the world totter and decay! We will dream on for ever in this changeless vale.' Then she put an inchanted ring upon his hand; so the years slipped from his shoulders and he stood before her in prime of youth and vigour. And she placed upon his brow a priceless golden crown of myrtle leaves and laurel, a crown no mortal treasure would suffice to buy—the Crown of Forgetfulness. Then Olger remembered no more the things which were past. His old loves, toils and battles faded from his mind; and in place of a dead memory a living love was given him, and he loved the fairy queen, and he was hers and she was his. Then she brought him to a palace where he found King Arthur healed of his wound, with whom he talked of knightly deeds and often rode with him in friendly justs against the forms of Sir Lancelot and Sir Tristrem, or the shapes of great giants and dragons which Morgan le Fay and her brother Oberon raised up by inchantment for their pastime.

Thus dwelt Sir Olger in a faery dream of love and pleasure in the land where there is no death and no time. And thus two hundred years passed by, like yesterday to him dreaming in the faery's lap.

But France fell into trouble. The enemy were on her soil. Battle raged, but there was none to lead her armies forth to victory. Chivalry was either dead or slept. On every side the Franks were beaten by their foes and driven back by Paynim and by Saracen, until it seemed that they would be blotted out from among the peoples of the world; and they cried for a deliverer. Morgan le Fay heard and pitied them; and though it grieved her sore to part with her own dear knight, she said, 'Olger must go back to battle again, for France and Christendom!' So she went to him and said,

'Dear one, do you know how long you have dwelt with me?'

'A week, a month, a year, perchance,' he answered, with a smile and kiss—'one does not reckon time in Paradise.'

Then she lifted the crown of forgetfulness from his brow and his memory came again.

'I must go back,' he cried, upstarting like one new wakened from a dream—'I have tarried here too long. Clarice will wonder why I stay, and Caraheu will think me wrecked. Peradventure Charles, my master, calls for Olger, and calls in vain. My sword, my horse, my spear! O let me go, sweet queen. Yet tell me, have I dwelt long in this fair garden?'

'Not long to me, dear knight—but you shall go,' she answered.

Then Morgan le Fay raised up his dead squire, Benoist, and brought his sword Courtain, and led forth Papillon for his steed.

'Guard well the ring upon your hand,' she said, 'for, wearing it, your youth and vigour will not fade.' She brought him moreover a torch, saying—'See that you kindle it not, so shall you live for ever; but if by mischance it should break out and burn, cherish the fire with care, for the measure of your days is the last spark of the torch.'

Then she threw a spell upon them all that they slept the while she carried them through the air to France. And when Sir Olger awoke he found himself lying by a fountain, his arms and armour at his side, and Benoist holding Papillon ready for him to mount: and all his life in Avalon seemed but a night's dream. Leaping to horse they rode into a city.

'What city is this?' asked Olger of a horseman whom he overtook.

'Montpellier, Sir Knight.'

'Oh, yes,' said the Dane, 'but I had forgotten. In truth I ought to know Montpellier well enough, for a kinsman of mine is governor of the city,' and he named the man he thought still ruled it.

'You are pleased to jest,' the horseman answered—'there was a governor of the city of that name two hundred years ago—the present governor is Regnier. But the man you speak of was a romance writer, wherefore I see you jest in claiming kinship with him. I need not tell you that he wrote the romance of Olger the Dane; a good story, though few believe it now, except perchance a man who goes about the city very often singing it, and picks up money from the crowd.'

The horseman slackened his pace a little till Benoist came up with him.

'Who is your master?' he whispered.

'Sir,' said the faithful squire, 'surely you must know him? He is Olger the Dane.'

'You malapert,' said the horseman, 'Olger the Dane perished in shipwreck two hundred years ago, and but for courtesy to the chevalier your master, I would make you pay dearly for jesting with me!'

Then the Dane and his squire rode on to the market-place of Meaux, where they stopped at the door of an inn which Olger well remembered.

'Can we lodge here?' he asked.

'Certainly, Sir Knight,' answered the innkeeper, 'and be well treated.'

'But I wish to see the landlord.'

'Sir?' said the innkeeper. 'I am the landlord.'

'Nay, nay,' answered Olger, 'but I want to see Hubert the Neapolitan who keeps this house.'

The man looked at him for a minute, and seeing the knight's countenance remain serious, he thought him nothing less than a madman. So he shut the door in his face, and having barred it, ran to an upper window and shouted into the street—'Here is a man who wishes to speak with Hubert, my grandfather's grandfather, who has been dead two hundred years. Seize him! He is mad or possessed with a devil. Send for the Abbot of St. Faron to come and cast out the evil spirit!'

A great crowd gathered about the inn and set upon the knight and his squire, harassing them with stones and darts; and an archer shot at Benoist and killed him. Then Sir Olger, grieving for the death of his squire, turned upon the crowd in fierce anger and leaped Papillon into their midst and cut them down on all sides till he had scattered from the market-place all those that were not dead upon its pavement. But so hotly burned his wrath that it kindled the torch he bare in his breast; wherefore he rode with it to the church of Saint Faron of Meaux. There the abbot met him.

Olger said, 'Is your name Simon? You at least should know me, for I founded this abbey and endowed it with lands and money.'

'Pardon,' answered the abbot, 'but I know little of those who came before me. Will you tell me your name?'

'Olger the Dane.'

'Strange,' thought the good man to himself, 'he calls me Simon when my name is Geoffrey, and the abbey charter certainly says that the abbot who lived in the days of Olger the Dane was named Simon, 'Sir Knight,' said the abbot aloud, 'do you know that Simon has been buried so many years that his very bones are long since crumbled into dust?'

'What! Simon gone? And Charles the Great, and Caraheu and my wife Clarice—where are they all? Not dead—it cannot be!'

'Dead—long dead—two hundred years, my son,' the abbot said. Then a great awe and wonderment fell upon Sir Olger as he thought that his dream of Avalon and Morgan le Fay perchance was true; and he followed the abbot into the church, scarce knowing whither he went, and there told all that had happened to him. And the abbot believed him and gave thanks to Heaven for sending back the redoubtable champion of France and Christendom. Then Olger told him the secret of the torch and begged him to make an iron treasure-house beneath the church, wherein so little air should come that the flame might dwindle to a single spark, and that spark being nursed and husbanded might smoulder slowly through the ages. Now this being done and the torch safely locked up and guarded, the abbot became very curious to take in his own hands the strange ring the knight wore on his finger; and Olger let him draw it off. Instantly his youth departed and he shrivelled into feebleness, a helpless withered husk of a man, with a skin like wrinkled parchment, and no sign of life save a quivering in his aged jaws. But his ring being restored, the Dane's strength and youth returned, and he leaped upon Papillon and rode off to fight for France.

The enemy was gathered at Chartres, a mighty host, and the flagging and disheartened Franks, broken into disorder, fled everywhere before the Paynim. Suddenly appeared in their midst a knight of mighty stature with a black eagle on his shield and riding on a great horse; a knight whose course about the battle-field was tracked with a long line of slain; and the frightened Franks seeing the marvels which he did, stayed in their flight, saying one to another, with bated breath for wonderment, 'It is Olger the Dane!' till the whisper grew to a cry, and the cry to a great battle-shout that rent the air, 'Olger the Dane! Olger the Dane!' as rushing fearless on the foe they swept the Paynim from the field as a tide sweeps litter from its course. Again and again did Olger lead the Franks to victory, nor rested he from battle till France was free again and Holy Church was stablished, and the spirit of chivalry had revived as in the olden time. While he fought the torch burned fiercely in the church of Saint Faron of Meaux, but when he stayed his hand it dwindled to a spark again.

Covered with glory and renown Sir Olger came at length to court. The King of France was dead, and the queen loved the knight for his bravery and gentleness. One day whilst he slept upon a couch within the banquet chamber of the palace, the queen came to him and one of her dames of honour, named the Lady of Senlis, withdrew the ring from his finger. They were frightened to see the strong man wither to an ancient dried-up skeleton. But the queen, knowing thereby of a truth that it was Olger the Dane, caused the ring to be immediately replaced and he regained his former youth. Howbeit the Lady of Senlis loved Sir Olger as well as the queen, and finding he cared nothing for her love, she determined at least to hinder him from wedding with her rival. So she sent thirty strong knights to waylay him as he passed out from the palace, charging them to seize Morgan le Fay's ring from his hand. But Sir Olger spurred Papillon among them, and with Courtain his good sword cut them down: neither helm, hauberk, nor shirt of mail, availed against his strong arm.

Now after this the queen would wed with Olger, for she said, 'He and no other shall sit upon the throne of Charles the Great, for he defended it of old and he has saved it now.' And Olger, flushed with the great honour of sitting on the seat of Charles his master, consented. So they made ready for the bridal, and all the lords and ladies of France came to be present at the marriage. Such pomp and ceremony was never seen since the crowning of King Charles. The church shone with the blaze of gold and heraldry, and glittered with the jewels of fair dames and the armour and the banners of brave knights. Stately music echoed through the aisles as a grand procession entered, and the trumpeters and heralds proclaimed the Queen of France and Olger king that shall be crowned. Then Sir Olger took the queen by the hand and led her through the bending throng till they came before the altar, and together kneeled upon the chancel pavement.

Suddenly there shone a light, brighter than all the gold and jewels, and Morgan le Fay, clothed in a shining kirtle so dazzling that none might bear to look thereon, floated down upon a white cloud, and caught away Sir Olger. And the cloud received them both, and wrapping them from mortal sight went up and waned into thin air and vanished in the church, so that whither they went no man can tell.

But Olger the Dane is not dead. For the torch still burns in the treasure house of the Abbey of Saint Faron of Meaux. He only dreams in the arms of Morgan le Fay in the faery land of Avalon, and one day he will waken and come back.

When men fail in the land of the Franks in time of sore distress, when her armies fall upon the field and the spirit of her people is all broken in the battle-flight, when there is none to lead her children against the stranger and the spoiler of her land, Morgan le Fay will pity her and raise up her old champion, and the Dane shall come back on his mighty battle-horse to trample down the enemy. Then shall the Franks again shout 'Olger the Dane!' and like an angry flood sweep down upon the foe.

HAVELOK.

THERE was once a king of England named Athelwold. Earl, baron, thane, knight, and bondsman, all loved him, for he set on high the wise and the just man, and put down the spoiler and the robber. At that time a man might carry gold about with him, as much as fifty pounds, and not fear loss. Chapmen and merchants bought and sold at their ease without danger of plunder. But it was bad for the evil person and for such as wrought shame, for they had to lurk and hide away from the king's wrath; yet was it unavailing, for he searched out the evil-doer and punished him, wherever he might be. The fatherless and the widow found a sure friend in the king; he turned not away from the complaint of the helpless, but avenged them against the oppressor, were he never so strong. Kind was he to the poor, neither at any time thought he the fine bread upon his own table too good to give to the hungry.

But a death-sickness fell on King Athelwold, and when he knew that his end was near he was greatly troubled, for he had one little daughter of tender age, named Goldborough, and he grieved to leave her.

'O my little daughter, heir to all the land, yet so young thou can'st not walk upon it; so helpless that thou canst not tell thy wants, and yet had need to give commandment like a queen! For myself I would not care, being old and not afraid to die. But I had hoped to live till thou should'st be of age to wield the kingdom; to see thee ride on horseback through the land, and round about a thousand knights to do thy bidding. Alas, my little child, what will become of thee when I am gone?'

Then King Athelwold summoned his earls and barons, from Roxborough to Dover, to come and take counsel with him as he lay a-dying on his bed at Winchester. And when they all wept sore at seeing the king so near his end, he said, 'Weep not, good friends, for since I am brought to death's door your tears can in nowise deliver me; but rather give me your counsel. My little daughter that after me shall be your queen; tell me in whose charge I may safely leave both her and England till she be grown of age to rule?'

And with one accord they answered him, 'In the charge of Earl Godrich of Cornwall, for he is a rightwise and a just man, and held in fear of all the land. Let him be ruler till our queen be grown.'

Then the king sent for a fair linen cloth, and thereon having laid the mass book and the chalice and the paton, he made Earl Godrich swear upon the holy bread and wine to be a true and faithful guardian of his child, without blame or reproach, tenderly to intreat her, and justly to govern the realm till she should be twenty winters old; then to seek out the best, the bravest, and the strongest man as husband for her and deliver up the kingdom to her hand. And when Earl Godrich had so sworn, the king shrived him clean of all his sins. Then having received his Saviour he folded his hands, saying, '*Domine, in manus tuas*;' and so died.

There was sorrow and mourning among all the people for the death of good King Athelwold. Many the mass that was sung for him and the psalter that was said for his soul's rest. The bells tolled and the priests sang, and the people wept; and they gave him a kingly burial.

Then Earl Godrich began to govern the kingdom; and all the nobles and all the churls, both free and thrall, came and did allegiance to him. He set in all the castles strong knights in whom he could trust, and appointed justices and sheriffs and peace-sergeants in all the shires. So he ruled the country with a firm hand, and not a single wight dare disobey his word, for all England feared him. Thus, as the years went on, the earl waxed wonderly strong and very rich.

Goldborough the king's daughter throve and grew up the fairest woman in all the land; and she was wise in all manner of wisdom that is good and to be desired. But when the time drew on that Earl Godrich should give up the kingdom to her, he began to think within himself— 'Shall I, that have ruled so long, give up the kingdom to a girl and let her be queen and lady over me? And to what end? All these strong earls and barons, governed by a weaker hand than mine, would throw off the yoke and split up England into little baronies, evermore fighting betwixt themselves for mastery. There would cease to be a kingdom and so there would cease to be a queen. She cannot rule it and she shall not have it. Besides, I have a son. Him will I teach to rule and make him king.'

So the earl let his oath go for nothing, and went to Winchester where the maiden was, and fetched her away and carried her off to Dover to a castle that is by the sea shore. Therein he shut her up and dressed her in poor clothes, and fed her on scanty fare; neither would he let any of her friends come near her.

Now there was in Denmark a certain king called Birkabeyn, who had three children, two daughters and a son. And Birkabeyn fell sick, and knowing that death had stricken him, he called for Godard, whom he thought his truest friend, and said, 'Godard, here I commend my children to thee. Care for them I pray thee, and bring them up as befits the children of a king. When the boy is grown and can bear a helm upon his head and wield a spear, I charge thee make him King of Denmark. Till then hold my estate and royalty in charge for him.' And Godard swore to guard the children zealously, and to give up the kingdom to the boy. Then Birkabeyn died and was buried. But no sooner was the king laid in his grave than Godard despised his oath; for he took the children, Havelok, and his two little sisters, Swanborough and Helfled, and shut them up in a castle with barely clothes to cover them. And Havelok, the eldest, was scarce three years old.

One day Godard came to see the children and found them all crying for hunger and cold; and he said angrily, 'How now! What is all this crying about?' The boy Havelok answered him, 'We are very hungry, for we get scarce anything to eat. Is there no more corn, that men cannot make bread and give us? We are very hungry.' But his little sisters only sate shivering with the cold, and sobbing, for they were too young to be able to speak. The cruel Godard cared not. He went to where the little girls sate, and drew his knife, and took them up one after another and cut their throats. Havelok, seeing this sorry sight, was terribly afraid, and fell down on his knees begging Godard to spare his life. So earnestly he pleaded that Godard was fain to listen; and listening he looked upon the knife, red with the children's blood; and when he saw the still, dead faces of the little ones he had slain, and looked upon their brother's tearful face praying for life, his cruel courage failed him quite. He laid down the knife. He would that Havelok were dead, but feared to slay him for the silence that would come. So the boy pleaded on; and Godard stared at him as though his wits were gone; then turned upon his heel and came out from the castle. 'Yet,' he thought, 'if I should let him go, one day he may wreak me mischief and perchance seize the crown. But if he dies my children will be lords of Denmark after me.' Then Godard sent for a fisherman whose name was Grim, and he said, 'Grim, thou wottest well thou art my thrall. Do now my bidding and to-morrow I shall make thee free and give thee gold and land. Take this child with thee to-night when thou goest a-fishing, and at moon-rise cast him in the sea, with a good anchor fast about his neck to keep him down. To-day I am thy master and the sin is mine. To-morrow thou art free.'

Then Grim took up the child and bound him fast, and having thrust a gag of clouts into his mouth so that he could not speak, he put him in a bag and took him on his back and carried him home. When Grim got home his dame took the bag from off his shoulders and cast it down upon the ground within doors; and Grim told her of his errand. Now as it drew to midnight he said, 'Rise up, dame, and blow up the fire to light a candle, and get me my clothes, for I must be stirring.' But when the woman came into the room where Havelok lay she saw a bright light round the boy's head, as it had been a sunbeam, and she called to her husband to come and see. And when he came they both marvelled at the light and what it might mean, for it was very bright and shining. Then they unbound Havelok and took away the gag, and turning down his shirt they found a king-mark fair and plain upon his right shoulder. 'God help us, dame,' said Grim, 'but this is surely the heir of Denmark, son of Birkabeyn our king! Aye, and he shall be king in spite of Godard.' Then Grim fell down at the boy's feet and did him obeisance, and said, 'Forgive me, my king, for that I knew thee not. We are thy thralls, and henceforth will feed and clothe thee till thou art grown a man and can bear shield and spear. Then deal thou kindly by me and mine as I shall deal to thee. But fear not Godard. He shall never know, and I shall be a bondsman still, for I will never be free till thou, my king, shalt set me free.'

Then was Havelok very glad, and he sat up and begged for bread. And they hasted and fetched bread and cheese and butter and milk; and for very hunger the boy ate up the whole loaf, for he was well-nigh famished. And after he had eaten, Grim made a fair bed and undressed Havelok and laid him down to rest, saying, 'Sleep, my son; sleep fast and sound and have no care, for nought shall harm thee.'

On the morrow Grim went to Godard and telling him he had drowned the boy, asked for his reward. But Godard bade him go home and remain a thrall, and be thankful that he was not hanged for so wicked a deed. After a while Grim, beginning to fear that both himself and Havelok might be slain, sold all his goods, his corn, and cattle, and fowls, and made ready his little ship, tarring and pitching it till not a seam nor a crack could be found, and setting a good mast and sail therein. Then with his wife, his three sons, his two daughters, and Havelok, he entered into the ship and sailed away from Denmark; and a strong north wind arose and drove the vessel to England, and carried it up the Humber so far as Lindesay, where it grounded on the sands. Grim got out of the boat with his wife and children and Havelok, and then drew it ashore.

On the shore he built a house of earth and dwelt therein, and from that time the place was called Grimsby, after Grim.

Grim did not want for food, for he was a good fisherman both with net and hook, and he would go out in his boat and catch all manner of fish—sturgeons, turbot, salmon, cod, herrings, mackerel, flounders, plaice, lampreys, and thornback, and he never came home emptyhanded. He had four panniers made for himself and his sons, and in these they used to carry the fish to Lincoln, to sell them, coming home laden with meat and meal, and simnel cakes, and hemp and rope to make new nets and lines. Thus they lived for twelve years. But Havelok saw that Grim worked very hard, and being now grown a strong lad, he bethought him 'I eat more than Grim and all his five children together, and yet do nothing to earn the bread. I will no longer be idle, for it is a shame for a man not to work.' So he got Grim to let him have a pannier like the rest, and next day took out a great heaped basket of fish, and sold them well, bringing home silver money for them. After that he never stopped at home idle. But soon there arose a great dearth, and corn grew so dear that they could not take fish enough to buy bread for all. Then Havelok, since he needed so much to eat, determined that he would no longer be a burden to the fisherman. So Grim made him a coat of a piece of an old sail, and Havelok set off to Lincoln barefoot to seek for work.

It so befell that Earl Godrich's cook, Bertram, wanted a scullion, and took Havelok into his service. There was plenty to eat and plenty to do. Havelok drew water and chopped wood, and brought turves to make fires, and carried heavy tubs and dishes, but was always merry and blithe. Little children loved to play with him; and grown knights and nobles would stop to talk and laugh with him, although he wore nothing but rags of old sailcloth which scarcely covered his great limbs, and all might see how fair and strong a man God had made him. The cook liked Havelok so much that he bought him span-new clothes with shoes and hosen; and when Havelok put them on, no man in the kingdom seemed his peer for strength and beauty. He was the tallest man in Lincoln, and the strongest in England.

Earl Godrich assembled a Parliament in Lincoln, and afterward held games. Strong men and youths came to try for mastery at the game of putting the stone. It was a mighty stone, the weight of an heifer. He was a stalwart man who could lift it to his knee, and few could stir it from the ground. So they strove together, and he who put the stone an inch farther than the rest was to be made champion. But Havelok, though he had never seen the like before, took up the heavy stone, and put it full twelve foot beyond the rest; and after that none would contend with him. Now this matter being greatly talked about, it came to the ears of Earl Godrich, who bethought him—' Did not Athelwold bid me marry his daughter to the strongest man alive? In truth I will marry her to this cook's scullion. That will abase her pride; and when she is wedded to a thrall she will be powerless to injure me. That will be better than shutting her up; better than killing her.' So he sent and brought Goldborough to Lincoln, and set the bells a-ringing, and pretended great joy, for he said, ' Goldborough, I am going to spouse thee to the fairest and stalwartest man living.' But Goldborough answered she would never wed with any but a king. ' Aye, aye, my girl; and so thou would'st be queen and lady over me? But thy father made me swear to give thee to the strongest man in England, and that is Havelok, the cook's scullion; so lief or loth to-morrow thou shalt wed.' Then the Earl sent for Havelok and said, ' Master, wilt wive?' ' Not I,' said Havelok— ' for I cannot feed nor clothe a wife. I have neither stick nor stem—no house, no cloth, no victuals. The very clothes I wear do not belong to me, but to Bertram the cook, as I do.' ' So much the better,' said the earl, ' but thou shalt either wive with her that I shall bring thee, or else hang upon a tree. So choose.' Then Havelok said he would sooner wive. Earl Godrich went back to Goldborough and threatened her with burning on a stake unless she yielded to his bidding. So, thinking it God's will, the maid consented. And on the morrow they were wed by the Archbishop of York, who had come down to the Parliament, and the earl told money out upon the mass-book for her dower.

Now after he was wed, Havelok wist not what to do, for he saw how greatly Earl Godrich hated him. He thought he would go and see Grim. When he got to Grimsby he found that Grim was dead, but his children welcomed Havelok and begged him bring his wife thither, since they had gold and silver and cattle. And when Goldborough came, they made a feast, sparing neither flesh nor fowl, wine nor ale. And Grim's sons and daughters served Havelok and Goldborough.

Sorrowfully Goldborough lay down at night, for her heart was heavy at thinking she had wedded a thrall. But as she fretted she saw a light, very bright like a blaze of fire, which came out of Havelok's mouth. And she thought 'Of a truth but he must be nobly born.' Then she looked on his shoulder, and saw the king-mark, like a fair cross of red gold, and at the same time she heard an angel say,

'Goldborough, leave sorrowing, for Havelok is a king's son, and shall be King of England and of Denmark, and thou queen.'

Then was Goldborough glad, and kissed Havelok, who, straightway waking, said, 'I have seen a strange dream. I dreamed I was on a high hill whence I could see all Denmark; and I thought as I looked that it was all mine. Then I was taken up and carried over the salt sea to England, and methought I took all the country and shut it within my hand.' And Goldborough said, 'What a good dream is this! Rejoice, for it betokeneth that thou shalt be King of England and of Denmark. Take now my counsel and get Grim's sons to go with thee to Denmark.'

In the morning Havelok went to the church and prayed God speed him in his undertaking. Then he came home and found Grim's three sons just going off a-fishing. Their names were Robert the Red, William Wendut, and Hugh Raven. He told them who he was, how Godard had slain his sisters, and delivered him over to Grim to be drowned, and how Grim had fled with him to England. Then Havelok asked them to go with him to Denmark, promising to make them rich men. To this they gladly agreed, and having got ready their ship and victualled it, they set sail with Havelok and his wife for Denmark. The place of their landing was hard by the castle of a Danish earl named Ubbe, who had been a faithful friend to King Birkabeyn. Havelok went to Earl Ubbe, with a gold ring for a present, asking leave to buy and sell goods from town to town in that part of the country. Ubbe, beholding the tall, broad-shouldered, thick-chested man, so strong and cleanly made, thought him more fit for a knight than for a pedlar. He bade Havelok bring his wife and come and eat with him at his table. So Havelok went to fetch Goldborough, and Robert the Red and William Wendut led her between them till they came to the castle, where Ubbe, with a great company of knights, welcomed them gladly. Havelok stood a head taller than any of the knights, and when they sat at table Ubbe's wife ate with him, and Goldborough with Ubbe. It was a great feast, and after the feast Ubbe sent Havelok and his friends to Bernard Brown, bidding him take care of them till next day. So Bernard received the guests and gave them a rich supper.

Now in the night there came sixty-one thieves to Bernard's house. Each had a drawn sword and a long knife, and they called to Bernard to undo the door. He started up and armed himself, and told them to go away. But the thieves defied him, and with a great boulder-stone brake down the door. Then Havelok, hearing the din, rose up, and seizing the bar of the door stood on the threshold and threw the door wide open, saying, 'Come in, I am ready for you!' First came three against him with their swords, but Havelok slew these with the door bar at a single blow; the fourth man's crown he brake; he smote the fifth upon the shoulders, the sixth athwart the neck, and the seventh on the breast; so they fell dead. Then the rest drew back and began to fling their swords like darts at Havelok till they had wounded him in twenty places. For all that, in a little while he killed a score of the thieves. Then Hugh Raven waking up called Robert and William Wendut. One seized a staff, each of the others a piece of timber big as his thigh, and Bernard his axe, and all three ran out to help Havelok. So well Havelok and his fellows laid about them, breaking ribs and arms and shanks, and cracking crowns, that not a thief of all the sixty-one was left alive. Next morning when Ubbe rode past and saw the sixty-one dead bodies, and heard what Havelok had done, he sent and brought both him and Goldborough to his own castle, and fetched a leech to tend his wounds, and would not hear of his going away. For said he, 'This man is better than a thousand knights.'

Now that same night, after he had gone to bed, Ubbe awoke about midnight and saw a great light shining from the chamber where Havelok and Goldborough lay. He went softly to the door and peeped in to see what it meant. They were lying fast asleep and the light was streaming from Havelok's mouth. Ubbe went and called his knights and they also came in and saw this marvel. It was brighter than a hundred burning tapers; bright enough to choose money by. Havelok lay on his left side with his back towards them, uncovered to the waist; and they saw the king-mark on his right shoulder sparkle like shining gold and carbuncle. Then knew they that it was King Birkabeyn's son, and seeing how like he was to his father, they wept for joy. Thereupon Havelok awoke, and all fell down and did him homage, saying he should be their king. On the morrow Ubbe sent far and wide and gathered together earl and baron, dreng and thane, clerk, knight, and burgess, and told them all the treason of Godard, and how Havelok had been nurtured and brought up by Grim in England. Then he showed them their king, and the people shouted for joy at having so fair and strong a man to rule them. And first Ubbe sware fealty to Havelok, and after him the others both great and small. And the sheriffs and constables and all that held castles in town or burg came out and promised to be faithful to him. Then Ubbe drew his sword and dubbed Havelok a knight, and set a crown upon his head and made him king. And at the crowning they held merry sports—justing with sharp spears, tilting at the shield, wrestling, and putting the stone. There were harpers and pipers and glee-men with their tabours; and for forty days a feast was held with rich meats in plenty and the wine flowed like water. And first the king made Robert and William Wendut and Hugh Raven all barons, and gave them land and fee. Then when the feast was done, he set out with a thousand knights and five thousand sergeants to seek for Godard. Godard was a-hunting with a great company of men, and Robert riding on a good steed found him and bade him come to the king. Godard smote him and set on his knights to fight with Robert and the king's men. They fought till ten of Godard's men were slain; the rest began to flee. 'Turn again, O knights!' cried Godard, 'I have fed you and shall feed you yet. Forsake me not in such a plight.' So they turned about and fought again. But the king's men slew every one of them and took Godard and bound him and brought him to Havelok. Then King Havelok summoned all his nobles to sit in judgment and say what should be done to such a traitor. And they said, 'Let him be dragged to the gallows at the mare's tail, and hanged by the heels in fetters, with this writing over him, "This is he that reft the king out from the land, and the life from the king's sisters."' So Godard suffered his doom and none pitied him.

Then Havelok gave his sceptre into Earl Ubbe's hand to rule Denmark on his behalf, and after that took ship and came to Grimsby, where he built a priory for black monks to pray evermore for the peace of Grim's soul. But when Earl Godrich understood that Havelok and his wife were come to England, he gathered together a great army to Lincoln on the 17th of March, and came to Grimsby to do battle with Havelok and his knights. It was a great battle, wherein more than a thousand knights were slain. The field was covered with pools of blood. Hugh Raven and his brothers, Robert and William, did valiantly and slew many earls; but terrible was Earl Godrich to the Danes, for his sword was swift and deadly as the levin fork. Havelok came to him and minding him of the oath he sware to Athelwold that Goldborough should be queen, bade him yield the land. But Godrich defied him, and running forward with his heavy sword cut Havelok's shield in two. Then Havelok smote him to the earth with a blow upon the helm; but Godrich arose and wounded him upon the shoulder, and Havelok, smarting with the cut, ran upon his enemy and hewed off his right hand. Then he took Earl Godrich and bound him and sent him to the queen. And when the English knew that Goldborough was the heir of Athelwold they laid by their swords and came and asked pardon of the queen. And with one accord they took Earl Godrich and bound him to a stake and burned him to ashes for the great outrage he had done.

Then all the English nobles came and sware fealty to Havelok, and crowned him king in London. Of Grim's two daughters Havelok wedded Gunild the elder to Earl Reyner of Chester; and Levive the younger, fair as a new rose blossom opening to the sun, he married to Bertram the cook, whom he made Earl of Cornwall in the room of Godrich.

Sixty years reigned Havelok and Goldborough in England, and they had fifteen children, who all became kings and queens. All the world spake of the great love that was betwixt them twain. Apart, neither knew joy or happiness. They grew never weary the one of the other, for their love was ever new; and not a single word of anger passed between them all their lives.

BEOWULF.

SCEF and Scyld and Beówulf—these were the god-like kings of the Gar-Danes in days of yore.

Upon the sea and alone came Scéf to the land of Scâni. He came in fashion as a babe, floating in an ark upon the waters, and at his head a sheaf of corn. God sent him for the comfort of the people because they had no king. He tore down the foemen's thrones, and gave the people peace and passed away.

From him proceeded Scyld the Scefling, the strong war-prince, wise in counsel, generous ring-giver. When Scyld grew old and decrepit, and the time drew near that he should go away into the peace of the Lord, he would be carried to the sea-shore. Thither with sad hearts his people bare him, and laid him in the bosom of a war-ship heaped with treasure of gold and costly ornaments, with battle-weapons, bills and spears and axes, and the linked war-mail. Rich sea-offerings of jewels and precious things they laid upon his breast. High over head they set up a golden ensign; then unfurled the sail to the wind, and mournfully gave their king and all his treasures to the deep and solemn sea; to journey none knew whither. Upon the sea, and alone, went Scyld from the land of the Scâni. He went in fashion as a king, floating away in his good ship along the track of the swans, his war-weeds and his battle-spoils beside him. He gave the people peace and passed away.

From him came Beówulf the Scylding, glorious and majestic, strong of hand, the beloved chieftain. He gave the people peace and passed away.

After the days of the god-like kings, the Danes chose Healfdene for their leader He ruled long and well, and died in a good old age, and Hrothgár his son reigned in his stead. To Hrothgár good fortune and success in war were given, so that he overcame his enemies, and made the Gar-Danes a powerful and wealthy people.

Now, in his prosperity, it came into Hrothgár's mind to build a great mead-hall in his chief city; a lordly palace wherein his warriors and counsellors might feast, they and their children for ever, and be glad because of the riches which God had given them. Biggest of all palaces was the mead-hall of Hrothgár; high-arched and fair with pinnacles. He named it Heorot, that men might think of it as the heart and centre of the realm; that, banded together in friendship at one common banquet table, they might talk of measures for the common good. With a great feast he opened Heorot the palace, with sound of harp and song of Skald, giving gifts of rings and treasure; so that all the people rejoiced and became of one mind, and sware fealty to him. Then Hrothgár's heart was lifted up because of Heorot which he had builded.

But far away in the darkness where dwell the Jötuns and Orks and giants which war against God, there abode a mighty evil spirit, a Jötun both terrible and grim called Grendel, a haunter of the marshes, whose fastnesses were dank and fenny places. Grendel saw the lofty palace reared, and was filled with jealous anger because the people were as one, and because there was no longer any discord among them. At night he came to the mead-hall, where slept the nobles and thanes after the feast, forgetful of sorrow and unmindful of harm; he seized upon thirty men and carried them away to his dwelling-place, there to prey upon their carcases. Bitterly mourned the Gar-Danes for their brothers when awaking in the morning twilight they saw the track of the accursed spirit, and knew that mortal strength availed for nought against their enemy. Next night Grendel came and did the like, and so for twelve years thereafter came he oftentimes and snatched the Danes whilst they slumbered, and carried them away to slay and tear them, neither for any ransom would he be prevailed upon to make peace. The houses in the land became empty, because of the counsellors and warriors that were swept away to the death-shade of the Ogre of the misty marshes. But like a shepherd for his flock grieved Hrothgár for the desolation of his people. Broken in spirit he sat in the many-coloured mead-hall, watching among his vassals through the night; but Grendel touched him not. To right and left of him the monster seized strong-hearted men, a helpless prey, but passed Hrothgár by. God set his finger on the king that the Jötun should not harm him. Hrothgár grew wearied that he was spared while his dear friends were taken; and when men came to him for counsel, he, the wise counsellor, had none to give but sat in silence, his head bowed in sorrow on his hands. Vainly the people prayed in the tabernacles to their idols that they would send a spirit-slayer down to save them.

Away to the westward among the people of the Geáts lived a man, strongest of his race, tall, mighty-handed, and clean made. He was a thane, kinsman to Hygelác the Geátish chief, and nobly born, being son of Ecgtheow the Wægmunding, a war-prince who wedded with the daughter of Hrethel the Geát. This man heard of Grendel's deeds, of Hrothgár's sorrow, and the sore distress of the Danes, and having sought out fifteen warriors, he entered into a new-pitched ship to seek the war-king across the sea. Bird-like the vessel's swan-necked prow breasted the white sea-foam till the warriors reached the windy walls of cliff and the steep mountains of the Danish shores. They thanked God because the wave-ways had been easy to them; then, sea-wearied, lashed their wide-bosomed ship to an anchorage, donned their war-weeds, and came to Heorot, the gold and jewelled house. Brightly gleamed their armour and merrily sang the ring-iron of their trappings as they marched into the palace; and having leaned their ample shields against the wall, and piled their ashen javelins, steel-headed, in a heap, they came to where sat Hrothgár, old and bald, among his earls. Hrothgár looked upon the Geátish warriors, chief of whom Hygelác's servant, the mighty son of Ecgtheow, towered tall above the rest, god-like in his shining armour and the dazzling war-net of mail woven by the armourer. Seeing him, Hrothgár knew that the son of Ecgtheow was Beówulf, raised up of God to be a champion against Grendel the evil spirit,—Beówulf the mighty-handed one, in the gripe of whose fingers was the strength of thirty men. And while wonderingly he gave him welcome, Beówulf spake, 'Hail, O King Hrothgár! Alone and at night I have fought with evil-beings, both Jötuns and Nicors, and have overcome; and now, in order to deliver the bright Danes from their peril, have I sailed across the sea to undertake battle with Grendel the Ogre. And since no weapon may avail to wound the flinty-hided fiend, I will lay by my sword and shield, and empty-handed go to meet him. I will grapple with him, strength against strength, till God shall doom whether of us two Death taketh. If I should be bereft of life, send back to Hygelác the war-shroud which Wayland forged to guard my breast, but make no corpse-feast for me: bury my body, and mark its resting-place, but let the passer-by eat without mourning; fate goeth ever as it must.'

Hrothgár answered, 'Well know I, O my friend Beówulf, of your bravery and the might that dwelleth in your fingers! But very terrible is Grendel. Full oft my hardy warriors, fierce over the ale-cup at night, have promised to await the Ogre with the terror of their swords and dare his wrath; but as oft at morning-tide the benched floor of the palace has reeked with their blood. But since your mind is valiant, sit down with us to our evening feast, where by old custom we incite each other to a brave and careless mind before night set in, and Grendel come to choose his prey.'

Then were the benches cleared and Beówulf and the Geáts sate in the mead-hall at the banquet with the Danes. Freely flowed the bright sweet liquor from the twisted ale-cup borne by the cup-bearer in his office, whilst the Skald sang of old deeds of valour.

Then said Beówulf, 'Full many a man of you hath Grendel made to sleep the sleep of the sword, and now he looketh for no battle from your hands. But I, a Geát, who in the old time have slain strange shapes of horror in the air or deep down underneath the waves, will encounter him, and alone; unarmed, I will guard this mead-hall through the night. Alone with the fiend will I await the shining of the morrow's sun on victory, or else sink down into death's darkness fast in the Ogre's grasp.' Hrothgár, the old-haired king, took comfort at his steadfast intent, and Wealtheow the Queen, so fair and royally hung with gold, herself bare forth the mead-cup to Beówulf, and greeted him with winsome words as champion of her people. Beówulf took the cup from Wealtheow's hands saying, 'No more shall Grendel prey upon the javelin-bearing Danes till he has felt the might of my fingers.' Happy were the people at his boldness, and blithe their joy over the well-served hall-cup.

Then King Hrothgár would seek his evening rest, for the wan shadows of night were already darkening the welkin. The company arose and greeted man to man, and Hrothgár greeted Beówulf and said, 'O friend, never before did I commit this hall to any man's keeping since I might lift a spear. Have now and hold this best of palaces. Be wakeful and be valourous, and nothing that thou mayest ask shall be too great a prize for victory.' So the king departed with his troop of heroes from the mead-hall.

Beówulf took off his coat of iron mail, loosed the helmet from his head, and from his thigh the well-chased sword; and having put aside his war-gear wholly, stepped upon his bed and laid him down. Around him in the dusk lay many well-armed Danes slumbering from weariness. The darkness fell, and all the keepers of the palace slept save one. Beówulf in a restless mood, naked and weaponless, waited for the foe.

Then in the pale night Grendel the shadow-walker rose up with the mists from the marshes and came to Heorot, the pinnacled palace. He tore away the iron bands, fire-hardened, wherewith the doors were fastened, and trod the many-coloured floor of the sounding hall. Like fire the anger flashed from his eyes, lightening the darkness with a hideous light. Terribly he laughed as he gloated on the sleeping Danes and saw the abundant feast of human flesh spread out around him.

Beówulf, the strong Waegmunding, held his breath to watch the method of the Ogre's onset. Nor did the fiend delay, for quickly seizing a sleeping warrior he bit him in the throat, drank the blood from his veins, and tare his limbs and ate the dead man's feet and hands. Then coming nearer, Grendel laid his hands upon the watchful champion. Suddenly Beówulf raised himself upon his elbow and clutched the Ogre fast; against the shoulder he fastened on the grim Jötun with his hands; and held him. Never before had Grendel met the gripe of hands so strong. He bent himself with all his might against Beówulf and dragged him from his bed, and toward the door; but Beówulf's fingers never slackened from their hold: he drew the Ogre back. Together they struggled upon the hall pavement till the palace rocked and thundered with their battle. Great wonder was it that the palace fell not, but it was made fast with well-forged iron bands within and without; yet many a mead-bench overlaid with twisted gold was torn from its place in the furious strife, and the ale spilled on the floor. But Grendel found the clutch of his enemy too strong; he could not loose it with all his wrestlings; and he knew that he must seek to flee away and hide himself in his marsh dwellings. But Beówulf griped him tight; and when the fiend would drag him down the hall he put forth all his strength into his clenched hands. Suddenly the Ogre's shoulder rift from neck to waist. The sinews burst asunder, the joints gave way, and Beówulf tare the shoulder and the shoulder-blade from out his body. So Grendel escaped from Beówulf's grasp and in his mortal sickness fled to the fens. There Death clutched him and he died.

Then in the morning many warriors gathered to the mead-hall; and Beówulf brought his trophy, Grendel's hand and arm and shoulder, and hung it high in the palace that all might see. So hard were the fingers and the stiff nails of the war-hand that no well-proven steel would touch them. Hrothgár thanked God and Beówulf for this deliverance, and having made the broken palace strong again with iron bonds and hung it round about with tapestry, he held therein a costly feast of rejoicing with his warriors and kinsmen, whereat many a mead cup was outpoured. To Beówulf he gave rich gifts: a golden ensign and a helm, a breastplate and a sword, each wrought with twisted work of gold, together with eight horses whose housings shone with precious stones. And when the lay of the glee-man was sung and the wine flowed, and the jocund noise from the mead-benches rose loud, Queen Wealtheow went forth under her golden crown and bare the royal cup to Beówulf to drink. A ring she gave him of rare workmanship all aglow with carven gems, likewise sumptuous dresses, rich with broidered gold and needle-work of divers colours. 'Be happy and fortunate, my lord Beówulf!' she said. 'Enjoy these well-earned gifts, dear warrior, for thou hast cleansed the mead-hall of the realm, and for thy prowess fame shall gather to thee, wide as the in-rolling sea that comes from all the corners of the world to circle round our windy walls.'

Then Wealtheow and her lord King Hrothgár departed to take their evening rest, and Beówulf went to a house appointed for him. But the warriors bared the benches, spread out their beds and bolsters, set their hard-rimmed shields at their heads, and lay down to sleep in the mead-hall. In their ringed mail-shirts they laid them down, ready for war, as was their custom in house and field; ready, if need should befall their lord. Good was the people. So darkness fell in the hall and the Hring-Danes slept, nor wot they that any were fated to die. But at midnight Grendel's mother arose from her dwelling in the cold streams, from her home in the terrible waters, and fiercely grieving for her son's death came and walked the beautiful pavement of Heorot. Greedy of revenge she clutched a noble, very dear to Hrothgár, and tare him in his sleep. Then while the Danes, waking in tumult, were yet smitten with the terror of her presence, she seized from its hanging-place the well-known arm and shoulder of her son, and passed out quickly with the prize. A great cry rose in the mead-hall. Beówulf and King Hrothgár heard it, and came hastily to Heorot.

When King Hrothgár knew what had been done, he said, 'O Beówulf, my friend; still sorrow for my people bindeth me. Æschere, my counsellor and war companion, hath been foully torn to death, nor can we tell whose shall be the next blood with which this new wolf-hearted fiend shall glut herself. Scarce a mile hence is her dwelling-place, a stagnant lake within a darksome grove of hoary-rinded trees whose snaky roots twine all about the margin, shadowing it. A foul black water, whereon fire dwelleth at night, a loathely lake wide-shunned of man and beast. The hunted stag, driven thither, will rather part from life upon the brink than plunge therein. Darest thou seek this place, to battle with the monster and deliver us?'

The son of Ecgtheów the Waegmunding answered, 'Yea, I dare. For to avenge a friend is better than to mourn for him. Neither can a man hasten nor delay his death-hour. Fate waiteth for us all; and he that goeth forth to wreak justice need not trouble about his end, neither about what shall be in the days when he no longer lives.'

Then King Hrothgár gave thanks to the mighty God, and caused a steed with curled hair to be bitted and led forth for Beówulf. With a troop of shield-bearers he accompanied the hero along the narrow path across steep stone-cliffs over-hung with mountain trees, till they came to the joyless wood and the drear water where Grendel's mother dwelt. Snakes and strange sea-dragons basked upon the turbid pool, and Nicors lay upon the promontories. Beówulf blew upon his horn a terrible war-dirge, and they sank and hid themselves. Then in his war-mail shirt which knew well how to guard his body from the clutch of battle, his white helmet, mail-hooded, on his head, and in his hand his hilted knife Hrunting, of trusty steel blood-hardened, Beówulf plunged into the slimy lake and the sea-wave closed above him. Long he swam downward into the dark abyss before he found the bottom. Grendel's mother lay in wait and grappled him in her claws, and bore him to her roofed sea-hall beneath the water, where gleamed a pale fire-light. Then Beówulf saw the mighty sea-woman, and furious, swung his heavy sword and brought it down with a crash upon her head. But the keen steel failed him in his need, for her hard skull turned its biting edge. So angrily flinging from him his twisted blade, and trusting wholly to his mighty hand-gripe, he caught the wolf-woman by the shoulders and bent her backwards to the floor. Fiercely she gave back his grappling, and wrestled him till from weariness he rolled and fell; then, drawing her brown-edged knife she sought at one blow to avenge her son. But the hard battle-net upon his breast hindered the entrance of the knife, and God who rules the firmament protected him, so that he gat upon his feet again. Then Beówulf saw hanging in the sea-hall a huge sword made by giants, a weapon fortunate in victory, doughty of edge, which none but he could wield. Hard grasped he the war-bill by the hilt, and whirled it savagely against the sea-woman's ring-mail in despair of life. Furious he struck, and the bone-rings of her neck gave way before it; so the blade passed through her doomed body, and, war-wearied, her carcase lay lifeless on the floor.

Long time with patience waited Hrothgár and his counsellors, looking into the dark lake where Beówulf went down. Noon-day came, and seeing the water stained with blood, they deemed their champion was dead, and sorrowfully gat them home.

But beneath the water was a great marvel. Beówulf cut off the sea-woman's head, but so hot and poisonous was her blood that the mighty sword which reeked therewith melted and burned away, all save the hilt. So it wasted like the ice when the sun loosens the frost-chain and unwinds the wave-ropes. Then Beówulf swam upwards with his heavy burden, the sea-woman's head and the sword-hilt, and having reached the shore he saw the lake dry up. By its hair he carried the woman's head, awful and glaring, to the mead-hall, and showed the wondering Danes the golden sword-hilt wrought in fashion as a snake, and marked with Runic characters wherein the history of its forging was set forth. Beówulf said, 'God and my strong hand prospered me and gave me victory. Yea, in my strength I have wrested away the sword wherewith the giants before the Flood defied the Eternal God! I have overcome the enemies of God, who have battled with Him unsubdued for countless years! Wherefore fear not, King Hrothgár, for thou and thine may sleep secure in Heorot which I have cleansed!'

The wise and hoary king, the mingled-haired, gazed long in silence on the sword-hilt, reading of the wondrous smiths that made it after the fall of the devils. Then he spake gently, 'O my friend Beówulf, great is thy glory and uplifted high, and wondrous are the ways of God who through the wisdom of His great mind distributeth so much strength to one man, making him a refuge-city for the peoples. But suffer a kindly word of counsel, dear warrior. When all things are subject to a man, when the world turneth at his will, he forgetteth that the flower of his strength and his glory are but for a little while before he leave these poor days and fade away forgotten and another come in his place. But the great Shepherd of the Heavens liveth on, and raiseth up and putteth down whom He will. Dear friend, beware of pride, which groweth up and anon beguileth the heart so fast to sleep that the warrior remembereth not how Death will overpower him at the last. So gloried I, when with spear and sword having freed the Hring-Danes from all their enemies under heaven, I built this mead-hall in my pride and reckoned not upon an adversary. But God sent Grendel many years to trouble me, till my pride was humbled, and He brought me a deliverer in thee. Wherefore I give Him thanks and pray thee to be like-minded, to bear thine honours meekly and to choose eternal gains. Go now with gladness to the feast, and to-morrow we will give forth treasure, the dear meed of warriors.'

Great joy was there in many-windowed Heorot, and when Night covered the land with her dusky helmet the warriors laid them down in peace and slept beneath the lofty arches, various with gold: no foe came near the noble dwelling-place; for Heorot was fully purged.

After that, when Beówulf would make ready his vessel to cross the sea again to his kinsman Hygelác, lord of the Geáts, King Hrothgár loaded him with a multitude of gifts of gold and rings and battle-harness, and made a treaty with him that there should be peace for ever betwixt the Gar-Danes and the Geáts, and that the treasures of both peoples should be held in common. So Beówulf and his companions entered their sharp-keeled ship and sailed to their home across the wide sea-plain, the seagull's path. Hygelác welcomed him returning spoil-laden from the game of war, and Beówulf shared his treasures with his friends and kinsfolk. Yet was it for a long time a shame and reproach to the Geáts that they held the might and courage of Beówulf in but little esteem, neither made they him a ruler and a chief among them. During many years the son of Ecgtheów grew old in good and quiet deeds; for he, the fierce in war, was gentle of mind, and meekly held the might and strength wherewith he was indued of God. But the Swedes came up to battle against the Geáts, and in his time of need Hygelác went to his treasure-house and brought forth Nagling, the wound-hardened sword, old and grey-spotted, of Hrethel, Beówulf's grandfather, and gave it to the strong Waegmunding, and made him captain over seven-thousand warriors and gave him a royal seat. So Beówulf went to battle and drave out the enemy. But Hygelác fell in the war-tumult. Thereby the broad kingdom came by inheritance into Beówulf's hand; and he was made king and held it fifty years with a strong arm against all foes, ruling wisely as a prudent guardian of his people.

Now, in those days, a terrible flaming dragon began to rule in the dark nights, a fire-drake which long had abode in the cavern of a rocky cliff hard by the sea, along a difficult and stony path unknown to men. All his cavern was full of ancient treasure in rings and vases and golden ornaments, which he had secretly stolen during a space of three hundred years. Folk missed their gold and jewels but knew not who the robber was, until one night a wayfarer by chance wandered into the cave and saw the precious

hoard and the dragon slumbering by it, and snatched a
golden drinking-cup from the glittering heap and fled.
Hot burned the dragon's anger when, awaking, he missed
the gold drinking-cup, and saw that his secret treasure-
hoard was known to men. He rose upon his flaming
wings each night and sped to and fro seeking the man
who had done him this evil; and where he went he consumed houses and people and scorched the land into
a wilderness. The waves of fire reached the palace and
destroyed that best of buildings, the fastness of the Geâts,
and the people trembled for fear of the terrible flyer of
the air. Dark thoughts came into Beówulf's mind, insomuch that he was even angry with the Almighty because
of the plague which visited the people, and in his bitterness he spake hard things against the Eternal Lord such
as befitted him not. Then he commanded to make a
variegated shield of iron, strong and well-tempered, to
withstand the fire-breath of the adversary, and having
put on his war-mail, he called together his warriors and
said, 'Many a battle, O my comrades, have I dared from
my youth up; many a warrior's soul have I loosed from its
shattered house of bone with my biting war-bill. Now
for the greater glory of my age will I seek this flaming
war-fly alone. Be it yours to abide afar off on the hill and
watch the combat, but take no part therein. The glory
and the treasure and the war are mine alone. Would I
might proudly grapple with nothing but my naked hands
against this wretch, as of old I did with Grendel! But
since the war-fire is so fierce and poisonous, I take my
shield and byrnie and my sword. Not a footstep will I
flee till Fate make up her reckoning betwixt us.'

Then arose the famous warrior, stoutly trusting in his
strength, and came to the hoary stone-cliff whence waves
of fire flowed like a rushing mountain torrent. Boldly
and with angry words the lord of the Geâts defied the
fire-drake to come out and face the thirsty steel of Nagling,
his sharp-edged blade.

Quickly the winged worm answered to his challenge. Bending itself together for the contest, and darting furious flames, it closed in battle with the haughty warrior; and they who beheld afar off saw nothing but the fire which wrapped the fighters round. The good shield guarded Beówulf's body less truly than he had hoped from the beams of fire. Nagling, the hard-edged, bit less strongly than the champion, who knew so well to swing the warbill, had need in his extremity: the keen sword deceived him as a blade of such old goodness ought not to have done. The fierce treasure-keeper, boiling with fury, flooded the plain in a sea of fire, so that the nobles which watched the combat turned and fled to the wood for safety. All turned and fled save one. Wigláf, son of Weohstán, a dear shield-warrior, only kinsman of Beówulf, saw his lord suffer in the bitter strife, and his heart could no longer refrain. He seized his shield of yellow lindenwood, and his old tried sword. 'Comrades,' he cried, 'forget ye all the gifts of rings and treasure we have received from Beówulf's hands at the daily out-pouring of the mead? Forget ye his past benefits and his present need?' Then he ran through the deadly smoke and the clinging fire to succour his dear lord. The flame burnt up his linden shield, but Wigláf ran boldly underneath the shield of his master and fought at his side. Then Beówulf, jealous for his single fame, though heat-oppressed and wearied, swung his great war-sword and drave it down mightily upon the head of the fire-drake. But Nagling failed him, and brake in sunder with the blow; for Beówulf's hand was too strong and overpowered every sword-blade forged by mortal man, neither was it granted to him at any time that the edges of the smith's iron might avail him in war. Wildly he spurned the treacherous sword-hilt from him, and furious rushed upon the fiery worm and clutched it by the neck in the terrible gripe of his naked hands. There upon the plain he throttled it, while the burning life-blood of the fire-drake boiled up from its throat and set his hands aflame. Yet loosened he never his gripe, but held the twining worm till Wigláf carved its body in twain with his sword. Then Beówulf flung the carcase to the earth and the fire ceased.

But the fiery blood was on his hands; and they began to burn and swell; and he felt the poison course through all his veins and boil up in his breast. Then Beówulf knew that he drew nigh the end of this poor life; and whilst Wigláf cooled his wounds with water, he said, 'Fifty years have I shepherded my people, and though so strong no king dared greet me with his warriors, I have only fought to hold my own. Neither have I made war on any man for lust of gain or conquest, nor oppressed the weak, nor sworn unjustly. Wherefore I fear not that the Ruler of men will reproach me with the doings of my life. But now, dear Wigláf, go quickly to the cavern and bring me of the gold and many-coloured gems that I may look thereon before I die; that so, feasting my eyes with the treasure I have purchased for my people, I may more gently yield up my life.'

So Wigláf hastened and came to the fire-drake's treasure-house; and lo! his eyes were dazzled with the glittering gold, the dishes, cups, and bracelets that were heaped within the cave and lightened it. Then he laded himself with gem-bright treasure, one trinket of each kind, and a lofty golden ensign, the greatest wonder made with hands, and a war-bill jewelled, shod with brass and iron-edged; and came again to his master. Fast ebbed the chieftain's life upon the sward. Senseless he lay, and very near his end. Wigláf cooled his fiery veins with sprinkled water, and the lord of the Geáts opened his eyes and gazed upon the golden cups and variegated gems. He said, 'Now give I thanks to the Lord of All, the King of Glory, for the precious riches which mine eyes behold; nor do I grudge to have spent my life to purchase such a treasure for my people. Bid them not to weep my death, but rather glory in my life. Let them make a funeral fire wherein to give my body to the hot war-waves; and let them build for my memorial a lofty mound to sea-wards on the windy promontory of Hronesnaes, that the sea-sailors as they journey on the deep may see it from afar and say, "That is Beówulf's cairn."'

Then from his neck he lifted his golden chain, and took his helmet and his byrnie and his ring and gave them to Wigláf, saying, 'Dear friend, thou art the last of all our kin, the last of the Waegmundings. Fate hath long swept my sons away to death. I must go and seek them!' So parted his soul from his breast.

Presently came the nobles which before had fled, and found Wigláf washing the body of their prince with water and sorrowfully calling upon him by name. Bitterly spake Wigláf to them. 'Brave warriors! Now that the war is over, have you in truth summoned courage up to come and share the treasure? You, who forsook the treasure-earner in his need; forsook in his extremity the high prince who gave you the very war-trappings wherein you stand? I tell you nay. You shall see the treasure with your eyes and hold it in your hands, but it shall not profit you. The Swedes beyond the sea who came against Hygelác and slew him, the same that Beówulf overcame and drave out, when they learn that our strong warrior has passed into his rest, will come again and snatch the land from your weak holding and carry you away into bondage, and seize the treasure. Let it be his who won it! Safer will he guard it in his sleep than you with feeble war-blades and weak javelins. Let the lord of the Geáts slumber with it in the cairn which we shall build for him; so shall men fear to touch the treasure as they would to snatch a sleeping lion's prey.'

So with one accord they bare the hoary warrior to Hronesnaes, and from the cavern drew out the twisted gold in countless waggon-loads.

Then for Beówulf did the people of the Geáts prepare a funeral pile, strong, hung round with helmets, with war-boards and bright byrnies; and weeping they laid their lord upon the wood. Eight chosen warriors walked with Wigláf round the pile with torches to kindle the bale-fire. The wood-smoke rose aloft, the noise of mourning of a people sorry of mood mingled with the crackling of the blaze, and the wind blew on the war-bier till the flames consumed the bone-house of the mighty-handed chief.

Then the Geáts wrought a great cairn beside the sea. It was high and broad, and easy to behold by the sailors over the waves. Ten days they wrought thereat, and built up the beacon vast and tall, and laid the ashes of their lord therein. Then they brought the rings and gems and ornaments and put them in the mound. No earl ever wore the twisted gold for a memorial, no maiden was made glad with the golden rings upon her neck, but the treasure sleeps in the earth with him who won it! Twelve nobles rode about the mound calling to mind their king in speech and song; praising his valour; even as it is fit that a man should extol his lord and love him in his soul after his body has become valueless and only his deeds remain.

So mourned the people of the Geáts for their dear lord. And they said of him that he was the mildest and gentlest of all the kings of the world, the most gracious to his people and the most jealous for their glory.

INDEX.

AAC

Aachen, 321 et seq.
Accolon, 20, 92, 101, 102 et seq.
Achar, 359
Achilleus, 17, 45, 58
Adam Bell, 15
Adonis, 37, 46
Æschere, 368
Æscingas of Kent, chronology of the, 6
Æsir, ship of the, 48
Aethlios, 10
Agamemnon, 75
Aglavale, 154
Agni, 18
Agravaine, 215 et seq.
Ahi, 56, 78
Ahmed and the Peri Banou, 52
Aigeus, 17
Aigyptos, 14
Aineias, story of, 2
Akrisios, 58
Alice, the Fair Pilgrim, 37, 156
Alisander, 37, 155 et seq.
Alkinoös, palace of, 79
Alkmênê, 16
Allah-ud-deen, ring of, 36
— sword of, 42
Allegorical visions, 51, 181, 183, 188, 190
Allegories, 179
Alory, 351
Alpheios, 38, 58
Alroy, forest of, 107
Al-sirat, bridge of, 95
Amaltheia, horn of, 47, 49
Amant, 153
Ambrose, 61
Amirannt, 313

ART

Amlethus, 73
Amphitryon, 16
Amphion, 14, 38, 76
Amulius, 57, 71
Amys of the Mountain, 310
Andred, 142, 150
Anelaphus, 73
Anglides, 155
Angys the Dane, 234
Animism, 48
Anlaf, 73, 315
Anlaf-cwiran, 73
Annowre, 148
Anseis, 322
Ansirus, 156
Anteros, 14
Anvil and sword, 16
Apples, golden, 12
Aragus, 318
Arbor vitæ, 49
Arethousa, 58, 67
Argentile, 72
Argo, 26, 48
Argus the dog, 62
Aries the cowherd, 22, 97
Aristhanas, 37, 71
Aristomenes, 49
Arjuna, 14
Artemis, 14, 24, 75, 76
Arthur, arguments for the historical character of, 2
— birth and early years of, 16, 82
— character of, 56
— crowning of, at Rome, 112
— the Emperor, 110
— expedition of, against the Roman Emperor, 2
— the giant-slayer, 111

ART

Arthur, grave of, alleged discovery of the. 3
— and Guenevere, 154
— supposed historical residuum in the story of, 4
— imprisonment of, 101
— loves of, 85
— and Mordred, 56 *et seq.*
— and Olger, 361
— φιλογύνης, 18
— story, origin of the, 7
— subordination of, 22, 44, 46, 64, 89, 152, 221
— sword of, 17, 19, 44, 82, 86, 102
— treachery of Lancelot to, 54
— and Tristram, 152, 160
— twelve victories of, 5
— visions of, 56, 226
— wanderings of, 27
— wedding of, 96 *et seq.*
— and the Weird Sisters, 47
Arundel, 62, 274, 282, 296
Ascapard, 62, 284, 290, 291
Ashera, 49
Asklepios, 37, 71
Asterodia, 10
Astolat, the Fair Maid of, 47, 205 *et seq.*
Astrabakos, 60
Astyages, 58
Asvins, the, 13, 23
Atalanta, 34
Athelstan, 301
Athelwold, 308
Athênê, ship of, 49
— Tritonis, 58
Attabiscar, song of, 66
Aubry, 309
Aulis, 76
Aurentil, 76
Aurilisbrosius, 234, 240
Avalon, or Avilion, Vale of, 58, 69, 229, 361
Azidahaka, 56

B

Baal, altar of, 49
Badon, Mount, siege of, 5, 6
Bagdemagus, 100, 178
Baldur, 29
Baldwin, 83, 111, 155
— son of Ganelon, 327

BRA

Baldwin, son of Olger, 355
Baligant, 341
Balin and Balan, 21, 22, 45, 55 *et seq.*, 115
Ban, 84
Barbarossa, 59
Barham Down, battle of, 226
Barnard, 314
Basant, 324
Baseborn boy, the. (*See* Boots and Beggars.)
Basil, 324
Bedegraine, Castle of, 85
Bedivere, Sir, 11, 227
Beggars in Mythology, 21, 62, 65, 71, 89, 371
Belingog, 262
Bellerophon, 43, 62, 276
Belleus, 117
Bellisande, 349
Bendelaine, 132
Benoist, 356
Beowulf, 28, 47, 73, 380 *et seq.*
Berchta, 12
Beranger, 332
Bernard, 204
Bernard Brown, 377
Bertram, 374
Berwick, 223
Bevis of Hamtoun, 46, 61 *et seq.*, 268 *et seq.*
Bheki, 63
Bifröst, bridge of, 95
Big Bird Dan, 42
Birkabeyn, 71, 370
Blaise, 85, 240
Blamor de Ganis, 140
Blancandrin, 320 *et seq.*
Blancheflor, 245, 300
Bleeding spear, the, 199
Blinnt, 169
Blood, the tribute of, 23, 195
Boabdil, 59
Boar, the, 273
— the wound of the, 46, 169
Boniface, 275, 283
Boots, 21, 29, 32, 71, 73, 75, 83, 86, 89, 118, 145, 231, 269
— of buffalo leather, 33
Borre, 85
Bors, 23, 50, 51, 84, 166, 206, 231
— temptation of, 190
Brademond, 273

Bradwin, 283
Bran, horn of, 46
Branquemond, 359
Breidablick, 22
Brengwaine, 140 et seq., 252 et seq.
Brennor, 141, 145
Briar-rose, 11, 34
Briseis, 65
Broceliande, 243
Broiefort, 70
Bruhier, 358
Bryant of Cornwall, 294
Brynhild, 34, 41 et seq.

C

Cacus, 78
Caerleon, 84
Camelot, 88
Canados, 263
Canterbury, bishop of, 226, 231
Carados, 114
Caraheu, 350 et seq.
Carbonek, 182
Carlisle, bishop of, 221
Cart, knight of the, 211
Curteloise, 195
Castor, 23, 170
Ceres, 12
Ceridwen, 46
Chandragupta, 8
Chapel, Perilous, 116
Charles the Great, 320 et seq.
Charlot, 353
Cheapside, Bevis in, 63, 294
Children, the fatal, 36
— slaughter of the, 19
Chochiluichus, 73
Chronology, artificial, 5, 6
Chrysâôr, 44
Chryséis, 73
Cinderella, 21, 32, 71
Clarice, 358
Claudas, 85
Cloudland, history of, 7
Colbrand, 315
Colgrevance, 192, 216
Conelaphus, 73
Conelocke, 73
Constantine, 111
Constaunce, 234
Corbin, the Maid of, 164
Correlative deities, 13, 14, 23

Corsuble, 350
Courtain, 354
Crux salutifera, 49
Cuaran, 73
Curan, 73
Cycles, mythical, in the Arthur story, 31
Cycle, I., Arthur, 31
— II., Balin, 31
— III., Lancelot, 31 et seq.
— IV., Gareth, 31 et seq.
— V., Tristram, 36 et seq.
Cyrus, the historical and mythical, 8, 15, 16, 21, 32, 37

D

Dahana, 58
Damas, 101
Dame of the Fine Green Kirtle, story of the, 28
Danaë, 35
Danaos, 14
Dannemont, 350
Daphné, 58
Darkness, myths of the, 57, 58
— snake of, 227
David, sword of, 195
Dawn, myths of the, 10, 17, 45, 56
Day and night, myths of the, 13, 14
Death, 45
Deianeira, 40
De la Rowse, Duke, 133
Delectable Isle, the, 47, 159
Delos, 11, 16, 22, 29, 58
Dêmêtêr, 12, 49
Devil's dam, 78, 388
Dew, myths of the, 10, 19, 58
Didier of Lombardy, 357
Diktynna, 18
Dimilioc, 81
Dinadan, 151, 155, 158
Dionysos, 29, 37
Dioskouroi, 14, 23
Divoun, 268, 286, 289
Dolorous Gard, 223
— stroke, 21, 23, 93
Dornroschen, 11, 34
Dragon-slayers, the, 38, 62, 63, 73, 164, 285, 307, 312, 394
Dragons and streams, 60, 64, 238
— of Cola and Calabria, the, 283
Drakôn, 3

DRO

Drought, myths of the, 13
Dumb Maiden, the, 164
Dummling, 29
Durendal, 17, 67, 232
Dwarfs, 12

E

Earth, 26
Ecgtheow, 383
Ector, 51, 82, 149, 232
Edenhall, luck of, 49
Edgar, 289
Eginhard on the death of Roland, 6
Eigil, 76
Elaine, the Fair Maid of Astolat, 42, 206 et seq.
— the mother of Galahad, 25, 42, 52, 165, 198
— the wife of Ban, 99
Eleusis, 11
Elf-child, the, 236
Eliazar, 199
Eliot, 155
Elizabeth, 135
Endymion, 10, 58, 59
Engeler of Gascoigny, 334
Eôs, 45, 65
Ephialtes, 75
Epimenides, 59
Epiméthous, 14
Erceldonne, Thomas of, 39, 59
Erl King, the, 38
Ermonie, 245
Ermyn, 271, 293
Ernis, 305
Eros, 14
Eteokles, 14
Ethel, 73
Ethiopians, table of the, 26, 49
Ettard, 108
Etymology, guidance of, in the comparison and interpretation of myths, 10–12
Euémerism, 4
Eurydikê, 74
Euryphassa, 22
Eurystheues, 14, 68, 75
Eve, spindles of, 194
Excalibur, 20, 58, 102, 105, 112, 228

GEO

F

Fafnir, 64, 78
Fairfine, 22, 71
Fair Gruagach, 28
Fair Rosamund, 3
Faith, ship of, 47, 194
Faithful John, 38
Faldrun, 336
Fancy, source of, 8
Faramond, 347
Fatal Children, 21, 36, 62, 68, 70, 135
— Sisters, 30, 47, 107, 229
Feinne, history of the, 61
Felice, 65, 297 et seq.
Five Kings, defeat of the, 100
Florentin, 261
Florentine, 284, 311
Fool, the Great, 71
Fools, in mythology, 21
Forgetfulness, cup of, 62
Fortager, 234 et seq.
— Castle of, 236
Frithjof Saga, 38
Frog Sun, Bheki, the, 63

G

Gabalatine, 114
Gaheris, 114, 219
Gaire, 304
Galagns, 100
Galahad, 21, 31, 46, 47, 51 et seq., 165, 173 et seq.
— and Lancelot, 196
— son of Brennor, 141
— well of, 199
Ganelon, 323 et seq.
Ganzblick, 22
Gareth, 32, 63, 117 et seq., 219
Garlon, 23, 93
Gaultier, 337
Gawaine, 21, 29, 31, 51, 97, 106, 218 et seq., 224
— death of, 226
— vow of, 177, 219
— wounding of, 224
Geáts, 383
Geoffrey of Anjou, 322
— Abbot of St. Faron de Meaux, 364
Geography, mythical, 84

Geraint, 2
Gerairni, 26, 50
Gerard, 323
Gerhardin, 263 et seq.
Gerin, 323
Giant who had no heart in his body, the, 13, 61
Giant-slayers, 63, 115, 281
Gilbert, 117
Glass Coffin, 62
Glauké, 40
Glaukos, 10, 14, 35, 45
Glenkundie, 38
Glorian, 347
Gloriande, 353
Godard, 37, 71, 370
Godfrey, 347 et seq.
Godrich, 71, 369
Gold Child, the, 32, 33
Goldborough, 71, 368 et seq.
Gorgons, 30
Gorlois, 16, 81
Gothic Princess, story of the, 60
Graiai, 30
Grail, the, 49, 165
Gram, the sword, 17, 20
Grander, 280
Graurock, 77
Green Lawns, Knight of the, 121
Grendel, 78, 382 et seq.
— mother of, 388
Grettir, exploits of, 5, 14, 28, 33, 43
— shortness of, 32
Grey frock, 77
Griffin, story of the old, 60
Griflet, 100
Grim, the fisherman, 37, 71, 371 et seq.
Gringamore, 127
Gonvernail, 250
Gudrun, 42
Guenevere, 24, 31, 36, 52, 96, 167, 202 et seq.
— and Lancelot, 202 et seq., 230
— and the lion, 146
— cruelty and sensuality of, 25, 41, 52 et seq., 213
— dower of, 25, 96
Guichard, 303
Guise, 332
Gunild, 380
Gunnar, 41
Gunter, 302

Gunthram, 63
Gurmoise, 309
Guy of Hamtoun, 268
— of Warwick, 61, 297 et seq.
— son of Bevis, 295
Gyges, ring of, 36

H

Hacon Grizzlebeard, 72
Hades, 10, 56
— cap of, 22
Hagen, 20
Haltelere, 336
Halvor, 32
Hameln, piper of, 38
Hamlet, 32, 74, 14
Hanelocke, 73
Harold, 70
Harpagos, 37, 71
Harp-i-chruti, 49
Havelok, 22, 28, 32, 37, 70 et seq., 371 et seq.
Healer, Arthur the, 46,
— Isolte, or Ysonde, the, 40, 265
— Lancelot, the, 46, 116
— Oinôné, the, 40
Healfdene, 382
Hedge of spears, the, 34
Hekaté, 10
Hektor, 20, 45
Helfled, 371
Helgi Hundingsbana, 24, 69
Helgis, the, 28, 59
Helen, 24, 41, 53, 54
Helené Dendritis, 75
Helios, 10, 14
Hellawes, 116
Henry II. and the grave of Arthur, 3
Heorot, 382
Hephaistos, 20
Herakles, 14, 26, 38, 40, 42, 56, 58, 68
— expedition of, against Ilion, 2
— madness of, 44
— poisoned arrows of, 40
— sleep of, 11
— twelve labours of, 5
Heraud of Ardennes, 297, 303, 307
Herb, the holy, 100
Hermanec, 46, 159
Hermes, 38, 76
— rod of, 49

HER

Heroes, bondage of, 74
— vulnerable only in one spot, 20, 77, 337
Herrise, 100
Hierodouloi, 26, 50
Higelac, 73, 383, 391
Hilda, 12, 67, 340 et seq.
Hjärrandi, 71
Hjordis, 20
Holda, 12, 67
Holger Danske, 68
Holy Coat of Treves, 77
— Grail, the, 26, 165, 168
Horn, the magic, 26, 46, 143, 330 et seq.
Horse, inchanted, 30, 360
Horselberg and Ercildoune, 59
House in the wood, 12
Howel, 135, 144
Hrethel, 383, 392
Hrothgar, 382
Hruodland, 6
Hrunting, 382
Hubert, 364
Hugh Raven, 376
Hugo, 302
Hunding, 59
Huon of Bordeaux, 26
Huron, myths, 13
Hygelac. (See Higelac.)
Hypnos, 10

I

Iamos, 60
Iasion, 12
Iduna, 11, 64
Igerne, 16, 81
Ikaros, 76
Iliad, 56
Ilion, myth of, 4, 45
Ill-tempered Princess, the, 12
Illugi, 14
Imagination, power of the human, 9
Incubi, 60
Indra, 18, 29, 58, 78
Io, 38
Iokasté, 18
Iolaos, 11
Iolè, 38
Iosca, 13
Ioskeha, 13
Iphigeneia, 24, 47

LAD

Iphikles, 14
Ironside, 129
Iron-stone, 62
Isis, ship of, 26, 49
Isolte (Ysonde) the Fair, 25, 36, 43 et seq., 157, 251 et seq., 261
— (Ysonde) of the White Hands, 42, 144 et seq., 261
Ixíôn, 13, 30

J

Jeffrey of Monmouth, 16
Jonas, 313
Joseph of Arimathea, 50, 199
— son of Jacob, divining cup of, 49
Josian, 63, 271, 290
Jötuns, 382
Joyous Gard, 157, 160, 220 et seq.
Joyous Isle, 171
Jung Frau Maleen, 12

K

Kalinak, 56
Kalypso, 59
Kamsa, 19
Karl the Great, 59, 348
Kay, 32, 82, 100, 115
Kehydius, 148 et seq., 163
Kephalos, 10, 18, 58
King of Ireland, 136, 140
— of the Lake, 100
Kinkenadon, Castle of, 117, 134
Kleopatra, 38, 65
Knapsack, Hat, and Horn, 33
Knight, the best in the world, 34, 95, 103, 164, 165, 174, 178
— of the Ill-shapen Coat, 33, 145 et seq.
— of the Red Lawns, 34
Knights who fail, the, 34, 125
Korônis, 38
Kreôn, 40
Krishna, 14, 18, 41, 56
Kyklôps, 17

L

Lad who knew not how to shiver, the, 32
Lady of the Lake, 20, 87, 90, 103, 109, 204

Index.

L

Laios, 18, 57
Lamorak, 26, 87, 145, 153, 159
Lancelot, 21, 24, 28, 34, 46, 51, 99, 112, 230, 232
— the best knight in the world, 34
— falsehood of, 25
— healing power of, 214
— humiliation of, 189
— madness of, 167
— and Olger, 161
— sensuality of, 31
— and Tristram, 152
Lanceor, 90
Lappenberg, arguments of, for the historical existence of Arthur, 2
Latmos, 58
Laurel, 134
Lavaine, 205, 215
Lavinium, Sow of, 2
Leodegrance, 28
Light and darkness, myths of, 14, 15
Linet, 34, 35, 123
Lingard, Dr., on the myth of Arthur, 5
Lionel, 23, 112 et seq., 190 et seq., 220
Liones, 123 et seq.
Loathly Lady, 83, 291
Lodbrog, Ragnar, 56
Logedas, Rajah, 62
Loki, 11
Lombard, Earl, 302
Lonazep, Castle of, 159
Loret, 305
Lorraine, Duke of, 309 et seq.
Lotos, 26, 49
Love-drink, 141, 252
Lovers of the Maidens, 18, 39, 41
Lucan, 57, 227
Luck of Edenhall, 26
Luxman, 14
Lykia, 10, 22, 45
Lykourgos, 3

M

Macduff, 37
Madhu, 19
Madness of Herakles, 44
— of Lancelot, 44, 167
— of Tristram, 43, 149
Mador of the Gate, 114, 203
Maidens, Castle of the, 179
Maidens, Lovers of the, 18, 39, 41
Maira, 75
Malgrin, 156
Manassen, 105
Marganices, 336
Marhaus, 29, 30, 39, 106, 109, 136 et seq.
Mark of Cornwall, 26, 37, 38, 41, 91, 136 et seq., 153, 247 et seq., 258
Marsilius, 320 et seq.
Maurice of Mounclere, 238
Medeia, robe of, 28, 40, 67
Meleagros, 38, 45, 65, 68, 362
Meliagrance, 25, 209 et seq.
Melias, 57, 178
Meliodas, 135
Meliora, 347
Meliot, 117
Memnon, 45, 55
Menelaos, 32, 54
Meriadok, 258
Miles, 291
Milo, 287
Mimir, well of, 17
Minos, 18
Mirandoise, 20
Mitra, 14
Modrain, 198
Moirai, 30, 68
Mombraunt, 279
Moon, myths of the, 10
Moradin, 359
Morage, 271
Moraunt, 249
Mordred, 18, 57, 88, 114, 215 et seq.
— and Gueuevere, 225
— death of, 228
Morgadour, 305
Morgan, 245
Morgan le Fay, 20, 46, 69, 92, 103 et seq., 143, 151, 156, 230, 317 et seq.
Morglay, 17, 273
Morloise, 195
Mother, the mourning, 11
Moyne, 234
Moysant, 359
Murdered and risen gods and heroes, 24
Myth and history, 15
Myths, Aryan and non-Aryan, 8
— comparison of, 7, 13

Myths, classification of, 14
— etymological explanation of, 10
— historical residuum in, 55
— modification of, 49, 51
— origin of, 8
— repetition of, 21, 27, 44
— of savage tribes, 9
— of the darkness, 57, 58
— of the dawn, 10, 17, 45, 56
— — — day and night, 13, 14, 45
— — — dew, 10, 19, 58
— — — drought, 13
— — — moon, 10
— — — spring, 11
— — — sun, 10, 28, 48, 65, 70
— — — winter, 11
Mythical cycles, 31
— heroes, madness of, 149
— — subordination of, 75, 78, 118 *et seq.*
— — temptation of, 182 *et seq.*
— names, 76

N

Nabon, 145
Nacien, 189
Nagling, 392
Names, mythical, 10
Naraka, 19
Narkissos (narcissus), the stupefying plant, 12, 59
Nature myths, 30
Naymes, 324 *et seq.*
Neleus, 14
Nennius, 61
Nessos, 40, 78
Nicors, 384
Niflunga, 42
Night, myths of the, 59
Nigramous, Castle, 116
Nimue, 98, 148, 230
Niniame (or Nimue), 243
Nix of the Mill Pond, 12
Norns, 30
Nuns, 26, 50

O

Oberon, 26, 361
— horn of, 47, 50
Ocresia, 71
Odin, 16, 17
Odysseus, 21, 32, 38, 46, 58, 62, 65, 70

Oidipous, 8, 16, 18
Oinônê, 40, 45
Old Griffin, story of the, 60
Old Soldier, story of the, 65
Olger the Dane, 28, 37, 62, 67 *et seq.*, 330 *et seq.*, 347 *et seq.*
Oliver, 322 *et seq.*
Omphalê, 28
One-eyed gods, 17
One-handed gods, 17
Ontzlake, 101
Ophelia, 75
Orendil, 70, 76
Orkney, King of, 92
— Queen of, 18, 85, 130
Orpheus, 38, 56, 76
Ortygia, 11, 38
Osile, 308
Otho of Pavia, 300, 302, 310
Otos, 75
Ottawa myths, 13
Ovand, 350
Oygel, 76

P

Palamedes, 42, 47, 137, 158 *et seq.*, 173
Palestina, 347
Pan, 38, 76
Panch Phul Ranee, 35
Panis, the, 45, 54, 78
Papillon, 360
Parallelisms of the Lancelot and Tristram myths, 36, 40, 42
Parcæ, 30
Paris, 40, 45, 54, 55, 58
Pase, Earl of, 156
Pasiphaê, 22
Patrise, 203
Patroklos, 20
Peirithoös, 14
Pellam, 93
Pelias, 14
Pellens, 108, 110
Pelles, 21, 50, 199
Pellinore, 22, 87, 92
Pendragon Castle, 147
— Uther, 16, 81, 234, 240
Penelopê, 38, 62
Porcivale, 21, 47, 51, 87, 183 *et seq.*
— sister of, 24, 47, 195
Perilous Castle, the, 35, 131

PER

Perilous chapel, the, 106
— pass, the, 121
— seat, the, 97, 164, 175
Perin of Montbeliard, 93
Peris of the forest, 115
Persant of Inde, 122
Persephoné, 10, 64
Perseus, 8, 17, 23
Pescheur, 180
Peticrewe, 259
Phaëthon, 14
Phallus, myths connected with the, 40
Philoktetes, 40
Phoibos, 14, 16, 18, 29, 44, 58
Pilgrim of love, 30, 77
Pillars or rods, 109
Pinabel, 344 et seq.
Pinel, 202
Poison, death by, 74
Poisoned weapons, 39, 137, 144, 250, 265
— robes, 28, 40, 61, 106
Pollux, 23
Polydegmon, 10
Polydektes, 75
Polyidos, 35
Polyneikes, 14, 18
Pomegranate, the, 12
Popular stories, classification of, 14
Potenhithe, 294
Prettyhands, 29, 32, 63, 71, 117 et seq.
Princess on the glass hill, 32
Pristina, 347
Prokles, 14
Prokris, 10, 18, 38, 58
Prometheus, 14
Protogeneia, 10
Punchkin, 13, 61
Python, 78

Q

Quails in mythology, 11
Queen Bride, 77
— of Eastland, 113
— of the Five Flowers, 35
— of Orkney, 130, 154
— of the Out Isles, 113
— of the Waste Land, 230

SAD

R

Ragnar Lodbrog, 20, 56
Rama, 14
Rapunzel, 35
Ravaná, 78
Raynburn, 318
Red City, the, 47
— Lawns, Knight of the, 29, 118, 122
Redesoun, 274
Regin, 21
Regnier, 300, 308
Relics, alleged evidence of, 2
Repetition of myths, 44
Reproduction, symbols of, 27, 36
Reyner of Chester, 380
Rhea, cup of, 49
Rhymer, Thomas the, 38
Rich Peter the Pedler, story of, 60
Ring, King, 38
— the magic, 35, 36, 69, 131 et seq., 279, 365
— of Allah-ud-Deen, 36
— of Gyges, 36
Rinkrank, 38
Robe, the poisoned, 28, 40, 67, 106
Robert the Red, 376
Robin Hood, 16
Rod of Wealth, 49
Rohand, 245, 248, 297
Roland, 6, 16, 65 et seq., 320 et seq.
Roland Rise, 245
Roman kings, artificial chronology of the reigns of the, 6
Rome, Emperor of, 86, 110
Romulus and Remus, 8, 14, 16, 32
Roncesvalles, battle of, 66, 329 et seq.
Rosamund, Fair, 3
Rose Maiden, the, 11
— of the Alhambra, 35
Round Table, the, 25, 36, 49, 96, 182, 242
— knights of the, 96, 177
Rudrau, 14
Rustem, 37
Ryons, 22, 88, 92

S

Saber, 62, 269, 291
Sadok, 37, 155, 303

SAD

Sadonae, 353
Sails, black and white, 265
Samson, 322
Sanam, daughter of Earl, 85
Sangreal, the, 26, 36, 46, 48, 165, 168, 180, 197
— achievement of the, 52
— etymology of the word, 27
Saramá, 54
Sarras, city of, 47, 195
Sarpedon, 10, 14, 45, 55
Saturnus, 12
Savitar, 17, 68
Scabbard, the magic, 88, 102, 105
Scef, 37, 47, 381
Scott, Sir Walter, novels of, 15
Scyld, 37, 381
Sebastian, 59, 70
Segard, 297
Segwarides, 39, 139, 145, 255
Segwin, 303
Seirens, 38
Seléné, 10, 59
Serapis, 49
Serpent of darkness, 56, 64
Servius Tullius, 37, 71
Seven Sleepers of Ephesus, 59, 69
Ship of Athêne, 49
— — faith, 149
— — Isis, 49
— — the dead, 46, 159, 208
Ships, Phaiakian, 48, 381
Shortshanks, 32
Siege Perilous, the, 97, 104
Sigmund, 16, 17
Sigrún, 24
Sigurd, 18, 37, 38, 45, 64
Simon, Abbot, 364
Sisyphos, 13, 30
Sita, 78
Siza, Pass of, 330 *et seq.*
Sleep, 15
Snake-leaves, the, 35, 128
Snakes, in mythology, 74, 278
— and weasels, 63, 227
Solar myths, imagery of, 29, 79
Solomon, bed of, 194
— ewer of, 49
Soma, 14
Soria Moria Castle, 32
Sisters, the fatal, 30, 47, 107
Spear, the mystic, 49, 166, 199
Spiritual place, the, 47, 195

TIN

Sphinx, 65, 78
Spring, myths of the, 11
Stauros, 49
Stone, the magic, 46, 279
Subordination of mythical heroes, 22, 44, 46
Sun, emblems of the, 49
— myths of the, 10, 28, 48, 65, 70
Sûrya, 14
Surya Bai, 12, 35
Swanborough, 371
Sword, the naked, 42, 174
— of Aigeus, 17
— — Arthur, 16 *et seq.*
— — Balin, 95
— — Bevis, 17, 273
— — Perseus, 17
— — Roland, 17, 67
— — Sigmund, 19
— — Sigurd, 41
— — Theseus, 17
— — Tristrem, 260
— — Volsung, 18
Syrak, 283

T

Taillefer, 347
Taliessin, cup of, 49
Tamlane, 60
Tanhaüser, 59, 69
Tantalos, 13, 30, 52
Tarnkappe, 23
Tawiskara, 13
Tedbald of Rheims, 323
Tegau Euroron, 46
Telephos, 8
Tells of Rütli, 59, 70
Terry, 277, 290
Thanatos, 10
Theseus, 14
— sword of, 17
Thestias, 26
Thetis, 20
Thierry, 63, 308
Thriai, 30
Thomas, True, or Thomas the Rhymer, 38, 69
Thorold, 300
Thrushbeard, 72
Thucydides, euemerism of, 4
Tierry, 344
Tintagel Castle, 81

Tithônos, 69
Tor, 22, 97, 100
Torch of Olger, 362
Tramtrist, 137 et seq., 251
Treasure, lost or stolen, 64, 78 et seq., 392
Treves, holy coat of, 77
Triamour, 259, 313
Tristram, 25, 28, 135 et seq., 245 et seq.
— and Arthur, 160
— — Lancelot, 152
— — Olger, 361
— — Palamides, 163
— banishment of, 150, 260
— death of, 217, 266
— madness of, 43, 149, 264
— φιλογύνης, 39
— sculptured hall of, 262
— sword of, 260
— treachery of, 257
— the dragon-slayer, 38, 252
— — harper, 38, 42, 136, 247
— — huntsman, 37, 136, 247
— — stranger, 265
— in the Norse ship, 246
— versions of the myth of, 38
Trinchenis, 280
Trojan War, versions of the myth of the, 4, 44
Trolls, 62
Turpin, 323 et seq.
Turquine, 114
Twelve Peers, the, 333 et seq.
Twin Deities, 13, 23
Two Brothers, 14, 38, 41, 94, 282
— Kings' children, 14
— Sisters, 14
— Swords, knight of the, 91
— wanderers, 14
Tylor, Mr. E. B., on the comparison and classification of myths, 2
Tyr, 17

U

Ubbe, 72, 377
Ulfin, 81
Una and the lion, 46
Urgan, 259
Uriens, 20, 92, 100
Urra of Hungary, 46, 214

Urry, 300
Ushas, 17
Ushasau, 14
Uther Pendragon, 16, 81, 234, 240
Uwaine, 30, 104
— les Avoutres, 189

V

Varuna, 14
Veillantif, 332
Venus, 60
Vestal virgins, 26, 50
Vikram, story of, 64, 65
Visions, allegorical, 239
Vivian, 347
Volsunga Saga, 16
Vritra, 78

W

Waegmundings, 77
Wäinämöinen, 38
Wanderers, in mythology, 27 et seq., 88
Wayland, 384
Wealtheow, 385
Weapons, mythical, 21, 22, 44, 70, 77, 82, 89, 174, 273
— poisoned, 39, 137, 144, 250, 266
Weasel, the, 314
Weeping Castle, the, 141
Wegtam, 29
Weird Sisters, 30, 47, 58, 107, 229
White Castle, 169
Widow's son, the, 32
Wight, Isle of, 291
Wiglaf, 394
William of Cloudeslee, 16
— of Malmesbury on the story of Arthur, 4
— Tell, 16
— Wendut, 376
Winter and Spring, myths of the, 11
Wishing Cup, 23
Wuotan, 16, 29

X

Xanthos, 10, 45

Y

Ynor, 279, 293
Yoni, 26, 49
Ysonde the Fair. (*See* Isolte)

Z

Zaleukos, 3
Zaragoz, 320
Zethos, 14
Zohák, 56

www.ingramcontent.com/pod-product-compliance
Lightning Source LLC
Chambersburg PA
CBHW030559300426
44111CB00009B/1035